Matthias Schwartz, Nina Weller (eds.)
Appropriating History

**History in Popular Cultures** | Volume 21

**Editorial**

The series **Historische Lebenswelten in populären Wissenskulturen | History in Popular Cultures** provides analyses of popular representations of history from specific and interdisciplinary perspectives (history, literature and media studies, social anthropology, and sociology). The studies focus on the contents, media, genres, as well as functions of contemporary and past historical cultures.

In der Reihe **Historische Lebenswelten in populären Wissenskulturen | History in Popular Cultures** erscheinen Studien, die populäre Geschichtsdarstellungen interdisziplinär oder aus der Perspektive einzelner Fachrichtungen (insbesondere der Geschichts-, Literatur-und Medienwissenschaft sowie der Ethnologie und Soziologie) untersuchen. Im Blickpunkt stehen Inhalte, Medien, Genres und Funktionen heutiger ebenso wie vergangener Geschichtskulturen.

The series is edited by Sylvia Paletschek and Barbara Korte (executives) as well as Judith Schlehe, Wolfgang Hochbruck, Sven Kommer and Hans-Joachim Gehrke.

**Matthias Schwartz** is head of the project "Adjustment and Radicalisation. Dynamics in Popular Culture(s) in Pre-War Eastern Europe" and co-head of the program area World Literature at the Leibniz Center for Literary and Cultural Research (ZfL), Berlin, Germany. His research interests include the cultural history of Russian and Soviet space flight, adventure literature, science-fiction and science popularisation, Eastern European youth cultures, memory cultures, and contemporary literatures in a globalised world.

**Nina Weller** is a postdoctoral researcher in the project "Adjustment and Radicalisation" at the Leibniz Center for Literary and Cultural Research. 2018-2022 she was the head of the BMBF project "Designing the Past" at the European University Viadrina in Frankfurt (Oder), Germany. Her research focuses on contemporary literature, popular culture, memory studies and representations of history in Eastern European cultures (Belarusia, Russian, Ukrainian).

Matthias Schwartz, Nina Weller (eds.)

# Appropriating History

The Soviet Past in Belarusian, Russian
and Ukrainian Popular Culture

[transcript]

Our thanks go to the German Federal Ministry of Education and Research (BMBF) and Leibniz Collaborative Excellence funding programme of the Leibniz Association for funding this publication. An electronic version of this book is freely available in Open Access thanks to the support of the Leibniz Open Access Monograph Publishing Fund of the Leibniz Association.

**Bibliographic information published by the Deutsche Nationalbibliothek**
The Deutsche Nationalbibliothek lists this publication in the Deutsche Nationalbibliografie; detailed bibliographic data are available in the Internet at https://dnb.dnb.de/

This work is licensed under the Creative Commons Attribution-ShareAlike 4.0 (BY-SA) which means that the text may be remixed, build upon and be distributed, provided credit is given to the author and that copies or adaptations of the work are released under the same or similar license.
https://creativecommons.org/licenses/by-sa/4.0/
Creative Commons license terms for re-use do not apply to any content (such as graphs, figures, photos, excerpts, etc.) not original to the Open Access publication and further permission may be required from the rights holder. The obligation to research and clear permission lies solely with the party re-using the material.

**First published in 2024 by transcript Verlag, Bielefeld**
**© Matthias Schwartz, Nina Weller (eds.)**

Cover layout: Maria Arndt, Bielefeld
Cover illustration: Illustration from the Ukrainian comic Buiviter, 1995, Konstantin Sulima
Copy-editing: Katharina Kelbler
Proofread: Charlotte Bull and Margarita Schäfer
Printed by: Majuskel Medienproduktion GmbH, Wetzlar
https://doi.org/10.14361/9783839460771
Print-ISBN: 978-3-8376-6077-7
PDF-ISBN: 978-3-8394-6077-1
ISSN of series: 2366-1267
eISSN of series: 2702-9441

Printed on permanent acid-free text paper.

# Contents

## Introduction

**Popular Culture and History in Post-Soviet Nation States**
*Matthias Schwartz and Nina Weller* .......................................................... 11

## I. Places of Longing: Yesterday's Tales, Melodramatic Lives and Astonishing Worlds

Chapter 1:
**More than Nostalgia**
Late Socialism in Contemporary Russian Television Series
*Mark Lipovetsky* .......................................................................................... 29

Chapter 2:
**Drawn History**
Ukrainian Graphic Fiction about National History
*Svitlana Pidoprygora* .................................................................................. 45

Chapter 3:
**Narrating Russia's Multi-Ethnic Past**
The Historical Novels of Guzel Yakhina
*Eva Binder* ................................................................................................... 69

Chapter 4:
**The Zone as a Place of Repentance and Retreat**
Chernobyl in Belarusian Films of the 1990s and 2000s
*Olga Romanova* ........................................................................................... 89

## II. Combat Zones:
## War Heroes, Resistance Fighters and Joyful Partisans

Chapter 5:
**Alternative Versions of the Past and the Future**
Soviet and Post-Soviet Pop Literature
*Maria Galina and Ilya Kukulin* .................................................................. 111

Chapter 6:
**Ludic Epistemologies and Alternate Histories**
The Soviet Past in Role-Playing Games
*Daniil Leiderman* ..................................................................... 133

Chapter 7:
**Partisan, Anti-Partisan, pARTisan, Party-Zan, Cyberpartisan**
On the Popularity of Partisanhood in Belarusian Culture
*Nina Weller* .................................................................................. 155

Chapter 8:
**Mummified Subversion**
Reconstructions of Soviet Rock Underground in Contemporary Russian Cinema
*Roman Dubasevych* ................................................................... 187

## III. Sites of Trauma:
## Horror Fantasies, Weird Sceneries and Realms of Terror

Chapter 9:
**Dealing with Cultural Traumas**
Popular Representations of the Past in Contemporary Belarusian Prose
*Lidia Martinovich* ................................................................... 207

Chapter 10:
**Nostalgia for Trauma**
Russian Prize Literature and the Soviet Past
*Valery Vyugin* ......................................................................... 225

Chapter 11:
**The Affective Landscapes of S.T.A.L.K.E.R.**
Domesticating Nuclear Disaster in a Video Game
*Oleksandr Zabirko* .................................................................. 241

Chapter 12:
**Come and See, Once Again**
A Russian Television Series on the Seventh Symphony in Defeated Leningrad
*Matthias Schwartz* .................................................................................. 265

# Epilogue

**Public History, Popular Culture, and the Belarusian Experience in a Comparative Perspective**
A Conversation
*Aliaksei Bratachkin in conversation with the editors* ........................................... 293

# Appendix

Acknowledgments ..................................................................................... 311

Authors ................................................................................................. 313

# Introduction

# Popular Culture and History in Post-Soviet Nation States

*Matthias Schwartz and Nina Weller*

## 1. The Post-Soviet Condition

Soviet history has been the subject of controversial debates in the spheres of history politics and commemorative culture from the moment the world's first socialist state finally collapsed. When on 8 December 1991 the heads of state of the Belarusian, Russian and Ukrainian Soviet Socialist Republics Stanislav Shushkevich, Boris Yeltsin and Leonid Kravchuk left the Soviet Union with the Belovezh Agreement and founded the Commonwealth of Independent States, this was the decisive move towards its end. A few weeks later Mikhail Gorbachev formally stepped down and dissolved the USSR. With this turning point, a radical revision of history began. Already in the final years of perestroika and glasnost, the previously taboo and bloody aspects of the 'red dictatorship' had been intensively examined and discussed. Now, an uncompromising renunciation of the failed state socialism and an unsparing reckoning with the crimes of communism were proclaimed. Boris Groys once described this turning away from the Soviet Union as a "post-communist condition", which resembled a "return from the future to the present" of the nation state. The utopian project of communism became once again an evil "spectre" for which nobody wanted to be blamed and that was imagined as an interruption of the natural cause of things, demonically supressing and destructing one's own nation and its allegedly essential development (Groys 2005: 35–49).

At the same time, the three countries, which actually had never existed as nation states for any length of time, set out in the early 1990s to search for an independent national history, for a 'national idea'. Particularly anti-communist narratives from the Cold War era circulating among the Belarusian, Ukrainian and Russian diasporas in the West, who then longed for a 'liberation' and 'rebirth' of their 'supressed' nations, became very popular among the new elites of the young post-Soviet countries. However, due to the close historical interconnections of the three newly founded states, this almost inevitably led to conflicts: To whom did the medieval feudal principality of Kyivan Rus' belong – Russia or Ukraine? Who had a claim to Crimea? Was the Tsarist Empire a colonial state of great-Russian dominance or a common heritage? Could Ukraine exclusively rely on the Habsburgian Galician period as a cultural heyday, or should it be understood as a multireligious, multicultural post-national state? (Hagen 1995) And which events, myths and figures could Belarus integrate into its self-image from the long history of the Lithuanian-Polish Commonwealth and later Tsarist rule, to which its territory belonged for centuries?

Yet, besides these debates among the political and cultural elites of how to construct their respective invented tradition, there was also a vivid interest among ordinary people in how to cope with the disruptions and upheavals of history, whose object and subject they themselves had become in the preceding years and decades. And they found possible answers in the then flourishing commercial mass culture, which developed particular appeal in Eastern Europe during the 1990s as a previously unknown phenomenon. Accordingly, in its widely consumed formats like evening talk shows, documentaries, feature films, nonfiction or fiction books and journals, it was not the search for a 'national idea' or pre-Soviet history that dominated, but all possible aspects of the Soviet past were the major topic. And the images and narratives distributed in these popular media very often sufficiently departed from what the respective official state history claimed in its new schoolbooks or at national curricula.

However, this history boom in popular media formats underwent significant transformations in recent decades. Not only the political circumstances changed, but also the increasing digitalisation and globalisation of all spheres of life transformed the forms and formats of popular culture sufficiently. The internet, mobile phones and social media enabled people even in the most remote provinces to easily create their own 'glocal' imaginary links to transregional events, histories and communities beyond centralised power structures. Thus, in the beginning of the new millennium, various imaginary "scapes" (Appadurai 1990) and affective affiliations arose, some of which ran counter to the state's contested attempts to establish a national history, while others reinforced it. This was by no means a phenomenon particular to Eastern Europe (cf. Korte/Paletschek 2007; Groot 2015), but within the context of the complete breakdown of the formerly canonised dogmatic Marxist conceptualisation of history, such tendencies developed their own specific dynamics of appropriating the formerly common past. A mass of mainstream films, novels, comics, television series, computer games, and music videos appeared, which generate, revise, perpetuate, dismantle certain notions of the past, and thus contribute to their affectively charged visualisation and virtualisation. And exactly these dynamics of 'appropriation' in Belarusian, Russian and Ukrainian popular culture are the subject of the essays collected in this volume. Their authors explore this changing tension between state history policy, popular historical myths and globalised entertainment culture in different media formats and art forms, particularly in the first two decades of the 21st century.

## 2. Popular Histories of the 1990s: Concealed Truths and Alternative Claims

When the Soviet Union was dissolved in 1991, this was not just a departure towards new nation states. It was also the so-called transformation period, when a chaotic privatisation of state property, Manchester capitalism, corruption and lawlessness prevailed, with all its enormous social and economic upheavals. Instead of prosperity and freedom for all, capitalism brought increasing economic inequality and the collapse of the social security systems (Ther 2014). Accordingly, the new political leaders – who mostly arose out of the old socialist *nomenklatura* – elected for the first time in free elections, quickly lost support. This disappointment about the promised better world of democracy and market economy also affected the common picture of history. The partly disastrous personal situation quickly led many people to long for the allegedly grey, but materially and in terms of everyday life reasonably secure stability of late socialism. 'Nostalgia' for the old days arose (Boym 2001).

It was at this specific moment of failing social 'transformation' and economic and political crises, that all kinds of alternative histories became extremely popular. Because official history politics had already been discredited under the communists for a long time, when in the name of Marxist historical dialectics only one ideologically reliable version was accepted, the newly established national 'mythologies' (Barthes 2006 [1957]) were soon disregarded as similar state propaganda. Furthermore, civil society activism, which focussed on a critical reconstruction of the past, had little to offer in the way of practical solutions for daily life. Against this background a new commercial popular culture quickly emerged that promised to provide all the answers that could not be found elsewhere. So-called New Chronologies, Eurasian genealogies and manifold conspiracy myths about secret powers behind the scenes attracted the broader public (Schwartz 2009; Suslov 2017).

Private television channels, tabloids, para-scientific periodicals or voluminous fantasy sagas were the media that fascinated the audience in the first post-Soviet decade. Among them were the "true story" of Stalin's crimes, "uncensored truths" from the Kremlin, "secret documents" from the KGB archives, "unbelievable stories" from the Gulag, but also sex and crime, love in concentration camps and scandals in the cosmos as well as Satanism and astrology, light and dark forces, puppet masters and masterminds. What really happened in the October Revolution? Who was to blame for the *coup d'état* in 1917: Russians, Germans, or the Jews? Was Lenin actually a spy? Did Stalin want to starve all Ukrainians to death? Was the Soviet Union the real aggressor in the World War II? What was the Space Race actually about? How many lovers did Gagarin have, why did he have to die? What are the real reasons for the Chernobyl accident? Would the Soviet Union have survived if Andropov had not been murdered? (Schwartz 2009) There has been no historical event, no famous personality, for which there have not been scandalous and voyeuristic revelations.

What these stories of the 1990s had in common was their scepticism towards official narratives. They looked for the plausible explanation behind the contradictory and the inconsistencies behind the seemingly self-evident: where the guilty party was established beyond doubt, they discovered unknown accomplices; where the perpetrator had long since been convicted, they found new evidence to the contrary; what was written in the Soviet or post-Soviet textbook had to be re-examined. Yet this popular cultural history writing was by no means always emancipative and rebellious; it was often deeply reactionary and xenophobic, following anti-Semitic conspiracy myths and nationalist resentments. However, they achieved their popularity less due to such sometimes radical political views but rather because of their distance, inherited from the late Soviet era, to any kind of official, generally accepted historical truths. And although this makes them eminently political, they have received little attention from political science, nor have literary and cultural studies taken much notice of the dynamics and pitfalls of these appropriations of history.

## 3. History Politics: Nationalising and Disintegrating a Common Past

With the turn of the 21st century, the political and technical conditions of history politics changed. Vladimir Putin won his first presidential election in 2000 in the Russian Federation, Aleksandr Lukashenko [Aliaksandr Lukashenka] in Belarus in 2001 started his second term as president, while Ukraine in 2004 underwent its first major political upheaval and mass pro-democracy protests with the Orange Revolution. The persistent 'nationalisation' of history policy, but also new media developments and the gradual establishment of authoritarian rule in Belarus and Russia have shifted the context for popular cultural activities massively. In the Russian Federation, the consolidation of Putin's power was accompanied by a change in official history politics (Kalinin 2011). Now a rehabilitation of the Red Army, the secret services and strong leadership found its symbolic expression in the renewed glorification of the victory in the 'Great Patriotic War', but also in the praise of supposedly great Russian statesmen and strong personalities as glorious forerunners of the president's own rule. Although it was not taboo to portray the darker sides of history in the media, such as the terror of the Cheka in the civil war or the crimes of the Stalin era, with increasing frequency at least since the 2010s they have been narrated as avoidable, if not excusable, excesses of a statehood in crisis (Scharlaj 2017; Weiss-Wendt/Adler 2021). This emerging new official narrative suggested that precisely in order to prevent such turmoil in the future, a strong hand was needed. At the same time, the Russian Federation was represented as a global political superpower following on from the Soviet Union, whose geopolitical interests outside its own country and especially in the 'near abroad' and vis-à-vis Ukraine have to be recognised (Saunders 2016; Szostek 2018; Borenstein 2019). State actors frequently saw Ukraine and Belarus as an integral part of the Russian multinational and multicultural empire since the 18th century.

Conversely, in Ukraine following the successful Orange Revolution in 2004 and especially after the so-called Euromaidan in 2013/2014, and in reaction to the annexation of Crimea by Russia and the war in the Donbass, a national historiography increasingly distanced itself from the overpowering neighbour (Kasianov 2022). The Ukrainian Institute for National Memory, founded in 2006, monitored the allegedly correct understanding of history and promoted, for example, the international recognition of the famine in the early 1930s caused by forced collectivisation as a genocide of the Ukrainian people, the so-called 'Holodomor'. Everything Soviet and Russian became designated negatively as alien influences of the centuries-old coloniser, occupier and aggressor from the East. The so-called decommunization laws banned nearly all Soviet names, symbols, legacies from the public space as a totalitarian criminal heritage. In contrast, the Western periods of rule from the Polish-Lithuanian Kingdom to the Habsburg-Hungary monarchy tended to be reinterpreted as positive, if not as periods of prosperity. Especially since President Viktor Yushchenko in 2010 officially declared Stepan Bandera a "Hero of Ukraine", for many he turned into an icon of the anti-Russian struggle for independence and liberation, whereby his collaboration with the Nazis and the anti-Semitic or anti-Polish pogroms committed by the Ukrainian Insurgent Army UPA were relativised as historical marginalia (Dubasevych/Schwartz 2020; Yekelchyk 2022).

While this extreme politicisation and polarisation of common Ukrainian-Russian history reached its tragic climax in Vladimir Putin's two speeches in February 2022 shortly before Russia's massive military attack on Ukraine, in which he attempted to justify this step with long historical digressions, the politics of history in Belarus is primarily based on domestic politics. National history became a contested subject in the conflict between President Aleksandr Lukashenko, who has reigned in an increasingly repressive and brutal way, and the opposition, which nowadays has been largely crushed, imprisoned or driven into exile. In order to justify its authority, the regime draws strongly, also symbolically, on Soviet historical narratives, but also uses national myths to distinguish itself from Russian influence (Goujon 2010; Rudling 2017). At the same time, the opposition tries to legitimise its actions partly by referring to the same everyday myths, but also seeks non-Soviet points of reference in history (Bekus 2017, 2018; Lewis 2017). A symbol for these different attitudes to history is the flag. While the official red-green state flag is clearly based on that of the Belarusian Soviet Republic, during its anti-government protests the opposition usually uses white-red-white banners originating from the Lithuanian Noble Republic. Soviet history has thus been moved back to the centre of power politics of the three newly formed independent states and is 'nationalised' in different and antagonistic ways.

These large-scale attempts at 'nationalising' history took place very much on a symbolic and ritual level, whereas the everyday experiences of people in late socialism are hardly represented here (Rutten et al. 2013). Yet, they went along with a change in the media formats to distribute und popularise these narratives: Print products play only an increasingly marginal role, and television has also largely lost its monopoly on audio-visual opinion-forming, at least among the younger generations. In contrast, various digital formats and genres are becoming more important. Digital search platforms, news portals, social media, messenger services or chat rooms, but also computer games, television shows and series are shifting the popular historical and alternative-historical discourses into virtual worlds, thus moving them from the local subcultures of fanzines and specialist circles into the mainstream of multiply linked communication spaces and discussion forums. This goes along with a gradual blurring of the boundaries between scientific and pseudo-scientific, journalistic and populist communication. Ordinary users have the potential to create their own niche on the World Wide Web, regardless of the language barriers that are becoming increasingly irrelevant thanks to AI translation programmes. But usually, the overall monitoring, commercialisation and surveillance of the digital sphere also channel users within their blurbs and target groups, which attracts state institutions that try to regulate this allegedly borderless information flow by IP addresses, national laws and ethical norms.

## 4. Popular Culture and History: Recoding, Normalising, Adjusting a Contested Past

In this field of tension between political nationalisation and media regulation, popular cultural appropriations of history are currently taking shape. They give history alternative affective and imaginary form and content, meaning and significance by transforming current fascinations and fears, desires and problems of the present into a historical guise. If one tries to grasp this phenomenon more accurately in theoretical terms, it is in particular the term 'popular culture' that has ambivalent connotations. Since modern times, popular culture has primarily been a term with negative connotations, functioning above all as a contrast to bourgeois high culture and classical art. The 'uncultured' peasants, soldiers and proletarians, in this view, were considered primitive, backward, barbaric, savage and tasteless.

With the emergence of industrial mass production, an additional difference has been made between a commercial and often state-controlled "culture industry" (Adorno/Horkheimer 2002 [1944]) on the one hand, which is shaped by the term 'mass culture'. and on the other hand, the much older notion of 'popular culture' of the lived and practised cultures of the common people, which goes back to fairy tales and folklore. While 'mass culture' stands for manipulation, propaganda, brainwashing, dumbing down and delusion 'from above' as modern 'opium of the people', 'popular culture' in contrast is associated with a rebellious, seditious, subversive, carnivalesque component of resistance 'from below' against the authorities. It is precisely the approach of the Birmingham School of Social Studies that has questioned such a schematic dichotomy between manipulation by the "state block" and resistance by the working classes and instead made strong the ambivalent and contradictory nature of urban, proletarian and youth subcultures (Hall 1981; Storey 1996).

Thus, further social and cultural research showed that instead of a simplified juxtaposition of above and below, manipulation and emancipation, reactionary and rebellious, a more dynamic and multidimensional understanding of popular culture is needed. Urban youth cultures 'from below' could also be reactionary, like the skinhead or hooligan scenes, just as, conversely, commercial Hollywood blockbuster movies 'from above' could certainly spread emancipatory and even rebellious narratives. In addition, in a globalised and media-networked world, there can be very different local appropriations of cultural and consumer products that turn the possibly intended function of artworks into its opposite in practice. For instance, during late Soviet times, entertaining TV series, soaps or melodramatic film comedies from India or Latin America with no political ambitions shown on state television developed an enormous cultural impact on the political imaginary. A completely different dynamic was taken on by the rebellious style and habitus of African-American hip-hop music that spread from New York across the globe at the end of the 20th century, which found many nationalist and even xenophobic adaptations in Eastern Europe without any emancipatory attitude (Oravcová 2016; Schwartz 2019). This means that popular culture today often constitutes its popularity not so much through their production sites (commercial vs. independent, state vs. dissident) but rather through the different forms of appropriation in specific cultural-political contexts.

However, the post-Soviet experience of Belarus, Russia and Ukraine also shows that this partly idiosyncratic appropriation and recoding by no means always has to happen with a clear political agenda, but that it is rather a kind of adjustment to given social and cultural conditions. Initially scandalous or tabooed topics and figures under different circumstances can lead to the normalisation of conventionalised narratives or images (Rosenfeld 2014), whereas apparently harmless youth cultures can suddenly become extremely political. This is especially true in times of war, when divergences in general are less tolerated and cultures tend to homogenise and erase ambivalences (Ugrešić 1998). In Ukraine, for example, this applies to the way in which the dark realm of Mordor and the malevolent Orcs from J.R.R. Tolkien's fantasy novel *Lord of the Rings* have become colloquially synonymous with Russia and its soldiers (Szczerek 2013; Yekelchyk 2022: 237–238). Conversely, in Russia, the so-called "popadantsy literature" about fantastic time travels to World War II, advertised by large commercial publishers, but read before the war only by a modest number of male lovers of military fantasy (Zabirko 2018; Galina 2021) prepared the ground for the imaginary commitment of many volunteers at the front, who see the attack on Ukraine as a decisive battle for the salvation of Russian civilisation.

But it would be premature to conclude from these examples that certain popular-cultural formats do have a somewhat predictable or even controllable effect on specific appropriations of history. Rather, the two examples show that popular culture develops its imaginary and affective power situationally. The fantasy boom in the decades before prepared the ground for an extremely heterogeneous and widespread reservoir of images and narratives open for subversive as well as for conformist notions (Schwartz 2016). Only through the Russian-Ukrainian war, the fantastic histories of Light and Dark forces fighting against each other gained a definite political meaning. Similarly, in Russian popular culture, alternative histories about World War II enabled diverse subcultures to articulate and constitute their personal "patriotism of despair" (Oushakine 2009: 2013) which only through Russia's military aggression gained its uncanny topicality (Noordenbos 2018; Makhortykh 2020).

In this way, popular appropriations of the past operate through various state and unofficial, commercial and independent media channels, constantly recoding, normalising and adjusting official narratives, alternate and fantastic histories and imaginary belonging (Brouwer 2016). They affect everyday routines, local subcultures and imaginary communities and gain political topicality within specific political and social conditions. It was probably not quite by chance that the role of a fictional history teacher becoming president in a popular commercial TV series called *The Servant of the People* (*Sluga naroda*), directed by Oleksii Kyriushchenko, paved the way for Volodymyr Zelensky to actually be elected as the real President of Ukraine in 2019 with an overwhelming majority.

## 5. Appropriating History: Entertainment and Estrangement

It is precisely these ambivalent and occasionally powerful aspects of popular culture that this book aims to address in focussing on its ways of dealing with the Soviet past. The editors have deliberately chosen the verbal noun *appropriating* in relation to history as the title. After all, the term 'cultural appropriation' in social and cultural studies signals a thoroughly problematic procedure in which, especially in (post)colonial power relations, a 'major' group or an institutional collective 'appropriates' and claims for itself styles, cultures, art forms of 'minor', often defeated societies, often against their will and without their consent. The term thus describes a cultural relationship of exploitation, where the 'appropriated' is powerless or at least inferior against the will of the expropriator (Young/Brunk 2012).

In our case, however, it is not a question of culture, but of history, and not that of appropriating something from another, foreign, 'exotic' culture, but of one's own history, which is, however, a divided and contested one: the common Soviet past of Belarus, Russia and Ukraine. This 'appropriation' process is on an affective and imaginary level a thoroughly violent and intrusive one, constantly splitting the past into what is one's own and what is alien, what belongs and what is rejected, what is approved and what is fought against. In this context, the term *appropriating* does not refer so much to a hierarchical, exploitive power relationship between different groups or societies (as in 'cultural appropriation'), but rather focuses on the competition of political and cultural actors for a contested 'heritage'. At the same time, in using the term in a more general understanding, we also want to emphasise the banal but significant fact that 'history' is not simply given, but is always made, questioning thus any form of naturalisation and essentialisation of 'national history'.

In this respect, the chosen approach focussing on appropriation of history also differs from a conceptualisation of dealing with the recent history of the 20th century that is widespread in memory studies. Memory studies often conceptualise 'collective memory' or 'cultural memory' as something that has existed within a specific community (a nation) for centuries, maintained by certain institutions, rituals, symbolic places that allow the inhabitants to reassure themselves as a collective and eventually to process traumatic events. In such a concept, Soviet history is often understood as an interruption of 'national' memory culture, forbidding and tabooing certain collective traits and traditions. Accordingly, Soviet history itself with its violent revolution, civil war and Stalinist terror is occasionally viewed as a process of permanent traumatisation and simultaneously tabooing everything divergent from its own ideology. "Warped mourning" (Etkind 2013) and unprocessed (national) traumata (Lugaric et al. 2017; Drosihn et al. 2020) are the consequence of this allegedly failed, false policy of memory (Schwartz et al. 2021). Through the gerund, "Appropriating History" emphasises that the alleged collective memory of such a 'nationalised' understanding of history is always an active, intentional process of construction that does not simply happen, but must be deliberately implemented and produced in order to be successful.

And it is precisely this active, productive appropriation of the Soviet past that characterises popular culture and essentially distinguishes it from alternative conceptualisations of collective cultural memory and state history policy: Popular culture never wants to permanently anchor a 'cultural memory' of certain historical events in the collective or enforce a specific 'national' understanding of history against other versions and views among the population, but constantly seeks alternatives, deviations, estrangements. Videogames are not about reenacting history, but about making well-known episodes and images enthralling and thrilling. Popular TV series are not about conveying official points of view, but about confronting individual fates with the unknown sides behind the façade. And bestselling literature does not aim to enlighten, but to shock and shake, to touch and comfort (Lovell/Menzel 2005; Borenstein 2011).

In doing so, popular culture reconstructs and varies the discontents and longings present in society, casts them in entertaining and exciting narratives and images and thus makes history accessible and transferable to daily life experiences (Shumylovych 2019). Thus, there is also a large number of state-sponsored, expensive, lavishly produced and widely promoted blockbuster films that fully correspond to the national-state view of Soviet history in Belarus, Ukraine or Russia, that never became popular culture. Like the widely promoted Canadian-Ukrainian melodramatic historical drama *Bitter Harvest* (*Hirki zhiva*, 2017, directed by George Mendeluk) about the 'Holodomor' or the Russian biopic about the heroic life of the first cosmonaut *Gagarin. First in Space* (*Gagarin. Pervyi v kosmose*, 2013, directedly by Pavel Parkhomenko), which both were a flop with viewers at the box office as well as on TV screens. In contrast, sometimes entertaining low budget movies that ridicule melodramatic and heroic narratives became a huge audience success, like historical comedies mocking Napoleon's Russian campaign *Rzhevsky Versus Napoleon* (*Rzhevskii protiv Napoleona*, 2012, directed by Marius Vaisberg), carnivalesque Cossack musicals *Like the Cossacks* (*Kak kazaki...*, 2009, directed by Igor Ivanov) or slapstick films about Hitler *Hitler Goes Kaput!* (*Gitler kaput!*, 2008, directed by Marius Vaisberg) or the film parody of the partisan myth *Party-Zan* (2016, directed by by Andrei Kureichik).

In summary, popular culture is formed in a dynamic process between producers and consumers, state and population, above and below, which constantly recodes, normalises and adapts historical narratives and images to the respective condition. These appropriations gain their attractiveness through the deviation from the norm: they make boring school knowledge or ideology exciting and entertaining by shedding new light on it, estranging it. Estrangement and entertainment succeed whenever they capture certain moods, discomfort, a *zeitgeist*, and turn them into catchy stories or plots, memes or icons. The specific characteristic of appropriating history in the post-Soviet countries of Belarus, Russia and Ukraine is that in 1991 there was no firmly consolidated official historiography or historical knowledge here. Thus, in all the three countries history became a subject of large-scale nationalisation and ideologisation on the part of the state. At the same time, since the 1990s there has been a mass of very heterogeneous, partly speculative and counterfactual interpretations on offer. Popular culture is a key player in this development because it generates dispositives that may become politically effective by reinforcing and radicalising emerging socio-political developments or, conversely, by undermining and recoding widespread notions of history. However, there is no automatism or determinism here according to which certain popular cultural tendencies inevitably lead to war or certain subversive practices necessarily result in revolt. Rather, the appropriations of history through popular culture are indicators and gauges of moods and resentments, they channel fears and desires, give them form and shape, but also offer imaginary escape routes and attractive alternatives to reality.

## 6. Outline of the Volume: Places of Longing, Combat Zones, Sites of Trauma

The present volume deals with works and phenomena of popular culture from the period before Russia's full-scale invasion of Ukraine on 24 February 2022. Initial ideas for its conceptualisation were discussed at the workshop *"History Goes Pop?" On the Popularization of the Past in Eastern European Cultures* organised by the two editors at the European University Viadrina Frankfurt (Oder) in December 2019. Accordingly, most of the essays collected here were written long before the war and partly impacted by the Belarusian protests in 2020 and 2021, although many were revised and, in some cases, supplemented afterwards. The aim of the volume is not to cover all areas of popular culture in all three countries equally, which would not be possible. Many formats of popular culture – like festivals, sport events, subcultures or religious movements – are not represented at all, others – like social media or popular music – are present in the individual contributions, but are not the subject of separate essays. The focus is on a literary, film and media studies analysis of audio-visual and textual formats, mainly fiction, comics, film, series and computer games.

The first part of the volume is dedicated to **Places of Longing**, events and periods of history with positive or negative connotations that are receiving new attention in popular culture. The emotional relationship to these places can hardly been described as nostalgic; popular culture engages rather with the conflict-laden aspects of the past in an immersive and empathic way, thus reinterpreting it for the present. While in the Russian Federation the reconstructive tendencies clearly predominate, fitting the Soviet into their own multinational and imperial self-image, the examples from Belarus and Ukraine demonstrate a more ambivalent imaginary relation to the socialist past, which often is imagined as contradictory to national identity. What all these reconstructive and wishful relations have in common is that they do not represent the past as something gone and distant, something irretrievably lost, but deal with Soviet history as something having continuous impact on the current reality. **Mark Lipovetsky** analyses the Russian television series *The Thaw* (*Ottepel'*, 2013), *Black Marketeers* (*Fartsa*, 2015), *Our Happy Tomorrow* (*Nashe schastlivoe zavtra*, 2016) and *Optimists* (*Optimisty*, 2017) to show how the rebels and outlaws of everyday Soviet life are presented here as heroes for the present. The series thus recode the fears and desires of contemporary viewers in a kind of retro-utopia with the aim of "symbolically protecting the viewer from the dangerous future and offer an escape from the present" (chapter 1). **Eva Binder** focusses on Guzel Yakhina's bestselling novels *Zuleikha Opens Her Eyes* (*Zuleikha otkryvaet glaza*, 2015), *A Volga Tale* (*Deti moi*, 2018) and *Train to Samarkand* (*Ėshelon na Samarkand*, 2021) to demonstrate how dramatic historical events such as the civil war, famines and the Gulag are brought to a contemporary readership in an exciting and entertaining way. Binder argues that this mainstream literature, which is committed to humanist values, follows a global popular realism in its style, but in contemporary Russia also has critical and enlightening impulses (chapter 3).

**Olga Romanova**, on the other hand, demonstrates through four Belarusian films about the consequences of the Chernobyl disaster, *The Wolves in the Zone* (*Volki v zone*, 1990), *The Atomic Zone Ranger* (*Reindzher iz atomnoi zony*, 1999), *I Remember/Father's House* (*Ia pomniu/Otchii dom*, 2005) and *Exclusion Zone* (*Zapretnaia zona*, 2020), how a critical and subversive impulse of repentance in the course of time gave way to a resigned retreat into the personal, a development that directly resonates with the political sphere in the country (chapter 4). In contrast, **Svitlana Pidoprygora** analyses dozens of Ukrainian comics and graphic novels from the last decade and concludes that in most of these works the Soviet past is largely made invisible and simply overwritten dominantly by fantastic alternative histories. Here, all kinds of superheroes, cyborgs, mythic warriors defend their nation against external enemies, which often resemble stereotypes about the Soviet Union and Russia. However, in particular graphic novels in the context of the Russian-Ukrainian war in Donbass since 2014 increasingly also emphasise the tragic and dramatic consequences of such violent conflicts for the own presence (chapter 2). These texts, films and series thus offer very different representations of Soviet **Places of Longing**, in which mythical fighters, cheerful rebels and melodramatic lone fighters provide often nationalised images and narratives for their own audience. Appropriated history here rarely displaces differentiated and educating aspects of the past, rather it adjusts it to present needs and demands.

The second part, **Combat Zones**, is not so much concerned with the structures of longing expressed in the appropriation of the past, but rather with the different types of protagonists and their function in the respective historical episodes. **Maria Galina** and **Ilya Kukulin** analyse Russian alternative histories of the Soviet Union, focusing on soldiers and fighters who are primarily concerned with avoiding the collapse of a mighty statehood. While in the 1990s the main subject of interest was to remove taboos from certain topics, more recent counterfactual works increasingly deal with an imagined revenge and a deep resentment against external enemies (chapter 5). **Daniil Leiderman** also analyses alternative histories, albeit in computer games such as 74 (1980s, 2017), *Red Land* (*Krasnaia zemlia*, 2011), *Atom RPG* (2018), and *Disco Elysium* (2019). These games, equipped with typical paraphernalia and landscapes of Soviet provenance, give players the opportunity "for examining and coming to terms with the complexities and contradictions of historical experience." This allows gamers to playfully reconsider and revise their own understanding and memories of the Soviet past (chapter 6).

**Nina Weller** looks at a special combatant figure from World War II, namely the partisan, who enjoyed enormous popularity in post-Soviet Belarus, both in official circles and among the artistic and political opposition. His tactics and strategies of subversion were appropriated and reinterpreted for the post-Soviet present in a wide range of media formats and genres, from large historical films to small forms of street protest (chapter 7). **Roman Dubasevych** discusses two recent Russian films about the *stiliagi* subculture of the 1950s and the Leningrad rock underground of the 1980s to exemplify that artistic and political reconstructions of Soviet heroic figures do not always aim at an active intervention into current conditions, but can also have the reverse effect of mummifying and depoliticising individual protest. Although the two sensational music films *Hipsters* (*Stiliagi*, 2008) and *Summer* (*Leto*, 2018), clearly focus on rebellious young people as likeable characters they are not staged as antagonists of a repressive dictatorship, but rather the plot and the visual aesthetics bring about an identification with hegemonic power (chapter 8). Thus, all four contributions demonstrate that the **Combat Zones** of history for popular culture function mainly as playing grounds for their protagonists to test various ways of action and behaviour that range from resentful imaginary revenge to playful and performative forms of negotiation and protest to an entertaining silencing of the historic conflict.

The last part of the book **Sites of Trauma** demonstrates that violent traumatic events in history have become an extremely successful and favoured topic in popular culture, which can be appropriated and narrated in very different ways. **Lidia Martinovich** discusses how "cultural trauma" has become an important medium for narrating national history in Belarus in recent times, analysing popular novels of the last decades. The "suffering Belarusian" has become a central figure to confront readers with different options for action and survival strategies in a historical guise, sometimes in a ridiculous, sometimes in a frightening way (chapter 9). **Valery Vyugin**, on the other hand, shows that the treatment of extreme violence is a thoroughly ambivalent phenomenon in Russian prize-winning literature nowadays. He argues that the depiction of traumatic events in Soviet history is increasingly losing its critical and enlightening function and is becoming more and more akin to non-political "recycling" for the purposes of entertainment, resulting in an increasing gamification of the past (chapter 10).

**Oleksandr Zabirko** observes a different phenomenon for the game series *S.T.A.L.K.E.R*, in which the apocalyptic zone of Chernobyl is depicted as an eerie and terrifying world populated by monsters and mutants from which there is no escape. This enormously popular model of reality has taken on a frightening topicality with Russia's attack on Ukraine (chapter 11). In the last chapter, **Matthias Schwartz** examines the multi-award-winning television series *The Seventh Symphony* (*Sed'maia simfoniia*, 2021) about the performance of Dmitrii Shostakovich's *Symphony No. 7* in August 1942 during the Leningrad Blockade to analyse how popular formats use traumatic historical experiences for the present as a multi-layered imaginary offer to come to terms with the ever more authoritarian and militarised regime in Russia (chapter 12). So, when in the 1990s the critical encounter with the tabooed and silenced traumatic aspects of Soviet history were highlighted primarily to uncover and demonstrate the failures and crimes of the Soviet system, nowadays **Sites of Trauma** mainly provide imaginary patterns and models for the present on how to act under situations of pressure, misery and danger. The volume concludes with a conversation with the historian and public history expert **Aliaksei Bratachkin**. In focussing on Belarus from a comparative perspective, he discusses how the use of popular cultural elements in public history has played a crucial role in post-Soviet nation-building since 1991. Historical themes in particular were promoted as didactic and educational tools by the state, but have also been used by opposition groups in competing national narratives, especially since 2020.

'Appropriating history' does not necessarily imply either critically reappraising and adequately remembering the past or, conversely, ideologically trivialising and relativising it; in popular culture, it means above all presenting dramatic episodes, dazzling figures and stereotypical images, which appeal in an entertaining way to the needs and desires, challenges and conflicts of the respective public. Especially in the nascent post-Soviet nation states, these entertaining representations often do more than government institutions, political parties or public educational organisations to shape ideas about how national belonging is articulated. Ideas about history and historical belonging sometimes have a strong effect in situations of political upheaval by fuelling rebellion and increasing bellicosity, as well as by exposing national myths or suggesting a retreat into the private sphere.

## List of Games

*74. Nastol'naia igra po sovetskoi istorii*, produced by Baryshnikova, Natalia/Vorontsov, Roman/Lomakin, Nikita/Starostin, Vasilii, Memorial, Tabletop RPG, 2017.
*Atom RPG*, produced by Atom Team, PC/Mac/Linux, 2018.
*Disco Elysium*, produced by ZA/UM (Kurvitz, Robert/Rostov, Aleksander), PC/Mac, 2019.
*Red Land* (*Krasnaia Zemlia*), produced by Shtab Dukhonina (Borkovskii, Egor/Trofimenko, Konstantin/Shalupaev, Mikhail/Ian'kov, Ivan), Tabletop RPG, 2010–2011.
*S. T. A. L. K. E. R. Shadow of Chernobyl'* (*S.T.A.L.K.E.R. Ten' Chernobylia*), produced by GSC Game World, PC/MAC, 2007.
*S.T.A.L.K.E.R. Clear Sky* (*S.T.A.L.K.E.R. Chyste Nebo*), produced by GSC Game World, PC/MAC, 2008.
*S.T.A.L.K.E.R. Call of Pripyat*, (*S.T.A.L.K.E.R. Poklyk Pryp'iati*) produced by GSC Game World, PC/MAC, 2009.
*S.T.A.L.K.E.R. The Cursed Zone* (*S.T.A.L.K.E.R. Prokliata Zona*) produced by GSC Game World, PC/MAC, 2013.
*S.T.A.L.K.E.R. 2: Oblivion Lost*, produced by GSC Game World, PC/MAC, 2015.
*S.T.A.L.K.E.R. 2: Heart of Chernobyl* (*S.T.A.L.K.E.R. Sertse Chernobylia*), produced by GSC Game World, PC/MAC, 2024.

## Filmography

*Bitter Harvest* (*Hirki zhiva*), dir. George Mendeluk, Canada/ UK 2017.
*Black Marketeers* (*Fartsa*), dir. Egor Baranov, Russia 2013.
*Exclusion Zone* (*Zapretnaia zona*), dir. Mitrii Semenov-Aleinikov, Belarus 2020.
*Gagarin. First in Space* (*Gagarin. Pervyi v kosmose*), dir. Pavel Parkhomenko, Russia 2013.
*Hipsters* (*Stiliagi*), dir. Valerii Todorovskii, Russia 2008.
*Hitler Goes Kaput!* (*Gitler kaput!*), dir. Marius Vaisberg 2008.
*I Remember/Father's House* (*Ia pomniu/Otchii dom*), dir. Sergei Sychev, Belarus 2005.
*Like the Cossacks...* (*Kak kazaki...*), dir. Igor' Ivanov, Ukraine 2009.
*Optimists* (*Optimisty*), dir. Aleksei Popogrebskii, Russia 2017–2021.
*Summer* (*Leto*), dir. Kirill Serebrennikov, Russia/France 2018.
*Party-Zan*, dir. Andrei Kureichik, Belarus 2016.
*Rzhevsky Versus Napoleon* (*Rzhevskii protiv Napoleona*), dir. Marius Vaisberg, Russisa/Ukraine 2012.
*The Atomic Zone Ranger* (*Reindzher iz atomnoi zony*), dir. Viacheslav Nikiforov, Belarus, Russia 1999.
*The Servant of the People* (*Sluga naroda*), dir. Oleksii Kyriushchenko, Ukraine 2015–2019.
*The Seventh Symphony* (*Sed"maia simfoniia*), dir. Aleksandr Kott, Russia 2021.
*The Thaw* (*Ottepel'*), dir. Valerii Todorovskii, Russia 2013.

*The Wolves in the Zone* (*Volki v zone*), dir. Viktor Deriugin, USSR 1990.
*Our happy tomorrow* (*Nashe schastlivoe zavtra*), dir. Igor Kopylov, Russia 2016.

**References**

Adorno, Theodor W./Horkheimer Max (2002): "The Culture Industry: Enlightenment as Mass Deception." In: ibid. Dialectic of Enlightenment [1944], edited by Gunzelin Schmid Noeri, Redwood City: Stanford University Press, pp. 94–136.

Appadurai, Arjun (1990): "Disjuncture and Difference in the Global Cultural Economy." In: Theory, Culture and Society 7, pp. 295–310.

Barthes, Roland (2006): Mythologies [1957], translated by Annette Lavers, New York: Hill and Wang.

Bekus Nelly (2018): "Historical Reckoning in post-Soviet Belarus." In: Lavinia Stan/Cynthia Horne (eds.): Transitional Justice and the Former Soviet Union: Reviewing the Past and Looking Towards the Future, Cambridge: University Press.

Bekus, Nelly (2017): "Constructed 'Otherness'? Poland and Geopolitics of Contested Belarusian Identity." In: Europe-Asia Studies, 69/2, pp. 242–261.

Borenstein, Eliot (2011): Overkill: Sex and Violence in Contemporary Russian Popular Culture, Cornell: University Press.

Borenstein, Eliot (2019): Plots against Russia. Conspiracy and Fantasy after Socialism, Cornell: University Press.

Boym, Svetlana (2001): The Future of Nostalgia, New York: Basic Books.

Brouwer, Sander (ed.) (2016): Contested Interpretations of the Past in Polish, Russian, and Ukrainian Film: Screen as Battlefield, (Studies in Slavic Literature and Poetics 60), Leiden: Brill.

Chertenko, Alexander (2021): "'[...] die Ideologie der Volksrepublik Doneck wird in der Abkürzung SSSR ihren Ausdruck finden'. Die Rekonstruktion der Sowjetunion in Zachar Prilepins 'Vsjo, čto dolžno razrešit'sja... Chronika iduščej vojny'. In: Iris Bauer et al. (eds.): Close Reading – Distant Reading. Spannungsfelder der slavistischen Literatur- und Kulturwissenschaften, Reflexionen des Gesellschaftlichen in Sprache und Literatur. Hallesche Beiträge 9, pp. 317–328.

Drosihn, Yvonne/Jandl, Ingeborg/Kowollik, Eva (eds.) (2020): Trauma – Generationen – Erzählen. Transgenerationale Narrative zum ost-, ostmittel- und südosteuropäischen Raum, Berlin: Frank & Timme.

Dubasevych, Roman/Schwartz, Matthias (eds.) (2020): "Einleitung." In: ibd. (eds.): Sirenen des Krieges. Diskursive und affektive Dimensionen des Ukraine-Konflikts, Berlin: Kadmos, pp. 7–46.

Etkind, Alexander (2013): Warped Mourning: Stories of the Undead in the Land of the Unburied (Cultural Memory in the Present), Stanford: Stanford University Press.

Galina, Maria (2021). "Post-Imperial Resentments: Alternative Histories of World War II in Popular Post-Soviet Speculative Fiction." *After Memory: World War II in Contemporary Eastern European Literatures*, edited by Matthias Schwartz, Nina Weller and Heike Winkel, Berlin, Boston: De Gruyter, pp. 171–196.

Goujon, Alexandra (2010): "Memorial Narratives of WWII Partisans and Genocide in Belarus." In: East European Politics and Societies: And Cultures, 24/1, pp. 6–25.

Groot, Jerome de (2015): Remaking History: The Past in Contemporary Historical Fictions, London; New York: Taylor & Francis Ltd.

Groys, Boris (2005): "Die postkommunistische Situation." In: Anne von der Heiden/Peter Weibel (eds.): Zurück aus der Zukunft: Osteuropäische Kulturen im Zeitalter des Postkommunismus, Frankfurt am Main: Suhrkamp, pp. 36–49.

Kalinin, Ilya (2011): "Nostalgic Modernization: The Soviet Past as 'Historical Horizon'." Slavonica 17/2, pp.156-66.

Kasianov, Georgiy (2022): Memory Crash: Politics of History In and Around Ukraine, 1980s–2010s, Budapest: Central European University Press.

Korte, Barbara/Paletschek, Sylvia (eds.) (2007): History goes Pop. Zur Repräsentation von Geschichte in populären Medien und Genres, Bielefeld: transcript.

Lewis, Simon (2017): "The 'Partisan Republic': Colonial Myths and Memory Wars in Belarus." In: Julie Fedor et al. (eds.): War and Memory in Russia, Ukraine and Belarus (Palgrave Macmillan Memory Studies), Cham: Springer International Publishing, pp. 371–396.

Lovell, Stephen/Menzel, Birgit (eds.) (2005): Reading for Entertainment in Contemporary Russia. Post-Soviet Popular Literature in Historical Perspective, München: Sagner.

Lugarić, Danijela/Car, Milka/Molnár, Gábor Tamás (eds.) (2017): Myth and its Discontents. Memory and Trauma in Central and Eastern European Literature. Mythos und Ernüchterung. Zu Trauma und (fraglicher) Erinnerung in Literaturen des zentralen und östlichen Europa, Wien: Praesensverlag.

Makhortykh, Mykola (2020): "Remediating the Past: Youtube and Second World War Memory in Ukraine and Russia." In: Memory Studies, 13/2, pp. 146–161.

Noordenbos, Boris (2018): "Seeing the Bigger Picture: Conspiratorial Revisions of World War II History in Recent Russian Cinema." In: Slavic Review 77/2, pp. 441–464.

Oushakine, Serguei (2013): "Remembering in Public: On the Affective Management of History." In: Ab Imperio 1, pp. 269–302.

Oushakine, Serguei (2009): The Patriotism of Despair. Nation, War, and Loss in Russia, Ithaca: Cornell University Press.

Oravcová, Anna (2016): "'Rap on Rap Is Sacred': The Appropriation of Hip Hop in the Czech Republic." In: Matthias Schwartz/Heike Winkel (eds.): Eastern European Youth Cultures in a Global Context, London: Palgrave Macmillan UK, pp. 111–130.

Rudling, Per Anders (2017): "'Unhappy Is the Person Who Has No Motherland': National Ideology and History Writing in Lukashenka's Belarus." In: Fedor, Julie et al (eds.): War and Memory in Russia, Ukraine and Belarus, New York: Palgrave Macmillan, pp. 71–105.

Rutten, Ellen/Fedo, Julie/Zvereva, Vera (eds.) (2014): Memory, Conflict and New Media: Web Wars in Post-Socialist States, London/New York: Routledge.

Saunders, Robert (2016): Popular Geopolitcs and Nation Branding in the Post-Soviet Realm, London: Routledge.

Scharlaj Marina (2017): "Krieg, Kommerz und Kreml-Konzerte: Geschichtsinszenierungen im heutigen Russland." In: Robert Troschitz/Thomas, Kühn (eds.): Populärkultur. Perspektiven und Analysen, Bielefeld: transcript 2017, pp. 157–180.

Schwartz, Matthias (2009): "Postimperiale Erinnerungsbilder. Zum Umgang mit der Geschichte in der russischen Populärkultur." In: Lars Karl/Igor J. Polianski (eds.): Geschichtspolitik und Erinnerungskultur im neuen Russland, Göttingen: V&R unipress, pp. 215–234.

Schwartz, Matthias (2016): "Utopia Going Underground: On Lukyanenko's and Glukhovsky's Literary Refigurations of Postsocialist Belongings between Loyalty and Dissidence to the State." In: The Russian Review 75/4, pp. 589–603.

Schwartz, Matthias (2019): "Ein Sumpf genannt Wirklichkeit. Patriotismus und Gegenkultur im polnischen Hip-Hop." In: Osteuropa 5, pp. 141–155.

Schwartz, Matthias/Weller, Nina/Winkel, Heike (eds.) (2021): After Memory: World War II in Contemporary Eastern European Literatures, Berlin: de Gruyter.

Shumylovych, Bohdan (2019): "Fragmenting Soviet Mythologies: Romantic Imagery and Musical Films in Ukraine." In: Studies in Eastern European Cinema, 10/2, pp. 111–128.

Suslov, Mikhail (2017): "The Eurasian Symphony. Geopolitics and Utopia in Oost-Soviet Alternative History." In: Mark Bassin/Pozo Gonzalo (eds.): The Politics of Eurasianism. Identity, Popular Culture and Russia's Foreign Policy, London/New York: Rowman & Littlefield International, pp. 81–100.

Szczerek, Ziemowit (2013): Przyjdzie Mordor i nas zje, czyli, Tajna historia Słowian, Seria Prozatorska I, Kraków: Korporacja 'Ha!art'.

Szostek, Joanna (2018): "The Mass Media and Russia's 'Sphere of Interests': Mechanisms of Regional Hegemony in Belarus and Ukraine." In: Geopolitics, 23/2, pp. 307–329.

Ther, Philipp (2014): Die neue Ordnung auf dem alten Kontinent: Eine Geschichte des neoliberalen Europa, Berlin: Suhrkamp.

Ugrešić, Dubravka (1998): The Culture of Lies: Antipolitical Essays, Pennsylvania: State University Press.

Yekelchyk, Serhy (2022): "Naming the War: Russian Aggression in Ukrainian Official Discourse and Mass Culture." In: Canadian Slavonic Papers, 64/2-3, pp. 232–246.

Young, James O./Brunk, Conrad G. (eds.) (2012): The Ethics of Cultural Appropriation, Chichester: WileyBlackwell.

Weiss-Wendt, Anton/Nanci Adler (eds.) (2021): The Future of the Soviet Past: The Politics of History in Putin's Russia, Indiana: Indiana University Press.

Weller, Nina (2019): "Gestern wird Krieg sein. Zeitreisen als neoimperiale Wunschmaschinen der russischen Erinnerungskultur." In: Riccardo Nicolosi/Brigitte Obermayr/Nina Weller (eds.): Interventionen in die Zeit. Kontrafaktisches Erzählen und Erinnerungskultur, Paderborn: Schöningh Verlag, pp. 167–198.

Zabirko, Oleksandr (2018): "The Magic Spell of Revanchism: Geopolitical Visions in Post-Soviet Speculative Fiction (Fantastika)." In: Ideology and Politics 1/9, pp. 66–134.

I. Places of Longing:
Yesterday's Tales, Melodramatic Lives
and Astonishing Worlds

## Chapter 1:
# More than Nostalgia
## Late Socialism in Contemporary Russian Television Series

*Mark Lipovetsky*

> Nostalgia is not always about the past.
> It can be retrospective but also prospective.
> (Svetlana Boym 2002: xvii)

## 1. Introduction

More than 20 years have passed since Svetlana Boym published her famous, now classic book *The Future of Nostalgia* (2002), in which she, on the one hand, defined nostalgia as the necessary shadow of modernity, and on the other hand, suggested a distinction between restorative and reflexive nostalgia.[1] While the former embodies the longing for a lost symbolic order, simultaneously (re)producing its idealised mythology, the latter "dwells on the ambivalence of human longing and belonging and does not shy away from the contradictions of modernity" (Boym 2002: xviii) – as exemplified by the works of Joseph Brodsky [Iosif Brodskii] and Ilya Kabakov [Il'ia Kabakov].

However, I would like to argue that since the second decade of the 21st century, the meaning of the representation of the late socialist past has drastically changed and no longer fits the concept of nostalgia, be it restorative or reflexive. One may find a telling example of this new quality of nostalgia in recent Russian TV series depicting the Soviet 1960s-80s. I will focus on several of them: *The Thaw* (*Ottepel'*, 2013, directed and produced by Valerii Todorovskii), *Black Marketeers* (*Fartsa*, 2015, dir. Egor Baranov), *Our Happy Tomorrow* (*Nashe schastlivoe zavtra*, 2016, dir. Igor Kopylov), and *Optimists* (*Optimisty*, 2017, dir. Aleksei Popogrebskii). There are certainly many more miniseries on the Thaw and

---

[1] This article is a shortened version of the article "Bolshe, chem nostalgiia. Pozdnii Sotsializm v Teleserialakh 2010-kh godov" [More than Nostalgia. Late Socialism in TV series of the 2010s"]. In: *Novoe Literaturnoe Obozrenie*,168/3 2021, 127–147, in co-authorship with Tatiana Mikhailova.

Stagnation that appeared in the 2010s, such as *Trouble in Store* (*Delo gastronoma no.1*, literary *The Case of Supermarket No. 1*, 2011, dir. Sergei Ashkenazi), *Furtseva* (2011, dir. Sergei Popov), *The Dark Side of the Moon* (*Obratnaia storona luny*, 2012, dir. Aleksandr Kott), *The Red Queen* (*Krasnaia Koroleva*, 2015, dir. Alëna Rainer), *Margarita Nazarova* (2016, dir. Konstantin Maksimov), *Liudmila Gurchenko* (2016, dir. Sergei Aldonin), *A Mysterious Passion* (*Tainstvennaia strast'*, 2016, dir. Vlad Furman), *Hotel "Rossiya"* (*Gostinitsa Rossiia*, 2017, dir. Sergei Sentsov), and *Little Birch Tree* (*Berëzka*, 2018 dir. Aleksandr Baranov) and many others.

All these series hardly fit a concept of nostalgia due to their focus on illicit, yet systemic aspects of the late Soviet lifestyle – black market trading, corruption, illegal business, bohemian freedom, or a semi-legal industry of glamour. Typically, the protagonist confronts Soviet authorities, while the latter are represented by various officers of the 'organs' and party apparatchiks. These TV series highlight and elevate those who were persecuted and humiliated in the 1960s-70s – the so called *stiliagi* (hipsters, dandies), *fartsovshchiki* (slang for black marketeers), *tsekhoviki* (colloquial term for black market producers) – as true heroes of their time and forerunners of the future (i.e., of the post-Soviet present). However, none of these films selects dissidents as their heroes – political opposition to communist ideology is not what they highlight, but rather capitalism and glamour *within* 'highly-developed socialism' (*razvitoi sotsializm*).[2]

## 2. An Aesthetic Utopia

Valerii Todorovskii's *The Thaw* was indeed a trend-setter, although Todorovskii did not hide the fact that he was directly inspired by Matthew Weiner's American television series *Mad Men* (2007–2015). *The Thaw* gained incredible popularity due to its tasteful and at the same time dazzling stylisation of the fashions, music, dances and even faces of the 1960s. Inspired by Todorovskii's suggestion, many critics initially interpreted *The Thaw* as the post-Soviet version of *Mad Men*, only to discover more differences than similarities with the AMC cult series.

First and foremost, Todorovskii only slightly imitates Matthew Weiner's retromania with his attention to minute details of the time. Todorovskii warned when the series had just been released: "I didn't try telling how it was in reality. There is documentary cinema and other directors seeking to reconstruct the epoch. And I have created a myth. For example, I decided that all women should be beautiful [in my film]" (Efimov 2013).

While creating his 'myth', the Russian director does not avoid stereotypes, rather he fills them with live energy and genuine charm. He openly constructs his series on the basis of a doubling between a film that the characters are producing, and their relations with one another that replicate the affairs of the personages in the film, but more brutally

---

2  One may point to Petr Buslov's *Vysotsky. Thank You for Being Alive* (*Vysotsky. Spasibo, chto zhivoi*, 2011) and Vlad Furman's *A Mysterious Passion* (*Tainstvennaia strast'*, 2016), but the representation of poets who personified the Thaw and Stagnation is so ridiculous in these films exactly because they are stripped of any depth and the protagonists are completely reduced to one-dimensional – flat according to Fredric Jameson – icons of glamour.

and with a greater psychological depth. Following the example of the cult film of the Soviet 60s, Federico Fellini's 8 $\frac{1}{2}$ (1963), Todorovskii blurs the border between filmic reality, artificially created in front of our eyes, and the personal dramas of the film characters. By doing so, he unnoticeably evacuates the characters' political and social troubles into the realm of fiction, thus removing the last obstacles for the representation of the Thaw as the triumph of style and elegance – in other words, as an *aesthetic utopia*.

*The Thaw* appeared in the atmosphere after the protests against the rigged Duma elections and the 'creative class's' attempt to formulate its political will in the winter of 2011–2012 were suppressed, and Todorovskii's series offered an answer to the despair following the failed revolution. The critic Ksenia Larina (2013) argues that Todorovskii depicts the world of Soviet filmmakers as the epitome of a parallel reality of freedom that cannot avoid compromises with the system but, nevertheless, heroically preserves its independence. Andrei Arkhangel'skii (2013), on the contrary, sees in this film a justification of conformism – "a non-ambiguous suggestion to revisit the contract between today's authorities and power and to reorganise it by using the Thaw as a model." In my view, neither of these critical assessments is accurate: indeed, Todorovskii seeks the origins of today's creative class, but he locates the intelligentsia's uniting platform not in its shared ideas, but in its shared lifestyle – chaotic, self-destructive, at times hysterical, at times sentimental, but always *aesthetically attractive*. Ilya Kalinin's analysis of the protest movement of 2011–2012 clearly demonstrates that *The Thaw* with emphasis on the stylistic appeal of the intelligentsia's lifeworld, indeed manifested the protest's actual "ideology", or rather, its substitute: "The political in this protest movement operated as just one other form of the stylistic, and the political protest served as the sign of the stylistic split between 'the cultured us' and 'cultureless them'." (Kalinin 2017) In Kalinin's opinion, this emphasis on style betrayed the elitist character of the protest, which, because of this, was doomed to failure.

In *The Thaw*, one may also detect the formation of the performative discourse for a sociocultural self-identification of the 'creative class' that emerged after 2012 and which Mikhail Iampol'skii has defined in his eponymous book of 2018 as a "park of culture" (*park kul'tury*): "the hipster lifestyle becomes the battlefield, while pogroms and arrests are irrelevant to it. [...] Violence not only coexists with the new lifestyle of today's Moscow; it constitutes its hidden but necessary component." (2018: 15, 29) This formula perfectly fits *The Thaw*, where the bohemian freedom of the filmmakers' circle is defenceless before the aggressive pressure and drunken invasions of the police investigator; where the film administrator never forgets his recent time in the prison camps of the Gulag, where gender repression is normalised, and where almost everyone is eager to turn away from the protagonist, a cameraman Khrustalev (Evgenii Tsyganov), when he is publicly shamed as a coward.

*Figure 1.1: Film still from Evgenii Tsyganov as Khustalev in the TV series* The Thaw *(2013)*

This penetration of violence within the television series into the lifestyle undermines the entire liberational project that this style is supposed to embody. Khrustalev and his friend, director Egor Miachin (Aleksandr Iatsenko) dream about the war film – judging by fragmentary references to the script, they have in mind something similar to Aleksei German's *Trial on the Road* (*Proverka na dorogakh*, 1971) with its stern monochromic style of 1960s 'severe realism'. However, the film that Khrustalev and Miachin are actually shooting within the twelve episodes of the series, whose hack dramaturgy creates counterpoints to the characters' stories and whose climactic optimistic song constitutes a very important part of the miniseries finale, belongs to a completely different genre, namely Soviet musical comedy. Its semi-parodic title *The Girl and the Brigadier* (*Devushka i brigadier*) refers to Ivan Pyriev's infamous musicals of the 1930s and 40s, while its musical style more resonates with Eldar Riazanov's *The Carnival Night* (*Karnaval'naia noch'*, 1956). If the dialogues and situations sound like a mockery, *The Thaw* stylised songs (composer – Konstantin Meladze) stick in the viewer's mind, shaping the series' long-lasting aftertaste.

Notably, both references to Pyriev's musical comedy films and *The Carnival Night* relate to the period preceding the time allegedly depicted in *The Thaw*. Since the drama about the partisan unit remains an abstract dream, and the hack comedy materialises in front of the viewers' eyes, it is the latter rather than the former that arises as the manifestation of Thaw cinema and art in general. This substitution is quite telling: while narrating his characters' artistic compromises for the sake of their future – yet unrealised – project, Todorovskii makes the Thaw, with its sexual freedom, irony and style, indistinguishable from late Stalinist aesthetics with its 'conflictlessness'. Notably, in *The Thaw*, much like in *The Carnival Night*, there is only one evil character – a police investigator Tsanin (Vasilii Mishchenko) – surrounded by various positive and invariably appealing personages.

*Figure 1.2: Film still from a scene from the fictitious comedy* The Girl and Brigadier *in* The Thaw *(2013)*

Indeed, in *The Thaw*, we are dealing with what Fredric Jameson in his *Postmodernism, or, the Cultural Logic of Late Capitalism* called "utopianism after the end of utopia" (1991: 160). According to Jameson, new utopian discourses that appear after the disappointment in leftist utopias of revolutionary change, display "the development of a whole range of properly spatial utopias in which the transformation of social relations and political institutions is projected onto the vision of place and landscape, including the human body" (ibid: 160). The crisis of leftist utopias in the West of the 1970s-80s is comparable with the disappointment associated with Perestroika and its liberational ideology that begins in the 1990s and reaches its peak in the 2010s. Hence, my hypothesis is that the TV series under discussion transform nostalgia into something more profound – a new utopian discourse, which, at the same time, is radically different from our traditional idea of utopia, as any example of 'utopianism after the end of utopia' would be.

The eight-episode television series *Black Marketeers* by the young film director Egor Baranov – later known for the mystical thriller *Gogol. The Beginning* (*Gogol'. Nachalo*, 2017) – is an illuminating case of such utopian spatialisation according to Jameson. The story is set in Moscow beginning with the protagonist's return from Siberia, where he spent a year at the construction of the Bratsk Power Station, which thanks to Evgenii Evtushenko's poem *The Bratsk Station* (*Bratskaia GES*, 1965) is a symbol of the Thaw itself. Even in the most dangerous moments, when an escape from Moscow would save them from trouble, the film's characters never leave the city – this idea literally never crosses their (and the filmmakers') minds. Moscow here emerges as the space of the materialised utopia filled with recognisable symbols of greatness and success (from the legendary opera and pop singer Muslim Magomaev to cosmonaut Iurii Gagarin) as well as with invariably beautiful and fashionable men and women. In the lavish Moscow setting, *Black Marketeers* portrays the life of black marketeers, producers of recordings 'on bones' (i.e., on X-ray film), and illegal hard currency traders, experienced by four young friends, as a series of exciting adventures. These adventures, according to the series' logic, initially stem from the idealistic cult of friendship, but more generally from the youthful desire to enjoy a fulfilled life. Accordingly, Andrei, the central character and the group's leader (played by Aleksandr Petrov), formulates the essence of the Thaw with Robert Rozhdestvenskii's poetic line: "zhit' vzakhleb" [to live fully, in full breath].

An interpretation of the protagonists' criminal business as a chain of exhilarating adventures is emphasised by repeated parallels between the four central characters and Alexandre Dumas' *Three Musketeers*, as well as by Andrei's affinity with D'Artagnan, an extremely popular figure in the late Soviet Union thanks to Georgii Iungval'd-Khil'kevich's television series *D'Artagnan and Three Musketeers* (*D'Artan'ian i tri mushketëra*) from 1978. Notably, the system of characters reminiscent of Dumas' *Three Musketeers* and of the Soviet TV adaption is characteristic of several contemporary TV series under discussion. It serves both as a sign of the characters' free spirit and their problematic relations with the system of power – both being subversive towards it and inseparable from it.

The protagonist of *Black Marketeers* is also an aspiring writer whose first story has been already published in the most popular literary journal of the Thaw period, *Iunost'* (*Youth*). This motif allows the filmmakers to engage the world of literary glamour, represented not only by a fictional femme fatale Valeria Lanskaia (Ekaterina Volkova) but also non-fictional, although highly stylised prototypes like the known authors Vasilii Aksenov, Gennadii Shpalikov, and Mikhail Svetlov. However, the meaning of the 'literary' motif is more substantial. When engaged in his life of adventures, Andrei either cannot write or writes poorly – obviously, his creativity is transferred elsewhere, or in other words, his life adventures substitute his writings. The writing, according to Jameson, also stands for spatialisation of the temporal and, like in *The Thaw*, suggests the evacuation of social problems from the realm of history to the realm of timeless fiction.

The impression that *Black Marketeers* is a timeless adventure rather than a historical narrative also suggests spatialisation instead of temporalisation. The effect of flatness increases with the growing significance of Pont, a larger-than-life villain, played by Evgenii Stychkin. In the film's finale, also in full accordance with the expectations inscribed into the adventure genre, Andrei is miraculously exonerated during the trial, which otherwise would lead to his long-term imprisonment and maybe even execution (as suggested by the story of a historical figure, famous black-market businessman Ian Rokotov, who was executed in 1961 and briefly appears in *Black Marketeers*, played by the star of *The Thaw*, Evgenii Tsyganov). As a *deus ex machina* a KGB officer appears (played by Timofei Tribuntsev): throughout the series he protected Pont as his informer and collaborator, but in the final episode, right before the verdict, he delivers materials to the court, pointing to Pont as the murderer and absolving Andrei. The evil character of the KGB officer thus becomes a saviour figure. This accumulation of improbabilities brings the impression of an adventure flatness to its maximum, only to be broken in the series' finale.

Andrei is exonerated due to his agreement to be a KGB informant and basically to become a new Pont. The viewers learn about this during the final scene, when Andrei's friends overwhelmed by joy meet him at the steps of the courthouse. Only Andrei's mother understands that his miraculous escape from imprisonment suggests a dramatic self-betrayal, and to his admission of guilt: "I've done so many horrible things", she responds bitterly: "And you'll do even more in the future."[3]

---

[3] All translations from Russian quotes are mine if not noted otherwise.

*Figure 1.3: Film still from* Black Marketeers *(2015)*

Only here the adventure narrative ends, and a different temporality takes an upper hand, but this is where the film ends too.

## 3. Remembrance of Idealism Past

In general, almost all the protagonists of these new Russian television series appear to be people who possess true creativity and seek ways to realise it. The viewer understands that only the rigidity of the Soviet system turns their creativity into a crime; under the post-Soviet condition it would be a secure foundation for their social success. However, the main utopian effect of these TV series seems to be associated with the decoupling of capitalism and cynicism, manifesting a tangible mirage of non-cynical profiteering and, by default, politics, conveniently situated in the late Soviet past.

Notably, all these series, with a varying degree of success, try to revive the moralistic narrative of the 1960s, according to which an ethical compromise is the worst crime a person can commit, and that the path of compromises inevitably leads to self-destruction. This narrative clearly represents an antithesis to cynical contempt towards moral values. In post-Soviet television it first reappeared in *The Thaw*, where Khrustalev loses everything, first and foremost the prospect of making his dream film, because during the war he had accepted his father's offer (or rather a plea) to save him from military service. In the climactic scene of *Our Happy Tomorrow*, the series about underground Soviet capitalists – the so-called *tsekhoviki* – in 1989, in the midst of Perestroika, the *tsekhovik* Lugovoi, who by now has lost all his wealth but won his beloved woman, with pathos suggests to his nemesis Kozyrev, a professional criminal, to ask himself: "At what moment did you betray yourself?" This narrative of moral betrayal in many ways resonates in the finale of *Black Marketeers*.

In Soviet films of the 1960s-70s, the function of moralists and guardians of idealism, was embodied by the officers of the organs – most frequently the Ministry of Internal Affairs or the KGB. In *The Thaw*, one such character appears, the aforementioned Tsanin, who investigates the death of the screenwriter Kostia Parshin and eventually rises as an epitome of entrenched Stalinism, systemic hatred towards the intelligentsia and its culture, and, generally speaking, becomes a personification of Soviet cynicism of power.

A similar character appears in *Black Marketeers*, and he openly represents the KGB. Timofei Tribuntsev plays Captain Ivanov as a disgusting character, and the film represents his villainy with almost a comical excess. Not only does he cover up for Pont, who pays him a significant fee for 'protection' – thus foreshadowing business practices of post-Soviet law enforcement officials, the so called 'siloviki' – but his henchmen also torture suspects imitating the Stalinist period. The KGB villainy is counterweighted in *Black Marketeers* by the moral authority and support provided by an honest policeman, who happens to be the father of the protagonist's love interest, German Mikhailovich Vostrikov, played by Aleksei Serebriakov. Notably, in *Little Birch Tree*, a 2018 TV series about the famed Soviet folk-dance ensemble, Serebriakov plays a KGB officer, who becomes the guardian angel for the ensemble and especially its director, while all villainy is delegated to a small clerk from the Ministry of Culture. From *The Thaw*, to *Little Birch Tree*, from 2013 to 2018, the power figure has accomplished a full transformation from a super-cynic to a guardian angel.

Such a 'splitting' of the figure representing the Soviet regime and its violence, into a grotesque villain and magic helper, is quite typical for all the series under discussion. It reflects filmmakers' ambivalence towards the Soviet system, or more generally, towards the Soviet past. On the one hand, the Soviet system serves as the obstacle to the protagonists' self-realisation. On the other, it stimulates their ingenuity and challenges their talents. The system harasses and represses them, while at the same time producing the *demand* for underground capitalist business and adding the significant *cultural capital* of rebellion and martyrdom to the transgressors, from *stiliagi* and modernist filmmakers to black marketeers. In short, this ambivalence reveals a co-dependence of the utopian non-cynical capitalism, as depicted in these films, and the repressive Soviet system, a co-dependence that deserves a closer look.

## 4. "A Deep State" of Late Socialism

On 11 February, 2019 Vladislav Surkov, at the time still Putin's closest aid, published an article titled "Putin's Lasting State". Among many suspicious claims about the greatness of Putin's state and its 'export potential', Surkov argues that this political order is more *honest* than its Western counterparts. Why? Because Western states apparently are secretly administered by the 'deep state' – an alliance of powerful agents and organisations, legal and illegal alike, that operates beyond democratic institutions and blatantly uses violence and corruption, alluding to a staple of multiple conspiracy theories. On the contrary, the Russian state is not split up into deep and external; it is built as a whole, with all of its parts and its manifestations facing out. The most brutal constructions of its authoritarian frame are displayed as part of the façade, undisguised by any architectural embellishments. The bureaucratic apparatus, even when it tries to do something clandestinely, does not try too hard to cover its tracks, as if assuming that "everyone understands everything anyway." (Surkov 2019)

If unpacked, Surkov's statement reveals an Orwellian paradox at its core: the Russian state is honest because it is openly deceptive and corrupt. Surprisingly Surkov's revelations did not cause much stir (if any) in the Russian media, apparently this logic has been adopted by contemporary Russian culture long before Surkov articulated it. More precisely, it has been cultivated by various means, including popular culture. It would not be an exaggeration to say that Surkov's self-righteous legitimisation of violence and corruption directly stems from the discourse shaped by the TV series I discuss here. The contemporary social, political and economic order is represented in them as the direct heir not to the formal Soviet system, as Western analysts frequently believe, but to the informal 'deep state' that was hidden underneath late socialism's surface and absorbed its brightest and most dynamic elements. By the means of this imagined genealogy, contemporary Russian social order is placed *beyond* any legal or moral judgment, as the 'third', hybrid and utopian, path, situated *between capitalism and communism*.

Another TV series, *Optimists* (2017–2021) based on the idea by Mikhail Shprits and Mikhail Idov, directed by the famous Aleksei Popogrebskii, author of the acclaimed films *Koktebel'* (2003), and *How I Ended this Summer* (*Kak ia provel ėtim letom*, 2010), highlights a connection between the imaginary Soviet deep state and contemporary Russia's politics. Notably, this TV series depicting Soviet diplomats in the early 1960s, received direct approval from the 'profile ministry' – in this case from the head of the Russian Foreign Office, Sergei Lavrov (cf. [Anon.] 2017). This is especially curious since at the same time as Lavrov's approval, *Parlamentskaia gazeta* published an angry letter from one of the Russian 'senators' Andrei Sobolev (2017), who felt offended by the fact that "in the difficult international situation of the 1960s Soviet diplomats are drinking vodka, sleeping around and endlessly smoking foreign cigarettes."

The series begins with the American exhibition in Sokolniki in 1959, which obviates the cultural gap between Soviet and American understandings of international politics. The *Optimists* are the staff members of the newly created Information-Analytical Group and their group's creator is an American communist of Latvian descent Ruta Blaumane (Severija Janušauskaitė, a future star of Tim Tykwer's *Babylon Berlin*). Their new boss Viktor Biriukov also features, a seasoned party apparatchik, with military experience not only from WWII but also from Budapest in 1956, he was one of those officers who crushed the Hungarian uprising (played by Vladimir Vdovichenkov, a former star of the TV series *Brigada* about 1990s gangster capitalism).

*Figure 1.4: Film still from Ruta and Biriukov in* Optimists *(2017–2021)*

Both Blaumane and Biriukov are transgressive, yet in a different way. As Popogrebskii explains, Biriukov from the very beginning is depicted as a seasoned Stalinist, while Blaumane is cheating on her husband, a heroic pilot, and without any hesitation writes a slanderous denunciation implicating Biriukov after their first rough encounter. Young characters are also far from being Soviet poster boys, in certain ways, they are borderline Soviet outcasts – a Jew, a son of reemigrants who perished in the Gulag, a secret American agent. Paradoxically, their marginality in relation to Soviet standards makes them most fitting for the role of transgressive reformers.

The first half of the series unfolds as a narrative about the 'westernisation' or, rather 'Americanisation' of Soviet diplomatic style – 'optimists' educate themselves and teach others how to utilise the media for political purposes and how to manipulate Western public opinion. These funny or not so funny episodes include storylines about the American pilot Powers, canine cosmonauts Belka and Strelka, or the media representation of Soviet fishermen lost in the ocean and found by Americans (an obvious reworking of the 1960 story about the Soviet Sergeant Ashkat Ziganshin and his crew). Apparently, Soviet diplomacy learns from the Western media how to do politics in the society of spectacle. Proudly and with panache, the series' protagonists demonstrate that the withholding and distortion of information is the most effective political tool and that it can produce a tremendous effect on the 'world's destiny'. This part of the film looks like clumsy advocacy for the 'spectacular' methods employed by Russian diplomats in the post-Crimean epoch and the heavy hand of the political commission from Lavrov's ministry is easily detectable here. However, despite a faithful reproduction of Cold War rhetoric, this series reveals the Soviet (and Russian) establishment's unrequited love for the West, hidden under the disguise of confrontation. The style and cut of Soviet diplomats' clothing, as well as their secret and not so secret sexual affairs with Westerners help to visualise this paradox.

Even more paradoxical is that while trying to act as real Westerners, the Soviet diplomats, in fact, act as imaginary devious capitalists lampooned by Soviet (and nowadays Russian) propaganda. At the same time, the series' authors present the adoption of dirty media tricks by the protagonists as proof of the true modernisation of Soviet international politics, which is confirmed by the verdict that comes from a highly placed Party functionary, a hidden Stalinist, who wants to disband the Information-Analytical Group: "Your department was created to convince our enemies that we are like them."

In the second part of the series, however, diplomats almost entirely forget about foreign affairs and find themselves fully absorbed by domestic politics. The theme of betrayal and self-betrayal begins to dominate the series' plot manifested by almost all central characters. In the beginning of the series, Blaumane writes a political denunciation of Biriukov, while having an affair with the KGB overseer of the ministry; and in the twelfth episode she has sex with Biriukov when her husband, half-paralyzed after the unsuccessful trial of a new fighter plane, falls and dies at home. Biriukov's secret love, a German journalist Gabi Getze (Karolina Grushka), is shot dead during a sting operation that he arranged, and the young son of his adversary dies after a car collision, organised on Biriukov's request. Andri Muratov (Egor Koreshkov) learns that his wife has denounced him to the KGB out of jealousy. A naïve and idealistic Arkadii Golub' (Rinat Mukhametov) is forced to take a bribe for his assistance in getting a foreign passport for a fictional Soviet genetics, Stanislav Pimenov, who will defect during a conference in Princeton. When arrested, Golub admits under pressure that he did this on Biriukov's orders (which is a lie). Even Lenia Korneev (played by Artem Bystrov, known by Iurii Bykov's film *The Fool* (*Durak*, 2014)), who seems to be a perfect example of the true Soviet diplomat – he is a street-smart former sailor, with rough manners – appears to be a victim of CIA entrapment: he agreed to collaborate with the US while in Cuba, and now the Moscow-based CIA officer reestablishes his connection with the former sailor who is beginning his career in the Soviet foreign ministry.

*Figure 1.5: Film still from three Soviet diplomats, three transgressors in* Optimists *(2017–2021)*

Considering the importance of the theme of faithfulness to oneself and one's ideals as the antithesis to today's cynicism in all the TV series under discussion, such a treatment of this motif in *Optimists* looks like an aberration. However, it is not. Rather, it reveals the true meaning of the alleged idealism of the past heroes in all these films. *Optimists* most openly, albeit in a caricature-like way, shows how the late Soviet 'deep state' functions by depicting a fictitious attempt of the anti-Khrushchev *coup d'état* in 1960. Until this moment, Biriukov devotedly serves the coup leader as his faithful lieutenant. However, when he learns that members in his group will be persecuted as traitors after the coup's success, Biriukov (with Blaumane's help) betrays his former mentor and protector by turning the same methods of media disinformation that they used on the international scene against the domestic conspirators.

Thanks to this mega-treason, all the film's protagonists, despite their own acts of betrayal, flourish in the film's finale and in the second season of the series released in 2021. Ruta Blaumane becomes the deputy minister of foreign affairs; Biriukov receives a post in the Central Committee; Arkadii Golub' is appointed as the head of the Information-Analytical Group instead of Biriukov; and Korneev ends up the chair of the KGB supervisor for the entire Ministry of Foreign Affairs. Notably, Muratov who did not betray anyone but was betrayed himself, is 'rewarded' in the least spectacular way – he is appointed to the Congo embassy where he departs together with his treacherous wife. In other words, after the defeat of old party apparatchiks, now they, young and transgressive, constitute the new deep state. Ignoring historical detail, the filmmakers make it clear that *this* deep state has assumed power after 2014.

From this perspective, the plot of *Optimists* – as well as other TV series of this kind – looks to be a rite of passage that the heroes need to undergo in order to join the new, post-Soviet, deep state. Alleged idealism helps the film's authors to justify the viewers' moral solidarity with these characters and their subsequent transformations. But it is the protagonists' ability to betray and to forget about their betrayals – i.e., to become cold and shameless cynics – that constitutes the critical condition for their 'admission' to the new order. In this respect, *Optimists* obviates the genealogy or contemporary power that is detectable in all of these series. Genealogy of power, according to Foucault (Rabinow 1998: 374), is based not on linearity but on ruptures and breakdowns – apparently, the moment of the betrayal of the former idealism imaginary constitutes the point of origin for the contemporary cultural, political and symbolic regime of power.

## 5. Retrotopia Unpacked

What is the new quality of nostalgia as manifested by these and similar TV series of the 2010s? One may define it with Zygmunt Bauman's term 'retrotopia' which he derives from Svetlana Boym's conceptualisation of nostalgia. He also cites Walter Benjamin's famous description of Paul Klee's *Angelus Novus* (1920) as the Angel of History whose face is turned towards the past, in which he sees nothing but "a single catastrophe which keeps piling wreckage" and who is smashed by the storm blowing from Paradise: "The storm irresistibly propels him into the future to which his back is turned, while the pile of debris [from the past] before him grows skyward" (Benjamin 1968: 249). In Bauman's words, nowadays this Angel of History is changing direction, he is caught in the midst of a U-turn, his face turning from the past to the future, his wings being pushed backwards by the storm blowing this time from the imagined, anticipated and feared in advance Hell of the future towards the Paradise of the past [...] The road to future looks uncannily as a trail of corruption and degeneration. Perhaps the road back, to the past, won't miss the chance of turning into a trail of cleansing from the damages committed by futures, whenever they turned into a present? (Bauman 2017: 2, 6)

In other words, in the retrotopian discourse the past has replaced the future. This concept resonates with the series under discussion. Both Mikhail Iampol'skii (2014) and Andrei Arkhangelskii (2013) suggest that these TV series attempt to cure the axiological disorientation experienced by post-Soviet people. The dominant ideological discourse simultaneously glorifies the Soviet period as the paradise lost and justifies neoliberal capitalism as the most effective economic order. On the contrary, the viewer of TV series about the Thaw and Stagnation finds the source of comfort in the realisation that the dreams of the miniseries' characters about foreign clothing and music, travel abroad and filming erotic scenes without the control of the Party has already been successfully accomplished in the present. Thus, what is indeed, albeit indirectly, glorified in retrotopias, is not the past but the present. Retrotopias, according to Bauman, offer "a firm ground thought to provide and hopefully guarantee an acceptable modicum of stability and therefore a satisfactory degree of self-assurance" (Bauman 2017: 8).

It would also be logical to explain the sense of post-Soviet confusion and identity splits with the contradictory or lost societal *telos*, which is also the reason for the absence of any captivating images of the future in contemporary Russian culture, both in social and literary discourses. Bauman's conceptualisation of retrotopia treats it as the modification of a traditional utopia. It was Northrop Frye, who famously compared the genre of utopia with the social contract offering the 'imaginative telos' to society:

There are two social conceptions which can be expressed only in terms of myth. One is the social contract, which presents an account of the origins of society. The other is the utopia which presents the imaginative telos or end at which social life aims. [...] The social contract, though a genuine myth which, in John Stuart Mill's phrase, passes a fiction off as a fact, is usually regarded as an integral part of social theory. The utopia, on the other hand, although its origin is such the same, belongs primarily to fiction. The reason is that the emphasis in the contract myth falls on the present facts of society which it is supposed to explain. And even to the extent that the contract myth is projected into the past, and so the myth preserves the gesture of making assertion that can be definitely verified or refuted. (Frye 1965: 323)

Not everything in this definition fits contemporary Russian retrotopias. First of all, they do not depict the utopian space and time of the past as rational, let alone faultless. On the contrary, they frequently emphasise negative aspects of the past, especially if these features seem not to be relevant for the present. Nevertheless, whether the heroes and heroines of the past fail or triumph in these miniseries, their performances create a utopian perspective on the past, not on the level of conscious goals but on the level of *affect*. This affect stems from the purely aesthetic aspects in the representation of the recent past, enhanced by the beauty of actors, elegance of settings and exoticism of clothing. These films, unlike classical utopias, do not situate a societal telos in the past, nor do they seek to provide "yesterday's solutions to today's problems", to use Bauman's expression, because as we know, affect is pre-cognitive, yet, it creates an illusion of knowing and understanding and thus is deceptive.[4]

However, and this is the most vital aspect of retrotopias – *they blur the distinction between the social contract and utopia*, or rather, present the affective utopia as a new social contract. Much like the latter, retrotopias project their myth into the past thus creating an illusion of historical evidence. But most importantly, retrotopian emphasis also "falls on the present facts of society which it is supposed to explain". Probably not only explain – but mostly justify, although this can be said about the social contract as well. This is not a neo-traditionalist, but a neo-conservative social contract that paradoxically reaches out to select transgressive and rebellious elements[5] of late Soviet history in order to validate today's status quo. By this means it simultaneously justifies the state repression and pardons citizens' legal nihilism, advocates obedience and absolves rebellion.

The emergence of retrotopias as a new social contract can be explained from various perspectives: either by the disappointment in 'traditional' utopias of a radiant future – whether communist or capitalist alike – or the instability of all social contracts, to which the ruling regime seemed to subscribe. Nevertheless, they provide a comforting effect. These retrotopias symbolically protect the viewer from the dangerous future and offer an escape from the present. In deep resonance with Adorno's and Horkheimer's description of the culture industry: "It is indeed escape, but not, as it claims, escape from bad reality but from the last thought of resisting that reality" (Horkheimer/Adorno 2002: 116).

## Filmography

$8\frac{1}{2}$, dir. Federico Fellini, Italy/France 1963.
*A mysterious passion* (*Tainstvennaia strast'*), dir. Vlad Furman, Russia 2016.
*Babylon Berlin*, dir. Tim Tykwer, Germany 2017–2023.
*Little Birch Tree* (*Berëzka*), dir. Aleksandr Baranov, Russia 2018.
*D'Artagnan and Three Musketeers* (*D'Artan'ian i tri mushketëra*), dir. Georgii Iungval'd-Khil'kevich, USSR 1978.
*Black Marketeers* (*Fartsa*), dir. Egor Baranov, Russia 2013.
*Furtseva*, dir. Sergei Popov, Russia 2011.
*Gogol. The Beginning* (*Gogol'. Nachalo*) dir. Egor Baranov Russia 2017.
*Hotel "Rossiya"* (*Gostinitsa Rossiia*), dir. Sergei Sentsov, Russia 2017.
*How I Ended this Summer* (*Kak ia provel étim letom*), dir. Aleksei Popogrebskii, Russia 2010.
*Koktebel'*, dir. Aleksei Popogrebskii, Russia 2003.
*Liudmila Gurchenko*, dir. Sergei Aldonin, Russia 2016.

---

4    Cf. Massumi 2002 on affective knowledge.
5    As noted by Ilya Kukulin, "performances of transgression in Russia's public sphere could be seen as elements of a shared system of public expression, almost unconnected to any specific political ideology and/or social stratum. These performances constitute the horizon of expectations for the conformist majority" (Kukulin 2018: 229).

*Mad Men*, dir. Matthew Weiner, USA 2007–2015.
*Margarita Nazarova*, dir. Konstantin Maksimov, Russia 2016.
*Optimists* (*Optimisty*), dir. Aleksei Popogrebskii, Russia 2017–2021.
*The Carnival Night* (*Karnaval'naia noch'*), dir. Eldar Riazanov, USSR 1956.
*The Dark Side of the Moon* (*Obratnaia storona luny*), dir. Aleksandr Kott, Russia 2012.
*The Fool* (*Durak*), dir. Iurii Bykov, Russia 2014.
*The Red Queen* (*Krasnaia Koroleva*), dir. Alëna Rainer, Russia/Ukraine 2015.
*The Thaw* (*Ottepel'*), dir. Valerii Todorovskii, Russia 2013.
*Trial on the Road* (*Proverka na dorogakh*), dir. Aleksei German, USSR 1971.
*Trouble in Store* (*Delo gastronoma no.1*, literary *The Case of Supermarket no. 1*), dir. Sergei Ashkenazi, Russia 2011.
*Our Happy Tomorrow* (*Nashe schastlivoe zavtra*), dir. Igor Kopylov, Russia 2016.

## List of Illustrations

**Figure 1.1:** Film still from the TV series *The Thaw* (*Ottepel'*), dir. Valerii Todorovskii, Russia 2013.
**Figure 1.2:** Film still from the comedy *The Girl and Brigadier* – film within the series *The Thaw* (*Ottepel'*), dir. Valerii Todorovskii, Russia 2013.
**Figure 1.3:** Film still from film *Black Marketeers* (*Fartsa*), dir. Egor Baranov, Russia 2013.
**Figure 1.4:** Film still from the TV Series *Optimists* (*Optimisty*), dir. Aleksei Popogrebskii, Russia 2017–2021.
**Figure 1.5:** Film still from the TV Series *Optimists* (*Optimisty*), dir. Aleksei Popogrebskii, Russia 2017–2021.

## References

[Anon.] (2017): "Lavrov nadeetsia, chto serial 'Optimisty' pomozhet molodezhi vybirat' professiiu diplomata." In: TASS, 25 April 2017 (https://tass.ru/obschestvo/4209864) [21 December 2022].
Arkhangel'skii, Andrei (2013): "Khrustalev, mashinku!" In: Kommersant, 9 December 2013 (https://www.kommersant.ru/doc/2358217) [21 December 2022].
Benjamin, Walter (1968): Illuminations. Edited and with an introd. by Hannah Arendt, translated by Harry Zohn, New York: Harcourt, Brace & World.
Boym, Svetlana (2002): The Future of Nostalgia, New York: Basic Books.
Bauman, Zygmunt (2017): Retrotopia, Cambridge: Polity.
Efimov Sergei (2013): "Valerii Todorovskii: 'Ia reshil, chto v 'Ottepeli' vse zhenshchiny budut krasivymi'." In: Komsmol'skaia Pravda, 2 December 2013 (https://www.kp.ru/daily/26166.5/3053484/) [21 December 2022].
Frye, Northrop (1965): "Varieties of Literary Utopia." In: Dedalus 94/2 (Spring), pp. 323–347.
Horkheimer, Max/Adorno, Theodor W. (2002): "The culture industry: Enlightenment as mass deception." In: Gunzelin Schmid Noerr (ed.): Dialectic of Enlightenment: Philo-

sophical Fragments, translated by Edmund Jephcott, Stanford: Stanford University Press, pp. 94–136.

Iampol'skii, Mikhail (2014): "Dvoiniki i zaemnoe ia." In: Seans, 28 March 2014 (https://seance.ru/articles/dvojniki-i-zaemnoe-ya/) [21 December 2022].

Iampol'skii, Mikhail (2018): Park kul'tury: Kul'tura i nasilie v Moskve segodnia, Moscow: Novoe izdatel'stvo.

Jameson, Fredric (1991): Postmodernism, or, the Cultural Logic of Late Capitalism, Durham: Duke University Press.

Kalinin, Ilya (2017): "O tom, kak nekul'turnoe gosudarstvo obygralo kul'turnuiu oppozitsiiu na ee zhe pole, ili pochemu, dve Rossii men'she, chem 'edinaia Rossiia'." In: Neprikosnovennyi zapas 6 (http://magazines.russ.ru/nz/2017/6/o-tom-kak-nekulturnoe- gosudarstvo-obygralo-kulturnuyu-oppoziciy.html) [21 December 2022].

Kukulin, Ilya (2018): "Cultural Shifts in Russia since 2010: Messianic Cynicism and Paradigms of Artistic Resistance." In: Russian Literature 96/98, pp. 221–254.

Larina, Kseniia (2013): "Chelovek idet za solntsem." In: The New Times 41/308 (https://newtimes.ru/articles/detail/75506/) [21 December 2022].

Massumi, Brian (2002): From Parables for the Virtual, Durham: Duke University Press.

Rabinow, Paul (ed.) (1988): The Essential Works of Michel Foucault, 2, Aesthetics: Method and Epistemology, edited by James Faubion, translated by Robert Herley et al., New York: New Press.

Sobolev, Andrei (2017): "Serial 'Optimisty' – paskvil' na otechestvennyi dipkorpus." In: Parlamentskaia gazeta, 28 April 2017 (https://www.pnp.ru/culture/serial-optimisty-paskvil-na-otechestvennyy-dipkorpus.html) [21 December 2022].

Surkov Vladislav (2019): "Dolgoe gosudarstvo Putina. O tom, chto zdes' voobshche proiskhodit." In: Nezavisimaya gazeta, 1 February, 2019 (http://www.ng.ru/ideas/2019-02-11/5_7503_surkov.html) [21 December 2022].

## Chapter 2:
# Drawn History
Ukrainian Graphic Fiction about National History

*Svitlana Pidoprygora*

## 1. Introduction

For centuries, the history of Ukraine has been the subject of interest for not only writers but also numerous artists, who have drawn upon varied styles, genres, and approaches to interest their readers and acquaint them with the past, draw parallels with the present, and point towards the future.[1] Naturally, the ideological conceptions of such works corresponded to the artists' worldview and the cultural-historical circumstances of their work and, in some instances, they played a key role for constructing an imagined national idea – as was the case with novels by Raisa Ivanchenko, Roman Ivanychuk, Ivan Bilyk, and others. When Soviet-era history books falsified the past, a sense of that history could be drawn from historical fiction. But it was only the boom in mass literature, which started in the early 1990s, that introduced historical images and themes that had otherwise been silenced to a broader public. In particular, Ukrainian crime novels, melodramas, women's literature, and thrillers prevailed and formed the basis for further popular engagement with the topic in comic books and graphic novels or graphic fiction. Thus, in the political circumstances of present-day Ukraine, comic books became a popular platform for the discussion of contested issues and formed a bridge between historical memory and the present through the close intertwining of words and pictures, i.e., visual images.

This trend corresponds to a general tendency in 20th century popular culture, where visual representations became increasingly more important than textual narratives. In a way, the visual became the calling-card of contemporary mass culture, as Fredric Jameson writes, whereas

---

[1]  This article uses materials from my monograph *Ukraïnska eksperymentalna proza XX – pochatku XXI stolit: 'nemozhlyva literatura'* (*Ukrainian Experimental Prose of the 20th and early 21st Centuries: An "Impossible" Literature*, 2018), particularly the sub-chapter "The Experimental Nature of Visual Literature and Graphic Fiction" (221–253).

the image, now liberated from complex temporalities of a plot you need to read and decipher, to reconstruct at every point, [began] to call for a different kind of visual attention [...] projecting something like a visual hermeneutic which the eye scans for ever deeper layers of meaning. (Jameson 1998: 127)

Late 20th century scholarship reacted to this tendency with the new research field of visual studies, which analyses visual artistic works (such as comics, graphic novels, video games, commercial ads, etc.) in relation to its implied ideology, social myths, and economics, focussing on the production and politics of signification within a given cultural context. This is especially true for graphic fiction, including comics and graphic novels, which often use visual metaphors to increase the images' variegated associativity, making them understandable within the context of the cultural, political or sociological situation of their own society. In this essay I will analyse some of these visual constructions of national history in Ukrainian comics and graphic novels as a specific form of national appropriation of the past.

## 2. The Comic Book. Cossacks in Ukrainian Comic Books

The comic book as drawn history has a long history – scholars trace it back to cave paintings, Egyptian hieroglyphics, Maya codices, medieval miniatures, illustrations of the Bible, and late 18th- early 19th century English political caricatures. The development of comics was enabled by a powerful explosion of mass culture on account of new technology that allowed the mechanical reproduction of images.

For a long time, professional academic analysis of comic books was hindered by the prejudiced opinion of it as a 'low' genre. However, starting from the mid-20th century, the comic book attracted increasing academic attention. We can find the beginnings of intellectual consideration of comic books in the works of such renowned semioticians as Roland Barthes and Umberto Eco. Eco views the comic book in the context of mythological narrative ("The Myth of Superman"). He posits that superhero comics – like ancient visual narratives – are meant to present the protagonist as a paragon of moral virtue and national pride (1979: 107–124). However, this does not preclude the fact that comic books comprise highly motivated signs, images and symbols, which generate meanings in various ways, creating a code for the reader to interpret.

International scholars conceptualise the comic as a 20th century cultural phenomenon that, despite its seemingly primitive nature, deserves serious attention as an indicator of social sentiments and tastes, a powerful tool of influence with profound communicative potential. Comics express the "word – symbol – image interaction" (Booker 2011: 958). They are not mere illustrations of the narrative, not just pictures accompanied by text, but a cohesive unit of word and image, a meaning-making interconnection. "Thanks to the interaction of verbal and nonverbal components," Liubov' Stoliarova notes, "the comic encompasses within itself a high volume of easily decipherable information" (2010: 384).

In the concluding decades of the 20th century, and the early 21st century, comics studies became especially popular in Western academic settings (McCloud 1993; Eisner

2008). A number of studies touched upon the question of the comic's evolution, its expression of national traditions, and view the comic in the context of visual rhetoric, multimodality, mediality and complex artistry.

In recent years, graphic novels especially have become increasingly popular in many countries, gaining recognition also with literary awards and artistic rankings. Also in post-Soviet space, with the lifting of state regulation and censorship, comics and graphic novels are gradually appealing to ever larger numbers of readers. Since 2010, Ukrainian literature has incorporated increasing amounts of various graphic literary works. A recent book market overview of Ukrainian comics lists several works that can compete with international products and are anchored in a national *Weltanschauung* and have a distinctly Ukrainian flavour, as one critique put it (Koval 2017).[2]

This 'Ukrainian flavour' is most clearly manifest in the themes of images in graphic fiction that highlight certain key events (periods) in the national history such as the Cossack age, the early 20th century 'national liberation struggle', the Soviet era or the war in Eastern Ukraine since 2014 to the present.[3] It is notable that not so many comics are dedicated to the treatment of the Soviet era (where national elements are not as prominent). Currently growing in popularity is a series of comics by Oleksandr Koreshkov entitled *Among the sheep (Sered ovets'*, 2018). The work's fictional space-time is full of signs marking Soviet realities of the 1950s through the 1970s: slogans like "Forwards to a Bright Future!", "The Party and the People Are One!", "Glory to Toil!", workers' grey uniforms, work passes, vigilantes, 'boy scouts' (pioneers) with red kerchiefs. In a playful, colourful, animation-like form, with animal characters like dogs, pigs or sheep, the comic offers a social satire of the Soviet reality, which, however, could be associated not only with the Soviet order, but with any form of violence against the individual. The anthropomorphism of the work, and the serious problems it touches on, is reminiscent of Art Spiegelman's style in his graphic novel *Maus: A Survivor's Tale* (1980). In the first book of Koreshkov's series, the canine protagonist (we are not told his name) is dismissed from factory work for being outraged with the director (a ram) who let him wait at his office door for a long time. He is intercepted and beaten up by vigilantes, asking why he is not at work; he witnesses a car crash when a drunken official (a hog) runs over a child at a station. The driver and the injured child are taken away by an ambulance, while a bystander is blamed in the news. These events force the protagonist to break with the usual scenario of being a silent witness to lies and they force him to overcome his own fear (Koreshkov 2018). In the comic, we trace an allusion to George Orwell's dystopia *Animal Farm* (1945), which uses animal protagonists as well as an allegory to expose the 'Soviet myth' of socialist life. Subsequent issues of Koreshkov's comic (four to date) discuss the protagonist's further resistance to

---

2   The market overview was done by *Chytomo*, an internet resource that publishes the latest information about the Ukrainian book market, events and projects, as well as analyses the development of Ukrainian book publishing https://chytomo.com/ [30 September 2023].

3   This article was written in November 2021, before the start of the full-scale war of the Russian Federation against Ukraine on February 24, 2022. Therefore, it does not discuss comics that appeared after the large-scale invasion and continue to emerge throughout the war. These comics now represent a significant layer of Ukrainian comic culture as of May 2024.

the system, his transformation from victim to a fighter and defender of others, a transition to active resistance.

Ukrainian contemporary authors of visual stories draw particular inspiration from the Zaporizhian Cossacks from the early modern period, interpreting this period anew in the context of contemporary mass culture. In particular, mythical Cossacks of strong character became the embodiment of the national superhero. Thus, it makes sense to view the comic as a mythological narrative that playfully offers positive role models to society, accumulates patriotism, awakens national pride for days of yore, thus striving to inspire heroic acts also in the present day. In doing so, these comics do not artificially construct a new Ukrainian narrative about the Cossack past, but rather revise and adapt these pre-existing narratives for the present, from post-independence (1991) to wartime (2014 onwards) Ukraine.

Comics dedicated to the fictional, legendary adventures of the Cossacks began to appear in Ukraine already in the 1990s, mostly in children's magazines. Thus, the newspaper *Robitnycha hazeta* (*Worker's Gazette*) published the *Buiviter* comic in 1995, written and drawn by Kostiantyn Sulyma.

In this story everything is aimed at fostering patriotism and praising the protagonists' courage, when the Cossacks in their conflict with *basurmany* (infidels),[4] *yasyr* (booty)[5] or magical monsters at last gain the obligatory victory for good. Accordingly, whereas an infidel gets his magical powers from a monster in exchange for his soul, the Cossack restores his power thanks to his native soil, and the holy cross. The structure of the comic is complicated by its narrative framing: the story of Buiviter's feat is told by a grandfather to his grandchildren, and in the end, it turns out that the grandfather himself is Buiviter's son. The young listeners understand their part in a struggle that is not complete – in the end, evil returns and the boys pick up Buiviter's magic sword. The striking drawings, the non-traditional placement of the frames (one drawing per page), the shading and colours (negative characters are depicted in dark colours, and as doing their dark deeds at nights, whereas Buiviter and the Cossacks are depicted in daylight and in bright colours), the negative caricature-like depiction of the infidel antagonists and the more realistic depiction of the Ukrainian Cossack protagonists, shapes the perception of an antithetical world, divided into good and evil, with Ukrainians standing unquestionably on the side of good. The comic also underscores important words with a larger font such as "Run for your life" and "Time". The rage of Khiz-Gireia and his yearning for revenge is emphasised by writing his remarks in white letters on a black background in the bubbles. This makes reading harder, thus deepening the prejudice against this character. The authors of the article "The history of Ukrainian comics" point out that "Buiviter became a Ukrainian superhero of a Ukrainian epic. The story became extremely popular, because there was no cult of a liberator hero in the country prior to

---

4   *Basurmany* is an archaic word once used to denote 'infidels', people of non-Christian faith; it was often associated with Tataro-Mongols, who raided Slavic lands, and who were eventually opposed by Cossacks. Later the term came to mean foreign enemies, or enemies of foreign faiths.

5   *Yasyr* is a term used (in the mid-15th to mid-18th centuries) to denote people taken prisoner by Turks and Tatars during fighting or raids on Slavic lands. Prisoners from the *yasyr* were intended to be sold at special markets for the trade of captives.

that. The clear image of the Ukrainian Cossack was turned into a superhero" ([Anon.] 2020). It was the first time in the Ukrainian cultural discourse that the Cossacks are viewed through the prism of superhero qualities. However, Buiviter can be seen as a protagonist adapting superhero qualities while not quite fully inhabiting it yet, because he lacks certain features that would allow us to classify him as such.

*Figure 2.1: Scene from comic* Buiviter *(1995)*

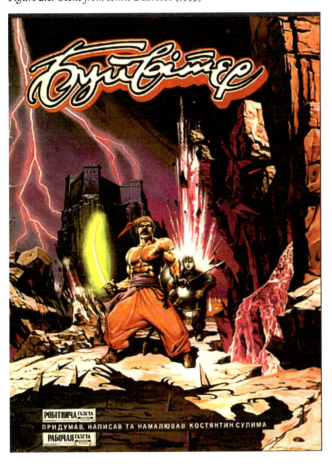

An attempt to publish a caricature comic, where the protagonists act, talk and are depicted in the manner of an animated film, was made by the Kozaky publishing house in 1992 in the comic *Marco Pyrih the Cossack. How Pyrih Became Pyrih* (*Marko Pyrih, zaporozhets'. Iak Pyrih stav Pyrohom*, 1992), written by Vadym Karpenko and drawn by Oleksandr Haiduchenko. The events of the plot are presented through the prism of burlesque humour. The heroes Marko Pyrih, Kharko Zhytymozhna, Koshovyi, Krutyviter, deacon Omel'ko, bard (*kobzar*) Zahrai inhabit an optimistic space, where even adversity is faced with levity and humour. The drawings of this comic are in a conventional style, the narrative is uncomplicated, however the characters seem to talk too much. The text in the speech bubbles disturbs the images, because at times every character in the frame has something to say on a given matter. The comic looks like a series of sketches from the *Krokodil*[6] and *Perets'* (*Pepper*)[7] magazines. No heroic image of Cossacks is presented here, rather they are shown to drink, play and engage in sport during peacetime, sometimes defending their everyday interests like inventive men who will always find a way.

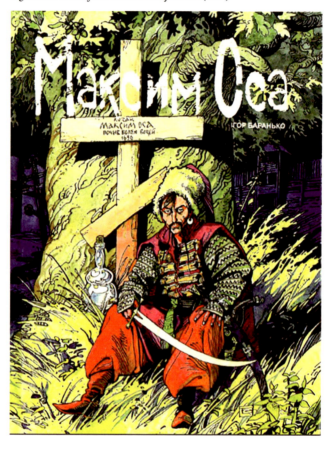

*Figure 2.2: Scene from comic* Maksym Osa *(2011)*

A different approach to the topic was chosen by Ihor Baran'ko, who in 2011 published his comic strip novel *Maksym Osa*. Baran'ko is a renowned Ukrainian author of international acclaimed comics, living abroad and working with multiple publishers in different

---

6  *Krokodil* was a "mass satirical journal founded in Moscow in 1922 as a supplement to the *Worker's Gazette*. From 1933 onwards it was published in the Pravda printing press. The pages of the publication gave the reader humorous and satirical words by I. Il'f and E. Petrov, M. Zoshchenko, V. Maiakovskii [...] and others, accompanied with sketches by artists D. Moor, V. Deni, the Kukryniksii group, etc" (Kovaliv 2007a: 533).

7  *Perets'* was a "popular bimonthly humor and satire journal, founded in Kharkiv in 1922 and based in Kyiv after 1941. Its pages [...] often contained caricatures" (Kovaliv 2007b: 203).

languages. The Ukrainian publication of the first volume of *Maksym Osa* was awarded the Ukraine-Europe 2011 diploma. The work had previously appeared in French, Polish, and Russian. The story describes the adventures of the eponymous Cossack protagonist. The historical surroundings, modernised by adding a 'whodunit' component makes the comic novel a lively read. Besides his skill as an artist, Baran'ko builds a tense detective narrative, full of intrigue. The quick and observant Maksym Osa cracks a hidden treasure mystery, finds a murderer and saves innocent lives. Essentially, Maksym Osa presents a favourable image of a Ukrainian with exclusively positive characteristics.

Furthermore, the full-colour adventure comic *Daohopak*, consisting of three volumes *Antalya Tour* (*Antaliis'ka hastrol'*, 2012), *Noble Love* (*Shliakhetna liubov*, 2014) and *The Secret of the Cossack Druid* (*Taiemnitsa kozats'koho mol'fara*, 2016), by Maksym Prasolov (script), Oleksii Chebykin (art), Oleh Kolov (text) deals with Cossack themes. The first volume was given the Jury Special Award for Best Illustrated Children's Book at the Book Arsenal festival. The authors of the 'blockbuster comic novel' succeeded in presenting the Cossack context in popular and modern forms. The work modernises national mythology and heritage, particularly the myths and legends of Cossacks with strong character and with special, seemingly mystical abilities. In the comic, three Cossack friends from the "knightly order of sorcerers and martial arts masters of the Zaporizhian Host" experience numerous mind-boggling adventures, endure hard battles and duels, astound enemies with their deftness, bravery, and invention. The work mixes the Ukrainian world with Eastern exoticism of places like Türkiye or Japan. The love story, a relationship between one male protagonist and a ninja woman, provides a clue to the book's title, a portmanteau of a Ukrainian martial art and an East Asian philosophy. The cast of characters is imbued with additional colour by adding talking and highly intelligent animals, such as the gander Husiar II and the tattooed hog Okist (meaning gammon). Animals are also involved in the Cossacks' various adventures. Overall, *Daohopak* is an amalgamation of various genres: adventure, fantasy, mystical, and historical fiction.

## 3. What is a Ukrainian Superhero Like?

The war in Eastern Ukraine boosted experiments in the superhero genre since 2014. Much like in the United States, in which the patriotic Captain America shows up in the dramatic period of World War II in order to oppose the Hitlerite coalition of powers, in Ukrainian comics, the threat of the conquest of the country by another state brings forth the image of a positive superhero, capable of opposing the military onslaught.

The colouring comic book series *Ukrainian Superheroes* (*Ukrains'ki superheroi*) with the volumes *To Save the Lark* (*Vriatuvaty zhaivoronka*, 2015) and *Invisible Island* (*Nevydymyi ostriv*, 2015) by Lesia Voroniuk uses the genre to educational ends in order to foster patriotism and Ukrainian national pride among children. Because, in addition to being a positive figure, the superhero must necessarily possess a set of qualities – have superpowers, wear a suit setting them apart from the public, and have a secret identity, i.e. lead a double life, hiding one's superhero essence (Duncan et al. 2015: 221–245). But, in contrast to their American models, Ukrainian superheroes often do not hide a secret identity or their supernatural abilities. Their identity is exclusively a heroic one, which is why they have no names other than the names that mark them as heroes.

Voroniuk's superheroes are faced with a task that is both difficult and ordinary for supermen – to save the Ukrainian world from perdition and to fend off the triumph of the forces of evil. The opposition between the positive and negative images transparently insinuate Ukrainian realities, in particular the Anti-terrorist Operation, which took place in the Donbas region from 2014 on, and the conflict between the national (Ukrainian) and the imperialist (Russian) worlds.

*Figure 2.3: Scene from comic* To Save the Lark *(2015)*

The names of the superheroes and their supernatural abilities betray the national cultural code, both historically, and in the present. Much like in the *Fantastic Four* of Marvel Comics, Voroniuk's superheroes are also four: Kobzar (Bard, leader of the superheroes who lost his sight as a Cossack on the island of Khortytsia, and has the ability to read minds and communicate telepathically), Vira (a student who believes in the all-conquering power of good), Kiborh (Cyborg, an unbreakable warrior with a human heart from Luhans'k), and Krip (Dill, a herbalist from the Carpathians, who uses herbs to heal or to make truth or memory potions). The heroes' outfits partially stress their national identity, underscore their abilities, their moral values and mode of being.

They do not, however, change over the course of the story, because life is not divided into 'heroic' and ordinary. Thus, the Kobzar wears a Cossack kaftan and jeans, his instrument, the *kobza*, which he plays when he is free to do so, is a necessary element of his image. The protagonists' blindness is also a homage to the traditional image of the blind *kobzari*, itinerant bards who wandered through Ukrainian lands in the 18th century and kept the memory of the past alive through songs. Krip wears an embroidered shirt and baggy Cossack-like trousers. He holds a dill plant in his hands. In addition to its healing significance, it gains a new connotation in the context of current events in Ukraine: The Russian word for dill, *ukrop*, has been used by Russian proxies to denote Ukrainian soldiers. Along with "ukr", this derogatory name is given a positive association here, with the dill plant that has a number of healing properties, and is an ingredient in many Ukrainian dishes. Kiborh's name and superhero origin story (once human, now a cyborg with a human heart and brain) has to do with events in the Donetsk airport in 2014–2015, where the Ukrainian military put up a defence so unexpectedly vicious that they were called cyborgs for their 'superhuman' strength and resilience. Kiborh, the cyborg, is essentially a robot made out of a super strong alloy, but his human nature is revealed through his heart, which is visible through clear material on the left side of his chest. Only the female character is depicted as wearing different outfits in the two volumes of the comic, which may identify her as a helper to the (male) superheroes. The distinguishing feature in her outfit is its green colour (green dress, green blouse), which symbolises hope, wisdom, calm, and optimism.

The three male protagonists have obvious supernatural powers – telepathy (Kobzar), healing (Krip), extreme physical strength (Kiborh). Their resistance to evil is an active one, they are always *doing* – running, fighting, playing a musical instrument (Kobzar), uncovering the enemy's plans. The female protagonist, by contrast, is static. Additionally, Vira's superpower is not that extraordinary, it is simply the belief in the triumph of good (her name, Vira, means "Faith" in Ukrainian), which all heroes ought to have. Vira accompanies the superheroes, her assistance takes the form of moral support – when Kiborh recalls the death of his wife after having found a "Faithful Heart" pendant he had given to her, Vira consoles him, saying "You did all you could" (Voroniuk 2015a: 10). Likewise, in *To Save the Lark*, it is Vira who figures out the code on the cage and lets the bird free. In *Invisible Island* the superhero men save Vira twice – Vira, again, not particularly strong, but serving here as an embodiment of all those for whose sake the superheroes fight evil, all those whose faith gives them strength.

Whereas the Ukrainian world is primarily represented by human characters, the enemy world is so repulsive and monstrous that it is represented by monsters, rather than people. The names and images of enemy monsters carry also a present-day political subtext. Dvorly [tweagles], the double-headed man-eating eagles, are an allusion to the double-headed eagle in the coat of arms of the Russian Empire and the Russian Federation; Vyrodky [bastards] are people who turned into monsters when they sold their soul and conscience for money. Vyrodky are traitors manipulated by Dvorly, who give them orders to destroy Ukraine. Visually, Vyrodky are reminiscent of Colorado potato beetles. They are also referred to by another name, Kolorady, which is a moniker for pro-Russian separatists and adherents of the 'Russian World' due to the similarity of the stripes of the St. George Ribbon to the yellow-and-black stripes of the beetle. In *Invisible Island* the superheroes fight a sea monster, Imperukha (a queen who was turned into a river monster for her heinous deeds), which also underscores the imperial ambitions of Ukraine's enemies.

The Ukrainian world is likewise represented through the images of a lark, cranes, Cossacks and a *kobza*, an embroidered shirt.[8] The superheroes make fairly quick work of the objectives facing them – they save the lark so that the sun may always rise above Ukraine; they save the Ukrainian soul embodied in a traditional *vyshyvanka*[9]: "The vyshyvanka is the soul of the Ukrainian people" – says the Cossack Keeper of the Soul, – "as long as we wear vyshyvanky we will be united and unbeatable" (Voroniuk 2015b: 10). The simple plot, clear drawings, the interactive, co-creative possibilities provided by the option of colouring the comic, clearly convey the main idea to the child reader – whatever happens, Good always defeats Evil, and Ukrainians will overcome any obstacles.

In a very similar way, the image of a Ukrainian superhero is modelled in the comic *The Patriot* (*Patriot*, 2016), which was written and drawn by Vadym Nazarov, stylistically resembling DC Action Comics. Notably, the comic is intended for a young adult audience, employing 17+ and 15+ age restrictions, as it features detailed depictions of graphic fight scenes, the cruelty of which is conveyed through torn-off limbs, bashed heads and 'creepy' elements. The comic complies with the three key elements of superhero characters: mission, power, and personality (Coogan 2006). Thus, an ordinary soldier – Sergeant Vidirvenko – gains supernatural abilities when he puts on the Patriot armour. The armour imbues him with extreme strength and speed to overcome evil. In armour, the sergeant also becomes impervious to bullets and able to jump off a helicopter without any harm to himself. But, like Superman, he is threatened by explosions, including grenade explosions: "Oh, damn... I don't like being blown up on grenades... Bullets, lasers, swords – I don't care... but not grenades..." (Nazarov 2017: 26). He performs a pro-social mission, fearlessly helping others as a warrior of light opposing the powers of darkness, which strives to conquer Ukraine, and then the entire world.

---

8   Linguistically, the comics draw upon Ukrainian folk expressions, sayings and spells ("[...] seeking out herbs, picking good health for the entire year", "come ye cranes, ye brothers, come and help good people", cf. Voroniuk 2015b: 3), which creates a positive national element, appeals to and envelops the reader with historical memory.
9   A *vyshyvanka* is a traditional element of clothing, a men's or women's shirt with ornamental embroidery. In fiction, it often serves the symbolic role of marking and keeping Ukrainian identity.

*Figure 2.4: Scene from comic* Patriot. Renegade *(2016)*

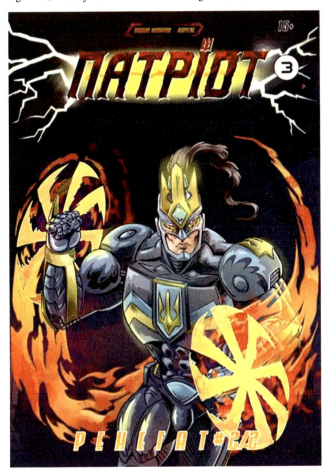

Whereas American superhero identity usually comprises "the codename and the costume, with the secret identity being a customary counterpart to the codename" (Coogan 2006: 32), in Nazarov's comic, the Patriot denotes the role he plays in the struggle against evil. The Patriot is, first and foremost, a Ukrainian, who loves Ukraine, has the mental fortitude and the belief in victory, which enables him to wear his armour. The Patriot's armour possesses national markers, which become more pronounced with each new issue of the comic. Thus, on the cover of the first issue, *Patriot. Attack of the Clones* (*Patriot. Ataka kloniv*, 2014), the suit is adorned with an abstract flag. In the second and third issues, *Patriot. Renegade* (*Patriot. Renehat*, 2016, 2018), the Patriot's armour exhibits a trident on his helmet, shoulders and chest, as well as the national flag – the armour is yellow and blue. Additionally, his weapon – the "Stinging Trident" sniper rifle – is reminiscent of a trident in shape, while the light billhook resembles the Old Kyivan *kolovorot/kolovrat* (spinning wheel), which hints at the Patriot's connection with ancient Ukrainian powers.

However, in contrast to Voroniuk's *Ukrainian Superheroes*, Nazarov's Patriot has a private identity. In daily life he has the name Sergeant Vidirvenko, which means "the Breakneck" and suggests the character's risk-friendly nature, his ability to make independent decisions according to the situation, and sometimes to ignore orders from his superiors, which always leads to positive outcomes. Whereas out-of-suit superheroes often feign some sort of weakness, Vidirvenko has no such weaknesses. The sergeant's physical power without his suit (which he must remove in enemy territory because light energy is blocked there, and the suit does not work) is demonstrated when he is depicted shirtless, with clearly defined musculature, and tattoos of a trident and the Kobzar (the 19th century Romantic poet Taras Shevchenko) on his chest. His image is crowned by his *oseledets*, the Cossack hair lock. In addition to his willpower and sense of duty, the sergeant is humble – he does not seek reward for his labours and has a sense of humour.

The three issues of the *Patriot* comic published so far put the struggle between Good and Evil into a more fantastical plane than the one we see in *Ukrainian Superheroes*, and a more large-scale one. The struggle of "Ukrainians against their enemies" becomes the struggle of "earthlings versus aliens". With every new issue, however, events of the comic are increasingly projected onto present-day Ukraine, including the war in the Donbas; and the conditional plane, where events unfold, betrays Ukrainian realities. The author stresses the comic's historical basis and the deliberate parallels with actual events and people with a note on the book's front endpaper: "Similarities to real persons and events in the comic are not always accidental." (Nazarov 2018)

In the first issue, *Patriot. Attack of the Clones* "the story's inception […] both in terms of the style of drawing, and the narrative manner, is reminiscent of a giant cartoon from the Perets' magazine" (Pityk 2019). By alluding directly to a potential real danger, it deals with the question if Ukraine is prepared to resist outside aggression and what is to be done when the threat becomes a reality. Will a hero turn up, one able to resist an invincible enemy? The comic uses humour and sarcasm to attempt to answer these questions. It tells the story of how Sergeant Vidirvenko has to try and infiltrate the enemy space station, "Phobos", which is hanging above Kyiv, and acquires armour and weapons. He even has to fight the clones of historical figures, such as Lenin, Stalin, Mao, as well as robots and aliens. It seems like the author deliberately saturated his comic with diverse antagonists to underline the multifaceted nature of the evil the protagonist is facing, as well as his extraordinary persistence and strength. Only after having overcome all obstacles, the sergeant becomes "the Patriot" – a defender of Ukraine and the entire world from the powers of darkness and evil. In general, as researchers of Ukrainian comics Anatolii and Kateryna Pityk note, "'Patriot. Attack of the Clones' is a sweet, benevolent, and at times naive mockery of the cliches of Communist inheritance and Russian propaganda, a fun black-and-white action comic." (2019)

The second (2016) and third (2018) issues of the *Patriot* comic comprise a separate story, "Renegade", and exhibit metamorphoses both formally, and content-wise. Unlike the first issue, these comics are full-colour, not black-and-white. The quality of drawing and artistic work with colour shows the author's prowess. The third issue opens with information about its characters, which again allows parallels to be drawn with contemporary reality. In particular, members of the Armed Forces of Ukraine and militants of the Donetsk People's Republic (DNR in its Ukrainian acronym), whereas the comic itself mentions "ukry" (derogatory term for Ukrainians/Ukrainian military used by separatist militants since 2014), "muscovites", the "ceasefire", the "ghostly peace and the exhausting

Svitlana Pidoprygora: Drawn History   57

invisible war", which situates the narrative clearly in the present. Among the *dramatis personae* are the Patriot, a.k.a. Sergeant Vidirvenko; Leutnant Kvitka, a servicewoman in the Ukrainian Armed Forces, and the Patriot's partner; Agent Franko, an undercover agent in the Ukrainian Armed Forces intelligence and others, who are set against the Bis (demon) – a werewolf and commander of DNR militants or a cap-wearing DNR militant who is a commander of a territorial checkpoint at a temporary frontline. The supervillain – the robotised demon-lord Pu, is not included in the list of characters, because, although he is the initiator of the aliens' attack, and a puppet master of the work's antagonists, he only appears on the final page with a promise to destroy the Patriot, which can be seen as hinting at further conflict, and the fact that the comic is incomplete.

*Figure 2.5: Scene from comic* Patriot. Renegade *(2018)*

The narrative of the *Patriot* comic clearly separates Ukrainian and enemy forces. Ukrainian forces are represented by people, who embody light, whereas the alien enemies feed on dark energy, turn people into renegades, and are monsters in terms of their physical form. Their misshapen nature is hyperbolised by the fact that they eat human flesh. Thus, Bis says "[...] leave a few warm ones for me [...] it's been a while since I've had any fresh meat!" (Nazarov 2016: 130). A renegade in the likeness of a little girl draws in children in order to eat them, and having seized a child, yells: "Won't! Mine! Won't! My toy! Must devour!" (Ibid. 2018: 33).

In general, both visually and verbally, the enemies in the comic are demonised and dehumanised. This shapes an unattractive image of the enemy in the mass consciousness. The antagonists are modelled in such a way as to provoke a negative attitude in the reader, to stress the enemy's physical and moral decrepitude, bizarre nature and opposition to the Ukrainian world. DNR militants are caricatures, their clothes mark the social groups making up their detachments – people with a criminal past (dressed in *vatniks* [cotton wool padded jackets], cigarettes between their teeth), the military (fatigues with no ID markings), Russian *kazaks* (*kubanka hats*). They have no names, only nicknames like "worm", "rat-eater" and the aforementioned "demon". The enemies' language is filled with curse words, criminal argot, *surzhyk*. The Russian language is provided in Ukrainian transcriptions, thus further stressing its 'otherness'. Incorrect speech patterns also stress the ethnic origins of those who fight for the enemy – such as Buryats or Chechens. Hitting the Patriot from a grenade launcher, a little man with a paunch says, in broken Ukrainian: "Take that, Ukropa. Batu[-khan] reward, Batu hero for Ukropa! Kobzon wife, kids shake hand for Ukropa! [...] You *shaitan* [...] flying Ukropa!!!" (Ibid. 2016: 11). The renegade's dehumanisation is stressed not only through a physical transformation into a monster, but also through the impoverishment of his speech: he speaks in simple sentences consisting of a single verb or noun ("toy", "girlfriend", "devour").

The events of *Patriot. Renegade* unfold in several locations: "Eastern Ukraine. Muscovite-occupied territory", "Department of Military Intelligence and Strategic Planning, Irpin, Ukraine", "somewhere in Kyiv, off the loud streets", "Not far from the frontline", "Armed Forces of Ukraine Military Base seized by pro-Moscow forces, Donetsk", "Somewhere in the nondescript ravines of the Donbas,", "Kremlin. Muscovy". Although the colour scheme of the entire comic is bright, there is still a light vs. dark contrast in the depiction of peaceful Kyiv, and the places where the enemy prevails. Eastern Ukraine is drawn in dark hues, with greens and browns, as a desolate, unpeopled territory – with bare trees, a human skull in the forefront, and a destroyed building in the background, where previously, a truck driver explains, "All this was villages! Neat houses in a row, and gardens blooming" (ibid. 2016: 1). The visual image of the separatist base is also dominated by darker shades, and the malevolent atmosphere of the events unfolding is underlined by making the bubbles red and pointy, rather than round. Red and shades of red accompany the appearance of the renegade in the image of a girl (red sky, red eyes) and his transformation into a red beast that shoots red snot at the Patriot. The Patriot, a warrior of the powers of light, is shaded in blue, yellow and orange hues. He performs his mission – rescuing rays of lights from occupied territory.

Among the comic's female characters, Lieutenant Kvitka (Flower) stands out. She is stereotypically sexually attractive, and lenient about the sergeant's jokes about her relationships with her subordinates. At a checkpoint, the Patriot notes: "You are a harsh mistress to your suitors, Lieutenant. It's a rare occurrence to see such a fine lady standing guard!", to which Kvitka replies: "Better bite your tongue, Sergeant, before I appoint you a costume for the canteen [...]" (ibid: 6). Leutnant Kvitka appears in an episode where children are being saved as a helicopter pilot, which causes a boy's admiration ("When I grow up, I'm going to be a pilot, like you!" (ibid. 2018: 40)). She assists the Patriot. However, it seems that the creation of an image of a Ukrainian female superhero is still in the future.

The *Patriot* comic is clearly oriented towards the contemporary political situation in Ukraine and fosters an optimistic agenda in the reader. The superhero lacks a secret identity (it is common knowledge that Sergeant Vidirvenko is the Patriot), which hints at the idea that Ukraine does not require a secret hero, but rather an obvious one, so that every person might believe themselves capable of an extraordinary feat, and that "the superheroes' true heroism is not in any supernatural ability, but in being unshakable in the face of overwhelming hardship" (Duncan et al. 2015: 252). At the same time, the comic divides the world into light and darkness, with the protagonists standing on the side of light, while their enemies represent darkness. This division and character of the struggle implies that the enemy is demonised. As a consequence, shaping a dehumanised version of the enemy also implies that one cannot negotiate with him; the only way to be safe from such an enemy is by destroying him.

A mixture of contemporary and Cossack narratives is also found in the comic *Victory. Savur-Mohyla* (*Zvytiaha. Savur-Mohyla*, 2015) by Denys Fadieiev. The comic deals with the fight for Savur-Mohyla in the summer of 2014, superimposing it on the Cossack age. According to legend, at this place the ottoman Sirko executed people who, after being liberated from Turkish captivity, decided to go back to the Turks rather than return to their homeland. In the comic Sirko judges: "Anyone who has rejected his home country, his native land, has no right to live! For there are no two Gods, no two suns [...] no two mothers" (Fadieiev 2015: 17). This exclamation is addressed also to present-day Ukrainians, while his art of combat is understood to inspire heroic acts and reawaken inborn national pride. In the comic, in particular a Cossack sword found during a battle during Ukraine's Anti-terrorist Operation, becomes a magical artifact that awakens national memory and turns ordinary persons of no particular moral courage into brave warriors with Cossack blood running through their veins. Notably, this present-day part of the narrative is told in Russian, whereas the Sirko story is told in Ukrainian.

Denys Fadieiev was also part of a script writing group for two issues of the full-colour comic *Volia: The WILL* (2017, 2018).[10] Rather than Cossack-era themes, this work

---

10   An entire collective of authors worked on *Volia: The WILL*. The scriptwriting group of the first volume comprised Denys Fadieiev, Oleksandr Fylypovych, and V'iacheslav Buhaiov; Roman Onyshchenko joined them to write dialogue; the group of artists included Oleksii Bondarenko, Maksym Bohdanovsk'yi, and Oleksandr Opara. The second volume was written by Denys Fadieiev, Oleksandr Fylypovych, Ol'ha Vozniuk, V'iacheslav Buhaiov; Anastasiia Fadieieva and Oleksandr Fylypovych joined in the writing of dialogues; the visual narrative was created by Ievhenii Tonchylov. Notably, the comics give separate credits to the artists of the historical pages (Victoriia Ponomarenko for the first volume, Maksym Bohdanovs'kyi – for the second) and historical consultants (Vladyslav Kutsenko, first volume; Ol'ha Vozniuk, second volume). The comic's language is diverse

addresses Ukraine's 'national liberation struggle' of 1917–1920, and projects alternative outcomes for those events. In the comic, the authors bring together a "historical basis, alternate history and superhero elements" (Il'in, 2018) and interrogate what would have happened, had events developed according to a different scenario. Additionally, the comic has no shortage of uncanny facets, portraying extensive steam-punk elements (steam machine technology, Industrial Revolution-era weaponry, the protagonists' clothes) and including various artistic styles, ranging from realism to caricature.

*Figure 2.6: Scene from comic* Volia: The WILL *(2017)*

The comic's characters include notable figures from Ukraine's history (Hetman Pavlo Skoropads'kyi; leader of an anarchist movement Nestor Makhno; Head of the Central Rada Mykhailo Hrushevs'kyi; first President of the National Academy of Sciences Volodymyr Vernads'kyi, inventor Ihor Sikors'kyi, Vladimir Lenin) who together with several other minor characters serve as recognisable historical figures that act according to widespread stereotypes and dominate the comic's narrative. Thus, the malevolent

---

and aimed at showing the characters primarily through a national lens. In addition to Ukrainian, the characters also speak Russian, Polish, and English.

nature of Bolshevik power is underscored by the images of Madame Blavatsky, who is brought back to life by magic, while Leon Trotsky resolutely implements the ideals of the October Revolution, by tearing out the hearts of dissenters and raising 'the Red dead' to fight.

These fantastic elements of the comic clash with the drawn parts of factual history – they are grayscale, realist-style sketches. The first volume places such history pages after every episode, the story of the second volume concludes with five history pages. They are meant to introduce little-known historical events, phenomena, inventions, and thus to familiarise the reader with the historical background.

The first part of *Volia: THE WILL* has a well thought out 'national' conception. The story begins on the front endpaper, which depicts an archangel striking a monster with a trident. The accompanying text serves as a starting point for the narrative:

> The young Ukrainian state arose from the ruins of an empire, as did its new and treacherous enemies. At the same time, a great war continues in Europe, the like of which the world had not yet seen, with spy intrigue, new mystical cults, and dangerous military technology. The freedom struggle continues, and the new history of the world begins in these pages. (Buhaiov/Fadieiev 2017)

Each episode of the comic is preceded by a segment of text introducing the reader into the action or foregrounding a key idea. Thus, the first episode opens with a text about World War I and the formation of the Ukrainian state under the leadership of Pavlo Skoropads'kyi. The second episode, "Ghost of the Past" ("Pryvyd mynuloho"), opens with a Ukrainian Sich Riflemen[11] song "Oh Ukraine! Beloved mother". The song's lyrics are a modified text of the *For Ukraine* (*Za Ukrainu*) poem by Mykola Voronyi, one of the founders of the Ukrainian Central Rada. Overall, the second episode, which was drawn by Maksym Bohdanovs'kyi, is executed in a Realist style, with many detailed mass scenes. The words of the song "For Ukraine, for her freedom / For honour and glory, / For the people" become the ideological lodestone of the narrative, which is based on the story of the Crimea Operation of 1918, when Ukrainian troops, headed by Colonel Petro Bolbochan, instituted Ukrainian authority on the peninsula, and created a Ukrainian navy. In the third episode, "A New Enemy", Oleksandr Oles' poem *Chains can never bind Ukraine* (*Vilnu Ukraïnu ne skuiut kaidany*, 1917) stresses the optimism and invincibility of Ukraine's defenders. The second volume has no such introductory element.

The opposition between national and enemy forces is constructed according to the conventions of the superhero genre, with a clear separation between good and evil, heroes, and villains, and with demonisation and dehumanisation of the enemy. On the side of the Ukrainian revolution are powerful weapons, the latest inventions, people with supernatural abilities – all of this is meant to help in the struggle against the Bolsheviks (Soviet Russia), who have mystical connections to evil spirits, can raise the dead as zombies to fight, subjugate the will of the living, and possess fantastical technology. This evil is fought by the Ukrainian 'cyborgs' Sich Riflemen, Maksym Kryvonis, Agnieszka

---

11   The Sich Riflemen are one of the detachments of the army of the Ukrainian People's Republic, formed in 1917 and notable for its organisation and effectiveness in combat.

the medium, the brilliant Professor Vernadskyi, who is developing a super weapon, and Ukraine's President Mykhailo Hrushevs'kyi, whose weapon is his book "The History of Ukraine-Rus".

In his meditations on the *Volia* comic, Vadym Il'in criticises the voluntarism of its superheroes, as "rather than to solve the problems that led to war, we are given a 'simple' solution – the removal of those problems through exclusively military means, through a superhuman technological effort" (2018). This bears the risk of forming "in the young reader a stereotypical, black-and-white idea of the events that do not actually fit into simple schemes" (ibid.). However, as a work of fiction the comic in no way aims at a truthful representation of real events, but on the contrary at strengthening the idea that victory over the external aggressor is possible, an idea particularly relevant in the political context of today's Ukraine.

## 4. *Dira (Hole).* A Graphic Novel by Serhii Zakharov

In the broad field of comics, cartoons, drawn picture stories and visual tales with its general orientation towards comicality, simplification and entertainment, it is only since the 1970s a distinct subgenre of the so-called graphic novel emerged, whose authors strove to separate themselves from the earlier genre development, modelling artistic reality in a different set of coordinates from that of the comic. Jan Beatens and Hugo Frey in their introduction to the Graphic Novel (2015) stress that the graphic novel is not merely a genre, but a medium that is part of other cultural fields and practices (graphic literature, visual narrative). They define the graphic novel and comics in general on four levels: 1. form; 2. content; 3. publication format; 4. aspects of production and distribution (cf. Baetens/Frey 2015). For instance, the distinctness of the form of the graphic novel is in the fact that its authors do not follow the established rules of comics, but rather create their own recognisable style, which does not necessarily mean an improvement to the traditional comic style. Authors of graphic novels prefer non-standard layout techniques, disrupting the usual net structure of the comic, or else return to a clear layout, so as not to distract from what they deem the most essential in their work. According to Baetens and Frey, in terms of narrative form, graphic novels often feature a narrator, where comics lack the visible involvement of one. On a content level, graphic novels deal with adult, or serious and complex themes that are largely uninteresting to a teenage audience. Authors stress realism or autobiography (like in *Maus: A Survivor's Tale* by Art Spiegelman, or *Persepolis* by Marjane Satrapi), turn to historicity and actuality (*In the Shadow of No Towers* by Art Spiegelman, *Last Day in Vietnam* by Will Eisner, etc.), mixing fictional and non-fictional, documentary narrative (ibid.).

One attempt to create a genuine Ukrainian graphic novel is *The Hole* (*Dira*, 2016) authored by the artist Serhii Zakharov, who had witnessed the events in Donetsk that had led to the proclamation of the unrecognised DNR in 2014. In response, Zakharov organised an art collective, entitled *Murzylka*, and created caricatures, street art, and graffiti portraying the infamous representatives of the new authorities. This artistic protest gained a worldwide response when the photographs were posted on the internet. The DNR authorities subsequently arrested Zakharov, imprisoned him and staged a shooting. But Zakharov managed to escape Donetsk and to move to Kyiv, where he processed his traumatic experience in graphics, which became the start of a graphic novel, and started to collaborate with the writer and journalist Serhii Mazurkevych, with whom he also started to work on the graphic novel *The Hole*.

*The Hole* was presented in Kyiv in 2016 and accompanied by the opening of an exhibition at the National Museum for the History of Ukraine, entitled *The Hole. 14 August... An Experience of Nonviolent Cultural Resistance*, where works by Zakharov were presented. The book immediately got a broad reception on the internet, underlining the fact that graphic novels disprove the idea that drawings can only entertain and amuse, but can open a much broader circle of subjects: "problems in the family, intolerance, the struggle for rights; genocide, as well as war" (Kalytenko 2017). Zakharov's works contains all central elements of the graphic novel, like a historical basis, autobiographical elements, the scale of the problems touched upon, the large book format (A4), and the orientation towards an adult reader. The topicality of the content in particular brings the work closer to non-fictional literature.

*Figure 2.7: Scene from graphic novel* The Hole *(2016)*

Particularly impressive is the layout of Zakharov's images, which, as indicated, he only later inserted into a plot in collaboration with Mazurkevich, supplementing them with new ones in order to make a story suitable for the form of a graphic novel. For this reason, the drawings, their situation on the page, their 'framing' are of utmost importance, they create an emotional visual arc, and reveal a person's feelings in a critical situation. In this respect the book cover, in shades of red and black, is impressive.

On an elevation in an urban landscape, a hole is drawn, into which the city is being pulled (high rise buildings, a stadium, train stations), but this process is incomplete. The hole symbolises a transition into a different space, which is likely unfriendly and has no future, which leads to emptiness, which is the unrecognised Donetsk People's Republic (DNR). At the top of the page, *Dira* is written in big black letters, drawn haphazardly – some spots are not filled with colour, the lines are clumsy as if pointing to the author's negative connotation of the word and what it stands for.

The plot is also typical for the graphic novel genre. From the very first pages the reader finds herself thrown into an uncanny world of violence, fear and lawlessness – a spread shows the barrel of a pistol, which conveys the impressions of someone faced with mortal danger. In the face of death, details become blurred, which is shown through a darkened backdrop in hatched lines. The large-scale image has no frame, it occupies the entirety of the available page space, including the margins. This technique of placing a single image on a two-page spread becomes the book's signature, literally signalling the huge scale of the disastrous events that took place in Donetsk in 2014. The blown-up close-ups (open-mouthed person in despair; someone with a gun; a protester, the artist himself; a scene of somebody being beaten up; the face of the victim of the beating) deepen and strengthen the sense of danger that rules in the city.

Another specificity of graphic novels is the framing of how many images are placed on one page, thus accelerating or slowing down the action, stressing at the same time its significance and tension. Scott McCloud distinguishes six types of frames: from moment to moment; from action to action; from object to object; from place to place; from detail to detail; with no visible connection. Whereas action frames predominate in American comics, making the narrative dynamic and keeping the reader in suspense, Japanese comics care more about condition, which is why they also have many "detail to detail" and "no visible connection" frames (McCloud 1993: 74–78). In the graphic novel *The Hole* it is not just the adventure that is of significance, but also the narrator's emotional state, so frames from action to action here alternate with frames that stress detail, and frames with no visible connection. These latter ones show how unbelievable and unreal everything happening to the narrator is, talk of his desire to break out of the closed space of unfreedom. Frames often include meaning breaks, which the reader is forced to fill for herself, thus supplementing events with own reflections and feelings, joining the process of making sense. Also, the shape of the frame matters, whether they are rectangular, star-shaped, heart-shaped, or something else. In *The Hole*, all the drawings are rectangular, however their frames are not differentiated, with them being situated on a black/white backdrop, or on full spreads without a frame, which further emphasises the bleak and depressive atmosphere.

Indeed, the author's use of black-and-white drawing is not accidental. The monochrome palette illustrates the absence of joy and hope, serves as a marker of cruelty, fear, moral degradation, and spiritual downfall. Gray people against the recognisable backdrop of the Lenin monument, with sticks in their hands, hands balled into fists, black mouths open, are reminiscent of a terrifying dark power. The author only captures negative emotions, depicting them schematically through an expressionist-influenced technique of hatching. The reader is faced with "strained hatch lines" and "black-and-white" silhouettes (Kalytenko 2017), a line technique which is reminiscent of delirium, of a nightmare, the narrator's refusal to believe that all of this is truly happening.

It is in particular the city of Donetsk where the destruction of peacetime life and its replacement with a state of war is happening: a pregnant woman in her kitchen, a grenade on the floor, blown up to an unrealistic size, children playing while a woman talks to an armed man; a person on their knees being beaten by sticks and brass knuckles; a foot on a person's face; drunken people – all of these are apocalyptic scenes that illustrate the arrival of an evil which awakens previously controlled aggression in people. At the centre of this kaleidoscope is a torn white space with a human silhouette in the middle – likely watching and realising the horror brought upon the beloved city This contrasts with the only full-colour object, a Ukrainian flag on the book's last page, which serves as a symbol of return from the 'uncanny valley' to the space of freedom and full-fledged life.

*Figure 2.8: Scene from graphic novel* The Hole *(2016)*

The narrative (both verbal and non-verbal) of Zakharov's *The Hole* is in the first person, in retrospect. Taking temporal distance from the traumatic events, the protagonist assumes the point of view of an outside observer and analyses the events from a remote perspective, strengthening the impression of the reliability of reported facts with its focus on abuses and human rights violations.

Another characteristic of the graphic novel in contrast to comics with its playful speech bubbles is that text is rather placed separately from the frame or atop the frame. This separation does not actually separate the whole but carries additional meaning. In *The Hole* the clarity of Mazurkevych's text with regard to place, time of action and the novel's protagonists is supplemented by Zakharov's expressive drawings. For instance, writing some phrases in uppercase, such as "It became clear on 12th of May, when the self-governance 'referendum' was held in the DNR" or "Is that you? Yes, it's me" underscores key plot twists. Moreover, the constant change between white letters at black background and vice versa makes reading harder and forces the reader to concentrate on emotionally challenging events.

Thus, by dealing with recent Ukrainian history, Zakharov's *The Hole* broadened the field of Ukrainian graphic literature both in terms of form and content. In the graphic novel, the narrative takes a serious register, and operates on more complicated levels than we have seen in comics. The work expresses the author's own traumatic experience, which he processes and addresses to an adult audience, an audience with its values and worldview already in place. The novel foregrounds the tragic, rather than the heroic. This, in turn, requires the use of specific artistic techniques, more attuned to tragedy, like the use of zoomed-in close-ups, grayscale, an expressionist drawing style, the lack of speech bubbles and a detached manner of first-person narration.

## 5. Conclusion

The modern Ukrainian comic is distinguished by original authorial techniques, a thought-out verbal component, as well as its relevance to the current needs of society. The comics make national history, in particular the Cossack past in its historical and mythological guise, but also the national liberation struggle of 1917, the Soviet era, the contemporary war in Eastern Ukraine relevant. They experiment with superhero, adventure, and mystery genres, as well as turning to alternative history and steampunk. A number of comics (*Ukrainian Superheroes*, *Patriot*, *Volia: The WILL*) model the image of a Ukrainian superhero, capable of opposing evil forces, which often carry markers of Russian expansionism. Through a number of visual metaphors and associations, the comics draw parallels to recent Ukrainian history – namely, Ukraine's conflict with the Russian Federation. Essentially, with its hyperbolised rejection of the enemy, the superhero comic serves as an answer to Russian propaganda in the current media communication field. More generally, contemporary Ukrainian comics and graphic novels construct all previous history as a 'national liberation struggle' opposing foreign, Russian oppressors.

The depiction of history through the prism of the struggle between Good and Evil, the separation of characters into clearly positive and negative, ignores the complexity and controversial nature of historical events and figures and contributes to forming a one-dimensional picture of the world in mass consciousness, and dichotomising, simplifying complex relationships. However, this form of national appropriation of history in comics is called to perform a higher-priority task – to create an optimistic and vibrant space for the victory of the national idea.

Whereas comics are distinguished by fantastical, fairy-tale elements and imaginary scenarios, or the modelling of a playful, entertaining representation of history, *The Hole* supplements and deepens the earnestness of its subject – namely the war in Eastern Ukraine, ongoing since 2014, and the proclamation of the unrecognised Donetsk People's Republic – via an autobiographical and 'documentary' narrative, as well as expressive drawings and an unusual page layout, thus addressing an adult audience.

But regardless of all the differences between the more simplistic superhero comics and the serious deeper genre of the graphic novel, they both have in common that they are concerned in depicting national history with the present-day political situation in the country and are intended to form an optimistic agenda among the reader, while bolstering the faith in victory in mass consciousness.

## List of Illustrations

**Figure 2.1:** Scene from comic *Buiviter* (1995).
**Figure 2.2:** Scene from comic *Maksym Osa* (2011).
**Figure 2.3:** Scene from comic *To Save the Lark* (*Vriatuvaty zhaivoronka*) (2015).
**Figure 2.4:** Scene from comic *Patriot. Renegade* (*Patriot. Renehat*) (2016).
**Figure 2.5:** Scene from comic *Patriot. Renegade* (*Patriot. Renehat* (2018).
**Figure 2.6:** Scene from comic *Volia: The WILL* (2017).
**Figure 2.7:** Scene from graphic novel *The Hole* (*Dira*), (2016).
**Figure 2.8:** Scene from graphic novel *The Hole* (*Dira*), (2016).

## References

[Anon.] (2020): "Istoria ukraïns'kykh komiksiv." In: UN (https://uncomics.com/ukranian-comics/) [16 January 2023].

Baran'ko, Ihor (2011): Maksym Osa [2008], Odessa: Ievgenios.

Baetens, Jan/Frey, Hugo (2015): The Graphic Novel: An Introduction, Cambridge: Cambridge University Press.

Booker, Keith M. et al. (eds.) (2011): The Encyclopedia of Literary and Cultural Theory in three Volumes, Hoboken: Blackwell.

Buhaiov, V'iacheslav/Fadieiev, Denys et al. (2017): Volia: The WILL, Knyha 1, Mikolaïv: Asgardian Comics.

Buhaiov, V'iacheslav/Fadieiev, Denys et al. (2018): Volia: The WILL, Knyha 2, Kharkiv.

Coogan, Peter (2006): The Superhero. The Secret Origin of a Genre, Austin: Monkey-Brain Books.

Duncan, Randy/Smith, Mattew J./Levutz, Paul (2015): The Power of Comics: History, Form, and Culture [2009], London: Bloomsbury Academic.

Eisner Will (2008): Comics and Sequential Art: Principles and Practices from the Legendary Cartoonist, New York: W.W. Norton.

Fadieiev, Denys (2015): Zvytiaha. Savur-mohyla, Mikolaïv: Asgardian Comics.

Il'in, Vadym (2018): "Komiks 'Volia: the WILL': nova mifologiia Ukraïns'koï revoliutsiï 1917–1921 rokiv". In: Spil'ne, 14 December 2018 (https://commons.com.ua/uk/komiks-volya-will/) [16 January 2023].

Jameson, Fredric (1998): Cultural Turn. Selected Writings on the Postmodern, London: Verso.

Kalytenko, Tetiana (2017): "Veseli kartynky pro nevesele: 4 komiksy pro viinu". In: Bokmal, 8 May 2017 (https://bokmal.com.ua/books/war-comics/) [15.01.2020].

Karpenko, Vadym/Haiduchenko, Oleksandr (1992): Marko Pyrih, zaporozhets'. IAk Pyrih stav Pyrihom: knykha-komiks, Kyiv: Kozaky.

Koreshkov, Oleksandr (2018): Sered ovets': komiks, Kyiv: Vovkulaka.

Koval', Nata (2017): "Made in Ukraine: komiksy velyki i malen'ki." In: Chtyvo, 25 August, 2017 (http://www.chytomo.com/issued/made-in-ukraine-komiksi-veliki-j-malenki ) [16 January 2023].

McCloud, Scott (1993): Understanding Comics: Invisible Art, New York: William Morrow.

Nazarov, Vadym (2014): Patriot. Ataka kloniv: Knykha 1. Navaleo.

Nazarov, Vadym (2016): Patriot. Renehat. Knykha 2. Samvydav.

Nazarov, Vadym (2018): Patriot. Renehat. Knykha 3. Samvydav.

Kovaliv, Iurii (2007a): Literaturoznavcha entsyklopediia: u dvoh tomah. Vol.1. Kyiv: Akademiia.

Kovaliv, Iurii (2007b): Literaturoznavcha entsyklopediia: u dvoh tomah. Vol.2. Kyiv: Akademiia.

Pidopryhora, Svitlana (2018): Ukrainska eksperymentalna proza XX – pochatku XXI stolit: "nemozhlyva" literatura, Mikolaïv.

Pityk, Anatolii/Pityk, Kateryna (2019): "Kvantovyi strybok Kapitana Ukraïna: koly chekaty na zoloty doby ukraïns'kykh komiksiv". In: Chtyvo, 18 March 2019 (https://chytomo.com/kvantovyj-strybok-kapitana-ukrainy-koly-chekaty-na-zolotu-dobu-ukrainskykh-komiksiv/) [16 January 2023].

Prasolov, Maksym/Chebykin, Oleksii/Kolov, Oleh (2012): Daohopak. Knyha I: Antaliis'ka hastrol'. Kyiv: Nebesky.

Prasolov, Maksym/Chebykin, Oleksii/Kolov, Oleh (2014): Daohopak. Knyha II: Shliakhetna liubov. Kyiv: Nebesky.

Prasolov, Maksym/Chebykin, Oleksii /Kolov, Oleh (2016): Daohopak. Knyha III: Taiemnitsa kozats'koho mol'fara, Kyiv: Nebesky.

Stoliarova, Liubov' (2010): "Analiz strukturnykh ėlementov komiksa". In: Izvestia Tul'skogo gosudarstvenogo universiteta. Gumanitarnye nauki 1, pp. 384–389.

Sulyma, Kostiantyn (1995): Buiviter: komiks, Kyiv: Robitnycha hazeta.

Umberto, Eco (1979): The Role of the Reader. Explorations in the Semiotics of text, Bloomington: Indiana University Press.

Voroniuk, Lesia (2015a): Ukraïns'ki supergeroï. Vriatuvaty zhaivoronka. Vypusk 1, Chernivtsi: Bukrek.

Voroniuk, Lesia (2015b): Ukraïns'ki supergeroï. Nevydymyi ostriv. Vypusk 2, Chernivtsi: Bukrek.

Zakharov, Serhii/Mazurkevych, Serhii (2016): Dira, Kyiv: Luta sprava.

Chapter 3:
# Narrating Russia's Multi-Ethnic Past
The Historical Novels of Guzel Yakhina

*Eva Binder*

> Honest novels about Soviet times are needed today in order to squeeze out the Soviet, even if only a drop at a time, and to finally leave it behind.
> *Guzel Yakhina (Iakhina 2021a)*

## 1. Guzel Yakhina: Success and Controversy

Within the space of a few years, the novelist Guzel Yakhina [Guzel' Iakhina] has achieved critical acclaim and great popularity among Russian readers. Following the tradition of the historical novel, Yakhina brings crucial and traumatic moments from the first two decades of Soviet power back to the public's attention. At the same time, Yakhina has been drawn into heated public debates on multiple occasions, which further raised her visibility. It turned out that criticism has been launched from opposing sides: Whereas conservative circles ranging from patriots to communists condemn her novels as a denigration of national history, liberal intellectual elites criticise her for romanticising and idealising the most traumatic moments of the Soviet past. The main question that inspired this article and therefore will be discussed in the following is what has made Yakhina one of the most widely read and publicly debated authors in Russia within just a few years. This question will be approached by focussing on the strategies Yakhina pursues in order to transform traumatic moments of the Soviet past into a contemporary reading experience that is as informative as it is entertaining.

In her historical novels, Yakhina draws on key elements of popular literature, such as protagonists who evoke empathy, conflicts that create tension, or the incorporation of popular genres by making use of melodramatic plotlines and adventure stories. At the same time however, Yakhina offers her readership more than mere divertissement. Besides being entertaining, historical novels have always opened up the possibility of presenting historical events from a critical distance and enabled reflection on the past from the perspective of the present. By fictionalising time and space, Yakhina recalls and reframes past realities and feeds them into present public debates. As will be shown, in her approach to history Yakhina attempts to balance opposing and conflicting ideological positions. She particularly addresses the egalitarian dimension of Soviet ideology and draws the readers' attention to questions of ethnic and cultural identity. This recognisable configuration on the level of content correlates with an equally recognisable form or style, which has been referred to as the 'cinematic quality' and which will be discussed hereafter in the context of realistic narration in mainstream literature and cinema.

Since personal identity and self-representation are significant factors of the mediated image of an author, some biographical information about Yakhina shall be provided prior to discussing her literary texts. Born in 1977 in the Tatar capital of Kazan' with a Tatar family background, Yakhina received her education from primary school to university in Russian (she holds a degree in foreign languages – in German and English). In 1999, she moved to Moscow, where she undertook a training course in screenwriting at the private Moscow Film School. As Yakhina has stated in numerous interviews (cf. Surikov 2021), she found the form for the story she had already had in mind by writing the screenplay for a full-length feature film. Out of the screenplay Yakhina finally developed her debut novel *Zuleikha Opens Her Eyes* (*Zuleikha otkryvaet glaza*, 2015),[1] which was published by AST, one of the leading and largest publishers on the Russian book market, in 2015. The novel immediately received the major Russian literary prizes – the Iasnaia Poliana Literary Award and the Big Book Award. From this moment on, the book's circulation figures rose from an initial 3000 copies to more than 600.000 to date. However, this impressive publicity was not gained by the literary text alone. Five years after its publication the story about a young Tatar peasant woman who fell victim to the so-called 'dekulakisation' of the 1930s was adapted as a TV miniseries for the Russian TV channel *Rossiia 1*. When the series premiered in April 2020, it garnered record-high viewing numbers and caused controversy across the political-ideological spectrum. The sudden media outrage came from different sides. Representatives of the Tatar community complained about the lack of a positive ethno-cultural Tatar identity and took particular offence at a brief sex scene in a mosque. The criticism from this side was particularly harsh regarding the two women involved – the author Guzel Yakhina and the actress Chulpan Khamatova, who were denigrated as traitors to Tatar culture. The Russian side raised no less vehement accusations of insult and slander. National patriots felt that the portrayal of history in the series offended their national pride, while communist sympathisers condemned the film as anti-Soviet. Above all, the sudden media outrage caused by the miniseries[2] demonstrated that Soviet history remains a contentious issue and a highly contested terrain in today's Russia.

---

1   *Zuleikha Opens Her Eyes* was translated into English by Lisa C. Hayden and published as *Zuleikha* in 2019, *Children of Mine* (*Deti moi*) was translated by Polly Gannon and published as *A Volga Tale* in 2023. All other translations from Russian are mine, if not stated otherwise.
2   For a close examination of the controversial debates cf. Anisimova 2020.

*Figure 3.1: Film poster for the TV series* Zuleikha Opens Her Eyes *(2020)*

Besides Yakhina's highly successful literary debut, the two novels that followed also managed to achieve a remarkable record on the book market. Her second novel *A Volga Tale* (*Deti moi*), which was published in 2018 also by AST, has a circulation figure of 260.000 copies. Her latest novel *Train to Samarkand* (*Ėshelon na Samarkand*) hit the market in March 2021 with an initial circulation of 75.000 copies (cf. Surikov 2021), and thereby exceeds the first edition of Evgenii Vodolazkin's *Laurus* (*Lavr*, 2012) or Zakhar Prilepin's *The Monastery* (*Obitel'*, 2014) fivefold, just to cite two of her well-known and critically acclaimed male colleagues.

Apart from the remarkable popularity of Yakhina's historical novels on the Russian book market, the author has attracted considerable attention from outside the country. According to Yakhina, by 2021 *Zuleikha Opens Her Eyes* has been translated into about 40 languages, her second novel *A Volga Tale* into about 14 languages, out of which half had been published by 2021 (cf. Surikov 2021). Due to its topic – the fate of the Volga Germans from pre-revolutionary time to World War II, her second novel received particular attention in Germany where in 2020 Yakhina and her translator Helmut Ettinger were awarded the prize for most promising work by the German Culture Forum for Central and Eastern Europe.

## 2. Diversity Beyond Postcolonial Discourse

In the three novels Yakhina has published so far, the author draws attention to the first two decades of Soviet power and the radical political and social changes the country and its population were subjected to. The dramatic and traumatic moments at the core of the narration are the 'dekulakisation' (*raskulachivanie*) of the 1930s (*Zuleikha Opens Her Eyes*), the tragic failure of the so-called Volga German Autonomous Republic (*A Volga Tale*), which existed from 1923 until 1941, and the famine in the Volga region after the civil war (*Train to Samarkand*). Apart from the historical time, the three novels share the geographic region in which the stories are set or which serves as a starting point for the journey within the plot. Yakhina's choice of the Volga region – in Russian Povolzh'e – can be regarded as a successful branding strategy. First, it fosters the public image and identity of the author who, by writing about the region she has been familiar with since her childhood, is seen to express her "love for the homeland" "(Pakhomov/Sadikov 2021). Second, Yakhina puts forward a geographic region that in public discourse tends to receive less attention than the imperial centres on the one hand, and the remote, culturally different peripheries of the country, such as Siberia or the Caucasus, on the other. Third, by highlighting the multi-ethnic population of the Volga region, Yakhina recalls the Soviet formula of the multi-national family and, at the same time, brings ethnic diversity in the present Russian Federation to the public's attention. As research on Russian mass media has shown, ethnic diversity appears to be, for various and complex reasons, not a major issue in public discourse (cf. Anisimova 2020: 110), although ethnic minorities constitute more than 20 per cent of the population of the Russian Federation (Protsyk/Harzl 2013: 2). Departing from ethnic diversity at the core of the narrative, Yakhina opens a perspective on cultural and social diversity in general by representing voices that in Russian public discourse are less audible than others. This can truly be said of women (*Zuleikha Opens Her Eyes*), children (*Train to Samarkand*) and of people whose voices were silenced and suppressed in the Soviet past, as is particularly the case with the German minority (*A Volga Tale*) after the Volga German Autonomous Republic was abolished in 1941.

The geographic and symbolic space of Yakhina's novels is determined by the Middle and Lower Volga – a region that is home to Volga Tatars as well as other numerous ethnic minorities and small languages. Accordingly, the city of Kazan' as one of the region's cultural and urban centres forms the point of departure for two of Yakhina's novels. As a member of the 'kulak' class, the pejorative Stalinist term for landowners, the heroine of her first novel is forced to leave her Tartar village Iulbash, and, together with the other deportees, is deported from Kazan' to the Siberian city of Krasnoiarsk and from there to the banks of the river Angara. In a similar way, the plot of *Train To Samarkand* is framed by Kazan' as the point of departure and a destination that is thousands of kilometers away from the central Russian Volga region. In Yakhina's third novel, 500 starving orphans are taken to the Central Asian city of Samarkand – "to the sun and bread" (Iakhina 2021c:

38), as it says in the novel. The journey is conducted under the surveillance of the young Red Army soldier Deev and the severe female commissar Belaia. The individual stages of this declared 'travel novel' (*roman-puteshestvie*) thus provide the structure for the narration with regard to place and (historical) time. The voyage along the railroad is outlined in the chapters' titles, as for example "Sviazhsk – Urmary" (chapter 2) or "Sergach – Arzamas – Buzuluk" (chapter 3). But although the geographic locations are real, the route itself is as fictional as appears to be the time – the year 1923. This obvious deviation from historical facts in *Train To Samarkand* – commonly the years 1921 and 1922 are regarded as the period of famine – made Yakhina, a year after the public outrage over the TV series, once again the target of media-fueled criticism. When the novel was presented in spring 2021, Grigorii Tsidenkov, a local historian from Samara, launched a harsh attack against the author, accusing her – besides historical inaccuracy and a lack of historical investigation – of plagiarising his own texts that he had published previously on his *LiveJournal* blog (cf. Samigullina et al. 2021).[3]

By fictionalising historical places and events, Yakhina ascribes symbolic significance to space and time. This becomes most obvious in the fictitious German village of Gnadenthal, where her second novel *A Volga Tale* is set. With its figurative name that can be rendered as "Valley of Mercy" in English, the village of Gnadenthal serves as a model of the historical German settlements on the Volga River (cf. Silant'eva 2020). In contrast to the other two novels, *A Volga Tale* is focused on a single place and a single male character: on the German schoolteacher Jacob Ivanovich Bach, who, due to the turmoil of the post-revolutionary years, falls silent but still manages to raise Antje, the baby left to him by his love Klara. The symbolic space in *A Volga Tale* is based on the dichotomy of the German colony on the right bank of the Volga River and the solitary homestead on the left bank where Bach lives. Here, the Volga functions as a border between a realistic and magic world (cf. Nabiullina 2019) or between a world of rapid historical changes (the village of Gnadenthal) and a world where time stands still (the solitary homestead). The river itself is presented through embellished descriptions that facilitate visualisation in the reading process, as the following quote illustrates: "[T]he Volga was so broad in these parts that, from the right bank, even the impressively large Gnadenthal houses looked like a smattering of colorful buttons, in the midst of which the belfry stuck out like a pin." (Yakhina 2023: 60)

Yakhina evokes the historical territory of the Soviet Union by combining fictitious places and travel routes with factual topography. Besides serving as a reference to the historical world, the accumulation of toponyms in the text stimulates the process of imagining space. Thereby, the toponyms themselves may take on a clearly marked poetic function by being displayed visually as words and phonetically as word sounds. The visual and acoustic effect these signifiers create is due to both their familiarity on the one hand and their non-Russian, foreign exoticism on the other. In her essay *The Garden on the Border* (*Sad na granitse*, 2016), Yakhina reflects upon the mere sound of non-Russian toponyms together with her subjective perception of space as a child:

---

3    For Grigorii Tsidenkov's attack on Yakhina including the untenable accusation of plagiarism see in particular: Shikhman 2021, 12:05-15:11.

> It is 800 kilometres from Kazan' to the Ural Mountains, just like to Moscow. When I was a child, I had this strange feeling: Siberia always seemed within reach, but the capital seemed infinitely far away. Siberia – that sounds familiar, similar to the Turkic languages: Ienisei, Baikal, Surgut, Kurgan; [...] the same wind-battered taiga as not far from Kazan', in Mari Ėl – the "Land of the Mari". And Moscow? Only the Kremlin smelling of printing ink as in school textbooks and the black-and-white pictures on television. Siberia is tangible and familiar, whereas Moscow is abstract and foreign. (Iakhina 2016)[4]

Besides the sound quality emanating from the place and river names from different languages the perception of space is intensified by sensory impressions and references to media representations. In *A Volga Tale*, one of the narrative digressions that feature Stalin describes how the great leader perceives his country from the air during his flight over the riverscapes of the Caucasus, Central Asia and Siberia, which provides the reader with a fictitious bird's eye view on the huge land mass of the Soviet Union. The scene is reminiscent of visual representations of space from the time in which the novel is set. Points of reference appear to be the numerous maps in political posters, as for example the 1951 poster *In the Name of Communizm* (*Vo imia kommunizma*), or the avant-garde cinema of the 1920s in general and Dziga Vertov's travelogue documentary *A Sixth Part of the World* (*Shestaia chast' mira*, 1926) in particular.

By making use of ostensive comparisons of the rivers with golden threads, white maines and blue ribbons, Yakhina merges the sentimental, subjective perception of space by a character, in this case by Stalin, with the objective perspective of cinematic and cartographic technologies. In addition, the accumulation of non-Russian toponyms intensifies the process of imagining the vast Soviet Empire:

> And *He* understood: under him was not one river, but dozens, hundreds of Soviet rivers, merging their waters together, and advancing forth. The Kura and Aragva, the Inguri and Khobi shone like finde golden threads in the current. The Katun and Karavshan and the Irtysh shook their white manes. The Enisei and Lena entwined their blue ribbons, and the Argun and Kolyma entwined their black ones. The varicolored streams ran at different paces – some rapidly, some more slowly. Some hardly crawled. [...] Breathless, *He* looked down at this incredible dance of the waters, at this symphony of hundreds of Soviet rivers. And, for the first time in many years, *He* felt the thrill of ecstasy in his chest, as *He* had felt long ago in his youth, listening to the poetry of Rustaveli and Eristavi. (Yakhina 2023: 280–281)

---

4 Yakhina's essay was published several times. It first appeared in print in the journal *Snob*, April-May 2016. In 2021, the text was republished in its Russian original together with a translation into German in the edited volume *Kulturen verbinden – Connecting Cultures – Sblizhaia kul'tury* (Fuchsbauer et al. 2021).

*Figure 3.2: Viktor I. Govorkov: In the Name of Communizm (1951)*

Besides imagining the space of the Soviet Union, Yakhina recalls the Soviet model of the 'friendship of peoples' and multi-national family in a positive egalitarian notion. The utopian conflict-free coexistence of different ethnic groups becomes most evident in the newly formed community of deportees in Yakhina's first novel. When the small group of those who survived the six-month-long deportation journey arrives at the desolate banks of the Angara River, we share, through internal focalisation, the perspective of the OGPU officer and camp commander Ivan Ignatov on the people who are now left to his sole surveillance and responsibility:

> As he peers into their faces, Ignatov recalls the names of everyone working in the camp. He finds them on the list, circles them with the charcoal, and counts again. There are twenty-nine people, including the Leningraders, Russians, Tatars, a couple of Chuvash, three Mordvins, a Mari woman, a Ukrainian man, a Georgian woman, and a German man whose mind is gone and has the fanciful and sonorous name Volf Karlovich Leibe. In short, an entire international organisation. (Yakhina 2019: 234)

Despite the ironic tone through which Ignatov's view of the group is rendered and which is particularly expressed in the phrase "polnyi internatsional"[5], the labour camp is presented here as an ideal type of Soviet microcosm of people with different ethnic backgrounds and from different social strata, ranging from the Leningrad intelligentsia (the so-called 'former people') to craftsmen, farmers and criminals.

---

5  In the English translation the irony expressed in the phrase "polnyi internatsional" which is rendered as "an entire international organisation" unfortunately gets lost, whereas it is well persevered in the German translation of "eine echte Internationale" (Jachina 2017: 266).

*Figure 3.3: Film still from group of ethnically different people in the TV series* Zuleikha Opens Her Eyes *(2020)*

Much later in the novel, which covers a time span of 16 years from 1930 to the postwar period, this idea of the multi-ethnic community recurs, this time with reference to the deportation of the Crimean Tatars in 1944. Here again, the multi-ethnic community is viewed from the derogatory perspective of the OGPU (which by this time had already been renamed to NKVD). Thereby, the narrative technique of internal focalisation allows for ironic distance and functions as a marker for Yakhina's critical position towards the represented historical events:

> In the spring of 1942, Kuznets makes a sudden appearance out of nowhere, as always. He's brought with him a barge packed with emaciated people who have dark-olive skin and distinct profiles: Crimean Greeks and Tatars. 'Ivan Sergeevich,' he says, 'these outsiders are to be taken into your charge. And provide security measures. After all, they're a socially dangerous element in large numbers and of excellent high quality.' He laughs. Non-natives were being deported from southern territories in case the region should be overrun with occupiers and minority nations, giving such people the opportunity to desert to the enemy. This measure was, as they said, a precaution. Well, Greeks are Greeks. Even if they're Eskimos with papooses, they're no strangers to Ignatov. Out of curiosity, he once counted up all the nationalities residing in Semruk and came to nineteen. This means there are two more now. (Yakhina 2019: 438)[6]

---

[6] The English translation of this passage is in fact erroneous. Therefore, a version that corresponds to the wording of the original shall additionally be provided here: "The Muslim southerners were deported from the southern territories as a precaution, not waiting until the territory was occupied by the invaders and the minoritiesand ethnic groups would take the chance to defect to the enemy – as they say, to avoid this. Well, the Greeks are the Greeks. But even if Eskimos and Papuans, Ignatov could not get used to it." (Cf. Iakhina 2015: 457)

In Yakhina's first novel, ethnic and social diversity is not only a central element for describing the scenery, but also determines the three main characters upon which the plot and narrative perspective rest. There is, first, the naïve perspective of the Tatar woman Zuleikha, whose sole narrow point of view defines the first chapter so that the readers perceive the degrading patriarchal world she inhabits. The hegemonic position is marked as male and Russian and is represented by the OGPU officer Ignatov, the murderer of Zuleikha's husband and her later lover. However, in the course of the plot Ignatov, who escapes the party purges only by being transferred to Siberia, becomes a victim of the Stalinist system himself and is thus transformed into a positive character with whom readers can sympathise. Third, there is the figure of Volf Karlovich Leibe who, as "a third-generation professor at Kazan University" (Yakhina 2019: 102), is reminiscent of the crucial role German scientists played in Tsarist Russia.

Whereas the plot as a whole rests upon the multi-ethnic triangle of Tatar, Russian and German, only the female character undergoes a fundamental personal development, which echoes the Soviet model of education, modernisation and cultural assimilation. This development is not only brought to the fore by realistic descriptions of the character's psychology, but is most concisely and densely rendered in the book's title, which is also the sentence with which the novel begins. Zuleikha opening her eyes describes both the literal everyday action of waking up and the personal growth of the female protagonist, who leaves patriarchal subjection and religious superstition behind and achieves inner freedom at the end. When Zuleikha opens her eyes for the first time, it is "as dark as a cellar" around her (Iakhina 2015: 9), and the reader is, as it were, trapped with her in an archaic peasant world. Until the end, this sentence recurs four times, and each time the world around Zuleikha or rather Zuleikha's perception of it appears brighter. Finally, she is surrounded by glaring sunlight: "Zuleikha opens her eyes. The sun is beating down, blinding her and cutting her head to pieces. The vague outline of trees all around her are quivering in a sparkling dance of sunbeams." (Yakhina 2019: 479)

Stepping out of the darkness into the sun and light is one of the most frequently invoked images of communist enlightenment. With regard to the supposedly backward nationalities of the Soviet East, this notion is rendered most vividly by the image of the Muslim woman casting off her veil. In this sense, Zuleikha opening her eyes functions as an icon, which in its form is reminiscent of the expressive close-ups of the Soviet film avant-garde[7] and in its meaning appears as a perfect metaphor for the liberation, emancipation and modernisation of the woman of the Soviet East. From a contemporary postcolonial perspective, however, Zuleikha's personal development very much resembles the colonial and imperial cultural logic, according to which universal subjectivity can only be achieved by discarding the traditional ethnic and religious identity. This logic was an integral part of the Soviet empire, although the Soviet nationalities policy was at the same time aimed at decolonisation and the formation of national identity among the non-

---

[7] The close-up of Zuleikha's eyes, which is also rendered on the book cover of the English translation, most closely echoes Dziga Vertov's film *Three Songs about Lenin* (*Tri pesni o Lenine*, 1934/35), in which the pioneer of documentary cinema presented an impressive montage sequence of pairs of eyes and women's faces.

Russian minorities.[8] As Anisimova has shown, Yakhina's approach to ethnic identity is most obviously rendered in the storyline of Zuleikha's son Iusuf, who grows up in the cosmopolitan atmosphere of the camp:

> [...] Iusuf's education fulfills the Soviet ideal of the transformation of an ethnic subject into a cosmopolitan Soviet intellectual, even if this personal growth emphasizes the humanist rather than the ideological influence of Soviet culture. Yet, to achieve this universal subjectivity, Iusuf has to reject his Muslim and Tatar identity. (Anisimova 2020: 118)

Whereas in *Zuleikha Opens Her Eyes* the particular constellation of the Tatar and Russian nationality sparked considerable criticism from the Tatar community, Yakhina's comparable approach to identity in her second novel passed unnoticed. In *A Volga Tale*, the author follows the same principle of positioning the universal model above the national(istic) mode of particularity and even goes a step further by promoting a hybrid model of cultural identity. The analogous character in *A Volga Tale* is Antje who was conceived in an act of rape and therefore is not the main protagonist's biological daughter.[9] Since the schoolteacher Bach fell silent, he cannot pass on his language – German – to the next generation. Instead of being endowed with the cultivated German language of her non-biological father, Antje learns to speak from Vasia, a vagrant boy who turns up at the homestead one day. Vasia is a typical representative of the so-called *besprizorniki*, the orphans and waifs produced by war and famine. The language Vasia, also called Vaska, speaks is "foreign", "unknown" to Bach (Yakhina 2023: 399) – not only because it is Russian, of Bach knows only a "few hundred words", but also because it does not correspond to the standard language:

> However, Vaska's words and phrases so diverged from the few hundred words of standard Russian Bach knew that they probably belonged to some unfamiliar language. *Shamat', kipishnut', shnyrit', styrit', xapnut', shibanut', kanat', volynit'* – clearly all words for pinching, or stealing, carousing, guzzling food and drink, etc. – but what kind of words were these? (Yakhina 2023: 398)

A still closer look shows that the language Antje learns from Vasia is not only substandard, but also a mix of numerous languages, just as Vasia himself is ethnically unidentifiable, of an unknown origin – whether from "a Kirghiz or Kalmyk yurt, or a Bashkir or Tatar peasant hut" (Yakhina 2023: 350). Vasia's language is expressive, emotional, inventive and

---

8   The numerous contradictions inherent in the Soviet approach to nationality are well described by the term "Affirmative Action Empire" which was introduced by the Canadian historian Terry Martin (2001). Martin sums up the tension between national identity on the one hand and the anti-national Soviet approach on the other as follows: "The Bolsheviks attempted to fuse the nationalists' demand for national territory, culture, language, and elites with the socialists' demand for an economically and politically unitary state. In this sense, we might call the Bolsheviks internationalist nationalists or, better yet, Affirmative Action nationalists" (15).

9   This shift from biological to social parenthood can already be observed in *Zuleikha otkryvaet glaza*, when Ignatov forges Iusuf's birth certificate and makes Iusuf his official son in order to give him the possibility to leave the camp.

thus diametrically opposed to the cultivated language Iusuf learns from the Leningrad intelligentsia:

> And it didn't matter whether Vaska was glad, angry, or afraid. The curses were always magnificent, of the highest order. He usually swore in Russian, but he was perfectly capable of swearing in Kirghiz, Tatar, and Bashkir. He knew abusive oaths in Mordovian, as well as Udmurt, Mari and Kalmyk. The epithets and the languages stuck to him like burrs to socks. Often, Vaska's lips scrambled all the idioms and dialects he knew, and the result was such an intricate mesh of curses that they astonished not only his interlocuters, but Vaska himself. (Yakhina 2023: 348)

To draw a first conclusion, we can say that Yakhina's notion of identity on which her novels rest echoes contemporary, liberal attitudes and thus does not conform to the system of conservative cultural and social values which has emerged since Vladimir Putin's third term as president and which, according to Katharina Bluhm, aims at "an authoritarian consolidation of national unity on the basis of social conservatism with repressive features" (2021: 13). Central elements of this conservative ideology are the invocation of the nation's "thousand-year history", as it says in Article 67 after the constitutional amendment of 2020, and the preservation of traditional family values and gender roles. At the same time, Yakhina's notion of ethnic identity does not correspond to postcolonial conceptions of identity but rather recalls the progressive and egalitarian tendencies within Soviet ideology and politics. In this way, Yakhina tries to find a balance between different ideological positions and strives for compromise, which is not only true for her understanding of ethnic identity, but also for her general attitude to Soviet history. The latter goes hand in hand with a clearly marked emotional distance to the Soviet past that in her literary texts is conveyed by irony and by switching the narrative perspective. In a commentary for the online platform *RBK Stil'*, Yakhina emphasises the need to face the Soviet past and to actively deal with it in order to finally gain sovereignty over it:

> Enough of watching – enough of being observers of our own country's history and our own lives. The Soviet is not an object, it is a subject: it lives in us and governs us, no matter how much we want to deny it. In our relationship with the Soviet past, we are the objects. As long as we are not aware of this. (Iakhina 2021a)

Yakhina clearly distances herself from any form of Soviet nostalgia and sees a possibility to gain critical distance by recognising what was achieved through Soviet modernisation. She views the secular and urban society of the present day as a direct result of Soviet education and enlightenment, of the struggle against religion as well as of the "then imposed scientific view of the world". At the same time, Yakhina clearly calls for the crimes and the perpetrators to be named:[10]

---

10 According to the historian and journalist Sergei Medvedev (2016), the sore point of dealing with the Soviet past is that violence has remained anonymous until the present day or, in other words, that with a few exceptions the Soviet perpetrators have never been named.

> We – as society as a whole and not just a small part of it – can already afford to call monstrous things monstrous (e.g. the mass famine of the 1920s). Crime a crime (e.g. the Great Terror or the deportation of peoples). A criminal a criminal (e.g. Joseph Stalin or Genrikh Iagoda). (Iakhina 2021a)

It is undoubtedly to Yakhina's credit that some of the crimes committed by the Soviet regime are named and fed into public debate. In doing so, she is successful by the mere fact that thousands of people read her books and millions of viewers have watched the TV series based on her novel *Zuleikha Opens Her Eyes* (cf. Revizor.ru, "Skandal rabotaet"). The public outrage the series sparked in 2020 can be explained – as paradoxical as it may sound – precisely by Yakhina's attempt to seek balance and compromise.[11] An answer to this paradox is provided by Alexander Etkind and his notion of the "multi-historical" condition in contemporary Russia. According to Etkind, historical memory in Russia is de-centred, deprived of social and political consensus: "Historical memory in Russia is a living, de-centered combination of symbols and judgments which are experienced simultaneously, all at once […] deprived of consensual anchors or reference-points" (2009: 190). In contrast to the persistent official complaints that young people had no or little knowledge of history, Etkind argues that "it is not the historical knowledge which is at issue but its interpretation" (ibid.: 193). In the past ten years since Etkind published his article on post-Soviet 'hauntology', which was followed by the book *Warped Mourning: Stories of the Undead in the Land of the Unburied* (2013), official as well as the people's interest in history has not decreased but rather increased. The interest of particularly young people in Soviet history is indicated, for instance, by the high viewing rates of Iurii Dud's documentary *Kolyma – Birthplace of Our Fear* (*Kolyma – rodina nashego strakha*, 2019) that has gathered more than 29 million views on YouTube. Although definitely more modest in numbers and reach, Yakhina's novels are both an expression of and a driving force for public interest in the country's recent history.

## 3. Camera-stylo Reversed: The "Cinematic Quality" of Yakhina's Novels

What the French film critic and filmmaker Alexandre Astruc claimed for cinema back in 1948 – the *camera-stylo* as a new auteur based, non-commercial direction in filmmaking – reappears in Yakhina's approach to literature in a laterally reversed way. The much-acclaimed "cinematic quality" as *the* attribute of Yakhina's writing style (cf. Anisimova 2020: 111) is literally placed at the beginning of her success as a writer. Her first novel was published with a preface written by Liudmila Ulitskaia, the grande dame of contemporary Russian literature. In her preface, Ulitskaia recalls the Soviet "pleiade of bicultural writers" from the Caucasian Fazil' Iskander to the Kyrgyz Chinghiz Aitmatov and regards the "young Tatar woman Guzel Yakhina" as someone capable of continuing this lineage. Ulitskaia highlights Yakhina's "somewhat cinematic narrative style" (Iakhina 2015: 5–6) as a

---

11 Due to the political and cultural situation in Russia since the full-scale invasion of Ukraine, Yakhina's attempt to seek balance and compromise is doomed to failure and further publications in Russia are called into question.

stylistic feature. Since then, literary scholars and critics (c.f. Abasheva/Abashev 2016) as well as the author herself have tried to comprehend the 'cinematic quality' and its implications.

When Yakhina's third novel *Train To Samarkand* hit the market in March 2021, some critics noted a change in her writing style and praised the use of language that appeared simpler and clearer in comparison to her first two novels: "But the language has changed. It is simple, clear and lucid. The reader does not have to fear the viscosity of metaphors and comparisons of the previous book" (Bashmakova 2021).[12] In the numerous interviews that accompanied the release of the novel, the author stressed that she felt the need to mitigate the "horrifying material" (Surikov 2021), to "lighten up the heavy narrative" and to "balance the grievous subject" by using artistic techniques that provide a serious counterweight (Pakhomov/Sadikov 2021). Yakhina herself associates these techniques with cinema, and invoked, first of all, the importance of genre: the genre of adventure (film), a series of minor adventures along the way, an integrated love affair, the children's world and children's playful, creative use of language with rhymes and nicknames (cf. ibid.). Besides genre, Yakhina refers to questions of narrative structure and gives priority to short and action driven scenes, to dialogues based on conflict or to the mimetic over the diegetic (cf. Kostiukovich 2021). Correspondingly, the sources Yakhina consulted are, besides dairies, memoires or letters, not the literary works of the avant-garde of the 1920s, but rather the works of artists and cinematographers, which means that her main reference points are visual rather than textual:

> And of course, there is another view, which I would call the view of the artist who lived in that era. Important to me is: the artist – not the writer. I try to avoid reading literary texts with regard to what I'm writing about, simply because their influence might be too strong. I'm particularly talking about related arts such as cinema. While working on "Train to Samarkand", I watched newsreels. This is not really an artist's perspective. But still, we can certainly call documentarians of that time, like Dziga Vertov, artists. (Surikov 2021)

With regard to textual structures and formal techniques, a better understanding of the much-acclaimed 'cinematic quality' of Yakhina's writing style can be achieved by taking a closer look at the way the author constructs narrative scenes. Yakhina works with visual effects by dynamically switching between distant and close views on what is happening. The technique of altering the perspective from distant views to close-ups works together with vivid descriptions of movement within the scene. Two scenes shall be singled out here in order to illustrate Yakhina's transmedial use of camera angles, camera movement and montage with which cinematic effects are achieved within the literary text. The first example is a hunting scene in *Zuleikha Opens Her Eyes*. The first winter in the taiga has come to an end and the deportees together with their commander Ignatov are starving. Ignatov goes hunting with the last remaining cartridge and can barely keep himself on his feet. In the following scene, we first follow the audio-visual perception of the hunter and, together with him, capture several details of a squirrel before it scurries up a tree.

---

12   The comment by Elena Kostiukovich for BFM.RU (2021) goes in the same direction.

Then we see his movements from an objective point of view and return to his subjective perspective, which now is a worm's-eye view of the sky and the treetops spinning faster and faster:

> There's a sudden rustling beside him. A squirrel is on a branch right next to Ignatov's face: it's thin, dirty gray, with scanty white fluff, yellow cheeks, and long scampish tassels for ears. Meat! A shining brown eye darts and – zoom! – it's up the tree trunk. Ignatov's shaking hand reaches upward with the revolver but it's instantly way too heavy to hold. A shabby tail like a miniature broom flashes mockingly up above, teasing as it blends in with brush-like branches, layers of bark, and needly sunbeams, before disappearing. The sky suddenly starts spinning faster and faster, and then everything's spinning, the treetops, the clouds [...]. (Yakhina 2019: 303–304)

Ignatov's gaze up into the spinning sky, which points to the danger that he may lose his consciousness at any moment, recurs several times while he moves, or rather crawls, up the cliff. At the top of the cliff, he is about to put an end to his life, but suddenly he looks up, the sky stops spinning and he sees "the long brown spot of a barge" in a perfect cinematic extreme long shot: "He looks up. In the distance, dark against the bright blue Angara water, is the long brown spot of a barge and a bold black dot alongside it. It's the launch." (Yakhina 2019: 305)

*Figure 3.4: Film still from Dziga Vertov's reference to the Soviet avant-garde in the opening frame of his film* Three Songs about Lenin *(1934/35)*

The recurring view up into the spinning treetops well deserves closer examination because it has a distinct reference point in photography and cinema. The image crystallises the Soviet avant-garde from the moment it was celebrated as a new art form to its obliteration in the 1930s and rediscovery in the 1950s. The genealogy of the gaze up into the branches of (pine) trees can be traced back to Aleksandr Rodchenko's photography "Pine Trees" ("Sosny", 1927). In the film *Three Songs about Lenin* (*Tri pesni o Lenine*, 1934/35) it takes the form of an implicit aesthetic and political statement, by which Dziga Vertov reaffirmed his avant-gardist approach.

*Figure 3.5: Reference to Aleksandr Rodchenko's photography* Pine Trees *in the film* The Cranes Are Flying *(1957)*

Finally, it recurs in the most prominent film of the Thaw – in *The Cranes Are Flying* (*Letiat zhuravli*, 1957) – as an explicit visual citation (cf. Stiegler 2009). Yakhina's reference to the spinning treetops as a sign of near death is formally and thematically most closely linked to the scene in *The Cranes Are Flying*, in which the positive hero Boris looks up at the treetops while he falls to the ground, having been hit by a bullet. In this moment, the image of the treetops literally starts to spin and other images of the melodramatic hero's projections of a happier future are superimposed onto it. In Yakhina's hunting scene, the gaze up into the treetops functions on several levels: it contributes to the cinematic style, enhances the melodramatic mode of the narrative, and – together with other references to the history of cinema such as the recurrent close-ups of Zuleikha's eyes – indicates the transmedial character of intertextuality in Yakhina's writing.

The second scene that will be discussed in order to illustrate Yakhina's use of cinematic techniques demonstrates how action and movement are conveyed by means of parallel montage. The scene from *Train to Samarkand* is placed at the end of the first chapter, when the train with the 500 orphans finally leaves the station of Kazan'. The commander of the train Deev is standing on the open steps of the carriage and looking back at the crowd of women, when, through the thick white steam of the engine, his gaze suddenly falls on a running figure that tries to catch up with the moving train:

> The wagon shivers underfoot. The rails clatter. The station building, the trees, the trains – everything floats slowly and drifts backwards. Thick clouds of steam fly over the ground, covering the crowd remaining on the platform more and more tightly from Deev. Suddenly a figure emerges out of the white wadding, someone running after the locomotive, headlong, as fast as possible. A woman! Her long skirt is fluttering as she runs, stretching up above her knees and exposing her skinny legs in huge shoes. Her braid, half grey, is flying in the wind. And in the woman's arms – a baby in scarlet. The train is picking up speed, faster by the second. And the woman is running – faster and faster. She stretches out her arms with the baby. [...] Her eyes gazing wildly. Her mouth open. She is reaching out the baby to him – with her bony, straight arms: take the child! (Iakhina 2021c: 77–78)

In comparison to the canonical gaze up into the trees, the scene of the departing train and a figure catching up with it does not recall a specific film or image, but rather appears to reference cinema as a whole and its ability to produce visual clichés. Although it can be argued that other contemporary authors make use of cinematic clichés as well,[13] the 'cinematic quality' ascribed to Yakhina's novels can be justified by the accumulation of formal devices that refer to cinema or, viewed from the perspective of reception, that contemporary readers are familiar with from cinema. Thereby, the cinema in question is not avant-garde or auteur cinema with its complex textual structures and formal experiments, but rather the technically well-made mainstream cinema based on realistic narration.

## 4. Conclusion

If we approach the question put forward at the beginning from the angle of Yakhina's cinematic style, then one answer to the question of Yakhina's popularity in present day Russia is the particular way the author narrates her stories. Yakhina's realistic narration can be illuminated by the notion of "popular realism" put forward by the German literary scholar Moritz Baßler (cf. 2011; 2021). According to Baßler, popular realism in contemporary literature implies a writing technique through which the reader is presented a diegetic world that practically anchors itself in space and that the readers perceive without being confronted with a complex literary form: "One reads. And understands." ("Man liest. Und versteht."), as it says in a teaser for the German novelist Bernhard Schlink (cf. ibid: 91). The characteristic features of popular realism include a language that is easy to comprehend – in contrast to the difficult, impeded language of literature in Viktor Shklovskii's concept. Furthermore, popular realism provides comprehensible plots, conflicts that create suspense and characters the readers empathise with (an effect that is achieved by, among others, the narrative perspective of internal focalisation (cf. ibid: 147; 2011: 101). However, popular realism provides both, a reading experience that is touching and profound at the same time (ibid: 137). For this tendency, Umberto Eco back in 1964 referred to Dwight MacDonald's stratification of high art, mass and middlebrow culture.

---

13   As Abasheva and Abashev (2016) have argued, also the novels of Aleksei Ivanov, another well-known and popular contemporary Russian author, show a certain *cinematic quality*.

Eco characterised MacDonald's "Midcult" as the interaction of form and content in order to sell the effects of art and "satisf[y] its consumer by convincing him that he has just experienced culture" (1989: 192). A characteristic feature of today's midcult or mainstream literature is, according to Baßler, the integration of "difficult" or "heavy" signs ("schwere Zeichen") in the text (cf. 2021: 145). For German culture such signs are provided by "the Nazi and Stasi period" (ibid. 2011: 100), with the Oscar-winning film *The Life of Others* (*Das Leben der Anderen*, 2006) as one prominent example. At the same time, Florian Henckel von Donnersmarck's highly successful feature film of 2006 demonstrates how popular realism as the dominant method of telling stories affects cinema and literature alike.

Viewed from this perspective, Yakhina's historical novels and the way they are received by literary critics in Russia clearly show that the general attitude towards mainstream literature has changed under the conditions of the globalised market economy of the last decades. Significantly, Galina Iuzefovich (2021) may criticise *Train to Samarkand* as "highly comfortable for the reader", rewarding the reader with "universal love", "compassion" and "the unity of all good people", but at the same time may stress the novel's necessity and relevance. Above all, Yakhina's novels themselves as well as the author's self-representation in the media bear witness to the fact that today's mainstream literature declares itself openly as popular and entertaining, on the one hand, and as profound and honest, on the other. At the same time, Yakhina's novels need to be assessed against the backdrop of a society, which is deprived of a consensual interpretation of Soviet history. In this context, Yakhina's Chekhovian aim to "squeeze out the Soviet, even if only a drop at a time" (Iakhina 2021a) appears as reasonable as it is courageous.

## Filmography

*The Cranes Are Flying* (*Letiat zhuravli*), dir. Mikhail Kalatozov, USSR 1957.
*The Life of Others* (*Das Leben der Anderen*), dir. Florian Henckel von Donnersmarck, Germany 2006.
*Three Songs about Lenin* (*Tri pesni o Lenine*), dir. Dziga Vertov, USSR 1934/35.
*Zuleikha Opens Her Eyes* (*Zuleikha otkryvaet glaza*), dir. Egor Anashkin, Russia 2020.

## List of Illustrations

Figure 3.1: Film poster for the TV series *Zuleikha Opens Her Eyes* (*Zuleikha otkryvaet glaza*), dir. Egor Anashkin, Russia 2020, https://www.kinopoisk.ru/film/1186153/posters/ [30 September 2023].
Figure 3.2: Viktor I. Govorkov: "Vo imja kommunizma" ("In the Name of Communizm"). 1951. Printed by courtesy of Klaus Waschik.
Figure 3.3: Film still from the TV series *Zuleikha Opens Her Eyes* (*Zuleikha otkryvaet glaza*), dir. Egor Anashkin, Russia 2020, (2019), https://www.kino-teatr.ru/kino/movie/ros/131459/foto/ [30 September 2023].
Figure 3.4: Film still from *Three Songs about Lenin* (*Tri pesni o Lenine*), dir. Dziga Vertov, USSR 1934/35.

**Figure 3.5:** Film still *The Cranes Are Flying* (*Letiat zhuravli*), dir. Mikhail Kalatozov, USSR 1957.

## References

Abasheva, Marina/Abashev, Vladimir (2016): "Kniga kak simptom. Kak sdelan roman Guzeli Iakhinoi 'Zuleikha otkryvaet glaza'." In: Novyi mir 5 (http://www.nm1925.ru/Archive/Journal6_2016_5/Content/Publication6_6342/Default.aspx) [30 September 2023].

Anisimova, Irina (2020): "From Celebrated Novel to Media Outrage: The Public Debate Surrounding the Miniseries Zuleikha Opens Her Eyes." In: Slavica Bergensia 13, pp. 107–127.

Bashmakova, Mariia (2021): "Ėshelon na Samarkand" kak ispytanie. Kakim okazalsia novyi roman avtora 'Zuleikhi…'." In: Fontanka.ru, 9 March 2021 (https://www.fontanka.ru/2021/03/09/69801017/) [30 September 2023].

Baßler, Moritz (2011): "Populärer Realismus." In: Roger Lüdeke (ed.), Kommunikation im Populären. Interdisziplinäre Perspektiven auf ein ganzheitliches Phänomen, Bielefeld: transcript, pp. 91–103.

Baßler, Moritz (2021): "Der neue Midcult. Vom Wandel populärer Leseschaften als Herausforderung der Kritik." In: POP. Kultur und Kritik 18, pp. 132–149 (https://doi.org/10.14361/pop-2021-100122) [30 September 2023].

Bluhm, Katharina (2021): "Sozialer Konservatismus und autoritäre Staatsvision in Russland." In: RGOW (Religion & Gesellschaft in Ost und West) 10, pp. 13–15.

Eco, Umberto (1989): "The Structure of Bad Taste." In: ibid.: The Open Work, Cambridge, Massachusetts: Harvard University Press, pp. 180–216.

Etkind, Alexander (2009): "Post-Soviet Hauntology: Cultural Memory of the Soviet Terror." In: Constellations 1/16, pp. 182–200.

Etkind, Alexander (2013): Warped Mourning: Stories of the Undead in the Land of the Unburied, Stanford: Stanford University Press.

Fuchsbauer, Jürgen/Stadler, Wolfgang/Zink, Andrea (eds.) (2021): Kulturen verbinden – Connecting Cultures – Sblizhaia kul'tury. Festband anlässlich des 50-jährigen Bestehens der Slawistik an der Universität Innsbruck, Innsbruck: innsbruck university press.

Iakhina, Guzel' (2015): Zuleikha otkryvaet glaza, Moskva: Izdatel'stvo AST.

Iakhina, Guzel' (2016): "Sad na granitse." In: Snob.ru, 2 May 2016 (https://snob.ru/entry/80811/) [30 September 2023].

Iakhina, Guzel' (2018): Deti moi, Moskva: Izdatel'stvo AST.

Iakhina, Guzel' (2021a): "Mozhem sebe pozvolit'. Kolonka Guzel' Iakhinoi o sovetskom vchera I segodnia." In: RBK Stil', 12 March 2021 (https://style.rbc.ru/impressions/604a3d789a7947c5b4cfd743) [30 September 2023].

Iakhina, Guzel' (2021c): Ėshelon na Samarkand, Moskva: Izdatel'stvo AST.

Iuzefovich, Galina (2021): "'Ėshelon na Samarkand': Guzel' Iakhinu obvinili v plagiate, no problema romana ne v ėtom. Tragediiu v Povolzh'e avtor prevratila v komfortnuiu skazku." In: Meduza.io, 13 March 2021 (https://meduza.io/feature/2021/03/13/eshelo

n-na-samarkand-guzel-yahinu-obvinili-v-plagiate-no-problema-romana-ne-v-etom) [30 September 2023].

Jachina, Gusel (2017): Suleika öffnet die Augen. Translated from Russian by Helmut Ettinger, Berlin: Aufbau Verlag.

Kostiukovich, Elena (2021): "Porazhaet sovershenstvom". Vyshel novyi roman Guzel' Iakhinoi "Eshelon na Samarkand." In: BFM.RU, 9 March 2021 (https://www.bfm.ru/news/466802) [30 September 2023].

Martin, Terry (2001): The Affirmative Action Empire. Nations and Nationalism in the Soviet Union, 1923–1939, Ithaca/London: Cornell University Press.

Medvedev, Sergei (2016): "Ėffekt Karagodina. Pochemu vlast' boitsia tomskogo filosofa?" In: Republic, 29 November 2016 (https://republic.ru/posts/76777) [30 September 2023].

Nabiullina, A. N. (2019): "Prostranstvenno-vremennye obrazy i motivy v romanakh G. Iakhinoi 'Zuleikha otkryvaet glaza' i 'Deti moi'." In: Aktual'nye voprosy sovremennoi filologii i zhurnalistiki 3/34, pp. 32–36.

Pakhomov, Vladimir/Sadikov, Aleksandr (2021): "Guzel' Iakhina govorit o romane 'Ėshelon na Samarkand' i otvechaet ego kritikam (i, konechno, rasskazyvaet o svoikh otnosheniakh s iazykom)." In: Rozental' i Gil'denstern, 15 March 2021 (https://tehnikarechi.studio/episodes/2021/03/15/guzel-yahina-govorit-o-romane-eshelon-na-samarkand-i-otvechaet-ego-kritikam-i-konechno-rasskazyvaet-o-svoih-otnosheniyah-s-yazykom) [30 September 2023].

Protsyk, Oleh/Harzl, Benedikt (2013): "Introduction." In: Oleh Protsyk/Benedikt Harzl (eds.), Managing Ethnic Diversity in Russia, New York/London: Routledge, pp. 1–12.

"Skandal rabotaet: Serial 'Zuleikha otkryvaet glaza' stal samym reitingovym teleproėktom s proshlogo goda." In: revizor.ru, 30 April 2020 (https://www.rewizor.ru/cinema/news/skandal-rabotaet-serial-zuleyha-otkryvaet-glaza-stal-samym-reytingovym-teleproektom-s-proshlogo-goda/) [30 September 2023].

Samigullina, Ėl'vira/Nigmatullin, Ajrat/Avakian, Diana (2021): "'Mne nuzhno vremia, chtoby vsë obdumat'": kraeved iz Samary obvinil Guzel' Iakhinu v plagiate." In: Biznes Online, 11 March 2021 (https://www.business-gazeta.ru/article/501964) [30 September 2023].

Silant'eva, Ol'ga (2020): "Tsentr malen'koi vselennoi." In: Moskovskaia Nemetskaia gazeta, 25 May 2020 (https://ru.mdz-moskau.eu/centr-malenkoj-vselennoj/) [30 September 2023].

Stiegler, Bernd (2009): "When a Photograph of Trees Is Almost like a Crime." In: Études photographiques [En ligne], 23 May 2009 (http://journals.openedition.org/etudesphotographiques/3422) [30 September 2023].

Surikov, Viacheslav (2021): "Guzel' Iakhina: 'To, chto proiskhodit seichas, – ėto prodolzhenie sovetskogo perioda'." In: Expert, 5 April 2021 (https://expert.ru/expert/2021/15/guzel-yakhina-to-chto-proiskhodit-seychas-eto-prodolzheniye-sovetskogo-perioda/) [30 September 2023].

Shikhman, Irina (2021): "'A pogovorit'?': "Guzel' Iakhina. Ėshelon na Samarkand. Plagiat, fal'sifikatsia istorii, golod v Povolzh'e." In: YouTube, 25 June 2021 (https://www.youtube.com/watch?v=KGV9WAOVA0c) [30 September 2023].

Yakhina, Guzel (2019): Zuleikha, translated from Russian by Lisa C. Hayden, London: Oneworld Publications.

Yakhina, Guzel (2023): A Volga Tale, translated from Russian by Polly Gannon, New York: Europa Editions.

## Chapter 4:
## The Zone as a Place of Repentance and Retreat
Chernobyl in Belarusian Films of the 1990s and 2000s

*Olga Romanova*

## 1. Introduction

The military invasion of Ukraine by Russian forces on 24 February 2022 began with the takeover of the Chernobyl nuclear power plant. The news of the outbreak of war in the former Soviet Union triggered a culture shock, part of which was the instant renewed fear of a new nuclear disaster and radioactive contamination that was reflected in the media – both among the populations of Belarus and Ukraine, which were most affected by the 1986 Chernobyl reactor explosion, and in Europe. News outlets and social media advised people to stockpile iodine pills and take a large dose if the level of background radiation rose to protect the thyroid gland, and rumours and fears were shared that the pills had disappeared from pharmacies. The panicked reaction that quickly spread through the internet suggests that both the memory and fear of a repeat of the Chernobyl disaster, despite the mothballing of the exploded reactor and complete shutdown of the nuclear plant, have become part of global contemporary culture in the 21st century.

And part of this global culture is the constant production of films and television series (as well as computer games) on the topic. Documentaries as well as feature films about the events at Chernobyl, the consequences of the nuclear explosion and the search for its causes have been released in various countries over the years. Among the feature films to date, there is a large number of both problematic and dramatic auteur films and genre films where the Chernobyl zone becomes the backdrop for a horror, thriller or adventure action plot.

In comparison, Belarusian feature films on the Chernobyl topic constitute only a small proportion of this group of films – from 1990 to 2020, only six feature films were released by independent studios and Belarusfilm. At first glance, this seems paradoxical, as for the small republic the radioactive contamination of parts of its territories became a national disaster and trauma. Belarusians are still facing the consequences of the explosion, for example, Belarus has a very high percentage of thyroid diseases. Moreover, the most famous book about Chernobyl was written by Nobel laureate and Belarusian writer Svetlana Alexievich [Svitlana Aleksievich] and *Chernobyl Prayer: A Chronicle of the Future (Chernobyl'skaia molitva. Khronika budushchego*, 1997) has been the source of plots for many films produced outside Belarus, like the famous HBO series *Chernobyl* (2019). But Belarusian feature film directors have never turned to this book themselves.

In order to understand this seemingly paradoxical situation, in the following section I will analyse Belarusian films from the 1990s-2000s about Chernobyl taking into account the closely intertwined cinematographic and political contexts. I will then offer an analysis of four genre films from different periods – the crime drama *The Wolves in the Zone* (*Volki v zone*, 1990), the action film *The Atomic Zone Ranger* (*Reindzher iz atomnoi zony*, 1999), the melodrama *I Remember/Father's House* (*Ia pomniu/Otchii dom*, 2005) and the thriller *Exclusion Zone* (*Zapretnaia zona*, 2020). In doing so, I want to trace the different meanings applied to the event that took place on the night of 26 April 1986, what political processes these meanings manifest, and how they are influenced by the genre format of the respective films.

## 2. Production Conditions and Policies

In 1986, in the wake of perestroika, a landmark event took place in Soviet cinema – the Fifth USSR Congress of Cinematographers in Moscow. It was held in a both revolutionary and romantic atmosphere under the slogan "to put an end to serfdom in cinema." At this convention a new leadership of the Union of Cinematographers was elected (Ėlem Klimov became the head), the abolition of censorship was declared, and the Union's republic cinema organisations proclaimed independence from the central USSR Goskino. A new film production model was established by the Council of Ministers' Regulation "On the Restructuring of Creative, Organisational, and Economic Activities in the Soviet Film Industry" in 1989, which in fact initiated a process of radical changes.

One of the results was the emergence of independent film studios, at least within the Belarusian film industry. A number of well-known Belarusian directors, mostly of the middle generation (like Viacheslav Nikiforov [Viacheslaŭ Nikifaraŭ], Valerii Rybarev [Valer Rybaraŭ] or Mikhail Ptashuk) left Belarusfilm, which until then had been the sole film studio, and established private film studios. By 1991, there were already eleven such studios, which is why "the period 1990–1992 is described by many as a boom of independent film production in Belarus" (Khatkovskaia 2010:108).

However, another result of the reforms was a crisis in the film industry, which was no longer financed from the Soviet budget: production declined, distribution problems were experienced, and the competition against Western films was lost, with these films often being imported by 'pirates', filling cinemas and video rental outlets, and being freely sold on videotape. After the collapse of the USSR at the end of 1991, the situation became even more critical. Independent studios had to master the market economy and secure funding for their films. They mainly depended on bank loans and subsequently were held financially responsible.

> This determined a lot of the specifics of the studio executives and their approach to what they did and how they did it. They had to calculate everything from the begin-

ning, stick to deadlines and budgets, combine the relative cheapness of the films' production whenever possible with their quality and appeal to the audience, and engage in marketing and self-promotion. They abandoned expensive projects, made low-budget films and experimented a lot. (Khatkovskaia 2010: 112–113)

At the same time, Belarusfilm remained the only production base in Belarus. However, its management did not consider it necessary to support 'independents' and charged very high rental prices. In addition, private film projects were heavily taxed and there were no tax breaks for Belarusian directors. In the light of high inflation, these conditions were very difficult. Yet in the early 1990s, it was the independent film studios that began to shape the face of Belarusian cinema.

These hard economic conditions explain why the films produced by the independent studios were mostly popular genre productions (like dramas, melodramas, comedies, detectives, action films) – directors had to ensure financial returns. However, experimental auteur films were also often private production projects. Thus, the first Belarusian feature film that was set in the Chernobyl region, the crime drama *The Wolves in the Zone* directed by Viktor Deriugin, was produced as an independent project. It was released in 1990 as a coproduction of two private film studios, the Belarusian Impul's, Minsk and the Russian Benefis, Leningrad. At the same time, the film can be interpreted as an authorial experiment, based on the search for a cinematic language to describe the Chernobyl disaster as a social and cultural trauma.

In total, several documentaries and only three feature films were made in the 1990s about life after Chernobyl, although the topic itself was still very present among the Belarusian public. Only one of the movies was produced by Belarusfilm: in 1993 it released the film *Black Stork* (*Chernyi aist*), the production of which was entrusted to the iconic Soviet Belarusian director Viktor Turov [Viktar Traŭ]. The film is characterised by its non-genre format, slow narration, symbolism and use of metaphor. The two other films are directed by Viacheslav Nikiforov, *My soul, Maria* (*Dusha moia, Mariia*, 1993) – a drama produced by the private studio Kadr, which had been led by Nikiforov since 1987. Nikiforov returned to the subject of Chernobyl once again with the action film *The Atomic Zone Ranger*. Released in 1999, it was a joint project of several Russian studios and was shot at Belarusfilm. Compared to *The Wolves in the Zone*, here the matrix of a Hollywood action film is adapted more explicitly and consistently, which gained the film a greater popularity.

But already by the mid-1990s, most of the Belarusian independent studios had disappeared from the cultural field.

The reasons for their self-liquidation are the lack of conditions conducive to their activities: an unformed legislative and legal framework, an unorganised banking system, credit and insurance systems, the absence of tax benefits and a policy of priorities for national cinema, and the absence of a coherent programme for the development of the national film industry itself. (Khatkovskaia 2010: 121)

In 1997, Belarusfilm was officially given 'national' status, and it returned to shooting films with state-funded money, just as in Soviet times.

> In the absence of opportunities for the further existence of independent studios in the country, the situation slowly starts to return [...] to a situation of administrative regulation of cinema and state funding, to a limited and easily regulated number of subjects of cinematographic activity. (Khatkovskaia 2010: 121)

Thus, it is no wonder that the period from 1986 to the mid-1990s was the most fruitful for Belarusian cinema in terms of social self-reflection. A number of films dealt with 'blank spots' of Belarusian history or sought to make sense of the late and post-Soviet present. They revealed the memory of traumatic experiences of various historical events of the 20th century seen from a national perspective like the Belarusian anti-Bolshevik resistance of the 1920s, the life of Belarusian Jews and the pogroms against them, the forced collectivisation or the post-war Stalinist repressions. All four feature films about the Chernobyl disaster made during this period are embedded in this context.

However, by the early 2000s, the work of cinematography engaged with the topic of national, historical and cultural traumas was artificially stopped. In this decade only a few Belarusian feature and documentary films that touched upon the subject of the Chernobyl catastrophe were produced. In 2006, Belarusfilm released the 'anniversary' film-melodrama *I Remember/Father's House*, directed by Sergei Sychev, which reflects on the state policy of memory and constructs a myth about the stable modern Belarus of the Lukashenko era. The main idea of this film is "You shouldn't look into the past all the time [...]," as one of its positive characters explains.

In 2020, following the success of the HBO series *Chernobyl*, Belarusfilm released the action film *Exclusion Zone*, directed by Mitrii Semenov-Aleinikov, where the Chernobyl territory becomes a springboard for a survival game of warring teenage heroes on a hunt for a bag full of money. The Russian TV series *Chernobyl* (produced by the Russian TV channel NTV, released in 2021) was also filmed in Belarus. Its plot is revealing, especially in light of the fact that a year later Russia would launch a 'special operation' in Ukraine with the passive support of most Russian TV viewers: Here KGB officers learn that foreign agents are interested in the Chernobyl nuclear power plant. An experienced CIA agent, suspected of espionage, is located in the town of Pripiat' and to find him, a Soviet lieutenant colonel of military counterintelligence arrives in the town. Soviet history serves as a blueprint for the present.

## 3. *The Wolves in the Zone* (1990): Mission Impossible

Although *The Wolves in the Zone* has been and still is advertised as a crime thriller, the criminal plot here seems less important than the author's statement with its surrealist climax and religious outcome of the storyline. Instead of a thriller, an existential drama of dehumanisation unfolds on the screen. The protagonist of the film is a former police captain called Rodion, who returns to the Chernobyl zone on a special mission. He was born there, was a liquidator in the aftermath of the Chernobyl disaster, damaged his health and was forced to leave on his own and take his blinded mother with him. These details are revealed in a dialogue in the first scene with the local policeman Stas, as well as the fact that a gang of looters ('wolves') has appeared in the zone – led by their mutual acquaintance Semën. Unlike the captain, who gained nothing from working for the state as a policeman, Semën lives richly and clearly bribes the local authorities so that he can sell goods taken from abandoned houses. This constellation is central for the whole plot contrasting the courageous Rodion with the neurotic Stas, who leads a cynical gang selling items contaminated with radiation all over the Soviet Union.[1]

This criminal plot in the following scenes, however, gives way to direct social and political denunciation. In the first scene, where Rodion and the viewer are immersed in the life of the zone, he witnesses a policeman stopping a peasant 'self-settler' (*samosel*)[2], who is driving a cart from his territory. Under the hay he is hiding radioactive cherries which he is taking to the market to sell. When the policeman proposes that the bearded man taste cherries, he spits them out in fright. Rodion also observes the liquidators burying food and machinery contaminated by radiation in a quarry, covering them with earth. "Battalion of death", says the liquidators' exhausted foreman, "working without gloves, naked [...]." A close-up shows the face of a twelve-year-old boy sitting behind the wheel of an excavator without any protective equipment.

Subsequently, we see some foreigners loading a car into a van, clearly taking it away to be sold. The next scene reveals that it is a joint business between Semën and the Soviet district leadership. After the deal, a representative of the nomenklatura goes out into the square "to the people," only after putting on boots with lead soles. "Quiet, comrades! Many authoritative scientists, authoritative commissions have come here. They've come to the conclusion: it's still possible to live!" Shouts can be heard from the crowd, separated by the police: "And why are the children sick?!" A little boy asks, "Uncle, when are we all going to die?"

*Figure 4.1: Film stills from the film* The Wolves in the Zone *(1990). Radioactive products in the burial ground; Speech by district authorities to local residents*

---

1   As the credits state, this film was actually even shot in an abandoned area of the Chernobyl nuclear power plant, and occasional documentaries are used and simulated to convey the atmosphere of the half-empty and radiation-contaminated area.
2   'Self-settlers' were locals who had voluntarily returned from evacuation to their homes in the radiation-contaminated area and were living in abandoned villages.

The three scenes are constructed using parallel editing, even though the story is told as taking place consecutively. This means that the director sees a connection between them, as well as a key to understanding the post-Chernobyl Soviet reality, which he paints as disintegrated and dehumanised.

Such a conclusion is also supported by a subsequent scene at the local market in a town near the border with the zone, where everything from food to white goods is sold. One resident walks around with a dosimeter, which shows high doses everywhere. "Put that gun away! Get out of here, you hooligan! Alcoholic!" a peasant yells at him who is bringing his radioactive cherries to the market. The curious citizen is grabbed and taken away by the 'market watcher' mafia, who works for Semën. Rodion stands up for him and is brutally beaten in an abandoned hangar. Semën, who fears the former captain will expose his business, warns: "If you get into trouble, you'll be buried yourself [...]." Rodion, beaten half to death, soon recovers – and this is perhaps the only sign that the viewer is facing a true hero of the criminal genre; in other scenes, the former captain is more often a silent witness rather than an active participant.

Obviously, these images of brutal mafia, corrupt police, cynical representatives of state power, who are opposed by a lone hero, are adapted from Hollywood action movies, which were well known to Soviet viewers and video parlour-goers from popular films in the late USSR with Sylvester Stallone (*Rambo. First Blood*, 1982), Steven Seagal (*Above the Law*, 1988), or Chuck Norris (*Code of Silence*, 1985). However, the emergence of these characters is also due to the social developments of the perestroika period. The criminal world as part of the 'decaying' Soviet reality had appeared in films since 1986, such as *Plumbum, or The Dangerous Game* (*Pliumbum, ili Opasnaia igra*, 1986), directed by Valerii Abdrashitov, *Assa* (1987), directed by Sergei Solov'ëv, *The Needle* (*Igla*, 1988), directed by Rashid Nugmanov [Rachid Nougmanov] or *My Name is Harlequin* (*Menia zovut Arlekino*, 1988), directed by Valerii Rybarev. Late Soviet daily life is represented here as false, implacably class-oriented, divided into rich and poor, province and the Moscow centre. Especially the common Soviet man is shown as drinking heavily, often a conformist and a latent Stalinist. Also, in *The Wolves in the Zone*, the ordinary Soviet facing the collapse of his country is portrayed as a looter or a cynical salesman of contaminated food, thinking only about his own well-being. The parallel motif of all these perestroika films is the violence that pervades Soviet society, as well as the cynicism of state power.

Very characteristic for this trend are two Belarusian films of this period – *Our Armoured Train* (*Nash bronepoezd*, 1988, Belarusfilm) and *Political Bureau Co-op or A Long Farewell* (*Kooperativ Politbiuro, ili Budet dolgim proshchanie*, 1992, Independent Studio), directed by Mikhail Ptashuk and written by Evgenii Grigor'ev. The latter was shot using private funds as an independent project already in 1990, but was released only two years later after the collapse of the USSR, when it finally received a distribution certificate from the Belarusian Ministry of Culture. *Political Bureau Co-op* begins as a satire of late-Soviet society: in the story, a resourceful entrepreneur creates a cooperative and hires doppelgängers of the civil war hero Chapaev as well as of Stalin, Khrushchev and Brezhnev. The theatre troupe travels to Belarusian towns where it draws full houses. The spectators of the play laugh at Khrushchev and Brezhnev, and then suddenly frantically applaud Stalin's appearance on the provincial stage. Satire is gradually replaced by tragedy. The turning point comes in the scene where two representatives of the provincial government order a Stalin impersonator into their mansion. He tries to play his role 'to order', but the situation changes: the owners begin to humiliate and mock the elderly actor and then they forbid the troupe from continuing their performances.

This turning point of the plot reveals the critical message of the film: encountering the Soviet authorities leads to inevitable humiliation, to discovering oneself as a subordinate, being at the bottom of the power hierarchy. However, the film protagonists also encounter the new 'masters of life', who turn out to be even more dangerous and frightening than the old ones. They are young racketeers who show up at the village hut and blackmail the outcast troupe into paying them protection money. On discovering that they have no money, they shoot all the actors, brutally torturing each one, before setting fire to a hut with the bodies of those killed. The gruesome finale of the burning village house, in which almost all the main characters die, reveals, according to the director, a symbolic meaning that characterises the whole country.

Thus, this film very vividly deals with the internal conflicts of late Soviet society and its fear of a post-Soviet future. The past is represented here by the figures of the leaders, the present by the 'Stalinist people' and the corrupted power, and the future by the young racketeers, the killers, who represent the dangerous nature of wild capitalism.

*Figure 4.2:  Film stills from the film* Political Bureau Co-op or A Long Farewell. *Aleksei Petrenko as Stalin's doppelgänger actor*

*The Wolves in the Zone* contains a very similar negative message that connects it to the theme of life after the Chernobyl disaster. Whereas in typical Hollywood crime thrillers or action films of the same period the protagonist is supposed to restore order and punish evil in a world that is falling apart, this exact mission proves impossible in late Soviet and early post-Soviet films. Just as the protagonist is defeated, the genre logic is also suspended here.

## 4. Symptoms of Cultural Trauma

In place of the typical climax of crime genre movies with a shoot-out between the hero and the antagonists, the central part in *The Wolves in the Zone* is a long and fraught sequence at night in a deserted town that has been cleared of residents. Rodion and Stas decide that it is impossible to deal with the gang through legal means, so they kidnap Semën from his cottage and take him to a place where no authority exists. We see documentary footage filmed at night of an abandoned town (most likely Pripiat' within the Chernobyl area, where all the inhabitants have been evacuated). This is followed by a scene in an abandoned flat after the evacuation, where the militia friends bring Semën as well as Stas's girlfriend, a nurse, whom they suspect of reselling looted items. In the meantime, Rodion goes off to look for his house. Spotting a marauder there trying to steal the family icon, he shoots him. It is at the house that Stas finally finds him. Rodion orders him to take the corpse out of his house and yells at his partner to leave as well. Then he looks at the photo album thrown on the floor. A close-up shows a photograph of Rodion as a child standing under a portrait of Stalin with a toy gun in his hands – a typical Soviet boy socialised with violence from early on.

The main emotional state of all those involved in the final part of the film can be described as fear, hysteria and madness. Also, all the characters who find themselves in the zone have nothing more to lose and nothing to hide; in the plot they are extremely open. In fact, the viewer hears a series of public monologues, which are constructed as a social denunciation and an exposé of the essence of the Soviet man. For example, Semën and a nurse are drinking vodka found in the flat. She complains about her very low salary and her longing for a child and justifies her collaboration with the looters entirely due to the circumstances of life: "Life is divided into before and after," says the woman. "We don't know what we eat, what we drink, what we breathe, what will happen to us. We are hostages. How can we keep ourselves safe? And there is no point." Semën's monologue is an ode to wild capitalism, denouncing the lack of initiative and the slavish obedience of the Soviet people. Rodion suddenly turns out to be a patriot for whom his homeland, the Soviet Union, is important. Stas's monologue is constructed as the self-disclosure of an ordinary Soviet man, as he shouts, "We are mutants, slaves, sheep!"

Then another man – a former intellectual, a former nuclear power plant worker – breaks into the flat. He claims to be the owner of the flat and suspects the guests of being looters, and they suspect him of the same. Rodion and Stas shoot both him and Semën, and are ready to shoot each other. It is dawn. Finally, Rodion imagines that the door of the room is slowly opening and a huge cactus, oversized due to the radiation, is reaching for him.

Thus, the viewer is immersed in a process of dehumanisation, where all the characters lose any sense of direction, easily kill each other and sink into madness. The zone is painted as a place where there is not only no power restraining people, but also no morality, and this is, according to the movie, the essence of what the Chernobyl disaster and the Soviet regime have done to people. This understanding is also supported by other individual fragments of the film and the glimpses of Rodion's flashbacks, such as in the picture showing him with a Stalin portrait. In this sense, he also represents the last post-war generation, being born still under Stalin's regime and in the present turning out to be criminal, deceitful and cynical. This is also true for the representatives of the district authorities, who began their ascent through the Komsomol and the Party. One of these nomenklatura representatives outright lies in a speech to the local population demonstrating no respect to ordinary Soviet people or to human life in general. In one of the flashbacks, Rodion recalls the evacuation of the population from the contaminated territories and thereby refers to the German occupation as one of the most terrible and tragic events in the memory of the Belarusians. The present authorities seem to be no better.

*Figure 4.3: Film stills from the film* The Wolves in the Zone. *Rodion and his memories of the evacuation*

Although these motifs are exaggerated and taken as a direct denunciation of perestroika-era cinema in general and the author's film concept, some of them are also heard in the testimonies recorded by Svetlana Alexievich for her documentary-fiction book *Chernobyl Prayer*. In the accounts of survivors – former liquidators or their relatives – parallels with the horrors and losses of war are often mentioned. For example, in the chapter "Land of the Dead" there is a story about the 'self-settlers', an elderly couple of peasants who went into the forest with their cow when the soldiers evacuated the village. "Like under the punishers," they explain. Other characters in the book also recall returning to their homes along familiar 'partisan paths'.

There are also witness accounts of looting and of locals removing both radioactive items and crops to sell in the markets. A former policeman recalls:

> They brought meat for disposal in the burial sites. The hips were missing from the beef carcases. The fillet. I filed a report. We had a tip-off that a house in an abandoned village was being dismantled. They were numbering and placing the logs on to a tractor with a trailer. We headed straight out to the address given. The raiders were arrested. They were hoping to remove the building and sell it as a dacha. They'd already received advance payment from the future owners. I filed a report. (Alexievich 2016: 88)

A recurring motif in *Chernobyl Prayer* is that the authorities explained nothing to the local population or the liquidators, gave no medical advice, acted in a domineering manner, hiding both the truth and their confusion, while the newspapers carried the traditional Soviet heroic narrative. In the part "The Soldier's Choir," the surviving liquidator soldiers recall the disenfranchised and hysterical atmosphere ("One guy, I think he was from Leningrad, was protesting: 'I don't want to die.' They threatened him with a court martial." (Alexievich 2016: 76) and how they were sent to the area with only shovels ("Did all the work by spade." (Alexievich 2016: 76)). At the same time, instances of heroism are also recalled when liquidators consciously sacrificed their lives.

Today we can view these monologues as evidence of the cultural trauma experienced by late Soviet society. As the central figure of "Monologue on a moonscape" reflected:

I began wondering why so little has been written about Chernobyl. Our writers keep on writing about the war, about Stalin's camps, but they're silent on Chernobyl. There are almost no books on it. Do you think that's just a coincidence? It's an episode still outside our culture. Too traumatic for our culture. And our only answer is silence. We just close our eyes, like little children, and think we can hide (Alexievich 2016: 98).

The Polish sociologist Piotr Sztompka (2001a; 2001b) suggests that any changes or events that shock society should be considered social trauma. In contrast to the medical or psychological understanding of the term, it refers to a "destructive impact on the social body." If trauma affects the cultural order, it can be called "cultural trauma," a symptom of which is the "disruption of normality:" a crisis of collective identity and a "disruption of the world of meanings," where both values and trust in authority are permanently undermined.

If disorder occurs, symbols take on meanings different from the ordinary signifiers. Values lose value, unrealistic goals are demanded, norms prescribe unsuitable behaviour, gestures and words signify something other than their former meanings. Beliefs are rejected, faith is undermined, trust disappears, charisma collapses and idols crumble (Sztompka 2001a: 11).

In the final scene of *The Wolves in the Zone*, Rodion races away in a military car, which he has stolen to get away from the site of the crime, having been shot by a distraught Stas. He then finds himself in the dugout of a strange man who all this time has been silently observing everything that has been going on in the zone and in the flat. In the corner of the dugout there is a candle and an icon:

– "Who are you?" Rodion asks him half-dead.
– "A Human. The zone," he replies.

And the viewer sees the man sowing the desolate land. It is commented on by a voice-over: "If a baby is taken away from its mother's breast, it will be sick. So it is with the man from whom God has been taken away."

This final moral can be seen in different contexts. On the one hand, it refers to the central idea of Georgian director Tengiz Abuladze's film *Repentance* (*Pokaianie/Monanieba*), which was filmed in 1984 but was not shown to a wide audience until after the Fifth Congress of Cinematographers in 1987. In its symbolic form it spoke about the victims of Stalinist repressions and the fact that they should not be forgotten either by the new generations of the Soviet authorities or by the people. The protagonist Ketevan, after the funeral of Varlam Aravidze (a symbolic figure who refers to both Stalin and Beria), digs up his corpse several times and throws it at the house of his wealthy heirs, son and grandson, and then tells the story of how Varlam destroyed their family by arresting his father and mother on a deliberately false accusation. The final scene of *Repentance* features a dialogue that has become famous and iconic primarily in the eyes of the late Soviet intelligentsia. An elderly woman asks Ketevan if this road will lead her to the temple: "– This street of Varlam, it will not lead to the temple. – Then what's the use of it? What's the road for if it doesn't lead to the temple?" asks the old woman and walks off into the distance. After the release of this film, the idea of repentance for the whole of Soviet society became, in a way, the project of the Soviet intelligentsia and was often called for in public statements. Behind this idea, presented in religious tones, was the hope for the 'spiritual renewal' of Soviet society and its morals.

At the same time, the final scene of *The Wolves in the Zone* captures the collapse of faith in Soviet science and the 'peaceful atom', which was its main symbol in the 1970s (the Chernobyl nuclear power plant was completed and started operating in 1977). Similar motifs are recorded in Alexievich's *Chernobyl Prayer*: one of the characters retells the popular version that the Chernobyl disaster was prophesied in the Book of Revelation:

> 'And there fell a great star from heaven, burning as it were a lamp, and it fell upon the third part of the rivers, and upon the fountains of waters; And the name of the star is called Wormwood: and the third part of the waters became wormwood; and many men died of the waters, because they were made bitter'. (Alexievich 2016: 74)

Chernobyl in Ukrainian is translated as "wild plant, wormwood," this is why the apocalyptic "wormwood star" has become a stable metaphor of the catastrophe in the journalism of the perestroika period and 1990s as well as in popular opinion. "You want to take her for science, but I loathe your science! Loathe it! First, your science took him away from me, now it's back for more. I won't give her to you!" (Alexievich 2016: 21) says another figure in the book whose monologue is a very painful story about how her husband died in agony (she recalls the doctors saying that he is now "a highly contaminated radioactive object" (Alexievich 2016: 16) and that she should take care of herself and her child, not to stay in hospital with him dying).

As Sztompka writes, any attempts to interpret a shock event that becomes symptomatic of cultural trauma do not arise in a vacuum: "There is always an available set of meanings encoded in the culture of a particular community (society). Individuals do not invent meanings, but select them from the surrounding culture, applying them to potentially traumatic events [...]" (2001a: 8). He also notes that these interpretations often manifest pre-existing cultural conflicts which, in my view, could include social stratification, the ritualisation of ideology, and grassroots condemnation of continued militarisation (like the 1979 invasion of Soviet troops into Afghanistan). These conflicts permeated the whole of the previous Brezhnev period (the period of Stagnation) and surely formed the increasingly indifferent, ironic or negative attitude towards Soviet power.

In summary, the crime movie *The Wolves in the Zone* and several other films from the perestroika period like *Political Bureau Co-op* deal with this cultural trauma, attempting to capture it on screen. In comparison, *The Atomic Zone Ranger*, another genre film made as an independent project but nearly ten years later, reflects very different cultural patterns and socio-political symptoms.

## 5. *The Atomic Zone Ranger* (1999). A Fantasy of a 'Strong Arm'

By the mid-1990s, the crime-adventure thriller, set against the backdrop of post-Soviet everyday life, was becoming a popular genre both in post-Soviet literature and in cinema, including Belarusfilm. *The Atomic Zone Ranger* was released in this context. Aleksei Kravchenko, a Russian actor who played the famous role of teenager Flora in Ėlem Klimov's war drama about the German occupation, *Come and See* (*Idi i smotri*, 1985), was invited to play the main character. Yet it was only after the release of *The Atomic Zone Ranger* that he changed his image and became the 'Russian Chuck Norris'.

*Figure 4.4: Film still of Aleksei Kravchenko in* Come and See *(left)*

*Figure 4.5: Film still of Aleksei Kravchenko in* The Atomic Zone Ranger *(right)*

In the film, Kravchenko plays a captain nicknamed Badger, who served on a nuclear submarine and later returns to Belarus to replace his father as a forester. He has to prevent timber from being exported from the Chernobyl zone for sale, and also runs into the local mafia, which is involved in drug trafficking and uses abandoned houses as a drug depot.

The main difference between the *The Wolves in the Zone* and a typical action film is that the latter usually promotes an incorruptible and strong hero who confronts the criminal world. This is commonly accompanied by a melodramatic love story, erotic episodes, a climax in the form of a shoot-out with the mafia and a happy ending. Accordingly, the grafting of the Hollywood genre canon onto post-Soviet soil requires a well-crafted and recognizable everyday background and a sympathetic protagonist that the public can identify with – fighting against antiheroes in a painful and unstable world. *The Wolves in the Zone* adapt many of these motifs, showing 'self-settlers' and looters in the zone or traders who sell radioactive goods on the market throughout the Soviet Union. Following the release of a series of Russian, Ukrainian and Belarusian films about Chernobyl and the publication of Alexievich's *Chernobyl Prayer*, these motifs became common patterns of description of the social consequences of the Chernobyl disaster. "We got a nuclear missile from ourselves. Now we'll be dealing with it for 300 years," the protagonist Ranger and his only associate in the fight against organised crime argue in one of their private conversations over a beer.

In addition to the motifs of lawlessness in the zone, realistic details of ordinary people's bleak, dreary everyday lives are shown, typical for 1990s perestroika films. The action film also portrays life in the provinces bordering the Chernobyl zone as poor and depressing. But there is no social and political criticism here anymore – the main trouble is not an indifferent or cynical state, but the mafia, the so-called 'New Russians' or 'New Belarusians'. Unlike the state, the mafia can be defeated – destroyed or imprisoned, and the evil will be punished. In this way, the genre formula of the crime thriller neutralises both social tension and fear of the future. *The Atomic Zone Ranger*, like other genre films of the period, adopts these motifs reproducing the post-Soviet audiences' fatigue from the shocking and demanding auteur cinema of the earlier perestroika period. As Russian film scholar Ian Levchenko aptly put it, "the Soviet cinema of the late 1980s [...] is ahead of its viewer, it wants too much from him. The need for a serious conversation in this viewer is more likely to arise out of inertia, on the wave of interest in the media. Unsupported by existential need, this interest fades quickly" (Levchenko 2007: 701).

This viewer fatigue regarding social and political criticism and self-criticism, as well as cultural products dealing with cultural trauma and fear is characteristic for the 1990s. Instead of thought-provoking pictures, genre cinema offered a schematic struggle of the strong hero against the mafia, which may be compared with the political call for a 'strong hand' of the authorities. In 1999, for example, Vladimir Putin declared publicly on central television with regard to Chechen fighters and justifying the Russian bombing of Groznyi: "We'll rub [mochit'] them out in the outhouse". The expression 'rub them out in the outhouse' instantly became an idiom, and permanently formed the image of the new Russian president as a strong leader. At the same time, in the second half of the 1990s, in independent Belarus, Lukashenko [Lukashenka] won wide popular support and was given the respectful family nickname of "Batska".

## 6. The 2000s: "You don't have to look back all the time…"

As one of the epigraphs to her *Chernobyl Prayer*, Alexievich chooses fragments from the article of the handbook *Chernobyl: A look back over the decades*, published in 1996, ten years after the disaster:

> On 26 April 1986, at 1:23 hours 58 seconds, a series of blasts brought down Reactor No. 4 of the Chernobyl nuclear power plant, near the Belarusian border. The accident at Chernobyl was the gravest technological catastrophe of the twentieth century.

> For the small country of Belarus (population ten million), it was a national disaster, despite the country not having one nuclear power station of its own. Belarus is still an agrarian land, with a predominantly rural population. During the Second World War, the Germans wiped out 619 villages on its territory along with their inhabitants. In the aftermath of Chernobyl, the country lost 485 villages and towns: seventy remain buried

forever beneath the earth. During the war, one in four Belarusians was killed; today, one in five lives in the contaminated zone. (Alexievich 2016: 1)

Twenty years later, Belarusfilm released the melodrama *I Remember/Father's House*. The main message is encapsulated in the description of one of the positive characters, a doctor-professor who monitors the health of the artist Anatolii, who as a child lived on contaminated territory and lost his parents and brother: "You shouldn't look back all the time, to the past. I understand, the people you loved are there, Chernobyl is there. But don't burn yourself to the ground! You're not a memorial candle." These words resound from the very first minutes of the film, which brings us to the key phenomenon of Belarusian state cinema of the 2000s: ideology is not camouflaged here, rather it is brought to the surface. It is articulated by the positive characters, supported by the plot, visuals and the final message – and none of it needs to be deciphered.

The professor's daughter Inna is Anatolii's former lover, who leaves him when she finds out she is pregnant and he is afraid to have a baby. In the end she leaves her job as curator of an art gallery and follows Anatolii to his homeland – to wait for the arrival of the baby in an abandoned village on the territory of the zone. The self-settled peasants have been living there for a long time. Sturdy, ruddy old men build a chapel in the zone to appease God, as one man says, "Chernobyl is a punishment for us for turning away from God," stating, "The soul is beyond control of radiation" and claiming that "nature itself has purified itself." Accordingly, Anatolii feels healthy and happy here, breathes the clean air of his native village and is reborn to a new life. It turns out that his illness was purely a product of nervous self-destruction.

Within this frame, the plot of the film is driven by a hardly camouflaged conflict. Anatolii discovers that cynical workers laid the floor of the house of the old Makarovs with radioactive planks taken out of storage from the zone. "That's a sin," says Anatolii's aunt. The narrator answers her: "Punishment. Let Comrade Makarov now walk on his floor and glow!" However, Anatolii sets out to find the house to warn the owner, but discovers that a young girl, Katia, who recently bought it, lives there. She tells him that the house has been sold because of the sudden death of Makarov, who used to live there with his grandparents. A further plot aspect develops as they attempt to find the cynical construction worker and punish him. At the end, a young businessman in love with Katia finds him through his connections and turns him in to the police.

The Belarusians portrayed in this film are mostly kind, naive and well-to-do people. They represent social stereotypes that have nothing to do with Belarusian reality. Thus, self-settled peasants are shown here as the most important national social group, 'stalwart in spirit' and religious, who have returned to the zone after evacuation and are convinced there is no longer any radiation. When Anatolii also decides to stay in his native village and to help paint the chapel, one of the old men says: "You should paint icons of us, so that our grandchildren will come here and pray". According to programmatic statements in the film, all problems are caused by 'spiritual mutation'. A bundle of dollars that passes from one character to another in order to help each other until it reaches Katia symbolises the solidarity that still exists among ordinary people.

In contrast to the early Christian idea of repentance, which appears in the finale of the 1990 film drama *The Wolves in the Zone*, here the religious morality refers to the Orthodox Church. It is also combined with traditional patriarchal relations in a romantic light: women treat men with love and sacrifice, Anatolii's bride Inna is ready to carry a child in the zone, and Katia keeps her chastity until her wedding – only towards the end she finally agrees to marry the businessman and tells him: "You will both feed and clothe me." References to orthodoxy, patriarchy and popular 'spirituality' are fragments of the eclectic ideology of the Lukashenko era. Its essence can be defined as the ideal of a pre-political stage of society, where the life of citizens is an adjustment to its urgent problems. As the film *I Remember/Father's House* suggests, the state is as if invisible here, as instead of by force, ideological constructs are presented here as 'coming from the people themselves'' and thus guaranteeing an imagined 'Belarusian stability'.

Repressive mechanisms are shown here only in relation to 'outsiders' who allegedly act against the interests of the 'common people' and their well-being. This notion of Belarusian authoritarianism allows the state to demand unconditional acceptance of any of its decisions. This became particularly obvious in 2008, when Lukashenko made the final decision to build a nuclear power plant on the territory of Belarus. The main objection from opponents to its construction was the fear of a repeat of the Chernobyl disaster. But other arguments like the ecological damage caused by transportation and processing of uranium and the problem of nuclear waste storage were also raised. "No atom is peaceful!", was one of the of the often-repeated slogans used by activists at the annual Charnobylski Shliakh protest action first held on 26 April 1989. Later in independent Belarus these marches and rallies in memory of Chernobyl became a form of political resistance and the one in 2008 was the biggest ever in the country, protesting against Lukashenko's policies, accompanied by clashes with police and arrests. This mass resistance against the construction of the nuclear power plant showed vividly that the authoritarian claim of an overall consent among 'common people' was false and that the distrust of citizens towards the authorities is enormous, especially because the Belarusian state never discusses its decisions with the public, does not engage in dialogue and responds to any protests with repressive methods.

The Belarusian revolution that erupted in August 2020, following the rigging of the presidential election results, the arrest of candidates, and the beatings and torture of protesters, finally exposed the mechanisms of violence that have always underpinned Lukashenko's rule. *I Remember/Father's House* is significant in this context and points to the model of relations between the state and the imagined people that the authorities are still trying to follow today, while no longer hiding their repressive nature and constantly pointing to internal and external 'outsiders' who threaten 'stability' and the 'Belarusian model'. It is worth noting that the inauguration of the first unit of the Astravets nuclear power plant, the construction of which began in 2008, took place on 7 November 2020 with the participation of Lukashenko, by then already an illegitimate president. Interestingly, the event was timed to coincide with the anniversary of the 1917 October Revolution, formally demonstrating the continuity of the Belarusian authorities with the Soviet authorities.

## 7. A Thriller Set against the Backdrop of Perestroika

*Exclusion Zone* is the last Belarusian feature film shot to date that takes place in the Chernobyl zone. It was shot at Belarusfilm, co-financed by the film studio with independent producers and released in Russia and Belarus in theatres and on streaming platforms. The aim of the project was to make an entertaining genre film that would be profitable, which has been a problem and a challenge for the national film studio for many years, as many of its films are still made for educational purposes, are not popular among Belarusians and do not pay off at the box office.

The result is a thriller with elements of slasher, horror film and survival drama. It takes place in 1989, three years after the Chernobyl accident and two years before the collapse of the USSR. The main characters – former classmates, two girls and four boys – set out on a hike along the Pripiat' River, and overnight their raft floats into the Chernobyl zone (the film was not shot there). The wild, desolate forest, swamps and abandoned houses become a disturbing backdrop for the unfolding plot conflict, in which only one heroine can survive and return home. A bag full of stolen money falls into the hands of the characters, when one of the classmates, Lësha, accidentally kills a man walking in the wood. The prospect of getting rich instantly changes the characters. They are all distinguished by several traits with an attempt at social typification. Lësha is back from the war in Afghanistan – to explain his easy-going attitude towards murder and corpses, the authors add another old criminal case and poorly controlled jealousy towards one of the heroines. If his first victim is accidental, the shooting of a former classmate Grisha is done on purpose. Grisha is a conventional rock music lover, who does not want to share the money nor conceal the accidental murder. The film also mentions that one of the girls was working 'on a panel', i.e., worked as a prostitute, which explains her passion for easy money. And the fun-loving guy Monia wants the money on his own to buy a flat, a car and to get married.

Among these protagonists there is also a boy and a girl who take their share of the money with a noble purpose: Artur is the son of an academic and needs the money for a heart operation abroad for his younger brother, whereas Lida, a student who wants to help him, gives him her share. Then an unknown person comes into play, who turns out to be the partner of the accidently killed man and who avenges him by killing two more of the classmates. In the final scene, Lida has to shoot the finally enraged 'Afghan' Lësha to prevent him from killing her friend Artur. In this way, the film obviously follows a formulaic model and keeps the viewer curious as to who will kill the next victim and satisfy the viewers' expectations. It is also likely that associations with computer shooter games like *S. T. A. L. K. E. R. Shadow of Chernobyl'* (*S.T.A.L.K.E.R. Ten' Chernobylia*, 2007) are intended, as the action is also placed in the 'zone'.

However, the real historical context of the late Soviet Union, although shown in a stereotyped way, as well as symbolic motifs are also characteristic for *Exclusion Zone*. For instance, the bag of money alludes to *I Remember/Father's House*, where a bundle of dollars also played a role, but back then the positive characters managed their problems without it. In contrast, closer to the finale, the survivors Artur and Lida learn that the money is radioactive, with the dosimeter from it going off the scale. "This is death. It must be destroyed," says Artur. But he has no time to destroy it, as he is killed in an absurd way on his way out of the forest, caught in a bear trap. Lida leaves the zone in a motorboat, along with the deadly radioactive money. The epilogue shows her spreading the money among Soviet citizens, and then someone handing Artur's mother a box of dollars for the treatment of her second son abroad.

Another typical characteristic of the movie is a certain nostalgia for Soviet values und relicts, which is also obvious in the motif of illicit and contagious money, which causes lust for profit and leads only to death, evoking the myth of the special morality of Soviet men. In another episode, the three heroes wander around the abandoned houses of Pripiat', where Monia throws stones and smashes windows, as he has "always dreamed of doing that." Then the glance of the protagonists stops at a red banner with the inscription: "Everything must be beautiful in a man: both his face and his soul, his clothes and his thoughts". In reality, such a slogan never existed, because Soviet banners bore short mobilisation formulas like "Peace for the World", "Peace. Labor. May" or "Decisions of the XXV congress of the CPSU Central Committee into life!". However, this quote about the beauty of a man from Anton Chekhov's play *Uncle Vanya* (*Diadia Vania*, 1898) was not unknown in Soviet culture and, for instance, a frequent topic of school essays.

*Figure 4.6: Filmstill from the film* Exclusion Zone. *A banner that is impossible in reality*

Instead of seeing this set-piece as a historical mistake by the filmmakers, it is rather a symptom of how Soviet ideals are represented here, ideals, which the protagonists are apparently deprived of, having lost their moral compass during the perestroika period. A more realistic banner would have been inappropriate and incomprehensible to the post-Soviet public. Whereas Alexievich's generation distinguished itself in opposition to Soviet morality, as she portrayed it in her book *Secondhand Time* (*Vremia sekond khėnd*, 2013), under the onslaught of capitalist cynicism, paradoxically the next, already post-Soviet generation is open for a certain nostalgia for the Soviet 'golden age', as it is summarised in a popular internet joke: 'the younger the blogger, the better the life he had under Stalin'.

Another characteristic of contemporary Belarusian films is the popular post-Soviet myth of the 'bandit 1990s'. Although the action in *Exclusion Zone* takes place before the collapse of the USSR, the motif of easy, bloody and bandit money is also omnipresent here. This myth is also actively used today in Russian and Belarusian propaganda. For example, after the 2020 revolution, Lukashenko has repeatedly frightened Belarusians in speeches that 'cynical businessmen' (aka 'bourgeoisie') who disagree with his policies want everyone to return to the 1990s, a time when they got rich and the main population starved and suffered. According to the official authoritarian narrative, Lukashenko personally prevented the country from being 'plundered' by destroying the bandits and keeping the collective farms and state factories. Thus, an analysis of this thriller through the prism of the political context and popular post-Soviet myths reveals a rather conservative and nostalgic morality, that is rather implicitly visible on the level of the 'political unconscious' than purposefully on the level of the entertaining plot.

In summary, one can conclude, that in order to fully understand the specific adaptation of formulaic popular genre cinema within post-Soviet culture, a detailed elaboration of the real context and psychology of the characters is inevitable, paying special attention to the way nodal symbols are implemented into the film plot. Thereby, the four Belarusian genre films about the Chernobyl disaster from different historical periods analysed in this essay, show a clear development from more critical attitudes towards the Soviet legacy to a rather distorting view on the recent past. Especially today, against the background of the renaissance of authoritarian and totalitarian ideologies in Russia and Belarus, it is most relevant to analyse late Soviet and post-Soviet movies through the prism of cultural trauma, taking into consideration ideology and political context.

When discussing the forms of social adaptation to cultural trauma, Sztompka, referring to Robert K. Merton's research, distinguishes between constructive active and passive adaptations. The former forms include *innovation* (cultural production) and *rebellion* (an attempt to radically change culture). The passive forms are *ritualism*, cultivating "unestablished traditions" as a way of hiding from trauma, and *retreatism*, ignoring trauma and attempting to act as if it does not exist (2001b: 9). Regarding Belarusian cinema, the situation of the 1990s can generally be characterised as an attempt at innovative cultural production and rebellion, while the path chosen by the state and, accordingly, by Belarusfilm in the 2000s rather resembles passive forms of retreatism. The critical message of films from the perestroika period and the early 1990s consisted in exposing totalitarian tendencies in power and in Soviet people. In spite of its journalistic, partly denunciatory form, the films of this period also expose the fear of impending capitalism and diagnose a value deadlock, trying to seriously cope with the near and distant past. Belarusian films of the following periods, with the exception of some independent productions, make an artificial break with this tendency, and instead present a both tendentiously ideological picture of reality, like in *I Remember/Father's House*, and politically unconscious genre plots as in *Exclusion Zone*.

## List of Games

S. T. A. L. K. E. R. *Shadow of Chernobyl* (S.T.A.L.K.E.R. Ten' Chernobylia), produced by GSC Game World, PC/MAC, 2007.

## Filmography

*Above the Law*, dir. Andrew Davis, USA 1988.
*Assa*, dir. Sergei Solov'ëv, USSR 1987.
*Black Stork* (*Chernyi aist*), dir. Viktor Turov, Russia 1993.
*Chernobyl*, dir. Johan Renck, USA, UK 2019.
*Code of Silence*, dir. Andrew Davis, USA 1985.
*Come and See* (*Idi i smotri*), dir. Èlem Klimov, USSR 1985.
*Exclusion Zone* (*Zapretnaia zona*), dir. Mitrii Semenov-Aleinikov, Belarus 2020.
*I Remember/Father's House* (*Ia pomniu/Otchii dom*), dir. Sergei Sychev, Belarus 2005.
*My Name is Harlequin* (*Menia zovut Arlekino*), dir. Valerii Rybarev, USSR 1988.
*My Soul, Mariia* (*Dusha moia, Mariia*), dir. Viacheslav Nikiforov, Belarus 1993.
*Our Armoured Train* (*Nash bronepoezd*), dir. Mikhail Ptashhuk, USSR 1988.
*Plumbum, or The Dangerous Game* (*Pliumbum, ili Opasnaia igra*), dir. Valerii Abdrashitov, USSR 1986.
*Political Bureau Co-op or A Long Farewell* (*Kooperativ Politbiuro, ili Budet dolgim proshchanie*), dir. Mikhail Ptashuk, Belarus 1992.
*Rambo. First Blood*, dir. Ted Kotcheff, USA 1982.
*Repentance* (*Pokaianie/Monanieba*), dir. Tengiz Abuladze, Georgia 1984.
*The Atomic Zone Ranger* (*Reindzher iz atomnoi zony*), dir. Viacheslav Nikiforov, Belarus, Russia 1999.
*The Needle* (*Igla*), dir. Rashid Nugmanov [Rachid Nougmanov], USSR 1988.
*The Wolves in the Zone* (*Volki v zone*), dir. Viktor Deriugin, USSR 1990.

## List of Illustrations

Figure 4.1: Film still from the film *The Wolves in the Zone* (*Volki v zone*), dir. Viktor Deriugin, USSR 1990.
Figure 4.2: Film still from the film *Political Bureau Co-op or A Long Farewell* (*Kooperativ Politbiuro, ili Budet dolgim proshchanie*), dir. Mikhail Ptashuk, Belarus 1992.
Figure 4.3: Film still from the film *The Wolves in the Zone* (*Volki v zone*), dir. Viktor Deriugin, USSR 1990.
Figure 4.4: Film still from the film *Come and See* (*Idi i smotri*), dir. Èlem Klimov, USSR 1985.
Figure 4.5: Film still from the film *The Atomic Zone Ranger* (*Reindzher iz atomnoi zony*), dir. Viacheslav Nikiforov, Belarus, Russia 1999.
Figure 4.6: Film still from the film *Exclusion Zone* (*Zapretnaia zona*), dir. Mitrii Semenov-Aleinikov, Belarus 2020.

## References

Alexievich, Svetlana (2016): Chernobyl Prayer [1997]. Translated by Anna Gunin and Arch Tait, London: Penguin Books.

Khatkovskaia, Inessa (2010): "Iz nedolgoi istorii belorusskogo nezavicimogo kino (1989–1997)." In: Perekrestki 3/4, pp. 98–133.

Levchenko, Ian (2007): "God zakrytogo pereloma." In: Novoe literaturnoe obozrenie 83/1, pp. 699–710.

Sztompka, Piotr (2001a): "Sotsial'noe izmenenie kak travma." In: Sotsiologicheskoe issledovanie 1, pp. 6–16.

Sztompka, Piotr (2001b): "Kul'turnaia travma v postkommunisticheskom obshchestve." In: Sotsiologicheskoe issledovaniia 2, pp. 3–12.

## II. Combat Zones: War Heroes, Resistance Fighters and Joyful Partisans

Chapter 5:
# Alternative Versions of the Past and the Future
Soviet and Post-Soviet Pop Literature

*Maria Galina and Ilya Kukulin*

## 1. Introduction

Alternate history is a special kind of contemporary fiction and, more broadly, narrative art.[1] It involves depicting historical events in the 'what-if' mode: how the modern world would have changed if one or more key events had played out differently than in reality. Broadly speaking, alternate history, overturning the famous thesis "history knows no subjunctive mood", is concerned with "a comparative analysis of precisely different possible alternatives" (Bestuzhev-Lada 1997: 112–122).

Usually, alternate history works are associated with science fiction and thus with mass culture, although intellectuals also draw upon this approach: in particular, Stephen Fry (*Making History*, 1997) and Philip Roth (*The Plot against America*, 2004), describe in their novels how countries, which in 'our' reality participated in the anti-Hitler coalition, begin instead to undergo political radicalisation in the 1930s-40s, taking on an overt resemblance to fascist regimes. It would therefore be more accurate to say that alternate history is a method of narrative construction, encompassing different types of literature, from mass to experimental. Alternate history echoes in terms of method the work of contemporary historians in the relatively new genre of 'thought experiments' or counterfactuals, which have a similar meaning but are written much more analytically and addressed to an audience of professionals in the humanities.

Furthermore, it is difficult to draw a precise line between ordinary historical novels and alternate history narratives, because any work of fiction with a historical theme is always based on fiction. As the American writer, literary scholar and sociologist Karen Hellekson puts it: a "mere" historical novelist may create a fictionalised maid to a real-life Queen Mary of Scots, but a "normal" narrative about the Queen assumes that her life

---

1   This essay partly draws on material in a chapter of a collective monograph: Galina, Maria/Kukulin, Ilya (2021): 155–186. Thanks to Vera Dubina and Andrei Zavadskii for permission to use materials from the chapter.

will end at the stake. However, if the novel, for example, reports that Mary defeated Elizabeth Tudor and became ruler of England and Scotland, then we are encountering an alternate history story (2001: 33). Hellekson suggests that alternate history is based primarily on nexuses of key events. In particular, many of the mass-cultural alternate histories in English-language literature rely on two well-known and mythologised nexuses: what would have happened if Germany had won World War II and what would have happened if Southerners had won the US Civil War in the North (Thiess 2015: 8–9).

Such literary works demonstrate, in a particularly poignant way, the creation of a "usable past". The creator of this term, the American critic and literary historian Van Wyck Brooks wrote in 1918 that the contemporary author should give the past a moral meaning that edifies people of the present. Alternate histories contribute to giving such meaning (and in this, writers can differ markedly from historians who create counterfactuals) on at least three levels.

Firstly, they most often portray fulfilled anti-utopias or – less frequently – utopias (Butter 2009), making our reality appear either as the best possible option or a result of an unfortunate accident in comparison with which the imperfections of 'our' world look especially frightening and, most importantly, changeable: had things been a bit different, 'we' could have lived a much better life! A 'past-turned-utopia', as we shall see later, could be the ideal imaginary space for escape from the discomfort of modernity. In cases of anti-utopias, reality is portrayed as relatively acceptable compared to the terrible disasters that could have occurred if events had gone differently.

Second, alternate history authors often establish implicit correspondences between events that actually took place and their 'alternate' versions. For example, Pei-Chen Liao draws attention to the 'realist' aspects of Philip Roth's novel mentioned above: his description of the persecution of the Jews in his fictionalised United States in the early 1940s clearly draws on Roth's experience of childhood suffering from grassroots anti-Semitism in America as described in his memoirs (2020: 11).

Third, alternate history sharply emphasises the impact of personal action and/or chance on large-scale social and political shifts. One of its earliest examples, Lyon Sprague de Camp's novel *Lest Darkness Fall* (1939)[2], tells the story of American archaeologist Martin Padway being transported by lightning from fascist Italy in 1938 to Rome in 535 AD, under the rule of the Ostrogoths. Padway helps the Ostrogoths to defend their kingdom against the Byzantines and the Lombards, thus preventing the onset of the Dark Ages. Obviously, at the time the novel was written, it was read as an allegory calling for personal opposition to fascism.

Accordingly, the American literary scholar Catherine Gallagher writes that alternate history has political significance: "the alternate-history impulse in the Cold War Period and after" was based on "the desire to see the logic of justice triumph over the dynamics of historical determination" (2010: 17). And since contemporary Russia is currently ex-

---

[2]   Hereinafter, except where otherwise stated, the year of the first publication of the work is indicated.

periencing a veritable boom in alternate history fiction (in the broad sense)[3], to which both authors with mass appeal and 'sophisticated' writers are contributing, it seemed worthwhile to investigate the socio-historical reasons for such an upsurge more closely. In doing so, we pursue the following initial hypotheses: Alternate history in contemporary Russia is, on the one hand, a special form of reflection on historical traumas, which is akin to the corresponding literature in the West, and, on the other hand, a form of phantasmatic, imagined historical revenge for all events which the authors consider as 'defeats' and manifestations of 'injustice' in relation to Russia.[4]

## 2. Background to Post-Soviet Alternate History

The thought experiment "what would have happened if" has been posed by many, from Titus Livy (59 BC – 17 AD), who speculated what outcome the war with Alexander the Great could have had for the Roman state, claiming that Rome had every chance of winning this war, to Aleksandr Pushkin in his note on the poem *Count Nulin* (*Graf Nulin*, 1827) (Leibov 2023):[5]

> Rereading Lucretia, Shakespeare's rather weak poem, I thought: what if Lucretia had thought to slap Tarquinius in the face? Perhaps this would have cooled his enterprise and he would have been forced to retreat with shame? Lucretia would not have been slapped […] and the world and the history of the world would not have been the same. (Kibalnik 1995: 64)

However, the French writer Louis-Napoléon Geoffroy-Château (1803–1858) was the first to publish a book of alternate history in 1836, his *History of the World Monarchy: Napoleon and the Conquest of the World* (*Histoire de la monarchie universelle. Napoleon et la conquette du monde*, 1812–1832) – an account of how Napoleon Bonaparte allegedly beat Russia, then conquered all the other countries and created a world state where the arts flourished.

In the first half of the 20th century, alternate history was developed and contemplated by both scholars and fiction writers, including Soviet writers: for example, in 1928, *The Reckless Novel* (*Bestseremonnyi Roman*), co-written by Veniamin Girshgorn, Iosif Keller and Boris Lipatov, was published. Its hero called Roman (in Russian, it is both a male name given to the character and also means "a novel") goes back in time to help Napoleon win the Battle of Waterloo.

In the 1920s, alternate history narratives in both Soviet and émigré Russian literature were perceived as a 'possible' extension of real history, where the course of events could be reversed by chance, as had been shown by the events of the two Russian revolutions of 1917 and of the Civil War. In 1922, the utopian novel *Behind the Thistle* (*Za cher-*

---

[3] See in particular the *Alternate History* (*Al'ternativnaia istoriia*) website https://alternathistory.ru/ [30 September 2023], which has been described as "the largest Runet blog". Runet is a common designation of the Russian sector of the internet.
[4] On revanchist motifs in fantasy literature and alternate history in the 1990s and 2000s, cf. Vitenberg 2004; Arbitman 2009.
[5] Our dating is guided by this work.

*topolokhom*) was published in Germany by Pëtr Krasnov, the recent leader of the self-proclaimed Cossack Don state who had just fled Russia. In his novel, he described a world where the Red Army perished under its own bombs and instead of Soviet Russia a patriarchal yet technocratic state emerged, "without foreigners, without speculators, without banks and without the dictates of Western Europe" (Krasnov 1922), but with television and airships to ferry whoever is needed to anywhere in the world. This narrative could be considered the first example of 'imagined historical revenge' in the history of Russian literature, which, as we shall see later, brings it close to post-Soviet mass-cult novels. For example, the commonplace accusation by conservative émigrés that there are too many Jews among the Bolsheviks takes on an inverted form in the novel:

"Do you have any Jews?" asked Diatlov.
"How not. They live among us. Where can they go? Only they don't rule over us anymore." (Ibid.)

If we talk about the USSR again, the publication of any works in the genre of alternate history since the 1930s became impossible for a long time. The Soviet authorities positioned science fiction as utilitarian literature, designed to call up young people to work on scholarly and technical innovations. Fiction had to serve propagandistic (educational and enlightening) goals and mainly portrayed the achievements of visionary inventors and the socialist economy. Of particular note are the fictional works depicting the victories of the Soviet Union 'with little blood' in the global wars of the foreseeable future, also a kind of alternate history, designed, however, to demonstrate not so much the randomness of historical choice, as the regularities of the Marxist-Leninist conception of the course of history.

Under these conditions, any somewhat daring intellectual experiments in science fiction were considered dangerous. However, during World War II, when the USSR became an ally of the United Kingdom and the United States, some works of English-language science fiction were published in Russian. Therefore, despite the postwar censorship bans, Soviet readers and writers had some idea of what sci-fi literature could be.

After Stalin's death in 1953, ideological prejudice against the 'dangerous genre' somewhat abated, but the artistic level of works of sci-fi remained very low due to the utter destruction of the genre. Attempts to change this tendency started in the late 1950s, mainly by Ivan Efremov and the brothers Arkadii and Boris Strugatskii. It is indicative, however, that it was precisely alternate history that continued to be perceived by the censors as an ideologically dubious – and therefore undesirable – field of literature. The Strugatskii brothers and Efremov preferred to transfer their dystopian models to imaginary planets – like in *Hard to Be God* (*Trudno byt' bogom*, 1963) and *The Inhabited Island* (*Obitaemyj ostrov*, also known as *Prisoners of Power*, 1969) by the Strugatskiis, or in *The Bull's Hour* (*Chas byka*, 1968) by Efremov – or to unnamed capitalist countries – like in the Strugatskiis' *The Final Circle of Paradise* (*Khishchnye veshchi veka*, also known as *Predatory Things of the Century*, 1965). Characteristic in this sense is the Russian translation of Arnold J. Toynbee's essay *If Alexander the Great had lived on* from 1969, published in abridged form in the journal *Znanie-*

*Sila* (*Knowledge is Power*) in 1979 (No. 12).[6] In this essay, the British historian returns to the thought experiment once set up by Titus Livy and presents a reality parallel to our own, in which Alexander the Great fulfilled all his plans of conquest, conquering the Qin Empire (the forerunner of China) and creating an everlasting state: Toynbee's narrator reports that he lives in the time of Alexander XXXVI.

This journal publication resounded with readers and, perhaps, also provoked the indignation of the ideological curators so that the editorial board had to hastily organise a round table dedicated to the topic "History – inevitable and accidental" in the next issue, gathering together "real historians" (Podol'nyi et al. 1980). The general verdict of this debate, as one of the participants, Professor G. A. Fedorov-Davydov, summarised it, concluded that "accidents speed up or slow down the course of history, but do not change its direction" (ibid.: 39), criticising Toynbee as an apologist of the decisive role of the individual in history. This critique was an ideological stigma in the USSR, because the crucial role of the masses in history was one of the key tenets of historical materialism (the official ideology of the time), where the individual could not be the creator of history (Marks/Ėngel's 1966: 175–176).[7] This dogma was ineluctable, even though this emphasis on the masses came into obvious contradiction with the cult of Lenin and, at the time, of Leonid Brezhnev.[8]

However, apparently by this time the most open-minded Soviet intellectuals were already seriously interested in the possibilities of depicting alternate historical events. Four years before Toynbee's translation was published, a book by the famous popular historian Nathan Eidelman, *The Apostle Sergei: A Tale of Sergei Muravyov-Apostol* (*Apostol Sergei: Povest' o Sergee Murav'ëve-Apostole*, 1975), had been released with a chapter entitled "Imaginary 1826", which described the success of the Decembrist rebellion of 1825 in Tsarist Russia. The chapter ended with a paragraph of two phrases: "It wasn't. Could have been" (ibid.: 264).

The persistent prejudice of Soviet censorship against alternative versions of history was later triggered by the *tamizdat* (foreign) publication of Vasilii Aksenov's novel *The Island of Crimea* (*Ostrov Krym*) in 1981 by Ardis Publishing, a publisher based in Ann Arbor (Michigan). In the novel, due to a number of favourable circumstances like the absence of the Perekop Isthmus and the decisive action of Aksenov's fictional Lieutenant Bailey-Land, during the Civil War the retreating White Army had defended Crimea against the Bolsheviks. Thus, it became a developed capitalist democracy and the object of envy, lust and hatred of the impoverished 'mainland' USSR. In doing so, Aksenov adopted some of the characteristic Cold War divisions to his alternate history novel, like those between North and South Korea, the FRG and GDR, or mainland China and Taiwan, which is most similar to the fictitious 'capitalist' Crimea. By analogy with the 'other China' that

---

6   We would like to draw the reader's attention to the fact that the publisher was a candidate (Ph.D.) of physical and mathematical sciences, rather than a historian belonging to the Soviet professional corporation.
7   First published in 1895 in *Der Sozialistische Akademiker*.
8   Since in Soviet times, the composition of journal issues was approved by the editorial and censorship authorities many months before the issue was printed, the publication bore all the hallmarks of an emergency response launched from above.

was booming in Taiwan, Aksenov came up with an 'alternative Russia'. Apart from the obvious 'anti-Soviet' message (the author portrayed the USSR as a country of total scarcity and the suppression of individual freedom), here the role of the individual is highlighted as the turning point in the Crimean campaign, thus obviously challenging the official Soviet notions of history (Aksenov 1983 [1981]). It sharply contrasts, for instance, with Sever Gansovskii's thought experiment *The Demon of History* (*Demon istorii*, 1968). In this story the protagonist, with the help of some mystical force, visits pre-World War I Austria-Hungary, eliminates the dictator who unleashed World War II, and in so doing brings Hitler to power. The message of this story is unambivalent: the course of history cannot be changed, one personality can be easily replaced by another.[9]

In this context, it is understandable that not only the outrageous *Island of Crimea* could not be published in the USSR until 1990 (in *Iunost/Youth*' 1–5), but also the classic examples of alternate history like Philip K. Dick's *Man in the High Castle* (1962). In this novel, a successful assassination attempts on Roosevelt changes history and leads to the Axis countries being victorious in World War II, an alternative that was categorically unacceptable to Soviet ideology, centred as it was on the irrevocability of the victory of the USSR.[10] Therefore, Dick's novel was only published in Russian translation in 1992 – that is, after the collapse of the USSR.

However, Ray Bradbury's famous story *A Sound of Thunder* (1961), in which history was radically changed by a minor intervention in the past, was promptly translated at the end of the Thaw, in 1963. This was possible since Bradbury did not deal with the events of Soviet or Russian history or with events that were somehow sensitive for Soviet propaganda.

## 3. Trauma and Resentment as a Driving Force of the Post-Soviet Russian Historical Novel

Although the domestic prehistory of post-Soviet alternate history, as we have seen, was sparse, in the post-Soviet space we are gradually beginning to observe its blossoming, unrestricted by censorship and – at first glance – ideological frameworks. This surge has several reasons.

The boom in the 'mass production' of alternate history novels in the former Soviet Union (but especially in Russia) in the 1990s was, of course, partly a 'response' to an unspoken ban on the genre in the USSR, but there were other reasons too. As early as 2002, Boris Vitenberg referred to alternate history in Russian as "a special genre, represented by dozens of names; the number of works of this kind is already in the hundreds." Among the reasons for this demand for the genre, the critic mentions "a natural feeling of dissatisfaction and disappointment caused by the brutal, sometimes simply monstrous and shocking realities of Russian history of the past century, which have become apparent to

---

9 Interestingly, a similar thought can be deduced from Stephen Fry's novel *Making History* (1996).
10 The USSR differed from other socialist countries in this radical extent of censorship: in Poland, for example, thanks to the efforts of Stanisław Lem, a translation of *The Man in the High Castle* was published.

the mass reader." The writings of contemporary Russian "alternative authors," Vitenberg writes, "are successful because they give rise to the pleasant and relaxing illusion that these sad events of the past could have been prevented in some way (ibid.: 315–327)."

The first text in the post-Soviet space that was broadly discussed and reviewed was a short novel by the St. Petersburg (Leningrad) writer Viacheslav Rybakov *The Gravity Plane Tsesarevich* (*Gravilët Tsesarevich*, 1993), which won several genre awards (including a personal award from the famous fantasy writer Boris Strugatskii, the *Bronze Snail*).[11] An anonymous synopsis of the novel, written in 2009 on a fanzine website summarises the novel's main message best and its depiction of a flourishing monarchical Russia in a thriving world:

[…] A world without World Wars I and II, which took the lives of millions of people.

A world without a Bolshevik coup in the early twentieth century. A world without communism. On this Earth, the Russian Empire is leading all countries towards a bright future through modern technology and true ideas of humanism. (Ruddy 2009)

This repetition of "without" in the description of the Russia of the future recalls the previously mentioned émigré novel by Petr Krasnov from 1922: "Russia without foreigners, without speculators, without banks, without the dictates of Western Europe." It depicts a world of high technology without great power rivalry, an arms race and everything we consider frightening but almost inevitable concomitants of modernity and progress.

Rybakov's main protagonist, the State Security Colonel Prince Aleksandr Trubetskoi, investigates the crash of an aircraft, a "*gravilët*" (i.e., with an anti-gravitation engine), which killed a crown prince of the Russian Empire. Trubetskoi discovers that the culprit of the *gravilët* accident was a communist named Kislenko, who staged an act of sabotage and acted in an apparent state of lunacy. Soon, several other distraught communists are caught by Trubetskoi's agents. However, in the world Rybakov describes, communists do not follow terrorist methods – communism is portrayed not as an ideology but a religion, peaceful and utopian, and the "patriarch of communism" is given physical features that resemble Mikhail Gorbachev. Therefore, the actions of Kislenko and other terrorists are clearly not motivated by communist ideology. Looking for the reasons for their lunacy, Trubetskoi arrives at the villa of a certain Albrecht Haushoffer – despite spelling the surname differently, apparently this character's name should refer to the son of the founder of geopolitics, Karl Haushofer. The real Albrecht Haushofer took part in the 20 August 1944 plot, the failed assassination attempt against Hitler, and was killed by the Nazis in Moabit Prison in April 1945 (in Rybakov's novel, Haushoffer's doppelganger was killed there in 1944). In the basement of an elderly aristocrat, Trubetskoi finds a strange construction:

---

11   Boris Strugatskii was one of the two Strugatskii brothers – the novels they co-wrote were arguably the most popular and well-known works of Soviet fiction. Arkadii Strugatskii died in 1991, Boris Strugatskii, who had since written two novels alone and a memoir about their common literary career, died in 2012.

> Almost the entire space of the room was occupied by a cast-iron monster standing in the middle – an incongruously and awkwardly huge one, [...] stitched with vertical lines of rivets, surrounded by a dishevelled tangle of thick and thin, straight and crooked pipes.
>
> It looked more like an enormous steam engine than anything else. It reeked a mile away of the wonders of Jules-Verne-like science. (Rybakov 1997 [1993]: 185)

It soon turns out that hidden inside this apparatus is a reduced, almost microscopic copy of the Earth, inhabited by microscopic human beings. These micro-humans are the guinea pigs in a gruesome experiment launched in the 19th century by Russian revolutionary-maximalist Pëtr Stupak and German scientist Otto Raschke. They created their "parallel world" in order to influence its inhabitants with chemicals and make them willing to give up any human attachments and go to their deaths for the sake of an idea. The beings created in this way inside the "cast-iron monster" unleashed the *real* history of the 20th century, with Lenin, Hitler and the concentration camps. As a result of the continued functioning of this "steam engine," negative psychic energy began to be transferred to the harmonious world of *"gravilëts,"* causing random victims to become existentially identified with the most militant inhabitants of "micro-Earth" and to be prepared to carry out unmotivated violent acts. In the novel's finale, Trubetskoi is about to address the UN Security Council with the question of what to do with this horrible device that is inhabited, however, by reasonable and morally responsible beings: technically it could simply be destroyed, but such a solution seems unacceptable to him.

The novel's message can be defined as both psychotherapeutic and escapist. Its main idea can be retold as follows: we live inside a global error, while reality is in fact incomparably more beautiful, albeit unattainable. With such an attitude to history, the authors of alternate history return time and again (a characteristic symptom of 'acting out' historical trauma) to the possibility of building a utopian Russia. They use a variety of events from the early 20th century as 'bifurcation points.'

It is indicative that almost all the changes introduced by the authors of contemporary Russian alternative history prose lead to a radical restructuring of the entire historical picture of the 20th century. Thus, in Iuri Arabov's novel *Collision with a Butterfly (Stolknovenie s babochkoi*, 2014)[12] Emperor Nicholas II did not abdicate in March 1917 and remained alive.[13] In the subsequent events of 1917–1918, history takes a completely different path: first the emperor arranges a secret meeting with Kaiser Wilhelm II in Finland and persuades him to agree to an armistice, and then forms an alliance with the Bolsheviks, as a result of which Lenin becomes head of government. Consequently, at the Ipatiev house it is not the royal family that is shot, but members of the anti-Lenin conspiracy, including Sverdlov and Stalin. Trotsky leaves to make a revolution in the United States, while Lenin, though wounded at the Michelson factory, recovers surprisingly quickly and, with

---

12   First published in *Oktiabr'* 2014: 1–2.
13   Arabov (who died in 2023) was better known not as a novelist, but as a frequent scriptwriter for the famous film director Aleksander Sokurov.

the support of the emperor, hopes "to restore the capitalist market in the country, connecting it with the Soviets" (Arabov 2014: 307) – as betting on the proletariat did not pay off.

At the same time, the Tsar's daughters grow up well. "Tatiana, who is enrolled on a sewing course, has an affair with a schoolteacher who teaches the history of the French Revolution" (ibid.: 309), while his other daughters also have a career. Olga works in the government office, Anastasia married a diplomat and went to England, only the beautiful Maria cannot find a path for herself and smokes "Herzegovina Flor" (ibid.: 310; in the USSR the cigarettes "Herzegovina Flor" were known as Stalin's favourite tobacco products). Moreover, the kolkhozes were never established and Lenin, transformed from a fervent revolutionary into a potential corruptor, "started taking bribes, and that has been the best news of recent months" (ibid.: 323). That is to say, all is not well, of course, but the alternative reality is still better than it could have been:

> The revolutionary impulse, like a volcano, went all to universal education and the GOELRO plan. The latter lit the 'Ilyich bulb' in the backwoods villages, while universal education taught the lazy but savvy people to read and write. Free medicine, run entirely by the state, put an end to malaria and typhus. Education in schools taught reading Tolstoy, Chekhov and Marx. What would emerge from this symbiosis, the Tsar did not know, and was a little worried about the future – was the pot boiling too quickly? The black dishes of loudspeakers hung in the village houses broadcasting news, folk and classical music. From the heights of telegraph poles, too, the radio shrieked. One peasant wrote to him in a letter: 'Put up the speaker. I want to speak into it myself'. (Ibid.: 324)[14]

At one moment, while the bed-keeper was preparing his bed for the night, Tsar Nikolai glanced through an economic report from the Office of the Council of People's Commissars, stating that 1926 industry had reached its pre-war level, i.e., had increased more than fivefold compared with 1921.

Nevertheless, Nikolai suddenly has an unpleasant dream that he signs a renunciation and he envisions everything that followed also in 'real history.' This 'return to reality' is a characteristic narrative move of alternate history. In Russian literature, it is often used as in *Gravilët Tsesarevitch* or in the finale of the novel *The Seventh Part of Darkness* (*Sed'maia chast' t'my*, 1997)[15] by Vasilii Shchepetnev, which will be discussed below.

As we can see from Arabov's novel, the theme of 'Russia without wars and revolutions' is addressed not so much by mass literature as by what might be called 'highbrow' fiction, perhaps because these 'peaceful' fictions do not offer any special adventures or action scenes, and mass literature is not too interested in 'adventures of the spirit'.

---

14   A twisted quote from Andrei Platonov's novel *Kotlovan* [*The Foundation Pit*], 1930: "Safronov listened with a sense of triumph, regretting only that he could not talk back into the speaker, to make known his readiness for all activity, for clipping horses, and his general happiness." (Platonov 1975 [1930], 56) This quote further emphasises that the 'alternative Russia' under monarchist rule has all the good that came – or seemed to come – in Soviet Russia thanks to the revolution.

15   First published in *Ural'skii sledopyt* 1998 8–19.

At the same time as *The Collision with a Butterfly*, the story *The Architect and the Monk* (*Arkhitektor i monakh*, 2013)[16] by the famous writer and journalist Denis Dragunskii was published. Here, in 1913 in Vienna's Café Versailles the young men Adolf Hitler and Iosif Stalin meet, talk, go to meetings in socialist circles along with Trotsky, they take turns in the bath, feel something like attraction for each other but it is not for certain, and they argue about a child's teardrop (in fact, Stalin did spend a short time in Vienna in 1913, where he met Trotsky). Trotsky is killed at Lenin's instigation with a meat cleaver, Lenin is drowned in a pond in revenge, Stalin is also hunted, but he escapes and finds refuge in God as a result of the shock. In 1922, terrorists attempt to assassinate not Lenin but the head of the country, Miliukov, who is shielded by Vladimir Nabokov Senior (as was the case in reality – but in Berlin, not Moscow), however, unlike in 'our' world, he survives and becomes Miliukov's successor. In 1937, Hitler is imprisoned for anti-state agitation, in 1938 he is released, meets Eva Braun and invents the "Viennese country style" (Dragunskii 2013: 271). Overall, Dragunskii's 20th century also looks cruel, but still less monstrous than in 'our' reality:

> And Metropolitan Joseph recalled his strange life in his dying hours. [...] The underground, emigration, the monastery. What a terrible century, what enormous revolutions and wars! [...] Why did they kill the Tsar and his family? Why were so many people put in jail and killed by Thälmann [the leader of the German communists Ernst Thälmann who in Dragusnkii's world came to power in Germany – M.G., I.K.]? And the Russian-German war! Only soldiers killed eight million people, and civilians – it is scary to imagine. And the fate of the Jews? Three million forcibly assimilated, one and a half million resettled, and another one hundred and fifty-six thousand eight hundred and six killed in the massacre of the forty-fourth year [...] Horrible, bloody, shameless, cynical and evil century. (Ibid.: 348–349)

Compared to the real losses of the 20th century, the losses of the alternative are more 'modest', but to the protagonist (the author's bitter irony) they rightly seem monstrous – there is nothing to compare them to.

In Aleksandr Sobolev's novel *Gryphons Guarding the Lyre* (*Grifony okhraniaiut liru*, 2020), which is more artistically complex and refined than Arabov and Dragunskii's novels, the action "takes place in Russia of the 1950s, but specifically in a Russia, where the Whites won, the Bolsheviks were expelled to Latvia and are stirring something up from there, where there was neither terror nor World War II and metro stations nestled among the unreconstructed Moscow squares" (Birger 2021). In general, it can be said that the alternative history of 'Russia without revolutions' in the post-Soviet space turns from a *literature of challenge* and *foresight* into a requiem for the unfulfilled golden 20th century, into the *literature of nostalgia*.

There are incomparably fewer sceptical alternative versions, like Vasilii Shchepetnev's story *The Seventh Part of Darkness*, 1997) about the *non-murder* of Stolypin in 1911, which leads to the preservation of the monarchy in Russia until at least 1933. But the result is not very comforting, as a newspaper review of the story summarised it:

---

16  First published in *Znamia* 2013 1.

There was no First World War, the country did not become Bolshevik. Emperor Alexei was not very confident but ruling, the biologist Vabilov [an allusion to the great Soviet botanist and geneticist Nikolai Vavilov who died of hunger in a Stalinist prison. – M.G., I.K.] is awarded the Nobel Prize for a universal vaccine, the husband of Nadezhda Konstantinovna [Krupskaia; allusion to Lenin. – M.G, I.K.] is floundering in the Comintern's Radio Liberty in Berlin under Lev Trotsky, Kaiser Wilhelm, who emigrated to Russia, is feeding at the Russian Tsar's court, and in America, the genius Einstein is working with his assistant Semen Blium to create a 'machine for travel through all dimensions', a zero-transportation machine [...]. Nevertheless, the alternative world is going down the drain. Russia, on the brink of a coup, is at war with Kuomintang China and the Comintern entrenched in Germany at the same time. The Russian General Staff, in alliance with Japan, plans to launch military operations against the United States, for which Russian scientists have already developed an 'atomic' (nuclear) bomb. There are plans for a global use of lethal bacteriological weapons created by the same Vabilov. All the main characters of the story are about to die [...]. Blium tries to reverse the course of events by sending 5.2 grams of lead from 1933 to 1911. Stolypin will be assassinated. World history will become what we know from the textbooks. (Larionov 2003)

It is only logical that in addition to 'revisiting the results of the revolution', the authors of alternate history in Russia also address another previously taboo subject: the victory of the Axis countries in World War II (let us call this subgenre alternative Reich studies). However, we do not always end up with the seemingly expected anti-utopia. Tellingly, even such a seemingly radical version ultimately leads in many narratives to a kind of 'humanisation' of the Third Reich.

It is common to trace the beginnings of alternative Reich studies in Russia to Andrei Lazarchuk's novel *The Other Sky* (*Inoe nebo*, 1993), subsequently revised into the novel *All Those Who Can Hold Arms* (*Vse, sposobnye derzhat' oruzhie*, 1997). The bifurcation point here is the successful German campaign of 1941 and Hitler's death in a plane crash in 1942. As a result, Göring takes over power, whose policy towards the conquered territories is much more lenient. By 1991, the world, according to Lazarchuk, is divided between the US and Britain, which is under their protectorate, Japan, which has annexed mainland China, independent Siberia and the Reich, which, as a state formation, is held until 1991 and falls apart as a result of a putsch (an obvious reference to the August Coup in the USSR). Already in Lazarchuk's works, it is depicted how the decrepit Reich gradually loses its aggressiveness.

A few years later, Sergei Abramov's even more radical novel *The Silent Angel Flew Over* (*Tikhii angel proletel*, 1994) appears. Here the USSR surrendered in 1942, but after Hitler's death from a heart attack in 1952, the country regains full independence:

Over the last twenty years, perhaps, Moscow has grown rapidly upwards; glass buildings, fragile to the eye, forty or more storeys high, impudently encircled the Boulevard Ring, with their golden mirror windows they looked over Chistoprudnyi Boulevard, Rozhdesvenskii Boulevard, Pokrovskii, Strastnoi, Tverskoi and other boulevards, but they did not enter the Ring with fear, the invasion had not yet taken place, the municipality firmly took the architectural virginity of the old center and did not sell any land there. [...] But a good deal of municipal money has been put to good use in the restoration of, for example, ancient walls, or on durable asphalt coverings of Moscow streets or on bright electric garlands decorating the eternal Moscow poplars on the same boulevards. So that, then, it was beautiful for all and convenient to live and rejoice... (Abramov 2015)

In other words, the National Socialist regime becomes first and foremost the guarantor of Russia's 'organic' development. The nostalgic message here is undeniable and may well compare with the alternate history versions that erase the revolution of 1917.

As a last example of this strand of literature, one could name the novel *The Sinologist* (*Kitaist*, 2016) by Russian Booker Prize winner Elena Chizhova. The same geopolitical outcome is modelled here with a protagonist, sent in 1983 from the Trans-Ural USSR to the territory invaded by the Reich, now called Russia, who is surprised to notice similarities, at least in the state rhetoric and symbolic language of both countries. In the finale, however, this hero stages a *coup d'état*, uniting the USSR and Nazi Russia into a non-contradictory totalitarian state.

In almost all the works mentioned, the victorious Third Reich is gradually transformed into a less bloodthirsty state. Probably, as observers point out, the belief that any repressive regime tends to soften in historical perspective, especially if it is surrounded by more liberal regimes with which it is forced to interact, is at work. Boris Vitenberg, for instance, directly links the humanisation of Hitler's regime in Lazarchuk's *The Other Sky* to the limited de-Stalinisation that took place in the USSR in the second half of the 1950s and the 1960s. But then he adds an important reservation: "It is indicative, however, that Philip K. Dick […], unlike the later Russian 'alternative', considered – most likely for moral reasons – a serious liberalisation of the Nazi regime, even decades later, almost impossible." (Vitenberg 2004).

However, Russian alternate history prose does not limit itself to the revision of the results of the 20th century, but the whole history of the Russian state is revisited in all kinds of utopia (or perhaps of retrotopia, to use Zygmunt Bauman's neologism). Rybakov, for instance, in co-authorship with the orientalist Igor Alimov under the pseudonym of Holm van Zaichik (in Russian, "zaichik" means "a little hare", and the whole penname imitates the name of the Dutch sinologist and writer Robert van Gulick, the author of detective novels about Chinese Judge Di) have presented the reader perhaps the most ambitious project of the 2000s in the alternate history genre, the seven-volume cycle *Symphony of Eurasia* (*Evraziiskaia simfoniia*) or *There are no Bad People* (*Plokhikh liudei net*, published by Azbuka, 2000–2005). Here the fork that directed the history of Russia in another – incomparably more favourable – way is based on the assumption that the son of the Golden Horde's Batu Khan, Sartaq Khan (died 1256), the sworn brother of duke Aleksandr Nevskii (1221–1263), was not poisoned by his own uncle Berke, but survived to old age, and as a result the Golden Horde (*Zolotaia Orda*) and Russia (*Rus'*) united into a single state Ordus' (van Zaichik 2000–2005).[17] A little later, China and vast territories in the Near and Middle East joined Ordus'. As a result, a great power with three capitals

---

17   However, modern historians of Medieval Eastern Slavs consider the 'twinning' of Aleksandr Nevskii and Sartaq a fiction put forward by Lev Gumilëv, the author of disputable works on historical themes.

appeared – Khanbalyk (Peking) in the east, Karakorum in the centre, and Aleksandria Nevskaia (St. Petersburg) in the north-west. It is a technically and socially super developed country, which considers the people of the West to be 'barbarians' but, in spite of its multi-ethnicity and tolerance, still bears signs of an archaic society. For example, public corporal punishment and polygamy are practiced here, although, according to the authors, the latter is humanised too.

Each novel in the cycle has a detective story, but as a whole the cycle is frankly presented as a postmodernist literary play, starting from the author's pseudonym to the ironic cultural references, such as the reference to a popular pop song "Unbreakable union of cultural uluses is united forever by Alexander and Sartaq"; these lines are a slightly modified opening of the Soviet Union's anthem (text by Sergei Mikhalkov and Ėl'-Registan). However, in spite of all these playful allusions, the cycle – quite in accordance with the title – can be considered a manifesto of new Eurasianism[18]: it describes a superpower based on the union of the peoples of Russia and Asia and at the same time – very importantly – directed against Western Europe and the ideas of liberalism and democracy associated with it. Regional rulers in Ordus' are not elected, but appointed by the capital's authorities, so residents of the relevant region can only ask the country's top leadership for one or another official to be placed above them – and they are all together called, respectively, not the electorate, but the "demanderate" – from the French verb *demander*, to ask. The state has a special kind of censorship which checks all foreign inventions for their usefulness to the state of Ordus'.

Boris Vitenberg (2004) in his article gives numerous examples of van Zaichik's anti-Western orientation: for example, the Balts deemed "practically barbarians", for they "drink strong alcoholic beverages in the middle of the day", and in general are "thieving people". As a consequence of the "barbarianism" of the Europeans, "the Atlantic world is increasingly becoming [...] a technological appendage of Ordus'", which, of course, is a long-standing dream of Russian nationalist technocrats.

The second novel in van Zaichik's cycle, *The Case of the Independent Dervishes* (*Delo nezalezhnykh dervishei*, 2004), combines satire of both supporters of Ukrainian independence and supporters of Chechen independence, for all the disparate nature of these movements and their consequences. The city where the action takes place is called Aslaniv: here the root of the Ukrainian name of Lviv, which in Slavic means "lion", is replaced by the Turkic translation of the same word – "a(r)slan". The Russian and Western human rights activists acting in Chechnya are portrayed in the novel in the comically grotesque image of a Western guest, Valeriia Kova-Levi (a portmanteau made up of the names of Russian journalist and political speaker Valeriia Novodvorskaia, human rights activist Sergei Kovalëv and French philosopher and social activist Bernard-Henri Lévy), who does not understand anything about Ordus' realities. All the opponents of empire in the novel appear to be criminal and dangerous and acting only for the benefit of their own selfishness.

The release of the novels in the Ordus' cycle was accompanied by a hectic publicity campaign and numerous reviews and public reactions. Irina Rodnianskaia (2002) published a review of the novel entitled "Trappers of Advanced People" ("Lovtsy prodvinutykh

---

18  On Eurasianism cf. Bassin, Glebov, Laruelle 2015.

chelovekov"). She characterises what is happening in Rybakov's and Alimov's novel cycle as "a connection of phobias: *anti-Americanism, Ukrainophobia, fear of radical Islam*; [...] *anti-Catholicism, eradication of words of foreign origin*", and comments: "not only Latinisms, Gallicisms and Anglicisms are eliminated [in the language of Ordus'], but also everything that links the Russian lexicon with Hellas – the common European cultural cradle [...]." The "phobias" mentioned by Rodnianskaia became dominant, "mainstream" in Russia in the second half of the 2000s and especially after 2014, when Ukrainophobia became part of Russian state policy and rapprochement with China became much more pronounced. In this sense, Holm van Zaichik's novels, whether inspired by political elites or written simply based on a spontaneous sense of conjuncture, anticipated earlier than many others some important political trends that emerged in the early 2000s. In contrast to Soviet times, a literary work of alternate history thus coincides with the state-backed political attitudes instead of contradicting them. But there is also another dimension that probably also contributed to the success of the novel, as Boris Vitenberg noted:

> The reason for the success of van Zaichik's alternative history [...] lies on the surface. It is, of course, the 'psychotrauma' of the collapse of the USSR. [...] This thoroughness, unhurriedness, paternal concern for citizens is well remembered from Soviet times. And many of its real characteristics as well. (Vitenberg 2004)

## 4. Our Women and Men Back in the Past

A very peculiar version of post-Soviet alternate history prose is the so-called *popadantsy* literature – a highly widespread phenomenon in Russian mass culture. The word *popadantsy* is derived from the verb *popadat'* (to find oneself somewhere), meaning someone accidently ending up elsewhere in time or space. By and large, there are several thousand novels on the theme of "our man in the past" in the post-Soviet space (Galina 2017). The concept of *popadantsy* is based on the fact that the protagonist in flesh, or by possessing the body of a historical character, gets to a key moment of history and changes the course of events, moving it in a more favourable direction for Russia's prosperity. Statistical calculations made by one of us (Maria Galina) show that the most frequently used periods in which the action of such novels takes place are the rule of Ivan the Terrible, the Time of Troubles, the Crimean and Japanese wars and – to a lesser extent – the October Revolution and the Civil War. We can assume that these periods are so attractive because they are perceived as the most traumatic for Russia's national self-perception – not per se, but thanks to the popular narratives created around them, and partly due to the underlying contradictions in these narratives: the October Revolution is supposedly benign because it created a Soviet state, but dangerous because it meant the destruction of the Russian empire.

However, two trends have been prevalent here in the last decades. One of them is the restoration of the USSR through the incarnation of the protagonist as a contemporary of the 1960s and 1970s. Here we should mention the novel by Sergei Arsen'ev *A Student, a Komsomol Girl, an Athlete* (*Studentka, komsomolka, sportsmenka*, 2012), with the revealing subtitle "Moscow, 1983. Bifurcation" and an equally revealing publisher's synopsis:

He has lived his life in Russia, which has fallen apart. He has no family or loved ones left. His son died fighting NATO peacekeepers in the streets of Moscow. His granddaughter was killed by thugs who went rogue. His present is poverty and death in the street from a heart attack. But as it turns out, he also has a future. And in that future he is given the opportunity to test whether one man can turn the machine of history around. Not just turn it, but do it without any superweapons or super-knowledge, by the power of his mind and a young girl's body. (Arsen'ev 2012)

Here, as we can see, the vector of resentment is directed not only at the "collapse of the empire", but also at imagined aggression by "NATO scumbags" (ibid.). Mikhail Koroliuk's trilogy on *Quintus Licinius* (*Kvint Litsinii*, 2014, 2016, 2018) with the subtitle "To Save the USSR" or Dmitrii Lazarev's novel cycle *It's Not Too Late* (*Eshche ne pozdno*, 2012–2015) as well as dozens of other novels and series follow the same direction (Viazovskii 2021). Almost all of them aim to save the USSR in one way or another, often by eliminating political reformers (Khrushchev, Gorbachev etc.).

However, the most popular of all historical periods within the *popadantsy* literature is without doubt World War II, of which there are over a thousand texts. These narratives can be grouped into themes, with its time-travelling protagonists being able to be divided into the categories of the intelligence officer, the tank driver, the counterintelligence man and so on. A separate topic are time-travellers visiting Hitler, like the radical nationalist novel duology by German Romanov *Comrade Führer. The Triumph of the Blitzkrieg* (*Tovarishch Fiurer. Triumf blitskriga*, 2012) and *Comrade Führer. Hang Churchill* (*Tovarishch Fiurer. Povesit' Cherchillia*, 2013), published with the following editorial synopsis:

A new fantasy thriller [...], breaking all limits of 'Political Correctness'! Our man at the head of the Third Reich! A Russian hitman in the body of Adolf Hitler! Will he be able to defeat England, carrying out Operation 'Sea Lion' – the invasion of the British Isles? Will he dare to lead a military coup to remove the Nazi Party from power and destroy the SS? Will 'Comrade Führer' be able to prevent a clash with Stalin by preventing Germany's suicidal war against the USSR? (Ibid.)

This is certainly an extreme example of rewriting the Soviet past, although it is not the only one. On the whole, however, the impression is that the majority of works in this pool are aimed at shortening the duration of the war and reorienting (in the most radical cases) the vector of resentment, but not at "abolishing" this historical cataclysm, despite its traumatic nature (Galina 2021). Because, according to sociologists, World War II and its victory – at least in mass consciousness – is the only undisputed "assemblage point" of the nation, a sacred and irrevocable event (Gudkov 2004: 20–58). Today this affective relationship to the past enters a new stage, as for the current Russian authorities the cult of victory in World War II has become a de facto civil religion, protected by a number of legislative acts. Alternate history can only adapt to this trend.[19]

---

19    One of the most active advocates of such a civil religion is Sergei Cherniakhovskii, professor of political science at Moscow State University and one of the ideologists of the Communist Party of the Russian Federation, who was already calling for it as far back as the mid-2000s. Of his numerous publications on the subject, see, for example: Cherniakhovskii 2005.

## 5. Conclusion

After the collapse of the USSR and the abolition of censorship, most novels in the alternate history genre manifested the idea of a 'lost paradise' or missed opportunities requiring 'correction'. Since the 1990s, a huge body of trash literature has been published in Russia dealing with the intervention of 'our men' (or women) in the past. Attempts to 'correct' the past, in particular to prevent the collapse of the USSR and, consequently, to change the present, have an openly neurotic and revanchist character. As a result, there is a nostalgic trend in both popular literature and more complex forms of fiction; however, popular literature adds a powerful vector of resentment and imagined revenge against Russia's 'enemies'.

This transformation of the alternate history genre into a 'weapon of imaginary revenge' and, ultimately, into a tool for anti-Western and anti-liberal propaganda has institutional backing, especially from big publishing houses aimed at the wider reading public. Unlike the USSR, where almost every version of alternate history contradicted the officially accepted interpretation of Marxist ideology, in contemporary Russia there is little confusion about the idea that history is infinitely malleable and changeable. The vector of resentment that can be traced in the vast body of popular literature in the 2010s and 2020s is very close to the narratives of the pro-state media. However, reviews of these novels on reader forums are markedly polarised, including in their assessments of the authors' political stance. Among the reviews there are quite favourable ones, alongside markedly critical ones, which is perhaps indicative of the fragmentation of the reading community.

In sum, we can say that post-Soviet Russophone alternate history narratives serve different functions, from experimenting with previously taboo topics to replaying traumatic moments of national history and imagining moments of 'historical revenge'. Recent trends put forward 'the logic of justice' and the nostalgic vector, dreaming of a restoration of the USSR and 'how it should have been in *reality*', including the infamous *popodantsy* literature about World War II.

## Postscript

This chapter was written prior to Russia's full-scale invasion of Ukraine. This invasion was accompanied by a major rebuilding of the Russian political regime, making it not only more aggressive toward other countries, but also more repressive toward many minorities within Russia – such as LGBTQ+ and transgender people, or Jehovah's Witnesses. The public support that the regime enjoyed in Russia during the first years of the full-scale invasion was largely based on the fact that state propaganda capitalised on – and continues to capitalise on – the emotions of post-Soviet ressentiment. Post-Soviet alternate history – as is now clear – was important because it expressed the emotions of the ressentiment in its purest form, except in rare instances of criticizing or analyzing them – in the novels of Elena Chizhova, Vladimir Sorokin, and Roman Arbitman – and, partially, Aleksandr Sobolev.

The term "ressentiment" as a sensible characteristic of the Russia's post-Soviet society was coined by the sociologists of Yuri Levada's circle. Following the annexation of Crimea and invasion in Eastern Ukraine in 2014, it determined the whole framework of their analysis of contemporary Russian society (Dubin 2014). In 2014, Lev Gudkov suggested that the ressentiment he described was the result of the development and delayed "aftereffect" of psychological processes that spread in Russian society in the early 1990s: "The collapse of the Soviet order caused extensive anomic processes and a prolonged state of mass disorientation, frustration and erosion of collective identity" (Gudkov 2022: 53–54).

While writing on the first stage of invasion of Ukraine in 2014, Gudkov states: "The traumatic consequences of the loss [...] have manifested themselves a generation later in the current explosion of patriotism, which makes sociologists think about the 'long-term' of social change" (ibid.: 127).

The transformation that Gudkov is talking about is worth considering from the methodological perspective of the history of emotions. One of the leading researchers in this field, William Reddy, introduces the concept of *emotive*, which is a description of emotion that simultaneously constructs emotion as a specifically cultural reaction in the consciousness of both the author of a statement (or a text) and his or her addressees (Reddy 2004: 96–111). Research in psychology and sociology shows that complex emotions are much more culturally constructed and much more the result of the subject's personal choices than was assumed previously (Scott 2015). Reddy reveals how a society's distinctive *emotional regime* is constructed, that is, a set of recognised, socially accepted emotional reactions tied to particular situations and communities and "guided" by emotives. The most important role in the production of emotives, as Reddy shows, is played by literature. Pop-cultural Russophone novels in the field of alternative history – not all, but many – can be understood today as *reservoirs of ressentiment emotives*.

The sociological significance of sci-fi for understanding ressentiment in post-Soviet Russia can be indirectly confirmed by the fact that back in 2014, some very popular authors of Russian sci-fi – for example, Sergei Lukyanenko or Vadim Panov – openly supported the war against Ukraine. Moreover, the popular and critically acclaimed science fiction writer Fyodor Berezin might be considered one of the scriptwriters of the early stage of this war – in his dilogy of novels *War 2010: Ukrainian Front* (*Voina 2010. Ukrainskii Front*, 2009) and *War 2011: Against NATO* (*Voina 2011. Protiv NATO*, 2010). These novels depict the takeover of Ukraine by Western countries and the struggle of Russian partisans behind the frontline between NATO and Russia. In 2014, Berezin became one of the leaders of the separatist movement in Donetsk (eastern Ukraine), and for several months was deputy to Igor Strelkov (Girkin) – the 'defense minister' of the self-proclaimed Donetsk People's Republic. In 2022, Igor Girkin was found guilty by a court in the Netherlands for destruction of the Malaysia Airlines' Boeing 777 crash: he ordered the plane to be shot down with a missile, believing it to be a Ukrainian military aircraft.

Berezin's role as a "scriptwriter of war" was first described by writer and critic Dmitry Bykov (2014), and soon later by journalists Kathy Young (2014) and Pëtr Silaev (2014). In 2016, *The New Yorker* published an interview with Berezin in which he referred to himself as a "Russian Tom Clancy," (Hitt 2016)[20] but articulated an obvious state of traumatic ressentiment:

> [The Soviet Union] was a special civilization, and now I mourn for it. Russia today is a capitalist country like the United States—not like the Soviet Union, which represented a new type of civilization in which you can live without undermining or exploiting other people. One day I hope it will be reborn. Maybe in some other country. (Ibid.)

One might see here an internal tension characteristic for the post-Soviet Russia's mass culture in general (L'vovskii 2011). Berezin regrets the collapse of the Soviet Union, but at the same time he tries to follow the style of American thriller novels, more precisely, the "technothrillers" of Tom Clancy, whose translations could not be published in the USSR because the writer publicly expressed his dislike for the Soviet leadership (Arbitman 1996).

By studying the evolution of post-Soviet novels in the realm of alternate history, one can reconstruct it as a transformation of ressentiment into the mode of imaginary revenge against the collective West. This visionary revenge was accompanied and fueled by Russia's real wars in Chechnya (1994–1996 and 1999–2009), Georgia (2008), Ukraine (since 2014) and Syria (since 2015).

*June 2024*

## References

Abramov, Sergei (2015): "Tikhii angel proletel." [1994] In: Ibid.: Trebuetsia chudo (Fantasticheskaia dinastiia Abramovykh, 7), Moskva: Sam sebe izd. https://publ.lib.ru/ARCHIVES/A/ABRAMOV_Aleksandr,_ABRAMOV_Sergey/Fantasticheskaya_dinastiya_Abramovyh._T.07.(2015).[rtf-ocr].zip [30 September 2023].
Aksenov, Vasilii (1983): The Island of Crimea [1981], New York: Random House.
Arabov, Iurii (2014): Stolknovenie c babochkoi, Moskva: AST.
Arbitman, Roman (1996): "Iz chego sdelano kreslo prezidenta SSHA." In: Novyi mir 5, (https://magazines.gorky.media/novyi_mi/1996/5/iz-chego-sdelano-kreslo-prezidenta-ssha.html) [1 June 2024].
Arbitman, Roman (2009): "Kroshka syn, papa Sėm i rzhavye grabli. Rossiiskaia fantastika kak Neulovimyi Mstitel'." In: Novoe literaturnoe obozrenie 1, pp. 223–228.
Arsen'ev, Sergei (2012): Studentka, komsomolka, sportsmenka, Moskva: Ėksmo, (http://samlib.ru/a/arsenxew_s_w/cbuffersvet22doc.shtml) [30 September 2023].
Bassin, Mark/Sergey Glebov/Marlene Laruelle (eds.) (2015): Between Europe and Asia: The Origins, Theories, and Legacies of Russian Eurasianism, Pittsburgh: University of Pittsburgh Press.

---

20   In our opinion, Berezin's self-comparison with the American writer is wrong, at least because Tom Clancy did not take part in the actions of terrorist groups, but only described their activities – and without much enthusiasm, to put it mildly.

Birger, Liza (2021): "10 knig, s kotorykh stoit nachat'." In: Pravila zhizni, 7 January, 2021 (https://www.pravilamag.ru/letters/233963-10-knig-s-kotoryh-stoit-nachat-2021-god/) [30 September 2023].

Bestuzhev-Lada, Igor (1997): "Retroal'ternativistika v filisofii istorii." In: Voprosy filosofii 8, pp. 112–122.

Brooks, Van Wick (1918): "On Creating a Usable Past." In: The Dial, 11 April 1918, pp. 337–341.

Butter Michael (2009): The Epitome of Evil: Hitler in American Fiction, 1939–2002, New York: Palgrave MacMillan.

Bykov, Dmitrii (2014): "Voina pisatelei. Ukrainskie sobytiia byli predskasany i osushchestvleny avtorami boevoi fantastiki." In: Novaia Gazeta 74, 9 July, 2014.

Cherniakhovskii, Sergei (2005): "Velikaia voina i grazhdanskaia religiia Rossii." In: Agentstvo politicheskikh novostei – Nizhnii Novgorod, 22 June 2005 (https://www.apn.ru/index.php?newsid=1447) [30 September 2023].

Dragunskii, Denis (2013): Arkhitektor i monakh, Moskva: AST.

Dubin, Boris (2014): "Nartsissizm kak begstvo ot svobody." In: Vedomosti, 27 August, 2014 (https://www.vedomosti.ru/opinion/articles/2014/08/27/narcissizm-kak-begstvo-ot-svobody) [1 June 2024].

Engels, Friedrich (1895): "Ein zweiter Brief von Friedrich Engels." In: Der Sozialistische Akademiker 20, pp. 373–374.

Galina, Maria (2017): "Vernut'sia i peremenit'. Al'ternativnaia istoriia Rossii, kak otrazhenie travmaticheskikh tochek massovogo soznaniia postsovetskogo cheloveka." In: Novoe literaturnoe obozrenie, no. 146, pp. 258–271.

Galina Maria (2020) "Ressentiment and Post-traumatic Syndrome in Russian Post-Soviet Speculative Fiction: Two Trends." In: Mikhail Suslov/Per-Arne Bodin (eds.), The Post-Soviet Politics of Utopia. Language, Fiction and Fantasy in Modern Russia, London/New York: I.B. Taurus, pp. 39–60.

Galina, Maria (2021): "Post-Imperial Resentments: Alternative Histories of World War II in Popular Post-Soviet Speculative Fiction." In: Matthias Schwartz/Nina Weller/Heike Winkel (eds.): After Memory. World War II in Contemporary Eastern European Literatures, Berlin/Boston: De Gruyter, pp. 171–195.

Galina, Marina/Kukulin, Ilya (2021): "Al'ternativnaia istoriia. Romany o 'popadantsakh'." In: Vera Dubina/Andrei Zavadskii (eds.): Vse v proshlom: teoriia i praktika publichnykh istorii, Moskva: Novoe izdatel'stvo, pp. 155–186.

Gallagher, Catherine (2010): "Telling It like It Wasn't." In: Pacific Coast Philology 45, pp. 12–25.

Gudkov, Lev (2004): "Negativnaia identichnost'." Stat'i 1997–2002 godov, Moskva: Novoe literaturnoe obozrenie, "VSTIOM-A".

Gudkov, Lev (2022): "Resentimentnyi natsionalizm." In: Lev Gudkov: Vozvratnyi totalitarizm. V dvukh tomakh. Vol. 1, Moskva: Novoe literaturnoe obozrenie, pp. 47–156.

Hellekson Karen (2001): The Alternate History: Refiguring Historical Time, Kent/Ohio/London: The Kent State University Press.

Hitt, Jack (2016): "The Russian Tom Clancy is on the Front Lines for Real." In: The New Yorker, 7 January, 2016 (https://www.newyorker.com/books/page-turner/the-russian-tom-clancy-is-on-the-front-lines-for-real) [1 June 2024].

Krasnov, Petr (1922): Za chertopolokhom. Fantasticheskii roman, Berlin: Izdatel"stvo Ol'gi D'iakoboi i Ko, (http://az.lib.ru/k/krasnow_p_n/text_0100.shtml)) [30 September 2023].

Larionov, Vladimir (2003): "Moglo byt' i khuzhe." In: Knizhnoe obozrenie 27, 27 January.

Leibov, Roman (2023): Poema Pushkina "Graf Nulin". Opyt kommentirovannogo chteniia. The University of Tartu Press.

Liao, Pei-Chen (2020): Post-9/11 Historical Fiction and Alternate History Fiction: Transnational and Multidirectional Memory, Switzerland: Springer Nature.

L'vovskii, Stanislav (2011): "A Crick in the Neck." In: Russian Social Science Review 52/6, pp. 91–98.

Marks, Karl/Ėngel's Friedrich (1966): Sochineniia. Vol. 39, Moskva: Izdale'stvo politicheskoi literatury.

Platonov, Andrey (1975): The Foundation Pit [1930]. Tanslated by Mirra Ginsburg, New York: E.P. Dutton & Co., Inc.

Podol'nyi, Roman et al. (1980): "Istoriia: neizbezhnoe i sluchainoe." In: Znanie – sila 1/631, pp. 38–40.

Reddy, William M. (2004): The Navigation of Feeling: A Framework for the History of Emotions, Cambridge: Cambridge University Press.

Rodnianskaia, Irina (2002): "Lovtsy prodvinutykh chelovekov. O 'Evraziiskoi simfonii' Khol'ma Van Zaichika." In: Russkii Zhurnal, 18 July 2002 (http://old.russ.ru/krug/20020717_rodn.html) [30 September 2023].

Ruddy (2009): "Comment on" Viachslav Rybakov's 'Gravilët 'Tsesarevitch'." In: fantlab.ru [n.d.] (https://fantlab.ru/work7303) [30 September 2023].

Rybakov, Viacheslav (1997): "Gravilët 'Tsesarevitch'." [1993] In: Sochineniia v 2-kh tomakh. Vol. 1, Moskva: Terra, pp. 7–205.

Scott, Harris (2015): An Invitation to the Sociology of Emotions, London/New York: Routledge.

Silaev, Pëtr (2014): "Kak fantasty predskasali voinu na Ukraine." In: Afisha Daily, 5 September, 2014 (https://daily.afisha.ru/archive/vozduh/books/kak-fantasty-predskazali-boi-za-vostok-ukrainy/) [1 June 2024].

Shchepetnev, Vasilii (2002): "Sed'maia chast' t'my." [1997] In: Temnye zerkala, Moskva: AST, pp. 5–210.

Thiess, Derek J. (2015): Relativism, Alternate History, and the Forgetful Reader, Lanham: Lexington Books.

Toynbee, Arnold J. (1969): "If Alexander the Great had Lived On." In: Toynbee, Arnold J. (ed): Some Problems in Greek History 4, Oxford: Oxford University Press, pp. 418–487.

Toynbee, Arnold (1979): "Esli by Aleksandr ne umer togda." In: Znanie – sila 12, pp. 39–42.

Van Zaichik, Kholm [Rybakov, Viachslav/Alimov, Igor'] (2000–2005): Evraziiskaia simfoniia, St. Petersburg: Azbuka.

Viazovskii, A. Garik (2021): "Polnaia ėntsiklopediia popadantsev v proshloe, 26-ia redaktsiia." In: Zhurnal "Samizdat": Litobzor, (http://samlib.ru/o/odinokij_gawriil/popadanec26.shtml) [30 September 2023].

Vitenberg, Boris (2002): "Ob istoricheskom optimizme, istoricheskom pessimizme i gosudarstvennom podkhode istorii (Po povodu novykh knig A.L. Ianova i Iu.N. Afanas'eva)." In: Novoe literaturnoe obozrenie 54/2, pp. 315–327 (https://magazines.gorky.media/nlo/2002/2/ob-istoricheskom-optimizme-istoricheskom-pessimizme-i-gosudarstvennom-podhode-k-istorii-po-povodu-novyh-knig-a-l-yanova-i-yu-n-afanaseva.html) [30 September 2023].

Vitenberg, Boris (2004): "Igry korrektirovshchikov (Zametki na poliakh 'al'ternativnykh istorii')." In: Novoe literaturnoe obozrenie 66/2, pp. 281–293.

Young, Kathy (2014): "The Sci-Fi Writers' War." In: Slate, 11 July, 2014 (https://slate.com/news-and-politics/2014/07/science-fiction-writers-predicted-ukraine-conflict-now-theyre-fighting-it.html) [1 June 2024].

Chapter 6:
# Ludic Epistemologies and Alternate Histories
The Soviet Past in Role-Playing Games

*Daniil Leiderman*

## 1. Introduction

This article explores the representation of the Soviet past and experience in contemporary role-playing games both in Russia and abroad. Scholars like Adam Chapman have argued the need to take games seriously as historical epistemologies, with a significant impact on how players enjoying such games perceive history (cf. Chapman 2016). My claim is that the epistemologies of role-playing games represent the Soviet historical experience quite differently from conventional academic and popular historiography by demanding that players take responsibility for the course and outcome of history as represented within the game. By making history playful, decoupling it from a commitment to the continuities and inevitabilities of history, such games paradoxically accentuate the role of personal agency.

Games appropriate history as a space for play with the experiences and identities any historical moment prescribes as possible, yet without necessarily demanding any commitment to accuracy: for instance, a medieval game setting might let you play as a knight, but what this means will be accurate in some respects (wearing armour and riding a war horse) and inaccurate in others (fighting dragons). Both the commitment to and the neglect of historical facts structure the fantasy – so you can have your horse and the dragon too. When games apply this paradoxical fantasy structure to the representation of specific and recent history, rather than vaguely defined distant history – for instance, setting the game in World War II instead of the 'medieval era' – the result is still both the verisimilitude of historicity and a departure from it (e.g., you fight against Hitler and his inner circle, but also defeat them with your own hands, and Hitler is a giant robot). The same dynamic of intermittent commitment to historicity applies however, so the appeal to history fuels the very fantasy calling for major changes to historical continuity. The more compelling a game's representation of a historical moment, the more interesting it becomes to intervene in it, to change what you know to have happened, and if to fail, then to fail meaningfully. History and historical continuity become territorialised in the game as interactive and explorable ludic objects, comparable to the kinds of traversable boards or maps that historically territorialise everything from adulthood to economics in various board games (*Life*, *Monopoly*, etc.).

This territorialisation of history does not have to be particularly accurate or truthful. It can be very rudimentary: for instance, a first-person multiplayer shooter representing World War I trench warfare, would use historical elements (e.g., World War I-era uniforms and weapons) and offer a specific historical experience (harrowing trench-to-trench combat, bayonets etc.), but no context or historicity otherwise (the player's avatar is a disposable body with no identity, past or future, when the avatar dies, the player keeps playing with another avatar). At the same time, there are also more sophisticated examples, which engage with history deeply, using ludic identity and the personal memory of ludic phantasmagoria as though they were primary experiences. Players live another life and its history as though it was their own, however simulacral, and make choices meaningful to themselves, but also inseparable from the representation of history framing them within the game. Such representations attempt to territorialise the confusing terrain of history, to take ownership of it in a way that both explores what actually happened, and intervenes in it, potentially creating an alternate history, but in either case offering a fantasy of sovereignty within history.

## 2. Playing with Alternate Histories

In her book, *Telling It Like It Wasn't: The Counterfactual Imagination in History and Fiction* (2018), literary scholar and historian Catherine Gallagher argues for alter-histories as an important form of moral argument, citing the example of when in

> [...] prosecutions of war crimes against humanity [...] prosecutors often respond by instancing people in similar situations who refused to cooperate with the criminal actions. They thus construct norms for alternatives in which the victims might have gone unmolested if the perpetrators held themselves to higher levels of accountability. And they often further claim that convicting the perpetrators will set a precedent for the adoption of new norms by the agents of the state, who will no longer consider themselves immune to prosecutions. (8)

Gallagher concludes that "the counter-factual mode's ambition [is] to shape history rather than merely record, analyze, or understand it" (ibid.). Thus, games employing counter-factual modes are directly invested in a historical exegesis or an ideological reckoning and are anything but frivolous in tackling the subject of historical memory and trauma. As historical representations, they can easily be faulted for being entirely focused on entertainment, with no interest in engaging with actual historical events as anything beyond a colourful backdrop. However, if Gallagher's argument is taken seriously, they should also be considered as shaping history and taking responsibility for it in a way that is not strictly about entertainment, or is about entertainment in a peculiar way – allowing for unusual fantasy realisation that is not simply oriented towards gratuitous violence, but towards viscerally imagining a historical moment, or even shaping that moment with your own hands. After all, a game that only offers violence as a fantasy does not need to go to the trouble of creating historical verisimilitude – there are plenty of such games set in zombie apocalypses, alien landscapes, abstract terrains and other settings that are not overdetermined with historicity. Instead, what becomes apparent is that there is a reciprocity in historical games: they produce historicity because the player demands it, needs it to realise a fantasy of historical agency.

This argument resonates strongly with philosopher C. Thi Nguyen's thesis about games as a whole, laid out in his book *Games: Agency as Art* (2020), where he writes:

> The designer creates, not only the world which players will act, but the skeleton of the players' practical agency within that world. The designer designates players' abilities and goals in the game. The designer's control over the nature of the players' agency is part of the game. The game designer sculpts the game's activity. The game designer crafts for players a very particular form of struggle, and does so by crafting both a temporary practical agency for us to inhabit and a practical environment for us to struggle against. In other words, the medium of the game designer is agency […] games are the art of agency. (17)

For C. Thi Nguyen, games' use of agency, however truncated, is the medium's definitive formal feature, but in the case of games attempting to territorialise history, Gallagher's model of the alter-historical becomes particularly important. If both scholars' arguments are valid, then such games not only engage agency, but moralise it with rhetorical appeals towards shaping history. If for Nguyen games are a medium of agency, historical games turn the full weight of that agency to the problem of what can be learned from history and what pleasures can be wrung from engaging with a distant historical moment.

## 3. Agency and Role-Playing Games

Role-playing games (hereafter RPGs) are a type of game that grew out of Gary Gygax and Dave Arneson's tactical fantasy dungeon-crawler *Dungeons and Dragons* (hereafter *D&D*) (1974), but today embrace a much vaster and more diverse set of possible games, play-styles and genres. There are both table-top RPGs and computer RPGs, but computer RPGs grew from the table-top legacy and often emulate or aspire to emulate table-top experiences, as table-top RPGs allow for far greater improvisation and freedom on the part of the player. Every table-top RPG works through collaborative storytelling constricted by a set of rules, which are either interpreted collectively, or in the case of computer RPGs, programmed into the game, with the game designers scripting the story and whatever choices it will permit. In a typical table-top game, one player takes charge as the 'Game Master' (hereafter GM) and describes a world and its inhabitants, troubles and obstacles, using the rules to arbitrate interactions within it for the other players. The other players use the rules to create characters (hereafter PCs for 'Player Characters') in that world, and play as those characters, making decisions and changes in the world represented by the GM.

All players roll polyhedral dice to generate random numbers, establishing the failure or success of their actions on the basis of the dice rolls and rules. In computer RPGs, the computer handles this aspect of the game. In both cases, the aim is to make the storytelling unpredictable, creating the drama and the pleasure of the game. While everyone involved has some fantasy of how the narrative ought to develop, the dice create the possibility of surprise (e.g., the players might fail to achieve their goals completely, and instead of a cinematic victory, suffer a crushing defeat). This makes the narrative interesting to the players, since they themselves cannot conclusively say how the game will end, and thus the risks they take within the game feel authentic and meaningful. Similarly, moral and ethical choices feel significant because they are not controlled by chance and allow for the expression and exploration of identity.

In *D&D*, players took the part of adventurers exploring a fantasy world full of treasure and dangerous monsters. *D&D* identities were limited by the genre of fantasy, but nevertheless became complex explorations of moral agency, with players able to play both traditional heroes and villains, or otherwise 'evil' characters, and pursue expressly evil goals within the game – e.g., raising armies of monsters to destroy society. This incorporation of moral and ethical dilemmas is consistent with other role-playing games, even as they represent totally different contexts, genres, or identities: from science fiction to contemporary life.

Gallagher historicises the origins of the alter-history to the work of Gottfried Leibniz, arguing that for this Enlightenment philosopher, the creation of alternate histories was an important way of imagining and rationalising the subjectivity of God:

> [...] [Leibniz] posited a new mode of being for all of those unrealized possibilities by locating them in 'possible worlds.' The invention of these realms was a way of reconciling the fact of evil in this world with God's omnipotence, omniscience, and unfailing beneficence, as well as with the freedom of both divine and human will [...] The Theodicy thus inspired later writers to combine counterfactual history with religious apologetics, explicating historical events, especially the most apparently incomprehensible and horrific, as preferable to other possibilities; and it also gave the enterprise its comparative emphasis [...]. (2018: 18–19)

Alter-history in Gallagher's reading of Leibniz tries to capture the perspective of God, anticipating or imagining an omniscience so as to understand and even justify it, gaining a clarity about real history. In games, however, this is further complicated by the player not only imagining this omniscience, but embodying it, through the ability to remember different outcomes in the same game, saving and reloading and other practices common to digital games. In table-top games, you subordinate yourself to chance as a player, but still exercise a divine perspective – for instance, if a character drinks wine from a goblet, they do not know if they have been poisoned or not, but the player playing them does with certainty, as the GM told them, and indeed they are likely responsible for making a note of it and keeping track of the poisoning in the game (or cheating and 'forgetting' about it until reminded by the GM). The divine gaze sought by alter-history, and the personal, individual gaze empowered with sovereignty by RPGs, here hybridise into a vantage point that combines the traits of both, despite their apparent irreconcilability.

You are omniscient, capable of quantifying and leveraging every aspect of your identity into shaping history as a sovereign agent, but you are also limited and prejudiced, locked within the historical contingencies and political inevitabilities spelled out on your character sheet. In a historical RPG, you are both the player who knows how history really went, and the PC, caught up in a whirlwind of historical events and desperate to change them to their will. This treatment of history entangles it in several contradictory modes of representation, interactively collapsing politics, ideology, history, and private subjectivity together. What is the goal of such a venture? Is it to clarify or obfuscate? To force history to make sense, or force the player to make sense of it?

## 4. The Objects of Study

I am going to explore four RPGs all of which represent Soviet histories and alter-histories, offering post-Soviet landscapes as a comparable terrain to the haunted dungeons of D&D. These games are all by East European designers, and all equally full of dangerous trials and weighty moral decisions, tailored to the ideological and historical trauma of the Soviet experience: 74 (1980s, 2017), *Red Land* (*Krasnaia zemlia*, 2011), *Atom RPG* (2018), and *Disco Elysium* (2019).

74 is a board game, initially created by anonymous Soviet nonconformists in the 1980s, and then donated to Memorial, which published 74 as both a board game and political work of art. It asks players to play through the whole of Soviet history, keeping a kind of familial record of the historical traumas experienced by the player's avatars.

*Red Land* is a historical RPG set in the revolutionary period of 1917–1924, where a magical anomaly gave everyone's political ideology magical weight, pitting Red revolutionary mad science against the angel-summoning of the White army, while demonically-possessed revolutionaries realise the metaphor in Fëdor Dostoevskii's *The Possessed* (*Besy*, 1872) literally. The warring ideologies are accentuated with magic, allowing for an exaggerated examination of revolutionary and counter-revolutionary values.

*Atom RPG* is a post-apocalyptic role-playing computer game, an explicit ode to the classic American series of post-apocalyptic role-playing computer games focused on 1950s America and the Western landscape (*Fallout* (1997) and *Fallout 2* (1998)), but about the USSR and the Soviet landscape. Like *Fallout*, *Atom* is loaded with historical references to the post-Soviet 1990s, effectively imagining the post-Soviet world as an apocalypse and demanding that the player make meaningful choices for the future of this world.

Finally, *Disco Elysium* is a critically acclaimed and philosophically complex mystery computer RPG created by an Estonian anarchist collective (ZA/UM), which imagines the post-Soviet world through the figure of an amnesiac policeman coming to terms with the complexities of ideology and identity in the wake of the collapse of communism under neoliberal forces.

I have chosen these four because they represent a vast spectrum of role-playing experiences and media, but all focus on Soviet and post-Soviet history as a central object of play and inquiry, and all directly hold players responsible for this history, whether as passive witnesses (who nevertheless have a responsibility to witness), or as active shapers, whose intervention not only explores history, but changes it, or responds to it with sovereignty and urgency regarding the contemporary moment.

The RPG as a genre promises a range of agency within the phantasmagoric world shaped by play, or perhaps even sovereignty over it – an allure key to the entertainment that they offer, as well as to the power fantasy. Faced with a nemesis, the PC might defeat them in combat, trick them with a clever ploy, join them in building their evil empire, perish while trying, or leave altogether. All options consistent with the emergent narrative are within the player's range of agency, limited only by their ability to narrate the decision, and carry it out using the power that the game mechanics offer their character – from martial skill to magic spells. RPG computer games have historically attempted to maintain this legacy: for instance, the aforementioned Fallout series is particularly notable for having multiple possible means of resolving challenges within the game (memorably, in *Fallout: New Vegas* (2010) persuading a reaving army that their economic model is unsustainable).

This leads to a ready contradiction in RPGs focused on or set in real history: a player in a fantasy game who just defeated a tyrannical dragon-king and liberated their kingdom is still within an internally consistent phantasmagoria – there are always more dragons to slay. But what if the game is historical, set in 1938, and the player characters just overthrew Stalin? How does the narrative of the game proceed from there, without exiting or rupturing the very historical context that originally defined the game's setting? There is an intrinsic friction as sovereign choice grates against the specific and stable circumstances of history necessary for organising a historical narrative or setting.

The private experiences of the PCs do not always collide with history in this fashion. Indeed, if we imagine the game described above playing out, before overthrowing Stalin, the players necessarily first inhabited the Stalinist setting for a meaningful period of time, both in the game and out of it, in their solitary day-dreams, and collectively, meeting for a few hours every week, establishing their world, their PCs' relationships and values, overcoming challenges and likely only overthrowing Stalin at the conclusion of a prolonged narrative arc. There would likely be tense coded conversations, close brushes with the KGB, perhaps a terrifying interrogation or the brutal death of either a player or someone close to the players. Players tend to consciously bring in familiar literary and cinematic tropes, while the randomness introduced by the dice makes the narrative emergent (does your character live or die, trick the interrogator, or break?) The experiences shaped by such play are alternate histories, but these alter-histories are peculiar for having been experienced personally, with players inhabiting or surviving a phantasmagoria of Stalinism in the 1930s, that they themselves imagined; likely both inaccurate, loaded with images from other fictional media, and still paradoxically earnest in the attempt to capture the historical moment, or bring it to life in the collective imagination of the players. The unpredictability of the emergent narrative nevertheless makes the experience feel less like literature or theatre, and more like life, defying scriptedness with turns of fortune or misfortune driven by the dice. Consequently, rather than feeling as though they have read a history, players feel as though they have lived one.

## 5. Witnessing History: Memorial's 74 and the Suspension of Sovereignty

The first RPG I would like to discuss is not entirely an RPG. It is a board game with a track and does not allow for too many meaningful choices – for the most part, players roll the dice and move the appropriate amount experiencing historical and personal events. This, as I will show, is an important component of its rhetoric, supplemented by a device from role-playing games, where at the conclusion of the game, players are asked to narrate their PC's personal history under the USSR. All RPGs are structured around a certain freedom of choice, while 74 (1980s, author unknown), is consciously choiceless, offering no opportunity to take agency, other than through this finalising narration that turns the game into a kind of family history. At the same time, unlike the racetrack board games whose formal structure it adopts, 74's track does not represent capturable territory, but rather a full span of history: 74's space can only be passed through, never won.

The currently available version of 74 was released and re-designed in 2017 and made available for download or purchase by Memorial, the human rights organisation declared a 'foreign agent' in Russia in 2016, and which was ordered to liquidate by the Supreme Court of the Russian Federation for alleged violation of the "Foreign Agent" Law on 28 December 2021.

The title 74 reflects the number of years that the Soviet Union lasted – the donated original was untitled. According to Memorial, 74 was made anonymously as a samizdat art project at some point in the 1980s ("74. Nastol'naia igra po sovetskoi istorii"). It is not clear how many copies of the original game were created, likely very few. The copy used as a basis for the 2017 release was gifted to Memorial in 2009 by Susanna Pechuro, who received it from Liubov' Kabo (ibid.). Memorial's 74 juxtaposes private existential experience and angst by framing it against the whole span of the Soviet experiment from 1917 to 1991, mapped onto a board game track. The overall structure of the game is a traditional racetrack, a genre of games commonly played by children who enjoy rolling dice until the game ends, but generally disliked by adults who want to make choices in their games. Here the game spatially begins in 1917 and ends in 1991, but everyone reaches 1991 in due time, making racing an unimportant part of the game, with the focus instead on the historical and personal experiences accumulated along the way.

In 74, players follow two courses – the personal and historical, with separate circular tracks marking off the chronotopes of the prison camp and the international trip, where player pieces may move due to events in the game. However, the major emphasis in 74 is on characters, as each player begins with a discrete profession – at first, Worker, Labourer or Past-Person (pre-revolutionary elite), and quickly accumulates new roles in response to historical events, becoming a Soldier, Expert, Chekist, Enemy of the People, or after de-Stalinisation, a Marginal.

*Figure 6.1: Cards from 74 (2017)*

Left: Chekist. Caption: Work in national security isn't for everyone, acquaintances behave carefully with you. In red: This character cannot go to jail. Arrest means execution by firing squad; Right: Enemy of the People. Caption: Political charges and the camps are a mark for life, and your health is ruined. In red: A player with this character cannot expend private life cards. All private life events affect the enemy of the people.

These accumulations of identities are accompanied and shaped both by historical events and private events which appear as the PCs traverse both the historical and personal tracks. Private events are by-and-large tragedies or problems, while historical events are not necessarily tragic, except insofar as they represent historical trauma. Thus, for instance, the card "1937: The Great Terror" demands that players roll a six-sided die, going to the camps on one to five as an Enemy of the People, or becoming a Chekist on a six. This means players fundamentally have no control over the vicissitudes their alter-egos suffer from history. This is clearly a device, as one of the consequences of becoming an Enemy of the People is being subject to all, rather than only some events on the personal track (and these tend to be terrible). In effect, the game models the experience of the Enemy of the People by having them experience more of the game directly – an intensification of the normal play experience – you are swept along by the waves of history more powerfully than the other players, but all of you lack control over where history sweeps you – to a camp or into the KGB – and that is the point.

This type of representation transforms the basic epistemology of the game into a personal narrative generator – players do not choose to join the repressive apparatus or perish heroically, it happens to them automatically, due to the roll of the dice, but chance here produces the distinct feeling of authenticity. It is no longer a stranger that dies in the camps or joins the repressive authorities – your fate is in play. The designers drive in this implication with their end-game rules which request that players go around the table telling their personal and typically tragic story of the Soviet experiment by reading their identity cards in sequence and filling in the details via improvised narration. This twist resonates with role-playing games, creating a fascinating situation where the delivery of an ideological or rhetorical message is not couched in a pedagogical tone of knowing authority, but offered first to chance and then to the players themselves for articulation. This recitation of the family history is a player's only opportunity to express their agency within the game, allowing for the greatest freedom in either coming to terms with their PC's actions and experiences, or framing them in a meaningful way. What seemed to be a representation of history as a torrent of chance and fate, detached from personal choice or responsibility transforms at the end, suddenly holding players personally responsible for witnessing and memorialising their alter-history.

74 is not about simulating the Great Terror – it is about simulating the life of ordinary people as the Great Terror passes over them, as they are threatened by the authoritarian apparatus or co-opted by it. Its epistemology is drastically different from the vantage point of traditional history, but it is equally different from that of the personal journal – juxtaposing the two, collapsing one into the other and, most significantly, investing the player with the obligation to make sense of it – to take up a fictional epistemology and make it compellingly their own. Sovereignty of choice appears to be a wilfully missing factor from the game play of 74, a fantasy that consciously will not be indulged. But isn't sovereignty the utopian promise of such games and their experiments with identities?

## 6. Exacerbating Politics with Magic: *Red Land's* Experiment with Ideological Identity

Numerous games from the post-Soviet world, however, have attempted to experiment with allowing sovereignty, even an excess of sovereignty that derails and destabilises history, once more relying on the devices of role-playing games, and thus the central device I located within 74: the juxtaposition of history represented as set in stone, or as an uncontrollable current, and the opportunities for agency offered by personal or private alter-histories. *Red Land* (2010–11) by "Shtab' Dukhonina", a Russian collective composed of Egor Borskovskii, Konstantin Trofimenko, Mikhail Shalupaev, and Ivan Ian'kov, is a particularly interesting example, because it further empowers this personal vantage point while exploring a discrete temporal territory – the Revolution of 1917 and the civil war that followed – through a role-playing game.

*Red Land* uses *Savage Worlds* (2003), an RPG rule system designed to be genre-neutral, accommodating every conceivable narrative, from superheroes to regular people's experiences, as a basis. *Red Land* adds its own content and tilts the *Savage World* system to represent the October Revolution and ensuing civil war. The rules thus encompass historically appropriate identities, professions, skills, weapons and munitions. However, *Red Land* also adds a supplementary magic system structured around the four playable factions within the Red Land: the "Reds" or Communists, the "Whites" or Monarchists, the "Greens" representing the vantage point of villagers advocating a traditional way of life, and the "Blacks" representing either anarchists or professional criminals. Players are to choose their PC's faction, and there is no obligation to choose the same faction – so players could both be collaborating and opposing one another, depending on the sort of story they are all interested in telling. Similarly, the role of magic is entirely up to the players: it is possible that a given group will either focus on magic or ignore it altogether. Nevertheless, the magical system complicates and accentuates the representation of the historical civil war. Ideologies are materialised and literalised here: for instance, a player whose character is a White cavalry officer, who in a moment of crisis prays for salvation from the godless Reds, might find an actual angel manifesting in accordance with the rules of the game.

This is the case for all the ideologies involved: Red magic relies on 'scientific' experiments using historical materialism and a lot of human blood, Marxist cyborgs and vampire-locomotives. White magic relies on summoning the ghosts of the Imperial past and terrifying Biblical angels, as well as on strict parochial social hierarchies. The magic of the "Greens" is all about rejecting industrial modernity for the united forces of Pan-Slavic witchcraft and paganism. Black magic is not represented as magic at all, rather as incredible luck that allows criminals and anarchists to escape prosecution but is also fuelled by actual demonic possession – an apparently conscious literalisation of Fëdor Dostoevskii's *The Possessed* (or *Demons*) on the part of the designers. The designers also added dozens of texts: faux-newspaper clippings, manifestos, underground agitation and others, both imitating historical materials and supplying alter-historical plot hooks and details hinting at the supernatural or magic.

Rather than playing conventional slay-the-dragon adventures, the game focuses on the historical events and scenarios of the Revolution and civil war. Instead of becoming knights and wizards, players become Bolsheviks agitating in revolutionary Petrograd, a band of Cossack bandits on the front, commissars rooting out counter-revolutionaries, a folk uprising in the shtetl – or any other conceivable scenario appropriate to the setting and exacerbated by the presence of ideologically-charged magic. Gameplay requires a particular commitment to a historical verisimilitude. In games like *74*, a roll of the dice is all it takes to become a Chekist or a political prisoner, in *Red Land* each player has to ask themselves what it means to be a Chekist or a political prisoner, and then act accordingly, as part of the collective fiction developing in the course of play. This verisimilitude is absolutely vital here, because otherwise you might as well be playing *D&D* and asking yourself what it means to be a wizard or elf – identities not intrinsically limited by 20th century political ideology and its onerous demands. It is the intensity of Revolutionary politics and the specificity of the historical moment, and the identities it allows and fosters, that define *Red Land* as a setting.

Historical consistency in *Red Land* is a double-edged sword. It delimits agency, for instance, by forcing players to act as a Bolshevik or White officer of noble birth would (or how they imagine they would), acting out their character's identity both to their benefit and their detriment. However, this consistency also permits meaningful interventions in history: successfully assassinating Lenin, or indeed making him immortal, or any other such acts are possible, provided the players act consistently with the established rules and fiction. This is in marked contrast to *74*, as the agency allotted to players is far greater, and with the addition of magic, so is their power to make an impact on the world. What if Lenin is attacked by the player characters and the ghosts of the monarchy that they summoned? What will the USSR look like under the rule of Baba Yaga?

*Figure 6.2: Flavour text composed of fictional newspaper clippings about occult subjects, juxtaposed with appropriated Revolutionary-era posters and photographs. Red Land, p. 151*

*Red Land* opens up history into a kind of playbox, providing opportunities for both actions that feel historically accurate, and that make history radically protean. *Red Land* attempts to territorialise history, turning it from a vast an unknowable territory of endless complexity, into a personal map and narrative shaped by gaming sessions and memories of various ludic accomplishments (e.g.: "remember when we helped Baba Yaga save Lenin's life at the Kremlin in 1924?") producing a multiplicity of alter-histories. As the space territorialised by games is necessarily composed of role-played characters inhabiting phantasmagoric historical chronotopes, the subjectivities shaped by *Red Land*'s territorialisation of history almost necessarily cross-contaminate personal vantage points and the vantage points of governmentality, producing an odd hybrid.

In *Red Land*, governmentality becomes a portion of your character profile – your commitment to the Reds, Whites, Greens, or Blacks and their respective political and governing ideologies is primary and definitive, describing your identity and, perhaps more importantly, your magic, which translates directly to agency within the world of *Red Land*. Within a game of *Red Land*, the PCs define the world and ideology alike: if all of the PCs are, for instance, communist revolutionaries, their narrative arc within the game will become a synecdoche for the entirety of the communist side within the Revolution and Civil War – they will be the heroes and their stories, successful or tragic, will frame the representation of their chosen ideology. They, and only they, end up defining what revolutionary communism looks like for everyone involved in the game. In a group where the player characters have mixed ideologies, this effect will only be intensified: a communist revolutionary, White spy, and an anarchist bandit playing together will consciously treat each other's PCs as direct representatives of their respective ideologies, accentuating their political differences for the sake of ludic drama, or having their political arguments inflect the decisions made during play. It is this ludic epistemology – the merger of individual fantasy and a governmentality located in some alter-historical phantasmagoria that I am denoting 'ludic sovereignty', to stress that I am both sceptical of how genuine this sovereignty is and compelled to call it that because of the complexity of the fantasies it evokes.

## 7. Responsibility and History: *Atom RPG* and Making Choices

*Atom RPG* (2018) by the Atom Team, a multinational game indie-development studio based in Poland, Ukraine, Russia, and Latvia, is an excellent example of the complexity and ambition of role-playing games' attempt to represent not only history, but genuine responsibility and agency within history. *Atom RPG* was successfully funded with a small Kickstarter campaign, but was published on nearly every platform, including iOS and the Xbox, a fairly impressive feat for a small indie title. *Atom RPG* uses the RPG form to attempt an exegesis of a confusing and difficult-to-represent historical moment: the collapse of the USSR and Perestroika. *Atom* is unambiguously an homage to another alter-history series of games: the 1990s American RPGs *Fallout* and *Fallout 2*, both predicated on a post-apocalyptic future as imagined in the 1950s – ray guns and talking household robots alongside cannibal gangs and radiation. *Fallout 1* and *2* were set in Southern and Northern California, respectively, as alternate American histories told largely through the landscape, whose recognisable names (Reno, San Francisco, and others) jarred with their post-apocalyptic terrain and mutated inhabitants. *Atom RPG* represents the same sort of post-apocalyptic world-building, but in Eastern Europe. The international team of designers did not follow *Fallout* in depicting a specific geography, instead attempting to capture a temporal terrain.

At first glance, their approach is to scatter various geographical references, making the territory of the game both recognisable and not. For instance, one of the major cities in the game is Krasnoznamensk, which is west of Moscow, while the starting hub is the village Otradnoe, near Sochi, but they are within walking distance in the game. The names do not reference the actual locations, instead acting as broad Soviet-style signifiers: Krasnoznamensk translates as "Redbannerton", the village – as "joyful". These names are chosen as generic markers of the socialist world. Visually, *Atom RPG* evokes an immediately recognisable East European terrain and Soviet architecture and naming conventions, one both totally phantasmagoric and familiar.

Instead of the 1950s, this alter-Russia is supposed to be the 1980s (following a nuclear apocalypse and the detonation of multiple atom bombs), yet in its jokes and references, *Atom RPG* instead allegorises the first post-Soviet decade. Such contemporary references were already present as small easter eggs and jokes in *Fallout*, but here they are exacerbated to the level of major factors in the game's plot. *Atom RPG* refers constantly to such diverse sources as Vladimir Sorokin's postmodern novella *Monoklon* (2010), post-Soviet hip-hop, Perestroika-era cults, and the Russian literary canon, all framed as encounters within a post-apocalyptic landscape, and effectively representing the collapse of the Soviet Union as an explorable geography.

One of the first non-player characters who can join the PC is the protagonist of *Grandfather Mazai and the Hares* (*Dedushka Mazai i zaitsy*), Nikolai Nekrasov's 1870s narrative poem commonly assigned to and read by Soviet school children. In the poem, Mazai is an old man who rescues hares from a spring flood. Here, he (and his hares), is the aging Soviet intellectual, fixated on the literary tradition and living ethically while still trying to build communism. In another scene, the protagonist goes to see the dead Lenin, or rather Lenin's mummy, who turns out to be faking his death (or just impersonating Lenin) for profit – Lenin lives! Immediately adjacent to Lenin is an obvious reference to Mariia Devi Khristos (born Marina Tsvihun), leader of the prominent early 1990s cult YUSMALOS, who is depicted in *Atom RPG* in her recognisable pose of offering a blessing to the audience.

So, what exactly is happening here? The player is exploring a post-apocalyptic Soviet wasteland, in a game set in an alternate history of the 1980s, but keeps encountering references to the post-Soviet world of the early 1990s, its politics, jokes, cults, and ideologies. *Atom RPG* is using the personal vantage point of the role-playing game as a mechanism for exploring and understanding the contradictory and messy post-Soviet moment and taking a sovereign position within it.

In one of the most telling scenes, the player encounters a madman who calls himself "Monoklon". In a scene directly parodying the scene in the New Testament, when Christ encounters a man possessed by enough demons to call themselves "Legion", the player avatar can choose to exorcise the Monoklon into a herd of pigs, by calling upon the spiritual power of communism, in a kind of perverse rite that sacralises socialist materialism: "By the will of the presidium of the Central Committee of the Communist Part of the Soviet Union, leave this proletariat, oh unclean ones! Begone!" In Vladimir Sorokin's novella *Monoklon*, the narrative proceeds as a dialogue between several wealthy and sophisticated individuals in their mansion. Towards the very end of the narrative, the mansion is suddenly invaded by armed people, who seem to have some sort of police authority, but speak in an utterly incomprehensible tongue, that nonetheless is unmistakably the language of brutal and immediate violence. The reference to Sorokin's novel evokes it as a representation of epistemological collapse – of meaning disappearing under a wave of violence, of words no longer making sense except as supplements to violence. The player's paradoxical ability to exorcise the confusion through the magic of communism is meaningful here.

This juxtaposition of the New Testament and Sorokin's postmodernist prose invests the jumbled setting with a clear purpose. *Atom RPG* represents the Soviet post-apocalyptic as concurrent with the post-Soviet day-to-day, as characterised by the fragmentation of meaning and sense, a multiplicity of narratives, voices and myths struggling for competition and creating a violent cacophony. However, the player's intervention in these narratives and their role as a territorialising agent, completing all the quests in one city and moving on to the next, clearing a particular zone of monsters and artifacts and moving on to the next, all the way until the conclusion of the game, allows a fantasy of organising and traversing the historical space represented. *Atom RPG* culminates with the player asked to choose to either empower the old forces of Soviet history, embodied by a cabal of authorities from the Soviet regime soldiering on in a military bunker in order to restore the old world, or support the new forces of post-apocalyptic change, embodied by a nomadic militant organisation capturing the post-apocalyptic world for the future. History here becomes condensed in a single decision enacted by the player if they successfully territorialise this strange new terrain.

*Atom RPG* tackles history as an impossible tangle of ideologies and utopian projects but offers this entanglement as a territory that can be travelled, captured, understood, and ultimately mastered. Sovereignty becomes a crucial factor here: in *Atom RPG*, you are sovereignly deciding how history ought to progress from the chaos of the post-Soviet 1990s, but the choice is reductive and achieved through violence. *Atom RPG* cannot articulate or imagine a sovereignty that is not made possible by the apocalypse – the collapse of all social structures, and a wasteland ruled by violence are necessary factors here. The end of the world removes those social institutions that *Atom RPG* ultimately asks you to judge – it is only possible to defeat the forces of the old Soviet world because the atomic apocalypse has locked them in a bunker. It is similarly possible to re-empower them. The players have to make the choice themselves.

## 8. Fragmentary Selves in Post-Soviet History

*Disco Elysium* (2019) the computer role-playing game by the Estonian anarchist art collective ZA/UM, is the unlikely case of a game developed as an art project, but that goes on to become internationally famous as both a cult hit and a bestseller with more than 40 million dollars in sales world-wide (cf. Game-Stats 2019). For an indie project developed by an Estonian anarchist collective, *Disco Elysium* was remarkably successful with both fans and critics, earning 10/10 reviews from virtually all prominent video game sites, and sweeping multiple video game awards in 2019. The primary writer behind *Disco Elysium* is Robert Kurvitz, who developed the elaborate setting and the history of the world within which the video game is set over the course of multiple table-top RPG campaigns conducted with friends in the last two decades and using an original RPG system designed by Kurvitz towards this end (cf. Apperley/Ozimek 2021).

*Disco Elysium* is not a typical role-playing game. It attempts a more ambitious ludic epistemology, exploring ideology, history, and memory from a non-violent vantage point and through doubling-down on the radical potential in the new and alternate identities and histories made possible by the role-playing game. There are no *D&D*-like monsters, or even combat mechanics in *Disco Elysium:* violence is possible, but it is represented as tragic, swift and devastating to every human being involved, and everyone involved (other than a hallucinogenic cryptid that is not easy to meet) is a human being. The game consists of territorial and psychic exploration. The protagonist is an amnesiac, possibly named "Harry", who awakens in a strange city from what turns out to have been a lengthy alcohol and amphetamine stupor, devoid of any memory of their world or themselves. You are told, however, that you are a cop, and are investigating a crime – a murder, in fact. The dead man still hangs in the courtyard of your motel when you awaken, it has been a week since the apparent lynching. You are told you have been drinking heavily, singing, and screaming that you "don't want to be this kind of animal anymore" for hours during the night, and days on end. Nothing else is known, at least, at the start.

Solving the murder, and the larger mystery of who you are, is the premise and plot of the game, but the focus is on the self – on the protagonist's lost inner world, their broken life, that they are desperate to recover and understand. The protagonist is not a singular entity. The character sheet within the game splits him into twenty-four distinct attributes, all of them individually voiced within the game as separate personalities. Each has demands, insists on its own importance, chatters, and offers insights. Your Encyclopaedia bombards you with irrelevant facts and trivia, your voice of Authority insists you flash your badge and remind everyone you meet that you are the law around here, your Electro-Chemistry really wishes that you did more drugs, or maybe just had another cigarette, your Inland Empire intuits that the murder victim was killed by communism. Can any of them be believed or trusted? Do any of them represent the authoritative voice of the authentic self? The player can expend their experience to improve these areas, strengthening some attributes and their insights, while dampening others. Whenever they encounter a challenge that tests an attribute, the game visibly rolls dice, and even if improved with experience, failure is always a possibility. The game changes as a result, in each case, with success and with failure, and with each choice – as each "Harry" played is different – an authoritarian bully for one player, a warm-hearted empath for another.

The game also encourages Harry to adopt a political stance, offering unique content depending on if Harry chooses communism, fascism, neoliberalism or "moralism" (a parody of status quo liberalism within the game). The murder at the centre of the plot is also directly historicised and politicised. The lynched man is a representative of the neoliberal forces that destroyed the revolution. The local socialist labour union takes responsibility for his lynching but is not actually responsible. The real murderer is a man still fighting for the communist revolution, as far as he is concerned, alone and without hope. The neighbourhood has anarchists and nazis, capitalists and thieves, all invested and involved. The identity chosen by the player is unambiguously political and has a direct impact on how the city's history continues to affect its present. In one game Harry will solve the murder and become a homeless alcoholic, in another they might become an artist, or rejoin the police force, or quit drinking, or accuse the wrong person of murder. Harry's many potential selves reveal him to be a synecdoche of his city, and his multivalence and potentiality signal the same multivalence and potentiality as the rightful inheritance of the post-Soviet world, for better or for worse.

The game adjusts to all such playthroughs: whatever the protagonist chooses to do with themselves and their future is supported by the game's flexible narrative. The documentary film *Making Disco Elysium: The Importance of Failure* (2020) by Outcast Docs, makes the case that the roll of the dice – that central ludic device drawn from role-playing games – is strategically and conceptually important in *Disco Elysium* (cf. Outcast Docs 2020). The documentary argues that rather than treating dice rolls as prompts to either succeed, moving forward with the intended and planned plot where Harry solves the murder, finds his identity and returns to the police, or failure, where the game stutters, and the player needs to try something different to get back on track, the game leans into failure. Through failure, the game embraces all outcomes, even those that in other games would represent the player's having failed to overcome a challenge or losing track of the 'proper' plot. In *Disco Elysium*, your failures accumulate as meaningfully as your successes, as points of contact, development and potentially growth for the ludic subjectivity that is Harry, and his voices and thoughts. This ludic epistemology constructed around failed rolls of the dice, allows ZA/UM to experiment with an antiheroic protagonist, tormented and vulnerable, someone whose personal life has failed, who is residing in a failed political state, threatened by global capitalism and a looming climate disaster, someone who will not be fixed by any solved murder, and almost certainly not by returning to the police force. Failure is crucial to the historical representation as well. The failure of the communist revolution to create a better world is key to the game's central problems and philosophical conflicts, thus the accentuation of failure as a ludic device must also be seen as a historical argument: the failure of the revolution is a ludic problem, play again and play it differently.

Accordingly, rather than abilities or powers, Harry accumulates beliefs, which join the "Thought Cabinet". These have a mechanical function, improving certain skills or granting other advantages or disadvantages to represent the political, social and emotional conclusions that Harry draws from his experiences: everything from deciding to quit drugs, to deciding to embrace them, to obsessive, haunting nostalgia for a lost love, to direct commitment to the political ideologies of fascism, communism, capitalism and others. All these are available as potential avenues for Harry to believe, internalise, discard, or replace. No ideology or value system is represented as intrinsically superior (though fascism is clearly mocked and denigrated, while communism is treated with both cutting irony and a palpable hint of sadness – ZA/UM had no intention of making an apolitical game or hiding their leftist commitments).

The character-building systems and epistemologies of the role-playing game here become a poignant metaphor for postmodern identity and identity formation, for the necessity of making political and personal decisions without having moral absolutes or essential origins to rely upon. Harry is contingent and patchwork, his memories and identity shift constantly as he tentatively explores the world around him, lying about what he knows and does not know, or honestly acknowledging his amnesia, grasping for meaning and purpose in a world where both meaning and purpose are clearly mediated by blind chance, and the decentred accumulation of experiences and failures in your character sheet.

*Disco Elysium* reflects on these dynamics directly within the narrative. If the player decides to explore one of the major buildings in the neighbourhood's top floors, Harry discovers the abandoned studio of a company that once developed role-playing games about identity. A bare trace of their ludic epistemology remains in a 20-sided die that Harry finds and pockets, a small symbol of his own search for identity, and the contingent and random meaning that will necessarily emerge from it.

At the conclusion of the game, a minor plotline culminates in an easily missed but crucial encounter, when after hearing myths of a cryptid living in the reeds around the city, Harry actually encounters it; a marvellous, hallucinogenic mantid. The cryptid speaks to Harry, expressing profound sadness and grief at the terrifying human condition. Harry calls the creature "insane", to which it responds:

"No. *You* are. The moral of our encounter is: I am a relatively median lifeform – while it is you who are total, extreme madness. A volatile simian nervous system, ominously new to the planet [...] You are a violent and irrepressible miracle. The vacuum of cosmos and the stars burning in it are afraid of you. Given enough time you would wipe us all out and replace us with nothing – just by accident. [...] Everything your eyes touch goes back there – behind the thought mirror. What if you blink? Are we still here? (Please don't blink). What if you misplace us all one day – or just forget?" (ZA/UM 2019)

This encounter articulates the model of the self that emerges from the ludic epistemologies of role-playing games: tentative, decentred, the fragmentary portrait of humanity not united by omnipresent heroic narratives of unity and fantasies of domination and power. An experimental and vulnerable alternative self, shaped acutely by meaningful and painful choices, still fiercely powerful, ruthlessly engaged, capable of rethinking, reassessing, transforming, and awakening the world around it – as dangerous as it is full of promise, as rudderless as it is driven. *Disco Elysium* evoked a powerful set of both critical and fan reactions, from serious discussions about drug abuse and alcoholism, which the game portrays both playfully and with stark tragedy, to critiques of its political and historical message.

In an article called "A Year Later, I Still Cannot Stop Thinking About Disco Elysium" (30 August 2021) for Kotaku.com, a popular gaming website, Renata Price stresses that the fragmentations of Harry and the city of Revachol are intimate allegories of trauma, as it reverberates in both history and private memory:

Martinaise, the Revachol district within which *Disco Elysium* takes place, is sick. There is a body hanging from a tree, it has been there for over a week now. This is not normal for Martinaise, but for most people it is acceptable. Children, trapped in a haze of drugs and trauma, treat it like a plaything. The district has been sick for a long time. The Antecellian Civil War destroyed Revachol's monarchy, so the rest of the world destroyed the city. Following a successful communist revolution, the Coalition of Nations (the game's U.N. equivalent) unleashed a swift and violent campaign known as Operation Death Blow. Martinaise was one of its primary targets. The district was all but obliterated by artillery, and it has not recovered in the five decades since. This was the trauma that has since seeped into the bones of the city [...]. (Price 2021)

*Figure 6.3: Alexander Rostov,* Disco Elysium, *main menu and loading screen showing the city from the vantage point of the murderer, 2020*

Harry is a synecdoche of the city and history of Revachol, the setting of the game that is as much a protagonist as Harry. Revachol's history is presented throughout the game: its communist revolution, both optimistic and terribly bloody, economically and militarily crushed by the 'Moralist' nations of the world, making Revachol a colony-state for capitalist enterprise. The district explored throughout the game still bear the traces of the bombardment, walls marked with the executions of the communards. It is also a city struggling for its identity and history between the push and pull of communist, capitalist, moralist and fascist pasts. Harry's identity struggles are thus a reflection of global issues – the personal is truly political here, and since the personal is the exact domain upon which the game focuses mechanically, its epistemology becomes an epistemology of political history after the collapse of communism. Just as the PCs in *Red Land* inevitably came to stand for their chosen revolutionary or counter-revolutionary ideology, so does each player's Harry-experience become a representation of the post-Soviet condition, and the trauma both of the communist experiment and its collapse.

Revachol's symbol is the statue at the centre of the game's urban centre. The statue is of the ex-monarch of Revachol, who was overthrown in the communist revolution. The statue was blown up by the communards, but during the counter-revolution, a Dadaist art group re-assembled the monarch's statue without restoring it, preserving the king in an on-going state of explosion. The patchwork king stands still, torn chunks of stone on metal wires, a symbol of eternal and unceasing revolution without resolution. This indeterminacy, in which players intervene through Harry's soul-searching and crime-solving, not only mirrors Harry's fractured subjectivity, but also invests it with distinct meaning, monumentalising the post-socialist moment when the king is neither overthrown, nor reigning, but is frozen in perpetual explosion and fragmentation, unable to either remain a statue or to become nothing. The indeterminacy turns this post-utopian or post-dystopian state into its own distinct era, as fractured and still as unitary as Harry himself, or as the player playing Harry.

Much of the game's political conflict is centred around the murder that Harry investigates. The murdered man is a mercenary working for a moralist corporation, ostensibly killed by the local socialist union, who are striking against the corporation. The actual murderer, however, is an old communard, who never stopped fighting the long-since-lost war against capitalism and imperialism, dementedly continuing the lost cause from a nearby lighthouse with a sniper rifle. He murders the mercenary while he is in bed with a local woman, seeing their consensual affair as a symbolic violation of Revachol's political history. However, the socialist union takes the blame, claiming to have lynched the mercenary as a rapist, due to a complex triangle of desire between the socialists' lead enforcer, the murdered mercenary, and the woman in whose arms he died. Failing to solve the crime adequately leads the corporation to send a fully armed mercenary squad against the socialists and their union, with tragic consequences for the entire neighbourhood and city. Here the personal and political are inseparable, not on the level of ideology, but on the level of sex, life and death, as personal conflict mirrors or exacerbates political history, bringing back old traumas and staging huge issues as personal interactions.

Price writes of the communard assassin:

You find an old man with a gun. He is broken by the world and full of bullets, almost like you, Harry. He lived the revolution, loved it actually. Married himself to it. And it was murdered. So he sits on this shitty little island, alone. He eats rations and watches the city through the scope of his rifle. He hates it. Every bit of it. He is a warning of what you might become. (Ibid.)

The old man is Harry if Harry hadn't lost his memory, hadn't surrendered to oblivion allowing for the clean, if broken slate upon which the game's narrative relies. The amnesia is structurally equivalent to beginning a new game here, with Harry wiped clean once more, but the player is not granted the same privilege as Harry, as they are repeatedly forced to make sovereign decisions within the game, remembering all outcomes, even as they reload or change their mind.

*Disco Elysium* affects the player through the constellation of two familiar epistemological vectors: that of the character sheet, which attempts to map personal identity, and that of the representation of the city itself, which is composed both of the explorable, interactive area in the game, and several aesthetic images of it within the loading screens and start screens of the game.

Aleksander Rostov, the primary artist behind *Disco Elysium*'s visuals, chose an expressionistic, even fauvist aesthetic of sweeping strokes, dissonant and unblended colours and physiognomic grotesqueries. The epistemologies of the character sheet and the visual dimension once more constellate the personal and political right from the start. The starting screen is a digital painting of a vista of Revachol, including all of the areas visited by the player during the game save one: the lighthouse where the communard and assassin is still fighting for communism one sniper shot at a time.

The assassin's location is identical to our vantage point in this image – we see Revachol as he would from his lighthouse – indeed, if we focus our eyes just to the left of the equine statue of the detonated king at the centre of the image, we will see a solitary sliver of light – the window of the hotel where the murdered man was shot. Our aesthetic gaze upon the landscape can readily become the murderous scope of the political assassin, and once more the personal and the landscape become equally relevant epistemologies of a historical moment. Both the total fragmentation of a unitary self and the total fragmentation of ideological clarity become equivalent terrains that *Disco Elysium* embraces as fragmentary, as broken, and yet as ludically redeemable, mappable, reconcilable through the act of play, which renders all such complexity legible and redemptive as either character sheet, or map or both: "All of it in service of producing narratives strong enough to cope with trauma after trauma, and realising that, despite all the broken things inside of you, you can still touch and be touched by other people." (Ibid.)

Memory is thus a crucial axis and motif within the game – Harry loses his and comes to terms with the fact that he may well have lost it for a reason. The world is losing memory too, quite literally, as the world of *Disco Elysium* is suffering from a slow apocalypse at the hands of a devouring fog called "The Pale", which is strongly implied to be the materialisation of the weight of human history, a destructive and corrosive process of erasure. Memory is also a crucial formal device. The structure of the game is such that the player is often tantalised by a particularly ludicrous choice, with having Harry misbehave or act outrageously. Often after reading Harry's outburst, or otherwise unacceptable act, the player feels a bit troubled, reloads and tries a different approach. It is possible to do many reprehensible things in *Disco Elysium*, from internalising fascism, to striking a child, to attempting suicide to make a point in an argument. All these potentialities are sustained by the memory of the player, who makes bad choices, and then must decide to either stick with them, maintaining the narrative course, or reload, trying for a different Harry and a different sovereignty. This is fundamental to the game, and central to its philosophical argument – just as Harry must decide who he is, deprived of memory, so do you, the player who possesses the means to turn back time and try a different approach, must decide what your game is, and why you are playing it.

## 9. Conclusion

The representations of history in these games demand that the player not only make meaningful ideological choices but take responsibility for how these choices affect the world. In the process, contingent, and phantasmagoric ludic histories become allegories for examining and coming to terms with the complexities and contradictions of historical experience. Whether by allowing choices, or restricting them, turning history into a map, a district, or an individual, games make arguments about the histories they represent. Such ludic epistemologies do not produce authentic historicity. The alternate histories these games generate are necessarily allegorical and symbolic rather than factual. Nevertheless, through conduct and play their allegories become existentially meaningful, convincing the player that they experienced something authentic within the fiction, compelled and tested as they were by their own sovereign choices and the weight of their own memories.

## List of Games

*74. Nastol'naia igra po sovetskoi istorii*, produced by Baryshnikova, Natalia/Vorontsov, Roman/Lomakin, Nikita/Starostin, Vasilii, Memorial, Tabletop RPG, 2017.
*Atom RPG*, produced by Atom Team, PC/Mac/Linux, 2018.
*Disco Elysium*, produced by ZA/UM (Kurvitz, Robert/Rostov, Aleksander), PC/Mac, 2019.
*Dungeons and Dragon*, produced by Gygax, Gary/Arneson, Dave, TSR, Inc., Tabletop RPG, 1974.
*Fallout series*, produced by Cain, Tom, Interplay Entertainment, PC/Mac, 1997–2004.
*Red Land (Krasnaia Zemlia)*, produced by Shtab Dukhonina (Borkovskii, Egor/Trofimenko, Konstantin/Shalupaev, Mikhail/Ian'kov, Ivan), Tabletop RPG, 2010–2011.
*Savage Worlds*, produced by Hensley, Shane Lacy, Pinnacle Entertainment Group, Tabletop RPG, 2003.

## List of Illustrations

**Figure 6.1:** Cards from 74 (2017). Left: Chekist. Right: Enemy of the People.
**Figure 6.2:** Text composed of fictional newspaper, Red Land (2010–2011), p. 151.
**Figure 6.3:** Main menu loading screen from the Game *Disco Elysium*, designed by Alexander Rostov, 2020.

## References

Apperley, Thomas/Ozimek, Anna (eds.) (2021): "Disco Elysium: Special Issue on Baltic Screen Media Review." In: Baltic Screen Media Review 9/1, (https://sciendo.com/issue/BSMR/9/1) [30 September 2023].
Chapman, Adam (2016): Digital Games as History: How Videogames Represent the Past and Offer Access to Historical Practice, London: Routledge.
Gallagher, Catherine (2018): Telling It Like It Wasn't: The Counterfactual Imagination in History and Fiction, Chicago/London: The University of Chicago Press.
Game-Stats (2019): "Disco Elysium – The Final Cut – Stats on Steam." In: Statson Steam (https://games-stats.com/steam/game/disco-elysium/) [30 September 2023].
"74. Nastol'naia igra po sovetskoi istorii." In: memorial.com (https://www.memo.ru/ru-ru/projects/boardgame) [30 September 2023].
Nguyen, C. Thi (2020): Games: Agency as Art, New York: Oxford University Press.
Outcast Docs (2020): "Making Disco Elysium: The Importance of Failure." In: YouTube, 11 November 2020 (https://www.youtube.com/watch?v=N3NY7PnPhwY) [30 September 2023].
Price, Renata (2021): "A Year Later, I Still Cannot Stop Thinking About Disco Elysium." In: Kotaku 30 August 2021 (https://kotaku.com/a-year-later-i-still-cant-stop-thinking-about-disco-el-1847585413) [30 September 2023].
Sorokin, Vladimir (2011). Monoklon, Moskva: Ad Marginem.

## Chapter 7:
# Partisan, Anti-Partisan, pARTisan, Party-Zan, Cyberpartisan
## On the Popularity of Partisanhood in Belarusian Culture

*Nina Weller*

## 1. The Partisan Myth

In August 2020, an amateur video circulated on Belarusian social media that had been recorded from the window of a private flat in Minsk during protests against the Lukashenko [Lukashenka] regime. The video shows a group of OMON riot police clad in black balaclavas,[1] who form a chain across a wide street, attempting to block protesters from passing. They do not get very far with this effort, however, because numerous seemingly random passers-by unexpectedly encircle them from all sides and push them away, rendering them incapable of action. With music playing in the style of a silent film, the sped-up film reel conveys amusement about the fact that this 'partisan tactic' was able to foil the state authorities at least temporarily.[2]

As a pattern of resistance action, partisanhood always refers to the unequal relationship between mighty power structures and their weaker opponents, between the dominance of 'regular' forms of combat and the undermining of it through 'irregular' combat strategies. As irregular fighters, partisans defend the territory defined as their own which lies within a space occupied by the other. Since the publication of Carl Schmitt's book *Theory of the Partisan*, the partisan struggle has been defined primarily by decentralised action, mobility, surprising shifts between attack and retreat, and political (never purely personal) motivations for their engagement (Schmitt 1963).

---

1　OMON (*Otriad mobilniy osobogo nasnatchenia*), also known in Belarusian as AMAP (*Atrad militsyi asobaha pryznachennia*) is a special unit of the militia.
2　Cf. video on BelsatTV channel on X-Twitter: https://twitter.com/Belsat_TV/status/1300366799985356810 [30 September 2023].

*Figure 7.1: Screenshot from Belsat-TV on X-Twitter: "Belarusian women against men from riot police"*

Partisan tactics as strategies of resistance against an opponent occupying one's own territory are characteristic of Belarus in the 20th and 21st centuries. Partisan fighting on the territory of present-day Belarus dates to the 19th century. But it was not until the Soviet-Belarusian partisan struggle against the German occupation in the 'Great Patriotic War' (World War II) – which became culturally entrenched in the 1960s as a national myth and to popularise and legitimise Soviet-Belarusian state politics of memory and history – that the partisan became a central point of reference in Belarusian discourses of identity. Yet for decades, partisan tactics have also informed the Belarusian population's resistance to the increasingly totalitarian Lukashenko regime, which culminated in protests in August 2020 against fraudulent elections, with protesters demonstrating for democratic change and against repressive violence. Since the beginning of the large-scale Russian attack on Ukraine in February 2022, partisan tactics have for the first time since World War II again become relevant in a concrete state of war, in the sense that self-proclaimed partisan groups are together resisting Russia's great power ambitions.

The partisan is, in line with Roland Barthes' *Mythologies*, a figure through which, in Belarusian culture, history is transformed into everyday mythologies and a simulation of the past is completed which can always be reproduced and transformed anew for the present day. In Barthes' understanding, the success of the mythology lies in the fact that its message is never directly questioned, but rather is taken for granted, and its unconscious collective meaning is constantly reinforced by new material, through which the myth fundamentally reproduces itself continually (Barthes 2006 [1957]).[3] This also holds true for the partisan myth. I will discuss this below by tracing how the myth of the heroic partisan and of Belarus as a 'partisan republic' has been, and continues to be, shaped and generated by media and repeatedly transformed in popular culture in ever-shifting forms of appropriation, recoding and counter-mythologising.

## 2. "Partisan Republic": The Partisan as National Myth

In Belarus to this day, the central pillars of official war remembrance are the victory of the Soviet Union over Nazi Germany and the Belarusian civilian population's tragic experience of violence and annihilation during World War II.[4] After the war, the embedding of these experiences and memories in the collective work of commemoration created official places of remembrance and of personal and familial grief, but also always served to stylise the war as a struggle in defence of the Soviet homeland.[5] It is well known that during World War II, Soviet partisans also fought against the Nazi occupiers in the Ukrainian and Baltic Soviet republics, in Crimea, in the Caucasus and in Russia. However, it is only in Belarus that the overarching Soviet cult of the Great Patriotic War came to focus so strongly on the partisan struggle as a patriotic justification for an autonomous national identity.[6] Thus emerged the mythology of the partisan republic, which continued to be cultivated after 1991 as a *raison d'être* (Lewis 2017: 377) and a "calling card" (Sitnikova 2008: 413) of the country.

This myth essentially rests on three ideological conditions: first, the idea that resistance against the occupiers was sustained by the unity of all the Belarusian people; second, the idea of the selfless heroism of the partisan fighters; and third, the idea that all Belarusians made an unparalleled sacrifice for the Soviet fatherland[7], and that this sac-

---

3   On the connection between myth, history and the political in popular discourse, cf. also Pfister (2015).

4   During World War II, one in four to one in three Belarusians lost their lives; the number of victims was estimated at 2.2 million, of which 1.4 million belonged to the civilian population. Some 290 towns and 9200 villages were destroyed in the course of the German occupation and extermination policy (cf. Sahm, 2010: 43; Goujon 2010: 6–12; Marples 2012, 2014).

5   Cf. for more detail: Rudling 2008; Goujon 2010; Marples 2012 and above all Lewis 2017, who wrote the first seminal article on the significance of the partisan myth in Belarusian culture in the 1990s-2000s.

6   This development is at best comparable to the Yugoslavian partisan cult, which also reaches from socialist culture far into contemporary popular culture (cf. Jakiša 2015).

7   "Vsenarodnost'"; "Samootverzhennyi geroizm"; "Bespretsedentnaia zhertvennost'" (cf. Sitnikova 2008: 413, 424).

rifice made a crucial contribution to victory.[8] However, the notion of regional partisan identity existed long before World War II. It can be traced back to the concept of Bolshevik nationalities policy which was essentially developed by Lenin during World War I in response to the nationalism of the workers, a concept which demanded along with the proletarian revolution a national liberation of the nationalities that had been repressed in the 'prison of nations' of the Tsarist empire; this included the Belarusians. The White Ruthenian Democratic Republic proclaimed under German occupation in 1918 was famously short-lived; however, by early January 1919, after the collapse of the German Empire, the Bolsheviks proclaimed the Belarusian Soviet Socialist Republic, which was to become a founding member of the Union of Soviet Socialist Republics (USSR) in 1922. In the first years of the Soviet Union, the young republic enjoyed a relatively large degree of autonomy, which was intended, in the spirit of Bolshevik "affirmative action policy", to foster the national liberation of the people on the path to socialism through comprehensive language and cultural education (Martin 2001). In the context of this nationalities policy[9], the figure of the Belarusian partisan, who from 1918 to 1921 had fought alongside the Bolsheviks in the civil war and especially in the Polish-Soviet War[10], proved to be an ideal projection surface for developing the notion of the Belarusian people as fighters for a bright socialist future. In 1929, for example, the partisan motif was one of six guiding themes of the Third All-Belarusian Art Exhibition. Many of the paintings exhibited there were devoted to the theme of the partisan as a specifically Belarusian topos, including famed paintings by Gavriil Vier [Gaŭvril' Vier, Gabriel Wier] (1927), Mikhail Ėndė (1928) and Valiantsin Volkaŭ (1928), all of which were entitled *Partizany*.[11] The art historian Siarhei Kharėŭski notes that these works display an established canon of iconography, showing "men in farmer's attire with an ammunition belt slung across their shoulder, weapon in hand, carrying an axe in their belt" against the backdrop of a stereotypical landscape, most often a forest in winter (Kharėŭski 1999, as cited in Sitnikova: 2008: 398). While cinema and literature of the interwar period focused more on the Polish-Soviet War or the resistance against the Polish occupation, in visual art the opponent or occupier against whom the partisan struggle was directed remained vague in most representations in the 1920s (Sitnikova 2008: 400).[12] Kharėŭski therefore refers to exemplary representations of a "Belarusian partisanhood that defends itself against outsiders" (ibid.). This non-specific representation of the Belarusian partisan, however, soon took

---

8   The fact that the partisan movements on Belarusian territory were anything but uniform and that there were also Belarusian national partisan groups fighting against the Soviets was and is largely excluded from the official discourse (cf. Chiari 2001; Musial 2007, 2009).

9   A phase of language and cultural Belarusification was followed by a change in the party line in the early 1930s and a campaign to combat 'local nationalism', as a result of which the Belarusian intelligentsia were subjected to a repressive policy of persecution (deportations and mass shootings).

10  On earlier partisan battles on Belarusian territory, cf. Akudovich 2013:58-69; cf. Artsimovich 2016 [2021].

11  Cf. Kharėŭski 1999; Arcimovich 2016 [2021].

12  According to Dar'ia Sitnikova, this was also due to the fact that it was unclear which country could be considered one's own and who was to be defined as a "foreigner" and "outsider" (whether Poles, Germans, White Guards or even Soviet Russia itself) and thus as an "opponent", which is why the Belarusians tended to play the "role of a spectator without a voice" (Sitnikova 2008: 401).

on a significantly more political cast in films, and the figure of the village activist, filled with Bolshevik ideals, who fights for a new classless society against imperial German and Polish oppression, began to appear with increasing frequency.[13] This also represented a shift in the image of partisans themselves: "in place of the 'insurgent masses of the people', a 'heroic (Belarusian) people' was needed. A new war was needed, so that the fable could finally become a myth" (Sitnikova 2008: 412).

This new war arrived with the German invasion of the Soviet Union on 22 June 1941: during the period of war and occupation, the Soviet press imbued the figure of the partisan with heroic and mythological traits. Ekaterina Keding uses representations of partisan warfare in the newspaper *Pravda* from July 1944 to show how it was now presented as a "particular expression of popular ingenuity, of agility, of slyness, of unstoppable courage and plotting" (Keding 2013: 82).[14] The German invasion was understood as an "attack on the historical right of the Belarusian people to their own statehood" and the partisan war as an expression of the "remarkable qualities of the Belarusian people, their bravery and their heroism" (Lindner 2005, as cited in Artsimovich 2016 [2021], cf. Richter 2014).

After the end of the war, references to the partisan struggle served, as Keding emphasises, "above all a function in the post-war society of integration, legitimization and mobilization": "The partisan was supposed to unify a people divided between resistance and collaboration and to mobilise the Belarusian people for the work of building the Soviet Union and for socialist ideals" (Keding 2013: 82, 85). At the same time, national rhetoric now receded, while the overarching popular myth of the Soviet Union as a whole came to the fore: the Belarusian partisans were presented as part of the collective struggle against fascism of all peoples of the Soviet Union, who in turn would not have been able to operate so successfully without the support and solidarity of the simple people in the countryside, who had given them shelter, food and support.

The 1960s saw the phase of constituting the partisan myth, which now referred almost exclusively to World War II, while earlier imagery and stories from the civil war faded into the background: in the Brezhnev era, according to Nina Tumarkin, the Great Patriotic War became a "sacrosanct cluster of heroic exploits that had once and for all proven the superiority of communism over capitalism" (Tumarkin 1994: 5). For the Belarusian Soviet Socialist Republic, this meant large-scale glorification of the partisan struggle, including in public spaces. Piotr Macherov [Mašėraŭ], who became the first secretary of the Belarusian Communist Party in 1965 and who himself had fought as a partisan in World War II, played a crucial role in this project. There was already a Belarusian Museum of the

---

13  For example, the films *Tale of the Woods* (*Lesnaia byl'* 1926, directed by Iuri Tarich), an adaption of the novel *Svinopas* by Mikhas Charot; *The Pines Are Noisy* (*Sosny shumiat*, 1929, directed by Leonid Molchanov), an adaption of the novel *Dva* (1925) by Anatol Volnyi; the play *Partisany* by Kondrat Krapiva (1937); the film *11 July* (*11 Iulia*, 1938, directed by Iuri Tarich) cf. Sitnikova 2008: 400) as well as the novel *Dryhva* (*The Quagmire*, 1934) by Iakub Kolas in which a Soviet partisan (Ded Talash) from the era of the Polish-Russian war in 1941 rejoins the partisans and is supposed to testify to the fact that the entire Belarusian people joined the partisan struggle (cf. Gorbunov et al. 1961: 454, quoted by Lewis 2017: 378).

14  The medal "To the Partisan of the Patriotic War", introduced in 1943, also indicates the important role the partisan struggle played in Soviet propaganda already during the war (cf. for more detail Keding 2013: 82).

Great Patriotic War and a victory monument dedicated to Soviet soldiers and partisans had been erected on Victory Square in Minsk in 1954. Now, however, numerous streets in Minsk and throughout the country were renamed after war heroes and additional monuments to partisans and victory were built in almost every city (Lastoŭski et al. 2010: 266). This era also saw the creation of major national memorials with an almost sacred character, such as the Khatyn Memorial complex (Memorialnyi kompleks Khatyn,1969), the Mound of Glory (Kurhan Slavy, 1969) and Brest Hero Fortress (Brestskaia krepost'[Brestskaia krepost'],1971). Additionally, in 1978 Minsk became the last of a series of Soviet cities to be bestowed the title 'Hero City'.

Even after the end of the Soviet Union, this tradition of official war memorials and heroes' memorials was carried on: along with the creation of numerous new war memorials, an outdoor-adventure memorial theme park was opened outside Minsk, on what was dubbed the 'Stalin Line'[15], in 2005 for the 60th anniversary of the war's end. The new theme park included a Stalin memorial and tourist attractions featuring military technology.[16] This new 'Stalin Line' shows that critical engagement with Stalinism is officially unwelcome under Lukashenko. Additionally, this positive framing of Stalin broke a taboo in post-Soviet commemoration practices, given that in 2005, creating new Stalin memorials, let alone placing them in a context of entertainment and leisure, would (unlike today) most likely have caused a scandal even within Russia (even the renaming of Volgograd as Stalingrad since 2013 has taken place only temporarily on the occasion of war remembrance days). In 2014, Lukashenko had a new museum of the Great Patriotic War built, which was intended to symbolically represent an independent Belarus's own perspective on war remembrance by taking up the Soviet narratives but adapting and modifying them to fit the national discourse. The Soviet representation of the heroic partisan struggle thus continues to this day to inform official state initiatives for the formation of national memory in Belarus, as attested to by the traditional cult of heroism that is evident on days of remembrance and in history books, museum presentations of partisans, and multimedia projects commemorating World War II.[17]

---

[15] The "Stalin Line" is the name of the Red Army's western defence line, which ran from Karelia to the Black Sea and along the former USSR's border with Poland. In contrast to Western Europe, where similar fortifications were demolished, much of the line remained or was largely ignored after the collapse of the USSR in 1991. Remains of the fortifications of the Stalin Line can be found today in Belarus, Russia, Ukraine and the Republic of Moldova.

[16] Official site of the Stalin Line Park: https://stalin-line.by [30 September 2023].

[17] E.g. shifting the National Day of Remembrance from 27 July (Independence Day) to 3 July (the day of the end of the German occupation in 1944); the newly built Museum of the History of the Great Patriotic War, built in 2014; the representation of partisan images in public spaces to mark "Victory Day"; the multimedia project "Belarus Remembers" ("Belarus pomnit"), produced to mark the 75th anniversary of the end of the war: http://storyofvictory.sb.by/ [30 September 2023], etc.

## 3. "Partizanfil'm": Partisans and their Heroism in Post-War Film

Post-war Soviet cinema played an important role in popularising the figure of the partisan as a war hero and folk hero. Along with literary non-fiction, memoirs and novels[18], (war) film was *the* medium that played an essential part in canonising the myth. The state film studios produced so many war films that the Belarusfilm studio, founded in 1926, was ironically dubbed the Partizanfil'm studio for its perceived high output of partisan films. It was alleged that one out of every two films produced there after the war was devoted to the war; this claim was in fact greatly exaggerated.[19] Most of the 17 partisan films created in total were produced between the end of the Khrushchev Thaw and the early 1970s, after which the studio's interests shifted towards mainstream genres such as comedy, melodrama and adventure films.

One of the first films produced by Belarusfilm in the post-war era was *Konstantin Zaslonov* (1949, directed by Aleksandr Faintsimmer and Vladimir Korsh-Sablin), which defined the format for the aesthetic treatment of the war theme in Belarusian cinema for years to come (Sitnikova 2008: 426; Lewis: 2017: 377).

The film tells of the legendary resistance activities of the real-life figure Konstantin Zaslonov, who commanded Soviet partisan units between 1941 and 1942 in the Orsha region. He appears in the film as a flawless fighter for the Soviet cause, who takes a stand both for country-wide resistance and for the Party line. This highly ideological film, which was awarded the third-class Stalin Prize in 1950, is one of few works to pass muster with the censors at the peak of post-war Stalinism and the Cold War.

The film *The Clock Stopped at Midnight* (*Chasy ostanovilis v polnoch'*, 1959, directed by Nikolai Figurovskii) likewise conveys the notion of the 'nationwide partisan war', now narrated through the more complex expressive possibilities permitted to films in the Khrushchev Thaw era. The plot centres on a real-life event: the September 1943 assassination of Nazi official Wilhelm Kube, the *Generalkommissar* of the *Generalbezirk Weissruthenien* region of occupied Belarus and the *Gauleiter* of occupied Minsk. The film stylises two partisans who carried out the attack while disguised as maids, Ganna Chërnaia [Hanna Chernia] and Marina Kazanich, as heroes of the people. The film thereby introduced two female protagonists to the partisan myth for the first time; however, it was not solely due to their individual achievements, but above all through the invoking of the collective

---

18    E.g. collections such as Unconquered Belarus: Memoirs and Articles about the Nationwide Partisan Movement in Belarus during the Great Patriotic War (Nepokorennaia Belorussiia. Vospominaniia i stati o vsenarodnom partizanskom dvizhenii v Belorussii v gody Velikoi Otechestvennoi voiny. 1941–1945 gg., 1962), The Nationwide Partisan Movement in Belarus during the Great Patriotic War. June 1941–1944 (Vsenarodnoe partizanskoe dvizhenie v Belorussii v gody Velikoi Otechestvennoi voiny. Iun 1941–Iul 1944), 1967–1982); Memoirs of partisan commanders such as Partisan Chronicle (Partizanskaia khronika, 1961) by Aleksandr Vaupshasov, Partisan Republic (Partizanskaia respublika, 1964) by Petr Kalinin or Faithful to the End and Special People (Veren do kontsa and Liudi Osobogo Sklada, 1973) by Vasili Kozlov among others.

19    Daria Sitnikova has pointed out that the numbers were different in reality: among the 250 Belarusfilm productions from 1946 to 1983, there were ultimately only 18 partisan films (including children's films), i.e. only slightly more than 7 per cent, in which the partisans were the main or key theme (Sitnikova 2008: 425).

struggle of the people as a whole, which transcended boundaries of gender and education, that they could be presented as heroes. The film attracted 34.8 million viewers (Kudriavtsev 1998: 419), making it a Soviet blockbuster and showing how much its subject matter resonated with audiences at the time.

*Figure 7.2: Film poster for the film* Konstantin Zaslonov *(1949)*

The Film also played a major role in shaping the image of the partisan struggle as a matter of intergenerational identification. Other extremely popular post-war films include *The Children of the Partisan* (*Deti partizana*, 1954) and *Girl Seeks Father* (*Devochka ischet ottsa*, 1959), both directed by Lev Golub, which expanded the partisan myth to the younger Soviet generation by focusing on children and young people.

*Figure 7.3: Film posters for the films* The Children of the Partisan *(1954) and* Girl Seeks Father *(1959)*

*The Children of the Partisan*, the first Belarusian colour film, is set in the post-war era, with a plot centred on honourable remembrance of partisans: the children of two partisan fighters who died in service of the fatherland are lured into a trap by a former Nazi collaborator who fears being exposed. But with the help of their grandparents, the children escape and bring the villains to justice; in the end, the rightful order is restored. The film *Girl Seeks Father* tells the story of the young daughter of partisan commander Bat'ka Panas. The girl is taken into the care of an old forester, then is captured by the Nazi occupiers, who want to use her to force the partisan leader to capitulate. A heroic sabotage operation by the shrewd partisans thwarts the Nazis' plan. Both films illustrate the intergenerational power of the partisan myth. The films' use of the myth brought enormous success, especially for *Girl Seeks Father*, which became one of the most popular children's films in the Soviet Union with some 35 million viewers (Kudriavtsev 1998: 418, 420) and was also well-received internationally (Beliaev 2023).[20] This success was surely due in part to the film's linking of the partisan theme with adventure motifs (searching for the father, freeing the girl from the Nazis' clutches) and was also related to the fact that in the Soviet

---

20   Cf. the list of the most successful Soviet films between 1940 and 1989, compiled and annotated by cinema critic Sergei Kudriavtsev on the basis of statistics. According to this list, *Girl Seeks Father* is, along with the film *What Is It, the Sea?* (*Kakoe ono, more*, 1964: Ėduard Bocharov), one of the two all-time most-viewed children's films in the Soviet Union (Kudriavzev 1997: 410–442). The film critic Vadim Beliaev lists the film as one of the top 10 Belarusian box-office hits and, referring to data from Goskino, rates it as a highly successful film internationally, with releases in 75 countries. Unfortunately, Beliaev's further information on Goskino, among others, is currently not available (Beliaev 2023).

Union, entire school classes and Young Pioneer groups collectively attended showings of films that were considered especially important ideologically and educationally. Through this, the film became widely known and made an essential contribution to the production of the myth.[21]

## 4. "The Cinematic Partisan": The Psychological Turn in War Films (1960s-1980s)

The partisan film peaked near the end of the Khrushchev Thaw period, amidst the entrenchment of the Soviet war myth in history and politics under Brezhnev and Masherov. In this era of "Kinopartisanstvo" (Sitnikova 2008: 426), the partisan myth developed a particular allure, as its cultural function was twofold: it was not only a projection surface for heroic Soviet-nationalist war memory, but also served as a site of individual and psychological grappling with traumatic experiences of the war and the occupation.[22] On one hand, this period saw the making of a number of "showpiece films" (*paradnyi*), which were marked by an epic "fusion of Stalinist placard heroism and mass tragedy" (Sitnikova 2008: 430).[23] They include works such as *Father* (*Bat'ka*, 1971, directed by Boris Stepanov), *Flame* (*Plamia*, 1974) and *The Black Birch* (*Chernaia berëza*, 1977, both directed by Vital' Chatsverykoŭ [Vitalii Chetverikov]), as well as the first made-for-TV works, such as the miniseries *Time Has Chosen Us* (*Vremia vybralo nas*, 1976–1979, directed by Mikhail Ptashuk). They typify the reproduction en masse of an entrenched partisan myth in these years.[24] A second direction evident in this period is the psychological partisan film, which more starkly centres the individual experience of war in its plot. Like the so-called 'lieutenant prose' of this era, these works explored personal dimensions and morally ambiguous victim-and-perpetrator stories that went beyond simplistic friend-or-foe constellations. One of the pioneering 'psychological' partisan films is Viktor Turov's *Through the*

---

21   Another indication that the film was produced with some effort is the fact that, according to Beliaev, around 900 children tried out for the role of little Lenochka. The role was played by the later well-known actress Anna Kamenkova, who had caught the eye of a crew member in the playground with her open-minded and dominant qualities (Beliaev 2013).

22   Regarding the psychological aspect, Sitnikova justifiably mentions in literature the widely distributed works of Vasyl Bykaŭ and Ales' Adamovich, and in art the famous paintings *Partizanskaia madonna* (1967) by Mikhail Savitskii (followed in 1978 *Minskaia partizanskaia madonna*) and *Belarus'-mat' partizanskaia* (1967) by the artist Mai Dantsig.

23   Cf. on the topic of public history and popular Soviet cinema as myth-maker Tumarkin 1994 and Youngblood 2001.

24   During this period the canon was expanded by historically and politically sacralised heroic places: numerous films from the 1970s contributed to the popularisation of the image of Brest as a place of heroic resistance against the German invaders in the first days of the Great Patriotic War, which only loosely corresponded to historical reality, such as the multi-part *The Ruins Are Shooting* (*Ruiny Streliaiut*, 1970–72, dir.: Vital' Chatsverykoŭ [Vitalii Chetverikov]) or the films *I Am a Fortress, I Stood my Ground* (*Ia – Krepost', Vedu Boi*, 1972, dir: Izrail Pikman) and *Brest Fortress* (*Brestskaia Krepost'*, 1975, dir: Pikman). The partisan of the cinema and TV epics of the time had, as Sitnikova aptly diagnoses, been transformed into a "simulacrum", into a "monumental, decorative façade that no longer conceals a powerful imperial ideology of a totalitarian kind" (Sitnkokova 2008: 431).

*Cemetery* (*Cherez kladbishche*, 1964), which was the first such film not to place a party functionary at the centre of its plot as the leader of the people's resistance and to eschew exaggerated heroism and optimism. Instead, it showed internally contradictory characters, who acted out of doubt rather than conviction.[25] Such films were able to connect the presentation of the Belarusian people's resistance struggle and their suffering in war with existential questions without being accused of "anti-heroism" by party loyalist critics (Sitnikova 2008: 428). In the 1960s, this formed the foundation of a humanist hero ethos, to which later generations also felt connected.

Two additional films by Viktor Turov played a key role in the development: his screen adaptations of Ales' Adamovich's duology of novels *Partisans* (*Partisany*), comprised of *War Under the Roofs* (*Voina pod kryshami*, 1960) and *Sons Go into Battle* (*Synov'ia ukhodiat v boi*, 1963), which appeared in 1967 and 1969. The films tell of the fate of a mother and her two sons, who join the partisans during the war. Both the novels and their film adaptations are still anchored in a heroic mode of storytelling in that their plots follow the traditional narrative of the sacrificial struggle for survival and resistance which is borne by the partisans and the general population together. But they also use family and neighbourhood entanglements to show the irreconcilable moral dilemmas and human depths of war.[26] The popularity of the films and of Adamovich's books[27] was amplified by the casting of high-profile actress Nina Urgant in the role of the mother and by the fact that the film featured music by Vladimir Vysotskii, arguably the most popular Soviet singer of the era. Vysotskii remained a cult figure even after his death; he was well loved for his blissful songs about the Great Patriotic War and for his critical, ironic lyrics about everyday life in the Soviet Union. His song titled *Sons Go into Battle* (*Synovia ukhodiat v boi*)[28] played a major part in the popularity of the second film.

However, the psychologically nuanced characters, especially in the first film, which was released in 1967, met with harsh criticism from the authorities and the State Committee for Cinematography. Turov and Adamovich (who had written the screenplay for both films) were accused, among other things, of lack of heroic pathos, preference for traitorous characters rather than strong ones, and failure to designate clear villains.[29]

---

25  In this film, "the individual stands above the social, the war and the occupation situation serve only as a backdrop to raise existential questions" (Sitnikova 2008: 427).

26  Adamovich's own mother served as a model for the psychologically illuminated fate of Anna Korzun, who actively supports the partisans despite the great risk and ultimately saves her sons from the Germans by joining the partisans together with them. The book and film represented a new look at the underestimated role of women in war and were to be a major inspiration for Svetlana Aleksievich's book *The Unwomanly Face of War* (*U voiny ne zhenskoe litso*, 1985). Aleksievich's famous title goes back to Adamovich's introductory motto to *War Under the Roofs*: "War has no female face. But no memory of this war was stronger, more harrowing, more terrible and more beautiful than that of the faces of our mothers" (Adamovich: *Voina pod kryshami*. Minsk 1960, 5).

27  Their popularity is not so much reflected in large audience or sales figures (they do not appear on the lists of Kudriavtsev et al.), but rather in terms of their canonisation in the field of psychological partisan films, to which frequent reference is made to this day.

28  A video of the song with film images is available on YouTube: https://www.youtube.com/watch?v=ounQy6JWQoo [30 September 2023].

29  For the argumentation of the criticism against Turov and Adamovich, see in detail: Historiya kinamastatstva Belarusi. 1960–1985 (2002: 100–103), quoted in Sitnikova 2008: 429 as well as Shal-

For the 1969 second film, then, Turov and Adamovich had to make compromises in the direction of a more heroic depiction of the partisan struggle[30], which did not hinder the popularity of the two films or the long-term expansion of the partisan myth to include psychological dimensions.

Ultimately, however, this psychology-focused approach persistently chipped away at the partisan myth. Two films that became classics of Soviet-Belarusian film history show this particularly clearly in that they address violence, fear and doubt, and show the surmounting of these without any resolution, also connecting these themes with religious motifs. The first of these is *The Ascent* (*Vozchozhdenie*, 1976) directed by Larisa Shepit'ko and based on the story *Sotnikaŭ* by Vasyl Bykaŭ, which tells of complicated confrontations between partisans, villagers and collaborators. Its protagonist does not follow the code of loyalty, but rather – entangled in moral doubt and hope for rescue – betrays both his comrades and his ideals. Despite the authorities' misgivings about the film, it debuted on 2 April 1977, and although there were few copies of it, was seen by more than ten million viewers within the Soviet Union (Vasil'eva/Braginskii 2012: 313). It was the first-ever Soviet film to be awarded a Golden Bear at the Berlinale.

The second such film, Ėlem Klimov's *Come and See* (*Idi i smotri*, 1985), likely the best-known of all Belarusian-Soviet anti-war films, focusses radically on physical and psychological experience of the horrors of war. The film was made in 1977 but was censored by the Soviet authorities before it was completed and was blocked from release for years, due to accusations of, among other things, "simplification", "abstract humanism" and a perspective "not related to class" (as cited in Stiglegger 2020: 170). Ales' Adamovich had written the film's screenplay, and elements of his short story *Khatyn Story* (*Khatynskaia povest'*), which was published in 1972, were incorporated into it. Klimov rendered the story with disturbing images and intense sound collages. From the perspective of a teenage boy, the film recounts the partisan struggle and the horrific massacres of Belarusian civilians by German troops, transposing the presentation of the war onto a reality where everything – people, animals and nature alike – is touched by utter destruction and moral despair. Here, the partisan is no longer a heroic figure, but rather both victim and perpetrator, and above all a human being who is bound up in the inescapable atrocities of war. After years of censorship, the film finally reached cinemas in 1985 as a co-production of Mosfil'm and Belarusfilm; it found an audience of almost 30 million people in the Soviet Union alone. It remains the most internationally well-known Soviet-Belarusian war film to this day and was re-released in a restored Blu-Ray version in 2020. In the film, little remains of the heroic dimension of the partisan myth, but its radical depiction of the abject abyss of war from the perspective of a child partisan carries on the figure of the partisan with merciless realism.

---

nuivski 1971, quoted in Sitnikova: 2008: 430 and in: Vse belorusskie filmy. Catalogue spravochnik. Vol. 1: Igrovoe Kino. 1926–1970 (1996: 222).
30   Cf. for more detail, among others Karpilava et al. 2002: 103.

## 5. Partisans in Films of the 2000s: Nationalisation, De-Glorification, Deconstruction

At the end of the Soviet Union, the heroism and psychology that had ultimately been two sides of the same mythological construction began to break apart. In the context of Belarus becoming an independent country, the partisan myth now took on its own dynamics: in the 1990s, film production at Belarusfilm, the country's only major film studio, largely collapsed, which was due in part to economic factors and the reorientation of the film industry and in part to the shift in the orientation of public discourses of history and memory. Other themes now came to the fore, such as the Grand Duchy of Lithuania as the foundational period for a new version of national history.[31] At the same time, the first publications by independent historians appeared, which sought to revise the partisan myth and also challenged the conventional narrative of the civilian population's unconditional support for the partisans (cf. Lindner 1999, 2001; Artsimovich 2021). The election of Lukashenko as president in 1994 brought an abrupt end to this shift in perspective in the public discourse of history.[32] While the state and those representations which conformed to the official politics of history took on the Soviet construct of nationality in modified form, others began to revise the partisan myth in various ways or even to reinvent it entirely. This trend became increasingly evident beginning in the 2000s and follows two strands in film.

The first strand recycles the partisan myth in a certain sense, along the lines of the alternative concepts to notions of 'nostalgia' or 'trauma' which Valery Vyugin proposes in this volume, according to which historical narratives are "reused and resold" as "a resource" and are shaped into new forms to fit current needs (cf. Vyugin, chapter 10 in this volume). Numerous publicly financed Belarusfilm war film productions of the 2000s carried on the traditional Soviet image of the Belarusian folk hero in a new patriotic guise and with updated film technology (Khatkovaskaia 2013: 435). Two examples of this are films that both represent the staging of official national politics of memory under Lukashenko as "memory events par excellence" (Etkind 2010: 4, as cited in Lewis 2012: 379): first, the war drama *Deep Flow* (*Glubokoe techenie*, 2005, directed by Margarita Kasymova and Ivan Pavlov), the first Belarusian film in Dolby Surround, which uses the example of a young commanding officer to tell of responsibly overcome difficulties of the partisan struggle early in the occupation period. Not coincidentally, the film is based on motifs from a 1949 novel of the same name by Ivan Shamiakin, which was celebrated by Soviet critics at the time as the first real partisan novel and was awarded the Stalin Prize.[33] The second example is the monumental blockbuster *The Brest Fortress* (*Brestkaia Krepost'*, also known as *Fortress of War*, 2010, directed by Aleksandr Kott), which was created in co-production with several major Russian studios. The film rehashes topoi of the Soviet war canon: the "heroic defence of Brest Fortress" and the tenacious Belarusian

---

31   Cf. Hansen 2008: 187–196; Krawatzek/Weller 2022: 27–40; Weller 2022: 59–74.
32   On the politics of history under Lukashenko, cf. Lindner 1999: 423–477; Goujon 2010; Rudling 2017: 77.
33   Inessa Khatkovskaia classifies the film as the first and only "true national" (partisan) film (Khatkovskaia 2008: 437).

resistance against the German Wehrmacht in June 1941. Despite the Soviet side's swift defeat at Brest Fortress, party ideologues constructed a heroic narrative soon after the war (Ganzer 2021) which connected the Red Army's defence of the Fortress with partisan resistance. It was not until the Khrushchev Thaw period, however, that this narrative became widely known through the books *Brest Fortress* (*Brestskaia krepost'*, 1957) and *Heroes of Brest Fortress* (*Geroi Brestskoi kreposti*, 1961), which were written by the famous war reporter and Lenin Prize winner Sergei Smirnov based on witness accounts and interviews, and which made the fortress a symbolic site of memory, particularly in Belarus (Lewis 2011: 379). The significance that the post-Soviet Belarusian state attached to the recycling of the Soviet partisan myth is also evident in the tremendous financial expenditure and organisational effort that was invested in the production and distribution of the two films. Both films were Belarusian-Russian co-productions and were produced under Lukashenko's patronage. According to Khatkovskaia, *Deep Flow* broke all records for state funding and was introduced by the President himself at its premiere at the October cinema in Minsk. As for *Brest Fortress*, its production costs totalled some eight million dollars, and the film's premiere was promoted as one of the most important events of the 2000s wave of war films. The premiere was laden with symbolism: timed to coincide with the 69th anniversary of the Nazi invasion of the USSR, it was held on-site at the Brest Fortress memorial, as part of a grandiose memorial ceremony.

A second direction in recent Belarusian film, on the other hand, continues an individualised and psychological mode of narrating the war; these films de-glorify the partisan myth and in some cases deconstruct it. While the characters in the previously mentioned blockbusters display psychological nuance and internal conflicts, distinguishing them sharply from the epic works of the Soviet era, this ultimately serves solely to attest to the heroic pathos of the collective struggle. By contrast, newer adaptations of literary works by Vasyl Bykaŭ and Ales' Adamovich tie in with the late Soviet film adaptations of these authors' work, which address the bleak and brutal aspects of the partisan struggle from the perspective of the individual. These include *Franz + Polina* (2006, directed by Mikhail Segal), a film based on Adamovich's novel *The Deaf* (*Nemoi*, 1993), along with several films and a graphic novel based on Bykaŭ's story *Ours* (*Svaiaki*,1966)**,** as well as the award-winning film *In the Fog* (*V tumane*, 2012) by Sergei Loznitsa, based on a story of the same name by Bykaŭ (1989). In the latter work, the Belarusian-Ukrainian director Loznitsa treats the partisan struggle as a mere backdrop for the unspectacular but existential conflicts of individuals in times of war: each of the film's three characters tries to follow their own moral compass, but none of them remain morally unscathed.

*Mysterium Occupation* (*Okkupatsiia. Misterii* [*Akupatsyia Mistėryi*], 2004) directed by Andrėi Kudzinenka, set a highly provocative new direction. Its radical aim of dismantling the heroic partisan myth opened a new chapter in Belarusian cinema (Khatkovskaia 2008: 469). Even the fact that it was not produced by Belarusfilm, but rather by the independent Navigator Studio, was a minor sensation.[34] The film not only rejects the

---

34  Other critical films about national historical themes and the Soviet past crimes –such as Igor Kuznetsov's TV-documentaries *Katyn'. After 70 Years* (*Katyn. Praz 70 gadoŭ*, 2010) – about the mass murder of thousands of Polish officers and intellectuals by the NKVD in April 1940) and *The Stalin Line on a Child's Palm* (*Liniia Stalina na dzitsiachai daloni*, 2015) – dedicated to the youngest members

heroic meta-narrative, but also radically dismantles the categories of moral value set forth in the Soviet-Russian canon.[35] In micro-histories, it shows how daily life in an occupied country is shaped by desires, irrational choices, instincts, violence and sadism, with nobody distinguishing themselves through any heroic acts. The Belarusian culture ministry therefore banned the film on the grounds that it was unpatriotic and destructive, denying it a distribution licence for years,[36] which only attracted more interest in it in Belarusian online spaces and at international film festivals.[37]

*Figure 7.4: Film still from the film* Mysterium Occupation *(2004)*

But *Mysterium Occupation* not only dismantles (neo-) Soviet partisan heroism; through the paratextual framing of the plot, it also accentuates a negative state of "Belarusianness" as the actual national catastrophe: such "Belarusianness" is the end, the non-existence of Belarusian culture, or, as Simon Lewis aptly puts it, "the postcolonial mourning

of the Stalinist terror) or Vasil Hryn's documentary oral history film *The Third Truth* (*Tret'ia Pravda*, 2010) – in which people from the Polesian region talk about their life during Polish and Soviet rule) could have been shown only in an informal setting in these years (Sahm 2010: 53).

35   For more details on the film, see inter alia Gusakovskaia 2008; Bekus 2010: 229–233; Lewis 2011.
36   The state press accused the film and its director of, among other things, "slandering the partisan movement", TV-Kanal Kul'tura, 24. 06.2004 [22 November 2022, link not accessible]. The Ministry of Culture justified its decision by arguing that: "The treatment of the partisan movement in the film contradicts the truth, can hurt the feelings of war veterans and can have a negative impact on the education of the younger generation and young people" (Khatkovskaia 2008: 439). The film was first shown in Minsk in 2010.
37   The film was first screened as a short film at Filmfest Rotterdam and was able to be extended to a 90-minute feature-length film thanks to an award from the Dutch Film Fund. The longer version of the film was shown at numerous international film festivals.

for a past that cannot return and a present that is in ruins" (Lewis 2011: 377). A text superimposed on the beginning of the film states:

> 500 years ago, they did not know they were Belarusians, but their country was the largest in Europe. When they realized this, they no longer had a state of their own, and others considered them to be either incomplete Russians or defective Poles. But there still were some Belarusians. They got lumped together with the Soviet people. And then the war and occupation started. After this there were very few Belarusians left. Now the Belarusians have their own state. But there are no more Belarusians. (*Mysterium Occupation*)[38]

Here, director Kudinenko is addressing another myth, one which traces Belarusian identity to the era of the Grand Duchy of Lithuania and Polish-Lithuanian aristocratic culture as an anti-programme to the Soviet concept of nationalities. Inherent to this model, which was put forth by exponents of 'Belarusian rebirth', is the projection of national history backward onto the period of the Grand Duchy and onto the Belarusian Republic which existed for a few months in 1918 under German occupation. According to this model, Belarusian identity has always been formed in contrast to the dominant population group or in resistance to the occupying power.

But what is truly provocative about Kudinenko's interpretation is that he turns the paradox of this Belarusian identity into its essence: it is at the moment when the population are repressed and destroyed that they first gain an awareness of themselves as Belarusians. In this 'decolonial' reading, then, the existence of the Belarusian Soviet Socialist Republic is also a period of non-existence, as it had no autonomy under Soviet power. Correspondingly, the re-founding of Belarus as a nation can only take place through a radical deconstruction of all that is Soviet and thereby also of the Soviet partisan myth. In the end, all that can remain of the myth is its mere form, 'partisanhood' as a form of resistance and a therapeutic model for grappling with the absence of Belarusianness.[39] In his 2007 book *The Code of Absence* (*Kod adsutnaci*, 2007), the philosopher Valiantsin Akudovich took up this notion, which Kudinenko had generated through direct engagement with the Soviet partisan myth, expanding it into a comprehensive concept of identity.

---

[38] See the introduction to the film on Youtube, minute 0:00-0:52: https://www.youtube.com/watch?v=_s3_HqpVtSs [30 September 2023]. I quote the translation by Simon Lewis (Lewis 2012: 377).

[39] "For Belarus, the occupation is the main theme of its existence because our country has always been under occupation … . We wanted to speak about a traditional theme for Belarusian cinema, but at the same time to do it in our own way. All Belarusians are partisans and the subject of partisans and war is a sacred theme for Belarus." Kudienko in interview at the Moscow International Film festival in June 2004 (Kudinenko 2004).

## 6. "I'm not there": 'Partisan Identity' and the Anti-Partisan

Since the early 2000s, the figure of the partisan has been increasingly present in independent Belarusian culture as a concept of identity that creates a sense of commonality and is directed against state appropriation of the Soviet myth. In this figure, the main topoi of the partisan have shifted: in particular, the topos of collective 'resistance' against the German occupation in World War II has been gradually expanded to encompass any kind of 'occupation' past or present (Oushakine 2013). Two conceptualisations of partisanhood have especially gained tremendous popularity with the consolidation of Lukashenko's authoritarian presidential system and of the resistance against his regime's repressive restrictions: firstly, Akudovich's notion of a specific "partisan mentality" as a concept of national identity, as set forth in his much-cited book *Code of Absence* (*Kod adsutnaci*, 2007). And secondly, the concept of the "partisan artist", which the artist Artur Klinaŭ outlines in his cultural project *pARTisan* and which is focused more on subversive artistic practice. What the two concepts have in common, and what has made them so influential in contemporary popular culture, is that they pointedly make reference to the Soviet partisan myth and understand it as the true deviation from the Belarusian national tradition, or, more precisely, as an artificial, imperial construct, something 'foreign' that was forced on the Belarusian people through Soviet-Russian colonisation. At the same time, however, they appropriate the figure of the partisan, which is at the heart of this myth, but which is now used on behalf of the idea of a national rebirth and an 'authentic' Belarusianness in opposition to the Soviet 'occupier'. This figure is imagined not as a heroic warrior, but as a fighter without a weapon in hand, who defends the homeland with tactics of resistance and perseverance. According to Akudovich, this figure is an almost sacred embodiment of the Belarusian people and is a form of anticolonial self-description. Partisan life in the underground and the background is reinterpreted to possess a special quality of 'active absence':

> For the Belarusians, the word 'partisan' has long possessed a sacred meaning, which even the Soviet myth of the partisan movement could not take away from it. The Belarusian is a 'partisan' by nature – in his private life and as part of history. ... a partisan is someone who always hides. Hide-and-seek is probably the only national sport of the Belarusian people. A partisan always says: I'm not there. A partisan shows himself only in the interest of sabotage; afterwards, he hides again beneath his mask of 'I'm not there'. (Akudovich 2013: 68)[40]

Akudovich's alternative conception, then, adopts the form of the Soviet myth but reconstructs its content metonymically. He removes the partisan's two defining habits – hiding and sabotage – from their Soviet war context entirely; beyond this, he also postulates the original setting of the Soviet post-war myth –World War II era – as the real distortion

---

40   The original edition in Belarusian was published in 2007 under the title *Kod adsutnatsi. Asnovy belaruskai mental'nastsi* by the Minsk publishing house Lohvinaŭ. The translations into English are based on the German edition.

of history. He argues that the Soviet partisan struggle was forced on the Belarusian people as a foreign and ultimately self-destructive movement, and that the 'partisan' form of presence – acting in the background and adapting oneself – is ultimately far older (Akudovich 2013: 62, 170). This twofold revision enables him to transfer the qualities of the partisan as an ontological foundation for Belarusian identity backwards onto the entirety of its history and culture, which he claims shapes civilian everyday life to this day. Akudovich declares partisanhood to be the *conditio belarus*, a timeless and "sacred" habit that is to be found in all life situations and periods of history of the Belarusian people. And even where it completely invisible, he argues, it remains present, as the partisan mentality as a fundamental national habit is characterised by its disguising of itself. However, with this central part of his argument, Akudovich in turn takes up typically pan-Soviet habits of disguise, which – as Sheila Fitzpatrick has shown – spread throughout the country beginning in the 1920s and especially during the terror of the Stalin era (Fitzpatrick 2005).

Klinaŭ's conception of partisanhood is very similar to Akudovich's in its form but refers less to a national identity imagined to be timeless and more to a specific artistic strategy. For him, the Belarusian 'underground man' is someone who has, by retreating to a territory which he will defend and by defending his own culture from external influences, strategically adapted to his own country being ruled by authorities perceived as foreign (Klinaŭ 2014: 31). "For more than two hundred years, partisanhood has been an indispensable strategy of self-preservation, the only available survival technique for Belarusian culture" (Klinaŭ 2014: 26).

For Klinaŭ too, the Soviet partisan myth plays a key role: he defines it as the "Great Partisan" and sets it in opposition to the figure of the "anti-partisan". The latter fights not for heroic victories, but rather in the counter-world of the underground, against an authoritarian state regime and for his own survival and that of Belarusian culture.

> But the partisan is not just the heroic type with a weapon in hand, the fighter for the national cause. He is also a diagnosis: a pathological state of consciousness, with deep-rooted fears in response to historical trauma… From a psychological perspective, the Belarusian partisan is an underground man. His mission is not to triumph, but to survive. (Klinaŭ 2014: 28)

But for Klinaŭ, survival also means deconstructing the system of the Great Partisan in order to preserve the cultural code of Belarusian culture. In this, Klinaŭ's conception differs fundamentally from Akudovich's in that, while he too regards the Soviet myth as an aberration, he does not discard it entirely as a colonial construct foreign to Belarusian identity; rather, he recognises it as a national product of its own. He writes, for example, that the "development of the mythology of the Great Partisan" was "the most distinctive Belarusian cultural achievement of the Soviet era" (Klinaŭ 2014: 8). For him, the antagonism between what is one's own and what is foreign is not an ontological state of national identities, but rather a matter of succession: the Great Partisan figure that emerged from the 'colonial' Soviet context is supplanted by the anti-partisan or 'artist-partisan', who must subversively emancipate himself from the authoritarian and heroic legacy of his predecessor, becoming the true partisan (Klinaŭ 2014: 14–26).

## 7. *pARTisan*: TheArtist-Partisan as a Rebel against State Ideology

In the early 2000s, Artur Klinaŭ programmatically expanded his concept of the artist-partisan. For Klinaŭ, what was at stake was no less than the reconquest of the Belarusian cultural space and with it a comprehensive concept of partisan art that fought by subversive means to gain artistic autonomy. In works such as his installation *Partisan Mobile Shop (Mobil'nyi magazin partizana*, 2003), Klinaŭ shows that for him this was from the outset also a matter of differentiation from the official state partisan myth. In the installation, he displayed the retro-Soviet ideology of the Belarusian state as a cheap nostalgia article, like an exotic attraction.

But the cornerstone of Klinaŭ's project was the *pARTisan* art and culture magazine, which was founded in 2002 and sought to gather the independent arts scene together for the first time under the partisan label. In the first issue of *pARTisan*, Klinaŭ articulated the qualities ascribed to this rebellious partisan in a sort of 'partisan manifesto':

> The appropriation of spaces that the system is not able to penetrate constitutes the strength of the partisan. These spaces, the zones of the irrational, are inaccessible to the system, because the system a priori moves within the framework of rational discourse. At the same time, the partisan is superbly able to find his way in the labyrinth of the system. Because he knows the system's vulnerabilities, he can puncture it with pinpricks, then disappear into his safe haven on the other side of the mirror... (Klinaŭ 2014: 24)

For Klinaŭ and the *pARTisan* project, then, much more was at stake than creating exclusive spaces for autonomous art or, like the heroes of the film *The Matrix* (1999), of which the quote above is strongly reminiscent, solely retreating into subversive actions. Rather, the project represents the presence of independent creative artists in the spirit of an 'alternative partisanhood' as an "intellectual front", as also articulated by the philosopher Maks Zhbankoŭ: "It is very simple: partisans only appear in those places where an occupation has occurred. And in a country that has long been under cultural occupation, partisans of the intellectual front consequently appear" (Zhbankoŭ 2014, as cited in Strocaŭ 2014: 75).

One important point of reference for the *pARTisan* project was the programmatic multimedia photography project *Light Guerrilla Movement* (*Lëhki partyzanski rukh* [*Tikhoe partizanskoe dvizhenie*]), through which the artist Ihar Tsishyn [Igor' Tishin] had made a name for himself in 1997. A series of black-and-white photographs shows a man in partisan attire with a machine gun in his hand inside a typical hut like those seen in countless partisan films. One photograph provocatively shows the weapon in a dysfunctional state. The man does not hold the weapon at the ready to defend himself or to attack. On the contrary, he lies passively on a table and holds the weapon lackadaisically in his hand, like a useless object that has grown obsolete. Around him, time appears to stand still and the table to be the last safe refuge. In other images from the series, he starts moving, first inside the hut, then outside it, but nothing happens. In place of the hero of the Soviet and post-Soviet partisan myth, who is perpetually ready to fight, this scene is marked by a sense of excessive helplessness. Tsishyn's project was greeted by many as a manifesto and his partisan as a metaphor for Belarusian artists, who found themselves at a point of absolute emptiness at the turn of the century: in the late 1990s, alternative cultural life had largely ground to a halt due to increasing repression under the Lukashenko regime. The partisan became a symbol of the artist whose world had shrunk to the dimensions of a 'dissident' kitchen table. In this period, Tsishyn and many other dissenting artists emigrated abroad, as they saw no future prospects for themselves in Belarus (cf. Arcimovich 2016 [2021]); Shparaga 2013: 7–10). Klinaŭ's *pARTisan* project represented an attempt to counter this trend by offering an alternative within the country.

Figure 7.5: *Cultural magazine pARTisan, 2010/22*

During the 2010s, there were multiple phases in which state repression receded to a certain extent and small pockets of an alternative cultural life appeared to take hold within the few free spaces that the state authorities permitted. In a few scattered cases, the alternative and official cultural spheres even inched a bit closer to one another, for example, when rock bands that had previously been banned from performing were now able to perform even on state television (cf. Petz 2013: 2–7) or when critical artists received public funding.[41] The clear boundaries between the state 'occupier' and the resistance 'partisan', which had been fundamental to Klinaŭ's and Tsishyn's models of the partisan, now appeared to be obsolete. Even Akudovich called for a change in strategy: "The war of those days is over. Because the war we chose ended long ago without us, we just didn't notice the end... That is why *pARTisan* needs a radical shift in strategy so that it can remain partisan" (Akudovich 2014: 154). This shift in strategy did indeed come to pass, albeit in a very different way than expected, when in 2020 the regime responded to declining support among the population by holding fraudulent presidential elections, which led to massive protests, which in turn again updated the Soviet partisan myth and appropriated it in a form that strongly modified some aspects of it.

## 8. Partisanhood Reloaded: Between Resistance, Protest and War

To understand the boom in partisanhood during the protests of 2020–2021, one must take into account that the Soviet partisan myth had been reappropriated in many ways not only in the alternative intellectual and art scene, but also in commercial popular culture, on major websites and on social media. For example, in the film *Party-Zan* (2016) by Andrėi Kurėichik, young actors provocatively parody the myth in a storyline in which some young people seize on the obsessive production of war films in Belarus and shoot their own partisan film as a moneymaking scheme.[42] As early as 1997, the rock band N.R.M. (*Nezalezhnaia Rėspublika Mroia/Independent Republic of Dreams*), one of the most popular groups in the alternative scene, released the song *Partyzanskaia* on their album *Made in N.R.M.* Beginning in the style of war partisan songs, then shifting to a hard rock sound, the song features Belarusian-language lyrics that express the speaker's aversion to the present-day occupiers, an unmistakeable reference to the Lukashenko regime.[43] In 1999, the poet and singer Andrėi Khadanovich wrote the humorous poem *Pesnia Belorusskikh Partizan (Song of the Belarusian Partisans)*[44], which uses absurd rhymes, a Belarusian-Russian hybrid language, and the rhyming of 'partisans' with 'Tarzans' to undermine the heroic pathos of the myth.[45] The theme was also taken up in performance art, too, such as in "I am not...", a 2008 performance action by the artist Mikhail Gulin, in

---

41  Such as Klinaŭ himself, who in 2011 participated in the Belarusian pavilion at the 54th Venice Biennale, which was funded by the Ministry of Culture, and triggered critical discussions about whether independent art should be allowed to cooperate with a regime that extensively fights the idea of autonomous art (reference Petz 2013: 6, interview Klinaŭ).

42  Simon Lewis aptly speaks of "near-total carnivalization of the partisan trope, satirically mixing Hollywood-style comic debauchery with a mocking treatment of the country's traditional obsession with World War II" (Lewis 2017: 391).

43  See the refrain: "We are partisans, forest brothers. We are partisans, on familiar terms with war. We are partisans, we love our country. We'll cleanse our country from foreign bands." Translation by Lewis 2017: 387; Original song and full text on YouTube: https://www.youtube.com/watch?v=MSvwNjYsXgE [30 September 2023].

44  The poem was first published in the online edition of the magazine ARCHE (2/3, 1999), one of the most important independent platforms: https://arche.by [23 March 2023].

45  Cf. "O, Tarzans, forest Tarzans!, Long live the monkey King Kong! Off to camp went the Partisans, Off to faraway Hong Kong!" (Khadanovich 1999, translation by Lewis 2017: 387).

which he walked through Minsk and other cities with a sign on his chest proclaiming his non-identification with certain stereotypical attributes: "I'm not an amerikos" ("Ia – ne amerikos"), "I'm not gay" ("Ia – ne gei"), "I'm not a terrorist" ("Ia – ne terrorist"). He began the series with a sign written in German, which read "Ich bin kein Partisan" ("I'm not a Partisan"), evoking the German occupiers' punishment of Soviet partisans during World War II.[46] Gulin's work thereby inverts the historical form of public denunciation, making it into a personal reclaiming of public space (cf. Šparaha 2014).

*Belarusian Partisan (Belorusski Partisan)*[47], an independent media platform critical of the government which was founded in deliberate contrast to the state-sponsored platform *Partisans of Belarus (Partizany Belarusi)*[48], likewise made subversive use of the partisan myth, publishing information about events in the country that was omitted from the official news.[49]

All these widely divergent reappropriations of the partisan myth in popular culture, art and politics had the effect that during the dramatic events of summer and autumn 2020, the myth also played an important role in the protests against fraudulent elections, within a dynamic of recoding and reappropriation. For example, in a symbolically charged act on 16 August, in front of the Museum of the Great Patriotic War on Victory Square, a crowd of people wrapped the Minsk Hero City Obelisk and the Motherland statue (*Радзіма-маці*) in the white-red-white flag of the protests. Such impactful "acts of re-signification" (Bekus 2021) also appeared when subsequent demonstrations – fol-

---

46   Cf. Mikhail Gulin: "Ich bin kein Partisan": https://www.youtube.com/watch?v=olG701ZaE6w [30 September 2023].

47   Launched by Pavel Sharamet and a group of independent journalists in 2005, this platform was dedicated to uncensored information about events in Belarus, which is why it was repeatedly accused of "defiling the fatherland" and subjected to accompanying restrictions before it was declared "extremist" in November 2021 and closed down, including all channels on social networks.

48   This is a state database and educational project supported by the state-affiliated publishing house *Belarus Segodnia* and the *National Archives of Belarus*. In addition to the archiving and search function for historical data and individual fates, the platform is intended not only to keep alive the "memory of the Belarusian partisan struggle against Nazism", but also to cultivate the "patriotic education of the youth" and to explore an "expansion of the patriotic level of the population", which means that it is still clearly marked by the Soviet narrative. Cf. the homepage: https://partizany.by [30 September 2023]. Cf. the description of the project on the homepage: "The Partisans of Belarus project has been set up to perpetuate the memory of the Belarusian partisans who fought against the Nazis during the Great Patriotic War, to educate young people patriotically, to raise the civil and patriotic level of the population, and to intensify the search operations": https://partizany.by/about/ [30 September 2023].

49   The restrictions were justified by typical schemes of complaints from the population: state media published two letters of complaint from veterans' associations accusing "Belorusskii Partisan" of insulting all citizens of Belarus and the honour of veterans through their activity. Cf. "Griasnaia striapnia na saite 'Belorusskii partisan', oskorbliaet vsech zhitelei Belarussi." In: *News.21.By*, 30 March 2010: https://news.21.by/society/2010/03/30/524231.html [30 September 2023]) and "Ne oskorbliate veteranov." In: *Belarus Segodnia*, 26 February 2010: https://www.sb.by/articles/ne-oskorblyayte-veteranov.htm [30 September 2023]. Between 2010 and 2021, despite a change of server, the site was blocked several times, prosecuted, and declared extremist in November 2021, and thus discontinued all activities.

lowing a ban on demonstrations at Victory Square – were moved to Partisan Avenue and renamed a "Partisan March" ("Partizanskii marsh").[50]

However, tactics such as those used in the street action described at the beginning of this paper and used in coordinating protest actions via the Telegram channel *Nexta* played an even more prominent role in the protest and resistance movement. Referring to the protest movements of the 2010s, the sociologist Almira Usmanava [Ousmanova] defined such tactics as follows:

> The art of coming from ten different directions to gather at a specific spot, striking as planned, then scattering as quickly and inconspicuously as possible, only to pounce again in another spot. (Usmanava 2014: 109)

This partisan tactic is a "response to the 'situation' created by the regime, in which all protest is regarded as illegitimate violence" (Usmanava 2014: 109). This tactic – for which a new word, the verb *partisanits* (rus. *partisanit'*), has been established – was also deployed in other forms of public protest and flash mob actions. These included inconspicuous distribution of flyers; flash mob choirs performing protest songs in public places such as metro stations and shopping centres[51] (some of which were songs from the international tradition of partisan songs)[52]; unannounced concerts by well-known bands; talks by creative artists in the rear courtyards of buildings; and the placing of banned protest symbols in locations where they were difficult to remove, as well as the documentation of laborious (and often failed) attempts by staff of the state authorities to remove these symbols.[53] The last example in particular shows that these actions were not solely a matter of symbolically attacking the system's vulnerable points, but also of demonstrating the dysfunctionality of a supposedly omnipotent apparatus of power, and ideally dismantling it from within.[54]

---

50   Cf. Khartyia '97: "Partisan March Held in Belarus", 10 October 2024: https://charter97.org/en/news/2020/10/18/397402/ [30 September 2023].

51   Cf. people singing the songs *The Almighty God* (*Mahutny Bozha*) and *The Chase* (*Pahonya*) at the Kupalovskaia metro station on the evening of 27 August, *Zerkalo*, Youtube: https://www.youtube.com/watch?v=TN-ZgjvX_Vc [30 September 2023].

52   An overview on the role of songs in the Belarusian protest movement in 2020 is given by the online magazine *Meduza*: "Belorusskiy protest v musyke: pleylist Meduzy", 16 August 2020 (https://meduza.io/slides/belorusskiy-protest-v-muzyke-pleylist-meduzy) [30 September 2023] and by Andrei Khadanovich in: "Smuggling Freedom: Belarusian Protest Songs", 31 December 2020 on online magazine *Cultura.pl*: https://culture.pl/en/article/smuggling-freedom-belarusian-protest-songs, in which he refers to the song *The Partisan* (originally: *La Complainte du Partisan*) by Anna Marly & Leonard Cohen. The project "Street of Freedom" ("Ulitsa Mira") and the singer Svetlana Ben performed the song in a natural open space, floating on a raft across a lake, Cf. Nenoev Kovcheg, Youtube: https://www.youtube.com/watch?v=32re2VAWMVw&t=21s [30 September 2023].

53   Such as colouring a frozen lake in the colours of the opposition or tying three pairs of underpants coloured red-white-red to a line high above a road, etc. Cf. pictures in journal *Nastoiashchee vremia*, 11 January 2021: https://www.currenttime.tv/a/belarus-2020-dno/31038555.html [30 September 2023].

54   A key role in coordinating the protest actions and informing people about the events was played by the Telegram channel Nexta, with over one million people registered on the channel. Cf. *NEXTA live*: https://t.me/nexta_live [30 September 2023].

One striking particularity of the Belarusian protest actions was their recourse to methods taken from alternative Internet artworks with 'partisan tactics': popular Internet art projects from the 2010s such as the websites *Lemons* (*Limony*) and *Belarusian Toad* (*Belarusskaia zhaba*) and *Free* (*Svoboden*), which are collections of ironic photomontages with Belarusian themes or caricatures of Lukashenko.[55] Most of these sites have since been shut down, but they were carried on in new formats during the 2020 protests, such as on the Twitter account and Telegram channel *Sad Kolenka* (*Grustnyi Kolen'ka*), where a character named after Lukashenko's oldest son comments sarcastically on current political events in a way that is critical of the regime.[56] After August 2020, the "war of internet memes" (Dawidowicz/Kharytonau 2021) grew into a veritable storm of digital protest art, which made it possible to expose the ruling ideology's crude mixture of pathos and absurdity and, as an earlier overarching description by Usmanava put it, "through parasitical participation in public discourse" to "split things from within, devalue the familiar words and images and thus make the ubiquitous official culture look not only absurd but also completely out of place" (Usmanava 2014: 108).

The dimensions of these appropriations of tactics and symbols of the partisan struggle once again shifted radically with the preparation and launch of the large-scale Russian attack on Ukraine in February 2022. For example, the anonymous regime-critical hacker group calling themselves *Cyberpartisans*, who had made a name for themselves in 2020 with coups such as hacking the databases of the Interior Ministry and other state-run websites[57], now joined forces with the self-proclaimed partisan groups *The Storks are Flying* (*Busly liatsiats'*) and *Resistance* (*Supraziu*), in order to fight in solidarity with the besieged Ukraine against the imperialist adversary, Russia, and its ally, the Belarusian government.[58]

---

55    All three sites are deactivated for political reasons and currently not accessible.
56    Before the channel was declared "extremist" in August 2023, it had almost 350.000 followers on X-Twitter (https://twitter.com/sadmikalai) and over 20.000 followers on Telegram (@sadmikalai). The online portal *Kyky*, which has been labelled "extremist" by the government since December 2022, regularly publishes a column under the hashtag Grustnyi_Kolenka: https://kyky.org/search_tag?tag=Грустный_Коленька [30 September 2023].
57    One of their best-known coups, apart from uncovering numerous intercepted telephone calls, was the hijacking of the Interior Ministry's computer systems, where they gained access to the wanted lists and unceremoniously placed the names of the Interior Minister and Lukashenko himself at the top of the list as "most wanted". Cf.: *Kyky*, 3 October 2020: https://kyky.org/hero/eto-lish-vershina-aysberga-kiber-partizany-rasskazali-kak-budut-sryvat-maski-s-silovikov [30 September 2023].
58    Members of The Storks are Flying group were sentenced from to 8.5 to 15 years in prison by a Minsk court in December 2022 on charges of participating in terrorist activities, according to, among others, the human rights organisation *Viasna*, September 28, 2022: https://spring96.org/ru/news/109227 [30 September 2023]. Via Telegram they mobilise Belarusians to join a volunteer battalion fighting on the side of the Ukrainians in the war.

*Figure 7.6: Screenshot Telegram Chanel* Cyberpartisans

The alliance between the *Cyberpartisans* and the group known as *Railway Partisans* drew a great deal of attention: beginning in January 2022, they jointly carried out numerous acts of sabotage against the Belarusian railway network to prevent the transport of Russian military equipment to Ukraine via Belarus (Perova 2022).[59] The continuity of their actions with the Soviet myth is evident – in World War II, partisans similarly sabotaged the railway lines of the German occupiers on the occupied territory. In March 2022 the opposition political and journalist Franak Viačorka posted on Twitter: "Belarus is a land of partisans. Our heroes stop Russian trains, damage Russian equipment, hand out leaflets to prevent Belarus troops from entering Ukraine."[60] In this way, symbolic art actions and philosophical treatises have swiftly given way to the return of real acts of sabotage, and in place of tactics of unarmed retreat and hidden survival, masked (cyber-) attacks and armed forms of solidarity are once again appearing.

---

59  These acts of sabotage were coordinated and supported by anonymous comrades-in-arms via the Telegram group *Belarusian Haiun* (*Belarusskii Haiun*, @Hajun_BY), which monitors military movements on Belarusian territory.

60  Cf. *PolskieRadio.pl*, 21 March 2022: https://www.polskieradio.pl/400/7764/Artykul/2924291,Belarus sische-Saboteure-helfen-den-Ukrainern [30 September 2023].

## 9. Conclusion

Strictly speaking, in contemporary Belarusian culture there have been two interrelated phases of the popularisation of partisanhood, which are superimposed over one another in their contradictory nature. In line with Roland Barthes' notion of mythologies, these are different phases of the 'naturalisation' of symbolic constructions of identity, which different actors repeatedly adapt to fit specific cultural and political constellations. The first crucial phase of constituting the partisan myth took place during the post-war era, when the characteristics of the figure of the partisan which had existed since the 1920s were attached to the struggle against the German occupiers during World War II and shaped into recurring attributes, images and narratives. Thus emerged the topos of Belarus as a 'partisan republic' which was presented as having made a decisive contribution to the Red Army's victory over Nazi Germany through its heroic resistance. This myth was spread in all mediums and in many popular films beginning in the 1960s, and – after a brief phase of upheaval in the 1980s and 1990s – continued to be constitutive of Belarusian state power in the post-Soviet era.[61] In the second phase, which began at the turn of the twenty-first century, oppositional and dissident conceptualisations of 'partisanhood' have been directed against the dominance of that which is heroic, Soviet and official and of the state. In the second phase, 'partisanhood' has served as *the* metaphor for the Belarusian 'mentality' and 'identity' and as the core of a fundamentally revised myth. On the one hand, this is a concept of not showing oneself, of making oneself invisible in the face of the insurmountable superior power of the adversary 'occupying' one's homeland, a stance which was also projected backwards all the way to the early modern era as a timeless quality of all Belarusian identity. However, an update of the myth which was more tailored to the specific situation of Lukashenko's Belarus also emerged at the same time: the figure of the partisan as an actor engaged in subversive artistic practises and artistic protest entered into the self-conception of independent creative artists. Partisanhood was now understood as the art of living (and survival) and as the only way out of a struggle – which had not been freely chosen – against the adversary (the state, ideology, official art). In light of the already extensive apparatus of repression in Belarus and the ongoing Russian war against Ukraine with the participation of the Belarusian state, this understanding has begun to shift both within Belarus and abroad in the past year and half: now self-proclaimed partisans place their own activities within a broader context as acts of solidarity with the decolonial resistance of Ukraine against the imperialism of Russia. It is thus apparent that the formal core of the myth initially installed by the Soviet state in the 1960s, a core which refers to resistance against external occupying powers, has developed enormous vitality and popularity in recent decades and has largely eliminated its 'Soviet' content, if not outright identified Sovietness itself as the real 'occupation'. In these reappropriations of partisanhood, however, the quality which Barthes identifies as so dangerous in mythologies remains evident: rather than differentiating or historicising, the mythology constructs Belarusian identity in a way that repeatedly operates through clear distinctions between what is one's own and what is foreign, between

---

61  For more detail on the role of the partisan battle in Belarusian memory politics, cf. Rudling 2008; Hansen 2008: 187–196; Sahm 2010; Marples 2012, 2014.

the national and the imperial, and between the colonised and the occupier. At the same time, however, the post-Soviet appropriations of the partisan myth in the alternative and dissident art scene and in oppositional protest culture show that these binary mythic dichotomies are tremendously flexible, and that, as a familiar repertoire of symbols and narratives, they can be subversively adapted and varied to fit a specific political situation and cultural environment.

Translated by *Jane Yager*

## Filmography

*Brest Fortress* (*Brestskaia Krepost'*), dir. Izrail Pikman, USSR 1975.
*Come and See* (*Idi i smotri*), dir. Ėlem Klimov, USSR 1985.
*Deep Flow* (*Glubokoe techenie*), dir. Margarita Kasymova/Ivan Pavlov, Belarus 2005.
*Father* (*Bat'ka*), dir. Boris Stepanov, USSR 1971.
*Flame* (*Plamia*), dir. Vital' Chatsverykoŭ [Vitalii Chetverikov], USSR 1974.
*Franz + Polina*, dir. Mikhail Segal, Russia 2006.
*Girl Seeks Father* (*Devochka ischet ottsa*), dir. Lev Golub, USSR 1959.
*I Am a Fortress, I Stood my Ground* (*Ia – Krepost', Vedu Boi*), dir. Izrail Pikman, USSR 1972.
*In the Fog* (*V tumane*), dir. Sergei Loznitsa, Belarus/Germany/Latvia/Netherlands/Russia/USA 2012.
*Konstantin Zaslonov*, dir. Aleksandr Faintsimmer/Vladimir Korsh-Sablin, USSR 1949.
*Mysterium Occupation* (*Okkupatsiia. Misterii* [*Akupatsyia Mistėryi*]), dir. Andrei Kudinenko Belarus 2004.
*Party-Zan*, dir. Andrei Kureichik, Belarus 2016.
*Sons Go into Battle* (*Synov'ia ukhodiat v boi*), dir. Viktor Turov, USSR 1969.
*The Ascent* (*Vozchozhdenie*), dir. Larissa Shepit'ko, USSR 1976.
*The Black Birch* (*Chernaia berëza*), dir. Vital' Chatsverykoŭ [Vitalii Chetverikov], USSR 1977.
*The Brest Fortress* [also known as *Fortress of War*], (*Brestkaia krepost'*) dir. Aleksandr Kott, Russia/Belarus 2010.
*The Children of the Partisan* (*Deti partizana*), dir. Nikolai Figurovskii/Lev Golub, USSR 1954.
*The Clock Stopped at Midnight* (*Chasy ostanovilis v polnoch'*), dir. Nikolai Figurovskii, USSR 1959.
*The Matrix*, dir. Lana/Lilly Wachowski, USA 1999.
*The Ruins Are Shooting* (*Ruiny Streliaiut'*), dir. Vital' Chatsverykoŭ [Vitalii Chetverikov], USSR 1970–72.
*Through the Cemetery* (*Cherez kladbishche*), dir. Viktor Turov, USSR 1964.
*Time Has Chosen Us* (*Vremia vybralo nas*), dir. Michail Ptashuk, USSR 1976–1979.
*War Under the Roofs* (*Voina pod kryshami*), dir. Viktor Turov, USSR 1967.
*What Is It, the Sea?* (*Kakoe ono, more*), dir. Ėduard Bocharov, USSR 1964.

## List of Illustrations

**Figure 7.1:** Screenshot from Belsat-TV on X-Twitter: "Belarusian women against men from riot police".
**Figure 7.2:** Film poster for the film *Konstantin Zaslonov* (1949).
**Figure 7.3:** Film posters for the films *The Children of the Partisan* (1954) and *Girl Seeks Father* (1959).
**Figure 7.4:** Film still from the film *Mysterium Occupation* (2004).
**Figure 7.5:** Cover from Cultural magazine *pARTisan*, 2010/22.
**Figure 7.6:** Screenshot Telegram Chanel *Cyberpartisans*.

## References

Akudovich, Valiantsin (2007): Kod adsutnaci, Minsk: Lohvinau.
Akudowitsch, Valentin (2013): Der Abwesenheitscode: Versuch, Weißrussland zu verstehen (translated by Volker Weichsel), Berlin: Suhrkamp Verlag.
Artsimovich, Tatsiana (2021): "Igor Tishin: Multimediinyi proekt 'Tikhoe partizanskoe dvizhenie' 1997." In: Mart. Sovremennoe belarusskoe iskusstvo 16, 10 August 2021 (https://www.mart.by/2021/08/10/igor-tishin-multimedijnyj-proekt-tixoe-partizanskoe-dvizhenie-1997/) [30 September 2023].[62]
Barthes, Roland (2006): Mythologies [1957] (translated by Anette Lavers), New York, NY: Hill and Wang.
Bekus, Nelly (2010): Struggle over Identity: The Official and the Alternative "Belarusianness", Budapest/New York: Central European University Press.
Bekus, Nelly (2021): "Historical Memory and Symbolism in the Belarusian Protests." In: Cultures of History Forum, 16 February 2021 (https://www.cultures-of-history.uni-jena.de/politics/historical-memory-and-symbolism-in-the-belarusian-protests) [30 September 2023].
Beliaev, Vadim (2023): "Top-10 samykh kassovykh belorusskikh filmov." In: Komsomol'skaia Pravda, 20 March 2023 (https://www.belarus.kp.ru/daily/27478/4734707/) [30 September 2023].
Chiari, Bernhard (2001): "Die Kriegsgesellschaft. Weißrussland im Zweiten Weltkrieg (1939–1944)." In: Rainer Lindner/Dietrich Beyrau (eds.): Handbuch der Geschichte Weißrußlands, Göttingen: Vandenhoeck & Ruprecht, pp. 408–425.
Dawidowicz, Maria/Kharytonau, Serge (2022): "The War of Internet Memes in Belarus Memes and identity in Belarus." In: Vishegrad Insight, 7 October 2022 (https://visegradinsight.eu/internet-memes-belarus-opposition-lukashenka/) [30 September 2023].
Goujon, Alexandra (2010): "Memorial Narratives of WWII Partisans and Genocide in Belarus." In: East European Politics and Societies and Cultures 24 1, pp. 6–25.

---

[62] First published in Belarusian in 2016 in *Kalektar.org*: http://zbor.kalektar.org/16/ [12 December 2021].

Gusakovskaia, Nadezhda (2008): "'Okkupatsia. Misteriia', ili Belorusy ne sushchestvuiut." In: Al'mira Usmanova (ed.): Belorusskii format: Nevidimaia real'nost', Vilnius: European Humanities University Press, pp. 488–496.

Hansen, Imke (2008): "Die politische Planung der Erinnerung Geschichtskonstruktionen in Belarus zwischen Konflikt und Konsens." In: Sapper, Manfred et al. (eds): Osteuropa 6/2008, Geschichtspolitik und Gegenerinnerung: Krieg, Gewalt und Trauma im Osten Europas, Berlin: Berliner Wiss.-Verl., pp. 187–196.

Jakiša, Miranda (ed.) (2015): Partisans in Yugoslavia: Literature, Film and Visual Culture, Bielefeld: transcript.

Karpilava, Antonina A./Krasinski, A.V./Ratnikau, G.V. (eds): (2002): Historyia kinamastatsva Belarusi. Vol. 2. 1960–1985, Minsk: Bel. Navuka.

Keding, Ekaterina (2013): "'Neues aus den Partisanenwäldern' – alte und neue Konstruktionsversuche belarussischer Identität." In: Thomas Bohn/Rayk Einax/Julian Mühlbauer (eds.): Bunte Flecken in Weissrussland: Erinnerungsorte zwischen polnisch-litauischer Union und russisch-sowjetischem Imperium, Wiesbaden: Harrassowitz, pp. 81–93.

Khareŭski, Siarhei (1999): "Mastatstva pra vainu." In: ARCHE 2–3/1999 (https://xn--d1ag.xn--e1a4c/pub/arche/html/2-1999/charew299.html) [30 September 2023].

Khatkovskaia, Inessa (2008): "'Nacional'nyj fil"m' v Belarusi: Vmozhno li mnozhestvennoe chislo?" In: Al'mira Usmanova (ed.): Belorusskij format: Nevidimaia real'nost, Vilnius: European Humanities University Press, pp. 434–487.

Klinaŭ, Artur (2014): "Partisan und Antipartisan." In: Taciana Arcimovič/Steffen Beilich/Tina Wünschmann/Thomas Weiler (eds.): Partisanen: Kultur_Macht_Belarus, Berlin: edition.fotoTAPETA, pp. 14–26.[63]

Kudinenko, Andrei (2004): "Zapreschennyi v Belarusi film 'Okkupatsiia' mogut sniat s konkursa na MMKF." In: Kinokadr, 8 July 2004 (http://www.kinokadr.ru/news/2004/06/08/370.shtml) [03 April 2024].

Kudriavtsev, Sergei (1998): Svoe kino: Obzor otechestvennych filmov (Chempiony sovetskogo kinoprokata/Tetrad'4), Moskva: Dubl-D.

Lastoŭski, Aliaksei/Kazakevich, Andrėi /Balachaitse, Rasa. (eds.): "Pamiats' pra Druhuiu susvetnuiu vainu u haradskim landshaftse uskhodniai Europy." In: ARCHE 3/2010, pp. 251–300 (http://palityka.org/wp-content/uploads/2012/06/Lastouski-Kazakievich.pdf) [30 September 2023].

Lewis, Simon (2011): "'Official Nationality' and the dissidence of memory in Belarus: A comparative analysis of two films." In: Studies in Russian and Soviet Cinema 5/3, pp. 371–387.

Lewis, Simon (2017): "The 'Partisan Republic': Colonial Myths and Memory Wars in Belarus.". In: Julie Fedor/Markku Kangaspur/Jussi Lassila/Tatiana Zhurzhenko/Alexander Etkind (eds.): War and Memory in Russia, Ukraine and Belarus, New York, NY: Palgrave Macmillan, pp. 371–396.

Lindner, Rainer (1999): "Besieged Past: National and Court Historians in Lukashenka's Belarus." In: Nationalities Papers 27/1999, pp.631-648.

---

63  First published: "Partyzani antypartyzan." In: pARTisan 1/2002, pp. 16–24.

Lindner, Rainer (2001): "Weißrussland im Geschichtsbild seiner Historiker." In: Beyrau, Dietrich/Lindner, Rainer (Hg.): Handbuch der Geschichte Weißrußlands, Göttingen: Vandenhoeck & Ruprecht, pp. 25–48.

Marples, David R. (2012): "History, Memory, and the Second World War in Belarus*." In: Australian Journal of Politics & History 58/3, pp. 437–448.

Marples, David R. (2014): "Our glorious past": Lukashenka's Belarus and the Great Patriotic War, Stuttgart: Ibidem-Verlag.

Martin, Terry (2001): The affirmative Action Empire: Nations and Nationalism in the Soviet Union, 1923–1939, Ithaca: London: Cornell University Press.

Musial, Bogdan (ed.) (2004): Sowjetische Partisanen in Weissrussland: Innenansichten aus dem Gebiet Baranoviči 1941–1944: Eine Dokumentation, München: R. Oldenbourg.

Musial, Bogdan (2009): Sowjetische Partisanen 1941–1944: Mythos und Wirklichkeit, Paderborn: F. Schöningh.

Oushakine, Serguei (2013): "Postcolonial Estrangements: Claiming a Space Between Stalin and Hitler." In: Julie Buckler/Emily D. Johnson (eds.): Rites of Place: Public Commemoration in Russia and Eastern Europe, Evanston: Northwestern University Press, pp. 285–314.

Petz, Ingo (2013): "Paranoia und Pragmatismus Die belarussische Alternativkultur nach 2010." In: Belarus-Analysen 12, pp. 2–7.

Perova, Anya (2022): "The Guerrilla War on Belarus's Railways." In: Meduza, 5 July 2022 (https://meduza.io/en/feature/2022/07/05/the-guerrilla-war-on-belarus-s-railways) [30 September 2023].

Pfister, Eugen (2015): "Das Politische im Populären Diskurs." In: ibid. (ed.): Politische Mythen im Digitalen Spiel, 21 October 2015 (https://spielkult.hypotheses.org/349) [30 September 2023].

Richter, Timm C. (2014): "Belarusian Partisans and German Reprisals." In: Snyder, Timothy/Brandon, Ray (eds.): Stalin and Europe, Oxford: Oxford University Press, pp. 207–232.

Rudling, Per Anders (2017): "'Unhappy Is the Person Who Has No Motherland': National Ideology and History Writing in Lukashenka's Belarus." In: Julie Fedor et al. (eds.): War and Memory in Russia, Ukraine and Belarus, New York: Palgrave Macmillan, pp. 71–105.

Rudling, Per Anders: "'For a Heroic Belarus!': The Great Patriotic War as Identity Marker in the Lukashenka and Soviet Belarusian Discourses." In: Sprawy Narodowościowe/Nationalities Affairs 2008, pp. 43–62.

Sahm, Astrid (2010): "Der Zweite Weltkrieg als Gründungsmythos: Wandel der Erinnerungskultur in Belarus." In: Osteuropa 60/5, pp. 43–54.

Schmitt, Carl (1963): Theorie des Partisanen: Zwischenbemerkung zum Begriff des Politischen, Berlin: Duncker & Humblot.

Shparaga, Olga (2013): "Vom Partisanen-Nomaden zum Aktionskünstler. Die belarussische Gegenwartskunst." In: Belarus-Analysen 12, pp. 7–10.

Šparaha, Volha (2014): "Das Politische ist das Private." In: Taciana Arcimovič et al. (eds.): Partisanen: Kultur_Macht_Belarus, Berlin: edition.fotoTAPETA, pp. 140–149.

Sitnikova, Daria (2008): "Partizan: prikliucheniia odnogo kontsepta v strane bol'shevikov." In: Usmanova, Al'mira (ed.): Belorusskii format: Nevidimaia real'nost, Vilnius: European Humanities University Press, pp. 397–433 (https://ru.ehu.lt/wp-content/uploads/2017/10/Belformat-s.pdf) [30 September 2023].

Stiglegger, Marcus (2020): "Komm und sieh/Idi smotiri (1988). R: Ėlem Klimov." In: Matthias Schwartz/Barbara Wurm (eds): Klassiker des russischen und sowjetischen Films 2, Marburg: Schüren, pp. 169–178.

Strocaŭ, Dźmitry [Strotsev, Dmitri] (2014): "Jod." In: Taciana Arcimovič et al. (eds.): Partisanen: Kultur_Macht_Belarus, Berlin: edition.fotoTAPETA, pp. 63–77.

Tumarkin, Nina (1994): The Living and the Dead: The Rise and Fall of the Cult of World War II in Russia, New York: *Basic Books*.

Usmanava, Almira (2014): "Anarchist, Partisan, Künstler: Von der Notwendigkeit, Situationen zu schaffen." In: Taciana Arcimovič et al. (eds.): Partisanen: Kultur_Macht_Belarus, Berlin: edition.fotoTAPETA, pp. 102–111.

Vasil'eva, Ekaterina/Braginskij, Nikita (2012): Noev kovcheg russkogo kino: Ot "Stenki Razina" do "Stiliag", St. Peterburg: Globus-Press.

Weller, Nina/Krawatzek, Félix (2022): "A Former Soviet Republic? Historical Perspectives on Belarus." In: Nina Friess/Félix Krawatzek (eds.): Youth and Memory in Europe: Defining the Past, Shaping the Future, Berlin/Boston: De Gruyter, pp. 27–40.

Weller, Nina (2022): "'Let's be Belarusians!' On the Reappropriation of Belarusian History in Popular Culture." In: Nina Friess/Félix Krawatzek (eds.): Youth and Memory in Europe: Defining the Past, Shaping the Future, Berlin/Boston: De Gruyter, pp. 59–74.

Youngblood, Denise J. (2001): "A War Remembered: Soviet Films of the Great Patriotic War." In: The American Historical Review 106/3, pp. 839–856.

Chapter 8:
# Mummified Subversion
Reconstructions of Soviet Rock Underground in Contemporary Russian Cinema

*Roman Dubasevych*

> We require a visible past, a visible continuum, a visible myth of origin, which reassures us about our end. [...] Whence this historic scene of the reception of the mummy at the Orly airport. Why? Because Ramses was a great despotic and military figure? Certainly. But mostly because our culture dreams, behind this defunct power that it tries to annex, of an order that would have had nothing to do with it, and it dreams of it because it exterminated it by exhuming it *as its own past*.
> (Jean Baudrillard 1993: 10)

## 1. Introduction

In contemporary Russian film the Soviet era is mostly appropriated in a nostalgic way. While conservative – often neo-imperial or nationalist – representations prevail, this essay focusses on two musical films, *Hipsters* (*Stiliagi*, 2008) by Valerii Todorovskii and *Summer* (*Leto*, 2018) by Kirill Serebrennikov, which, on the contrary, explicitly celebrate moments of anti-authoritarian subversion and change. Both films express a strong nostalgia for the non-conformist subcultures and countercultural movements – the post-Stalinist hipsters, the so-called *stiliagi* of the 1950s, and the late-Soviet punks, the so-called 'nonformal' youth of the 1980s. However, despite all sympathy one can have towards the depictions of the open, liberal, underground and youth cultures in these two films, the two clearly nostalgic reconstructions of Thaw and perestroika rebels reveal significant contradictions or more precisely: a remarkable tension can be detected between the longing for moments of political emancipation and their simultaneous renunciation and mitigation.

Working on my material, however, I realised that the paradoxical self-induced neutralisation of subversive, countercultural messages had a significant political dimension: the films in question construct a surprising opposition between a rebellious, creative (and materially mostly unconcerned) minority on the one hand, and an indifferent, degenerate *seraia massa* (grey mass) of ordinary (Soviet) citizens on the other. Remarkably, this sort of elitist dichotomy undermines the democratic appeal of both the rock-n-roll of the 1950–60s (*Hipsters*) or the songs of the legendary rock bands *Kino* and *Zoopark* with their front men Viktor Tsoi and Maik Naumenko (*Summer*). Moreover, the striking division into the proud rebels and servile conformists not only resonates with a deep-rooted Russian fatalism – the long tradition of cultural inferiority complex and political resignation. My main thesis is that such antisocial modelling of countercultural groups, confirms traditional Russian topoi about the impossibility of change due to the 'national character' and apathetic masses, and thus plays into the hands of the current regime, because it disables solidarisation across rapidly growing social divides and, as a result, impedes the consolidation of a future opposition.

A prominent example for such an alienation between the high and low classes of Russian society, despite the overall critical tendency, is provided by Kirill Serebrennikov's dystopian drama *Yuri's Day* (*Iur'ev den'*, 2008) which brings its female protagonist, a cosmopolitan Russian opera star Liuba, to her provincial birth town where she experiences a nightmarish survival tour amid her lower class compatriots. Though expressing valid concerns about the growing distance between the glitzy metropolitan Russian centres and its dilapidated hinterland, *Yuri's Day* is also marked by palpable estrangement and disdain towards the pauperised and 'degenerated' strata of society.

Such a radical social othering significantly contrasts with the film's late-Soviet templates, for instance, Karen Shakhnazarov's remarkable phantasmagorical comedy *Zerograd* (*Gorod Zero*, 1988), where alienation and empathy function not exclusively but rather complementarily, reinforcing the absurd poetics of the plot and the helplessness of the protagonist. The film's crescendo with its celebration of the rock-n-roll pioneer of the dystopian 'City of Zero', a former police officer, provides an important intertext to both post-Soviet musicals: here, in the late-Soviet context, the reception of rock-n-roll articulates an ambivalent aura surrounding the popular Western music in Russian culture – an irresistible impulse to enjoy and rebel as well as the anxiety in this way to succumb to hedonism, amnesia and hegemonic power. In the post-Soviet situation, this ambivalence has turned into open contradiction, and the shock of Serebrennikov's 2008 protagonist Liuba and her barely hidden contempt for the decaying inhabitants of the eponymous provincial town in *Yuri's Day* can only be redeemed through her highly unrealistic and patriarchal transformation from an international opera star to a virtuous nurse, healing the putrid wounds of incarcerated criminals, suffering from venal diseases and tuberculosis.

Although the topos of an unbridgeable gap between liberal-democratic, pro-Western elites in the form of the paradigmatic former 'audience of the Ėcho Moskvy' or the TV channel Dozhd' on the one hand, and those indoctrinated by state television – the infamous *zomboiashchik* (zombie-box) – on the other, had been extant long before the Russian attack on Ukraine, the alienation between the oppositional elites and masses has reached its peak after February 2022 when, in the face of the state-initiated aggression and warcrimes, the expected mass protests arose only in some large cities and in diaspora.

Thus, instead of speculating about the abysses of the 'Russian soul' or a momentum for resistance, a stronger focus on the social alienation and contempt encoded in these two films, could contribute to a better understanding of the present defeat of liberal-democratic forces and the 'shocking' silence of the Russian majority as well as the absence of active large-scale resistance. For sure, the inactivity of broad strata of the population certainly has complex reasons. Yet, the contempt of the post-Soviet (neo)liberal elite for the 'degenerate' masses undoubtedly played its part in driving them into the hands of an authoritarian and conservative ruler like Vladimir Putin, who could always profile himself as the advocate and protector of the 'ordinary' or 'little Russians,' accepting them without any socio-cultural conditioning.

Current Western research on reconstructions of the past in post-Soviet cinema often deals with the imperialist or nationalist mythologies. It usually discusses how dramatic historical events in Central and Eastern Europe are instrumentalised for political legitimisation and the formation of national or 'imperial' collectives, but also for the repression of the unwelcome past events and voices. In particular, historical traumas from World War II like the battle of Stalingrad, the defence of the Brest fortress (*The Brest Fortress*, also known as *Fortress of War*, *Brestkaia krepost'*, 2010, Aleksandr Kott) or the Volhynian massacre (*Volhynia*, also known as *Hatred*, *Wołyń*, 2016, Wojciech Smarzowski), but also the state-initiated famine of 1932–33 Holodomor (*Mr Jones*, *Obywatel Jones*, 2019, Agnieszka Holland) or the Holocaust (*Ida*, 2013, Paweł Pawlikowski) have been broadly appropriated in the contemporary Russian, Belarusian, Polish and Ukrainian collective imagination.

In contrast, attempts to reconstruct subversive episodes which seem to openly question the hegemonic consensus have received much less consideration. But how to reflect critically on artworks which use cultural-historical turning points and phenomena to challenge the authoritarian narratives and mythmaking? Since both films discussed in this essay depict youth counter- or subcultures of the Soviet era, they stand, at first glance, for an ideological and aesthetic alternative to such highly mythologised Russian renderings of history such as the historical dramas *Admiral* (2008, Andrei Kravchuk), *Stalingrad* (2013, Fëdor Bondarchuk), *Panfilov's 28* (*Dvadtsat' vosem' Panfilovtsev*, also known as *Battle for Moscow* and *Thunder of War*, 2016, Kim Druzhynin/Andrei Shal'opa), but also to contemporary Ukrainian historical dramas *Firecrosser* (*Toi, shcho proishov kriz' vohon'*, 2011, Mykhailo Illienko), *The Guide* (*Povodyr*, 2013, Oles' Sanin), *1918 The Battle of Kruty* (*Kruty 1918*, 2019, Oleksii Shapariev), *Black Raven* (*Chornyi voron*, 2019, Taras Tkachenko) or Tatar films like *Haytarma* (*Qaytarma*, 2013, Akhtem Seitablaiev).

In the following I will discuss how the films *Hipsters* and *Summer* try to reanimate the traditions of nonconformism and the underground. In doing so, I will analyse to what extent these reconstructions of protest subcultures ultimately fail and even lead to their surprising neutralisation, to a trivialisation or even subtle affirmation of repression. Thus, I will argue that the films seem, more unwittingly than not, to inscribe themselves into the hegemonic order complicit with the current regime and its ideological bonds, for instance, through the idealisation of the USSR and commodification of its underground cultures. In referring to Fredric Jameson's critique of conservative aspects of postmodern nostalgia and Jean Baudrillard's observations on the postmodern media, I will also discuss the respective aesthetic characteristics of this tendency – *Hipster*'s carnivalisation and 'Americanisation' of the post-Stalinist era as well as *Summer*'s monochrome 'documentary' style and "hipsterization" of the Soviet 80s. Particular attention will be paid to the hyperrealism in the depiction of both historical periods which results in a paradoxical relativisation of their subversive cultural semantics. Finally, in the first approach these ambiguous phenomena will be tentatively described with the notion of 'mummification' – a metaphor which surely requires further elaboration.[1]

## 2. Valerii Todorovskii's *Hipsters* and the Challenge of the Philistines

The film *Hipsters* by Valerii Todorovskii, the son of the renowned Soviet-Jewish filmmaker Pëtr Todorovskii, became one of the most successful productions in the history of post-Soviet Russian cinema. It was due both to its theme – the rediscovery of the nonconformist youth culture of the Soviet era – and to the structural factors – the box office success of *Hipsters* – that, together with the popularity of such films as *Brother I/II* (*Brat I/II*, 1997/2000, Aleksei Balabanov), *Brigada* (2000, Aleksei Sidorov), as well as the international success of *The Barber of Siberia* (*Sibirskii Tsiriul'nik*, 1998, Nikita Mikhalkov) or *Night Watch* (*Nochnoi dozor*, 2004, Timur Bekmambetov) – was seen as a long-awaited recovery of the Russian film after the collapse of the state-subsidised Soviet film industry. The new self-confidence of Russian filmmakers also developed in a complex relationship as apprentice and rival to the West, especially given the global domination of Hollywood cinema. The claim of *Hipsters* was precisely no less than to realise a local historical theme in one of the most traditional and conventionalised Western film genres, the music film.[2]

As the title suggests, the movie tells the story of the Soviet hipsters *stilagi* (the "styled" or "style-conscious") – a youth culture of the late 1950s that, despite the Cold War, took its cue from the rock-n-roll and jazz music seeping through the Iron Curtain. The action takes place in 1955, just on the eve of the Thaw, a brief period of liberalisation introduced by Stalin's successor Nikita Khrushchev, notably by his criticism of the so-called 'cult of personality' at the 20th Party Congress of the CPSU in 1956. The film's protagonist, student Mėls Biriukov, is an average Soviet citizen who initially succumbs entirely to the regime's ideological indoctrination. As a volunteer team member monitoring public order and morality (*druzhinnik*), he actively participates at its lowest level of social control. In the course of a raid on an unofficial rock-n-roll dance party in Moscow's Gor'kii Park, he pursues and falls in love with his victim, a young woman Polina (Pol'za, eng. "utility"), who, along with her friends, mostly children of the Soviet upper class – diplomats, party and industrial nomenclature – indulges in the frowned-upon Western lifestyle.

After several attempts, which demand much energy, creativity and, not least, purchasing power, Mėls finally becomes a member of the adored clique. The admission means not only an erotic but also a social initiation for him. The timid and naive young

---

1   Speaking about the reference to the practice of 'mummification' also hints at a conspicuous tension between its deep roots in Russian Orthodox and Soviet traditions on the one hand, and the contemporary stage of capitalist media development on the other, a question that due to space restrictions cannot be explored further here. On the impact of the Orthodox tradition on the post-revolutionary cult of Lenin and his mummification see the talk by J. Arch Getty "Dead Man Talking: Lenin's Body and Russian Politics" (Getty 2016).

2   A detailed and systematic analysis of Todorovskii's effort to revive the genre and its Russian remarketing is offered by Rimgaila Salys (2016: 114–135).

man gradually develops into a self-confident consumer and adherent of an alternative, Western lifestyle, learning even to deal with the underground economy that supplies *stiliagi* with the coveted Western items. Mėls' new status is also underpinned by self-taught saxophone lessons, an instrument that the authorities deemed bourgeois and ideologically reprehensible,[3] and which the protagonist acquires at great risk on the *barakholka*, the Moscow black market.

However, his conversion from an obedient *homo sovieticus* to a defiant *stiliaga* is only one aspect of the film's story. Its climax is the protagonist's second and final initiation – the confrontation with the secondary or semi-fictional character of the *stiliagi* lifestyle. When Mėls' mentor Frėd, now a career diplomat, returns from a tour of duty in the US, both men escape from the confines of a claustrophobic family apartment onto the streets of Moscow to talk openly about Frėd's experiences in the country of their dreams, in particular about his impression of American hipsters. Mėls former role model visibly struggles to share his insight with his mentee – the *stiliagi* culture they idolised does not exist there. America, Frėd confesses, is much more conformist than they ever imagined. Accordingly, their entire hipster lifestyle was based on fiction, and is a simulacrum.

Mėls shock is intensified by Frėd's disillusionment and transformation from a flamboyant *stiliaga* and representative of the transgressive Moscow jeunesse dorée to a cynical and conformist Soviet functionary in fine American garments. Frėd's revelations trigger almost a violent backlash from Mėls, who, horrified about the shattering of his ideals, sends his former mentor packing and strides off in the opposite direction. Here, in the public space of a Moscow boulevard, the film completes a time jump that catapults Mėls into the present. Suddenly, the protagonist, who has paid such a high price to preserve his ideals, is no longer a loner – as Mėls steps into the empty middle of the boulevard, the colourful crowd of various youth subcultures grows around him. The song accompanying this triumphant march of diversity calls for the rest of society to treat the noisy and disruptive youths mildly and with understanding. Amid this carnival of youth non-conformism, Mėls' lover Pol'za also finds him, and they together stride towards a free and bright future.

Perhaps the most surprising thing about the reception of *Hipsters* was the enthusiastic reactions from critics in and outside the government camp. The notorious regime's TV presenter and Kremlin chief propagandist Vladimir Solov'ëv, noted at the time:

> I was stunned. There hasn't been a film like this in Russia for a long, long time, both in terms of genre and the quality of the script, the direction, the superb acting, and the camerawork... The film is so ideologically crucial that I would ask everyone to see it. It's about individual freedom, the right to be different, to be unlike others. I don't think the "Nashi" movement would like it very much. (Solov'ëv 2008)[4]

---

3   The complex dynamics of Soviet jazz and negotiations accompanying its status in Soviet society is highlighted by Gleb Tsipursky (2016: 332–361).
4   Cf. also the responses on the movie website Beliy.ru (Otzyvy): https://www.beliy.ru/work/stilyagifilm/index-48.htm [09 April 2023].

One of his antagonists from the opposition, the renowned music critic Artemii Troitskii even praised the film as "absolutely anti-state" and "freedom-loving": "'Stiliagi' is actually a very valuable appropriate and beautiful excuse to talk about other things, namely, once again, about freedom" (Vorob'eva 2009).

The enthusiastic consensus of both political antagonists Solov'ëv and Troitskii is significant in so far as it indicates the default agreement among post-Soviet Russian elites. The point of their paradoxical convergence is an elitist pathos of individuality opposed to the conformist 'gray mass' of the ordinary people. However, as the film shows, the nostalgic celebration and even carnivalisation of the still highly repressive Soviet power of the first post-Stalin years ultimately results in a trivialisation and surprising normalisation of the Soviet reality and its modern equivalent – the Putin regime of the early 2000s.

Without doubt, Todorovskii successfully communicates the central message of the depicted globalised subcultures – of rock-n-roll and jazz. The individuation process, the pathos of liberation of sexuality and creativity from traditional and collective constraints that characterised the original American model resonate remarkably well with the Soviet context (Bielefeldt 2017: 25–30). Despite all the systemic differences, the McCarthy and Eisenhower eras, with their Cold War paranoia and mass cultural pressures, bore some similarities to the Soviet regime, which sought openly to determine its citizens' leisure activities and consumption: yet while in the Soviet Union this control was exercised by state dictatorship, the laws of the market also had their norming effects. Though the film takes great effort to accurately depict the historical atmosphere, it reduces erotic, social and even political protest and transgression to the triumph of popular music.

Thus, *Hipsters* at first sight expresses a strong criticism of Stalinism, the ideological and social repression of the Soviet regime. Obviously, it can and should be interpreted allegorically and, in a counter-presentist way as a growing unease with authoritarian development under Vladimir Putin's second presidency. Yet, despite its general or manifest liberal tenor, the film's message contains significant contradictions, making the current regime and its historical correlate sometimes appear as almost harmless, even supportive towards its citizens, in a way representing its victims as its potential winners and true 'shareholders'.

Notwithstanding the criticism of uniformity, *Hipsters* strongly essentialises and simplifies the origins and dynamics of Soviet society. Todorovskii's music film establishes a seductive dichotomy: here the flamboyant individuals from the *stiliagi* camp, there a grey, jaded *seraia massa* (gray mass) of Soviet philistines, whom the young hipsters refer to with the pejorative slang term *zhloby* ("greedy persons"). Although the mainstream's hatred for *stiliagi* is shown as almost instinctual, 'zoological' in nature, its sociological or ideological causes are hardly elucidated. As a result, all the rage of the faceless proles is directed against the exterior forms of the protest – clothes, hairstyles, and music. The whole complexity of the Soviet experience, its tensions and paradoxes, adaptations and resistances as well as epoch-specific shifts are reduced to a conflict of lifestyles and consumer cultures, between style and stylessness. This is the more surprising as it was precisely during Khrushchev's Thaw that fundamental cultural and political issues became much more expressible and important than questions solely of looks and habits. The de-Stalinisation manifested itself, inter alia, in the emergence and growing popularity of the so-called 'poetic clubs' or the development of the author song, popularised by such bards as Bulat Okudzhava, Iurii Vizbor, Vladimir Vysotskii, Iulii Kim and others.[5]

The ideological and social struggles of the time are also well documented in the iconic movies like Aleksandr Zarkhi's coming-of-age drama *My Younger Brother* (*Moi mladshii brat*, 1962) which clearly departs from the heroic scripts of the Stalin era. Travelling for vacation from their native Moscow to the 'westernised' Estonia, its protagonists routinely go the pubs, listen to jazz music, work on the black market or even discuss the contemporary 'bourgeois' philosophers like Jean-Paul Sartre. The other paradigmatic social movie drama of the time, *Il'ich's Gate* (*Zastava Il'icha*, 1965) by Marlen Khutsiev, includes even a documentary episode with the legendary poetic readings at Moscow Politechnical Institute which hosted such important voices of the generation as Ievgenii Ievtushenko, Bella Akhmadullina or Robert Rozhdestvenskii. In contrast to Todorovskii's post-Soviet film, in Khutsiev's movie precisely ordinary young people like the working-class protagonist Sergei attend such readings, thereby clearly distancing themselves from the social narcissism and consumer-oriented lifestyle of the Soviet nomenclature children.[6] But instead of presenting in a similar way a nuanced picture of the contradictions within the alleged Soviet 'uniformity', the various forms of state control and strategies of resistance in which its 'silent majority' engaged, Todorovskii's *Hipsters*, except for the scene with Bob's Jewish parents and Gulag returnees, trivialises Soviet daily life into a harmless cat and mouse-game of flamboyant teenagers with clumsy authorities and their dumb and literally unstylish personnel.

As a result, the lack of sensitivity towards the historical and intellectual climate of the late 1950s is compensated within the film with an ardent attention to the material environment. The obsession with period fashions, hairstyles, old radios and cars virtually absorbs the viewer, turning the totalitarian Soviet Union into a mirror image of the golden American 1950s, the Perestroika period or even the Moscow night life of the 2000s. This impression is particularly reinforced by the numerous musical soundtracks, all by famous rock bands of the 1980s like *Mashina vremeni*, *Chai F* or *Kino*, which make the still highly repressive post-Stalin years feel even like the much more liberal Gorbachev era, transforming the risky actions of its protagonists into an exciting adventure game. At this point, paradoxically, the film's anti-authoritarian pathos tips over into an affirmative stance; the vibrant *stiliagi* subculture is represented as an archipelago of freedom and intrinsic part of the regime itself. Accordingly, it creates the impression that this epoch of authenticity, a real sense of community, destination and outstanding technical-industrial achievements actually was not so bad, but a time of great and pristine feelings, joyful improvisation, modesty and finally a meaningful way of life.

Thus, behind the untroubled dance life of the Soviet hipsters of the 1950s, one can easily recognise the attitudes of the early 'golden' 2000s which, in the Russian case, for

---

5   On the intellectual and artistic climate of the time, especially on the role of poetry in the anti-authoritarian resistance, see the memoirs of the author, translator, and literary scholar Vladimir Britanishskii [n.d.]: http://www.ruthenia.ru/60s/kritika/britanish_stud.htm [11 April 2023].

6   According to Vladimir Semerchuk, *Il'ich's Gate* enjoyed the status of a manifesto for the "sixties," especially due to its problematisation of a deep crisis of Stalinist identity model and its collectivist orientation (Cit. Kun 2012: 223).

large sections of the population were indeed characterised by increasing prosperity, living standards, and consolidation of state authority. The newly acquired self-confidence (and narcissistic self-referentiality within the film) arose out of the belief in irreversible economic advancement, but also out of the feeling of Russia's comeback as a great geopolitical power that, despite its authoritarian drift, still allows considerable freedom and leeway for art and business. Locating the film within this cultural-political frame, however, does not explain why the non-conformist *Kulturträger* in the film see as their primary opponent not so much the authoritarian regime, but the heavily homogenised mainstream society. Moreover, the ordinary Russians, increasingly excluded from participation in political and economic life, appear as phantasmatic, zombie-like, grey and obedient *homines sovietici*, incessantly stalking and harassing the colourful hipsterian dandies.

Such a limited, reductive portrait of the Soviet hipsters not only itself cuts away their characteristic oscillation between popular and countercultural, nonconformism and conformity, but leads to their depoliticisation and excessive aestheticisation. The important anti-racist as well as social message, accompanying the US-rock-n-roll wave due to its blues origins and numerous Afro-American performers, such as Little Richard and Chuck Berry, also gets lost in Todorovskii's transposition into the Russian context. Though its hybrid roots were hinted at by the female heroine's love affair with an exotic Afro-American visitor of the VI. World Youth and Student Festival in Moscow 1957, one can barely take seriously the smooth acceptance of the extramarital child by Mėls and his family. Supported by his father, a revered and open-hearted veteran, such an inclusivity rather coalesces with the regime's upcoming instrumentalisation of the Great Patriotic War, represented by such historical dramas like the *In August of 1944* (*V avguste 44*, 2004, Mikhail Ptashuk) or *Burnt by the Sun 2* (*Utomlënnye solntsem 2*, 2010) by the prominent 'court-filmmaker' Nikita Mikhalkov. At the same time, the film's unwillingness to confront the racial issue more seriously contrasts with the persistent xenophobia towards migrant workers from the former Caucasian or Central Asian republics which is depicted so vividly in Balabanov's iconic *Brother* dilogy. In addition, the final scene, in which Frėd delivers to Mėls the shattering news of the invented nature of their rock-n-roll lifestyle, can also be interpreted as a warning to Russian culture against trusting Western ideas too much.

Moreover, one of the film's pictorial leitmotifs – old x-ray films used for the pirate copies of rock-n-roll vinyl records – can even be interpreted in a self-revealing way. Lighthearted dancing to the sounds from the clinical x-ray pictures in a metaphorical sense discloses the symptomatology of the film itself: its frivolous treatment of a dramatic historical period appears now almost like literal dancing on the bones of the (dead) witnesses and victims of the regime, an impression, intensified, amongst others, by the choice of the music film genre for representing the early post-Stalin era. Though the recycling of the medical celluloid is historically accurate, the presence of the bones and skeletons amidst rock-n-roll-carnival cannot but evoke subtle associations with decadence, death and decay. While the unhomely black-and-white colour scheme of the x-rays also resonates with the film's schematic characterisation and Manichean dichotomies, bereft of the 'flesh' – human complexity and depth[7] – one is even tempted to see them as a metaphor for a surprising mortification of the film's genuine impulse to revive the spirits of non-conformism and resistance.

## 3. Reanimating the Protest Traditions during Vladimir Putin's Fourth Term

> Neither Naumenko, nor Tsoi, nor Serebrennikov are fighting the system. They simply live and create as if it does not exist, and the music of T. Rex easily drowns out the thunderous anthem of the USSR. It is precisely this position that makes them alien and hostile to any power, Brezhnev's or Putin's. (Dolin 2018)[8]

While the reception of *Hipsters* undoubtedly benefited from the cinematic legacy of the Todorovskii dynasty, especially the extraordinary success of Petr Todorovskii's perestroika dilogy *Intergirl* (*Interdevochka*, 1986) which broke ground with such explosive issues as illegal valuta, prostitution and emigration, the reception of another famous Russian musical film *Summer* (*Leto*, 2017) is hardly conceivable without the context of the late Putin-regime, particularly the persecution of its producer, the Moscow theatre director Kirill Serebrennikov. The art director of the renowned Moscow Gogol' Centr theatre since 2012, he gained his reputation with bold stage experiments collaborating, however, also in opera productions in famous state-sponsored institutions like the Bolshoi (Moscow) and Mariinskii (St. Petersburg) theatres. Apart from that, the versatile artist made successful films such as *Yuri's Day*, which earned him awards at the prestigious Locarno, Warsaw and Cannes Film Festivals. Yet, despite Serebrennikov's genuine liberal stance, his Gogol' Tsentr also staged authors loyal to the regime such as Zakhar Prilepin, who due to his key role in Kremlin propaganda warfare and the separatist fight for Donbas, was even appointed in 2018 a deputy art director of another renowned venue, the Maxim Gorkii theatre.[9]

---

7   Remarkably, the *Hipster's* ambivalent semantic structure is reproduced by some critical comments. Stating on the one hand that the film avoids the dangers of idealisation, Yana Meerzon surprisingly realises at the same time that it can be instrumentalised by the Kremlin power elite: "In other words, Todorovsky's film Stilyagi not only celebrates the Soviet musical underground as a tool of liberation and an expression of nonviolent resistance but also establishes present-day Russian youth as a target for new ideological narratives. It provides the Russian post-communist ideologists […] with a propaganda tool directed at glorifying the experience of the powerless" (Meerzon 2011: 479–510).

8   As Anton Dolin, one of the most renowned oppositional film critics in Russia continues: "*Summer* needs an adequate viewer who is able to remove the film from its many contexts (historical, human rights, festival, etc.) and enjoy it – like a concert of old, beloved, familiar music that suddenly sounds fresh, as if it were being played for the first time" (Dolin 2018).

9   The most significant controversy, however, was sparked by the rendition of the novel *Okolo nulia* (*At Zero*, 2009), published under the pen name Natan Dubovitskii. This nom de plume concealed Vladislav Surkov – a shrewd Russian apparatchik who, after his successful career as a PR manager in private business, rose to the rank of Russia's deputy prime minister. A 'creative head' behind the political scene of Putin's regime, Surkov is the one who allegedly invented, inter alia, the latter's party United Russia and led the Trilateral Contact Group for the peaceful settlement of the situation in eastern Ukraine.

In view of Serebrennikov's complex interaction with Kremlin elites, his arrest on charges of embezzling state funds from a theatre production came as a great surprise inside of the country – the harsh treatment of the star director stirred up tempers insofar as Serebrennikov, like Todorovskii a decade before him, had been considered the living proof of a certain leeway within the regime – a showcase of paradoxical coexistence of political paternalism, oil and gas based economic stability and some artistic freedoms that characterised the regime until the annexation of Crimea and its involvement in Donbas separatism. Thus, the filmmaker's detainment, despite numerous protests at home and abroad, marked a new stage of political repression.[10] Serebrennikov's persecution was immediately perceived as a warning signal to potential troublemakers among the Russian beau monde, and the sign of the growing dominance in the Kremlin's power hierarchy of the *siloviki* – officials associated with the state security apparatus – over the quasi-neoliberals.[11]

While *Hipsters* reflected in a counter-presentist manner the flaring up of tentative hopes for liberalisation under Vladimir Putin's co-regent Dmitrii Medvedev (2008–2012), culminating in the peaceful and partly festival-like Bolotnaia protests against the fraudulent parliamentary elections to the Russian Duma in December 2011, *Summer* could be attributed to the second, post-carnivalesque protest phase, in which the desire for change, especially after the violent crackdown on the protests, was growing ever more desperate but has been suppressed even more drastically. In this respect, the shift in Serebrennikov's music film from the politically relatively benign rock-n-roll or jazz to the much more explosive punk-rock and the band *Kino* with its charismatic front man Viktor Tsoi fits in well. *Kino*'s songs, especially its hit *I Want Change!* (*Khochu peremen!*) reached the general public with Sergei Solov'ëv's cult film *Assa* (1986) and its eponymous refrain, becoming the anthem of the perestroika.

Tsoi's cutting voice and Asian appearance transformed the singer with Korean roots into a multi-layered symbol. Embodying a dual Russian-Soviet and Eurasian subaltern, who, after decades of social and political estrangement, started 'singing back' against the corrupt empire and demanding a say. Respectively, Tsoi's final performance in *Assa* expressed the sensibility of a whole generation, craving changes to the corrupt system, in which no mediation existed between the new, often murky elites and the rebellious avantgarde of rock musicians.[12] Generally, Serebrennikov's *Summer* does not deal with the later fame of Viktor Tsoi as a rock and film star but with the beginning of his career.

---

10  Obviously, it was also an escalation of internal power struggle within the regime hierarchy which satirist Viktor Shenderovich pointedly and frequently dubbed "spider fights in a jar" (Maiers 2023).

11  The insurmountable antagonisms within Soviet society that were exposed through the looming collapse of the Soviet Union was mediated in *Assa* by the biblical Flood allusions and parallel historical narrative of Emperor Paul I's murder. Moreover, the death of the main protagonist of *Assa*, the frontman Bananan, at the hands of an ambitious mafioso Krymov as well as the circumstances of historical fratricide of Paul I by the future emperor Alexander I, appear, retrospectively, as a gloomy prediction of the future failure of systemic change and the subsequent marginalisation of Russian civil society in its desperate struggle with the country's multiple authoritarian pasts.

12  See: Shada 315 (2018); Andrei Burlaka is an independent producer, eco-activist and historian of the Russian rock, still working as an editor of several St. Petersburg-based rock-n-roll websites.

Yet Tsoi's first steps to the all-Soviet stardom are only one aspect of the film which programmatically sets out to illuminate the larger context – the socio-political climate on the eve of perestroika. Its goal was also to draw a collective portrait of the Leningrad rock underground of the early 1980s, which included such pioneers of the genre as Maik Naumenko (*Zoopark*), Boris Grebenshchikov (*Akvarium*), Andrei Panov aka "Svin" (*Avtomaticheskie udovletvoriteli*) or the famous rock critic and promoter Artemii Troitskii.

The film's major narrative line is the artistic friendship between the already established 'master' Naumenko and his talented 'apprentice' Tsoi which unfolds against the backdrop of Leningrad's rock underground. This tale of a creative tandem of once again two great male artists is repeatedly overshadowed by a parallel romantic story – a triangle between Maik, his wife, Natal'ia (Natasha) and the young Viktor. In this respect, *Summer* could also be seen as a film about love and creativity, a cinematic coming-of-age and artist's novel (*Entwicklungs- und Künstlerroman*) in one.

Surprising about Serebrennikov's approach to this period is, however, the absence of the major political, social and cultural currents of the time. Instead, the film plot focuses on private and small places like communal or private apartments where the legendary *kvartiniki*, house concerts took place, or the gloomy backyards of St. Petersburg's old town. The performances in the cradle of the movement – the Leningrad rock club on Anton Rubinshtein Street with its relatively limited public – is also part of the somewhat claustrophobic film chronotopos. Though a few sequences in which the television or radio run in the background evoke a certain *Zeitgeist*, they have a rather decorative, ornamental character and reveal often no specific relationship to the film narrative.

The absence of the ideological atmosphere of the time within a film which raised expectations of a cultural and political manifesto contrasts instead with an overabundance of material details – from the beautiful but dilapidated fabric of St. Petersburg's buildings to old-school music equipment, tape recorders, furniture and Soviet interiors. Like *Hipsters*, *Summer* repeatedly creates the impression that historic artefacts and non-discursive media are much more important than the cultural-political circumstances of the time. The fixation on iconic Soviet commodities feels almost like a metropolitan second-hand store – a biotope of modern hipsters rather than the history-laden time of the looming perestroika.

This incongruity between this highly stylised 'vintage' world on the one hand, and the testimonies and remembrances of witnesses on the other, provoked a heated public debate. As one of the film's protagonists and forefathers of Russian rock Boris Grebenshchikov bitterly remarked on *Summer*:

> His script features hipsters, typical, today's Moscow hipsters, who except to fuck at someone else's expense, do nothing at all. It has nothing to do with Maik, Tsoi, Natasha, or any of us. The man who wrote this script, he wasn't even on this planet. (Roads L. 2018)

However, it would be too easy to attribute Grebenshchikov's scathing comment just to the jealousy of the witness who knows better. Other reviewers like the aforementioned critic Artemii Troitskii, who also appears as a protagonist in the film, saw the accusations of historical inaccuracy as a fundamental misunderstanding, praising it above all as a good piece of entertainment.[13] Similarly, the renowned St. Petersburg cineaste and producer Sergei Sholokhov highlighted the "amazing" quality of the camera and the "joyful affects" conveyed by the film: "Our joy in cinema has disappeared. In this film, despite the fact that it talks about some terrible years of stagnation, there is no terribleness" (Telekanal Sankt-Peterburg 2018).

This depoliticisation and privatisation of *Summer*'s story line lends the film an aura of ahistoricity which is reinforced by some of its formal features, above all, by its colour tone – the nostalgic, 'old-school' aesthetic of black-and-white pictures. However, the intention to create in this way an accurate and 'authentic' sense of the late Soviet Union, to provide its specific "world view" or "structures of feeling" (Raymond Williams) paradoxically tips into its opposite. First, the switch to the monochrome picture itself causes some confusion since by the early 1980s the majority of Soviet films were already released in colour. Serebrennikov's decision was apparently dictated by the desire to create an aura of documentary accuracy, and underground atmosphere. Yet, this technique is contradicted by the fact that the movie is shot in modern monochrome perfection instead of the characteristic Soviet film and photo tonality – for instance the typical irregular, 'amateurish' contrast structure and softness of the Soviet Svema tapes, produced at the Shostka factory in the Soviet-Ukrainian Donbas. This impeccable digital black-and-white aesthetic imparts to the film a surprising coldness and timeless rapture which tellingly correlates with its 'hipsterian' content.[14].

This aesthetically and content-wise historically oblivious approach to the past is not, however, a unique post-Socialist Russian phenomenon, but a general postmodern tendency prominently problematised by Fredric Jameson. In the US-American cinema of the 70s, he observed a remarkable retro wave – a tendency for idealized reconstruction of the 'golden American' post war-era, epitomized in such films as, for instance, in the films *American Graffiti*, 1973 by George Lucas, or *China Town*, 1974 by Roman Polanski (Jameson 1991: 19). The critique relates these nostalgic representations to a fundamental change in the regime of postmodern signification which, respectively, reflects the recent, "purer", post-industrial stage of capitalist development (ibid: 35–36). Accordingly, the main distinction between modernist and postmodernist art lies in different types of representation which Jameson subsumes under the opposition between the depth and surface of

---

13   Troitskii 2018.
14   A close friend of Tsoi and co-founder of *Kino*, author and filmmaker Aleksei Rybin observes in relation to *Summer*, albeit with a telling slip of the tongue: "A film is made by a director. All questions to the director. [...] The screenwriter there is simply diabolical [adov], Idov is his last name, but in my opinion, it's diabolical, a simply diabolical man. This man, he should only write series called '80s'. What I saw in the film *Summer* is absolutely one of these '80s' series, which he did, as a matter of fact. Completely unlike the real 80s, not even close" (RTIVi Novosti 2019). Rybin refers here to popular series launched by Russian television between 2012 and 2016 which generally offered an idealised and nostalgic picture of the late Soviet period. Interestingly, in this interview with Rybin both interlocutors agree that the number of fictional elements depends on the genre. While Troitskii, who briefly advised the *Summer* film team, still tries to justify its playful treatment of historical background by stressing its generic nature as a music film, Rybin is much more critical. The reaction of Andrei Tropillo, the legendary producer and promoter, the "godfather of the Russian rock", turned out to be even more devastating. Cf. Unamusic 2017.

an object. Whereas modernist art like Vincent van Gogh's famous *Peasant Shoes* (1888) reflects not only a specific stage in aesthetic development like the ground-breaking usage of colour, but also the social world of the French peasantry, postmodern art, like in Andy Warhol's *Diamond Shoes* (1980) is characterised by pure self-referentiality, free of any historical relations, and hence remarkably silent. Even more, the "flattening" of Warhol's picture, its two-dimensional quality results into a "waning of affect" (ibid: 10), "a new kind of superficiality" which Jameson diagnoses as "the supreme formal feature of all postmodernisms" (ibid: 9). In contrast to van Gogh's *Shoes*, which renders to the spectator the severity of the peasant's life, Warhol's painting conveys fragmented, fetishised and thus mortified reality. Similarly, through their nostalgic character and fixation on the material surface, the postmodern cinematic reconstructions of the US-post-war years produce idealised, fictitious worlds; signs bereft of the complex historical reality and authentic historical setting – a simulacrum (ibid. 10).

Despite its conservative tinge, the idea of postmodern simulacra can be productively applied to the carnivalesque setting of *Hipsters* as well as of *Summer*. Todorovskii's musical film with its glaring bright colours and consumer goods (fancy clothes, cars etc.) strikingly contradict the harsh everyday conditions of the post-war Soviet Union. In the same way, Serebrennikov's film, despite its opposite aesthetic strategies of reductive and monochrome perfection, ends up with an analogous loss of historicity. A loss that is already suggested by the very title "Summer", which, on the one hand, connects the birth of Russian rock to the high season of vacation, enhancing its de-temporalisation and de-historisation. As a result, the evocations of the eternal, carefree lifestyle of the Leningrad's rock bohemians differ considerably from such groundbreaking cinematic testimonies of the time and milieu as Aleksei Uchitel's film *Rock* (*Rok*, 1988).

It is telling that the escape from history and social reality into a purified, careless and isolated bohemian universe also correlates with the extensive presence of nature – *Summer* begins in a picnic atmosphere of a Baltic beach where the nascent rock scene celebrates its parties. In addition, the beautiful shots of the pristine pine forests and Baltic Sea coast, now stylised as a monochromatic Soviet Woodstock, work as a counterpoint to the claustrophobic spaces of the decaying collective apartments (*kommunalkas*), belle epoque buildings with their deep, shady backyards and dilapidated staircases. The escape from history thus coincides with an escape from the modern city.

## 4. Conclusion: Showbiz Logic and the Mummification of Subcultures

> There were no admirers [...] In those rock-club days there were no admirers. It's a stupid word, admirer... You know, there were like-minded people or people who shared the same worldview... (Shevchuk/Zhang 2022)

The differences between the present and the past, the consistency of certain historical references are blurred in both *Hipsters* and *Summer* not only on an aesthetic and narrative level, but also in terms of ideology. In Serebrennikov's case, the most problematic ideological inconsistency is certainly the projection of several features of modern showbiz back into the Soviet 1980s. For example, the Leningrad rock scene, which according to contemporary witnesses had horizontal and rather rhizomatic forms of organisation, is presented in *Summer* as a hierarchical, competitive, and star-centred world, strictly divided between the 'genius' and his enchanted entourage. Respectively, the film abounds in episodes with ecstatic female fans whose reaction is often the only way to indicate artistic quality; by the same token, Maik Naumenko, who in real life was notorious for his shyness of publicity, modesty, and self-irony, appears as a taciturn, lofty enigmatic guru who does not care much about his surroundings. The band leader, who actually was highly sceptical towards the commercialisation of rock and the lures of the emerging Soviet music industry, is presented as an impresario who encourages his younger follower Tsoi by sharing with him his exquisite collection of Western records and supporting him as a co-producer in his first successes. Such a showbiz reinterpretation manifests itself, for example, in the rendering of Tsoi's debut in the rock club which is dramatised as an absolute turning point in his artistic career. Here it is not his performance that first excites the reluctant audience, but only the appearance of the older 'master' Naumenko which breaks the ice bringing the predominantly female fans to a frenzy and thus setting the stage for a happy ending.

At the same time, Serebrennikov is very inventive in the ways he stages and narrates the relations between the 'old master' Naumenko and 'to-be-master' Tsoi; with great intermedial sophistication he shows how certain moods, everyday situations or phrases, casually picked up on the street, may transform into songs. He, for instance, presents facsimiles of the original songs and blends them with quasi-documentary material such as faked amateur recordings to highlight the explosive, bifurcatory dynamics of the song writing. Communicating mostly without words, sometimes via chords, the creative exchange between two rock musicians is thus given an almost mystical aura of silence and non-verbal agreement. Yet all these scenes with the two protagonists are presented in such a speed of sequences, including various multimedia effects, that the viewer is rather overwhelmed, getting no time for imaginary immersion or, in Jamesonian terms, for developing any deeper affect and identification. Even more: the cross-fades, quick cuts, cartoon elements or other defamiliarising devices in a way marginalise the archival material aesthetically, covering its poetic function behind the perfect modern orchestration and montage.

This aesthetic choice of accelerated perfection influences also the depiction of the protagonists, which follows a certain showbiz logic. Generally, Serebrennikov's characters are rather emotionally flat and unconvincing: On the one hand, there is the Leningrad 'John Lennon' Naumenko, who lives in his genius bubble, neglects his family and balances on the verge of creative exhaustion. On the other hand, the younger Tsoi, also withdrawn and solitary, but taking touching care of Naumenko's young son and his wife Natal'ia, a detail that Serebrennikov develops into a magesterial plot line which totally contradicts the biographies of his historical prototypes.[15] Especially the speed

---

15   Remarkably, it is precisely the love triangle between the two icons of Soviet rock culture that earned Serebrennikov the most criticism. Although Nataliia Naumenko admits in her interviews and memoirs a short-lived, platonic affection for the young and inexperienced Tsoi, the love affair highlighted in the film fails to convince and only distracts the attention from its central message: the testimony of intense aesthetic and ideological innovation. Cf. Kushnir 2018.

with which Natal'ia's love oscillates between Maik and Viktor presents an Eros who like a radar follows the creativity of the (male) rock demiurges. Moreover, the female muse operates as an irrational force that knows no constancy in feelings and attachments but wanders after the (floating) symbolic capital, mirroring and reinforcing the male creative genius. Driven by this relational logic, Natal'ia acts pretty much in line with the 'the winner takes it all' principle of showbiz. Consequently, the rising leader of the Leningrad rock scene (Tsoi) wins not only the hearts of the audience but also the rival's lover (Natal'ia), turning history into a perfect Hollywood style success story.[16]

If we look at this aesthetic strategy in a broader theoretical perspective, it almost literally echoes Jean Baudrillard's critique of the postmodern stage of media development – its "precession of simulacra" (Baudrillard 2006 [1994]: 8). According to the French thinker, instead of a positive "lively, dialectical, full dramatic relation" to reality, postmodern cinema is characterised by "an inverse, negative" one, aiming at a more perfect picture of the world than the original itself and thus leading to an abolishment of the historic referent (ibid: 47). Striving towards such "an absolute correspondence with the real" (ibid.), which Baudrillard calls "a strategy of the real, neo-real and hyperreal," (Baudrillard 1993: 197) this fading of the historical referent results in a characteristic postmodern heightened self-referentiality and the respective nostalgia for a lost reality we discover in Serebrennikov's *Summer*. The described postmodern symptoms manifest themselves particularly in the metareflexive commentaries added in certain critical moments of transgression, when the present threatens to replace the fictionalised past too blatantly. Then the figure of a chronicler appears who repeatedly exclaims: "All this did not exist!" ("Étogo vsego ne bylo!"). This demonstrative negation of the film's narrative has seemingly the rhetorical goal to parody the attitude of a sceptical – Soviet or contemporary – and indoctrinated petite bourgeois who stubbornly denies the uncomfortable and subversive past or present reality. By contrast, for a more sophisticated audience it signals ironic distance to this utterance, asking for a sympathetic and winking acceptance of Serebrennikov's version of the events, now validated by negation.

However, this apparently sophisticated self-referential postmodern irony is not only unhistorical and superficial, but also bears an antisocial impulse, very similar to Todorovskii's othering of the Soviet 'grey masses' in *Hipsters*. This tendency culminates in an episode with the suburban regional train, the *elektrichka*. After a short peaceful ride in the eponymous vehicle of Soviet culture, the young rockers start brutally mocking and threatening ordinary Soviet citizens, who are going to their *datchas* or elsewhere. Instead of mild irony and sympathy for their elderly fellow countrymen, known from such pretexts as Venedikt Erofeev's ground-breaking novel *Moscow-Petushki* (1973)[17] or the already mentioned drama *City Zero*, the urge to scandalise and provoke finally prevails and becomes an end in itself.

However, this transgressive behaviour of the rebellious heroes together with the ostentatious character of the meta-commentaries do not automatically elicit unconditioned sympathy with the nonconformist characters: The portrayed quasi-artistic

---

16   This may be the reason behind Grebenshchikov's harsh critique of the Leto production team which completely misunderstood his circle, namely that it was not all about money (Roads L 2018).

17   *Moskva-Petushki* is also known as *Moscow to the End of the Line* or *Moscow Stations*.

excesses and provocations in the suburban train after a certain moment start to undermine the human dignity, solidarity and the very critical common sense they appeal to. Given the disdain and aggressive behaviour towards their fellow citizens, intensified by the exorbitant use of the multimedia montage, the 'ordinary' viewer rather involuntarily feels empathy with 'declassed' 'common people,' scared and stressed by aggressive punk performances.

Thus, the contradictory ambivalent rhetoric and aesthetic structure of both films – their simultaneous impulse to preserve and replace, to remember and to forget – leads to a paradox self-sabotage of the intended subversion.

Remarkably, the intense mythologisation and reification of the non-conformist youth cultures as well as the idealisation of the Soviet everyday life in Summer and Hipsters, promote rather the forgetting of its burdens and a paradox nostalgia for the very political system – the Soviet regime – they set out to dismantle. With their hyperrealist claim to surpass the historical past, to achieve a 'higher' verisimilitude, particularly on the level of protagonists, material decorations or formal perfection, both films lead to a striking mortification or even 'mummification' of the non-conformist content. Despite all painstaking efforts to recreate and reanimate the historical body of the Soviet rock culture, it – very much like the efforts to preserve Lenin – remains lifeless. In this way, both movies reflect something deeply symptomatic for a specific authoritarian context of Putin's Russia and beyond – a kind of Stockholm syndrome, an identification with the hegemonic power – a tragic turn against oneself.

## Filmography

*Admiral*, dir. Andrei Kravchuk, Russia 2008.
*American Graffiti*, dir. George Lucas, USA 1973.
*Assa*, dir. Sergei Solov'ëv, USSR 1986.
*Black Raven (Chornyi voron)*, dir. Taras Tkachenko, UA 2019.
*Brigada*, dir. Aleksei Sidorov, Russia 2000.
*Brother I (Brat I)*, dir. Aleksei Balabanov, Russia 1997.
*Brother II (Brat II)*, dir. Aleksei Balabanov, Russia 2000.
*Burnt by the Sun 2 (Utomlënnyie solntsem 2)*, dir. Nikita Mikhalkov, Russia 2010.
*China Town*, dir. Roman Polanski, USA 1974.
*Firecrosser (Toi, shcho proishov kriz' vohon')*, dir. Mykhailo Illienko, UA 2011.
*Haytarma (Qaytarma)*, dir. Akhtem Seitablaiev, UA 2013.
*Hipsters (Stiliagi)*, dir. Valerii Todorovskii, Russia 2008.
*Ida*, dir. Paweł Pawlikowski, Poland/Denmark/France/United Kingdom 2013.
*Il'ich's Gate (Zastava Il'icha)* dir. Marlen Khutsiev, USSR 1965.
*In August of 1944 (V avguste 44)*, dir. Mikhail Ptashuk), Belarus/Russia 2004.
*Intergirl (Interdevochka)*, dir. Petr Todorovskii, USSR/Sweden 1986.
*Yuri's Day (Iur'ev den')*, dir. Kirill Serebrennikov, Russia 2008.
*Mr Jones (Obywatel Jones)*, dir. Agnieszka Holland, Poland/Ukraine/United Kingdom 2019.
*My Younger Brother (Moi mladshii brat)*, dir. Aleksandr Zarkhi, USSR 1962.
*Night Watch (Nochnoi dozor)*, dir. Timur Bekmambetov, Russia 2004.

*Rock* (*Rok*), dir. Aleksei Uchitel, USSR 1988.
*Stalingrad*, dir. Fëdor Bondarchuk, Russia 2013.
*Summer* (*Leto*), dir. Kirill Serebrennikov, Russia/France 2018.
*The Barber of Siberia* (*Sibirskii Tsiriul'nik*), dir. Nikita Mikhalkov, Russia/France/Italy/Czech Republic/USA 1998.
*The Brest Fortress* [also known as *Fortress of War*] (*Brestkaia krepost'*), dir. Aleksandr Kott, Russia/Belarus 2010.
*The Guide* (*Povodyr*), dir. Oles' Sanin, UA 2013.
*Volhynia* [also known as *Hatred*] (*Wołyń*), dir. Wojciech Smarzowski, Poland 2016.
*Zerograd* (*Gorod Zero*), dir. Karen Shakhnazarov, USSR 1988.
*Panfilov's 28* [also known as *Battle for Moscow* and *Thunder of War*] (*Dvadtsat vosem' Panfilovtsev*), dir. Kim Druzhynin/Andrei Shal'opa, Russia 2016.
*1918 The Battle of Kruty* (*Kruty 1918*), dir. Oleksii Shapariev, UA 2019.

## References

Baudrillard, Jean (1993): "The Evil Demon o,f Images and The Precession of Simulacra." In: Docherty, Thomas (eds.): Postmodernism. A Reader. New York: Columbia University Press, pp. 194–199.

Baudrillard, Jean (2006): Simulacra and Simulation [1994], Ann Arbor: The University of Michigan Press.

Bielefeldt, Christian (2017): "Rock-n-Roll." In: Hecken, Thomas/Kleiner, Marcus S. (eds.): Handbuch Popkultur, Stuttgart: Metzler, pp. 25–30.

Britanishskii, Vladimir (1996): "Studentskoe poėticheskoe dvizhenie v nachale ottepeli." In: Ruthenia.ru [n.d] (http://www.ruthenia.ru/60s/kritika/britanish_stud.htm) [11 April 2023].

Dolin, Anton (2018): "'Leto' Kirilla Serebrennikova: kollektivnyi son o minuvshei epokhe. V Kannakh pokazali fil'm arestovannoho Kirilla Serebrennikova o Viktore Tsoe i Maike Naumenko." In: Meduza, 10 May 2018 (https://meduza.io/feature/2018/05/10/leto-kirilla-serebrennikova-kollektivnyy-son-o-minuvshey-epohe) [08 April 2023].

Getty, Arch J. (2016): "Dead Man Talking: Lenin's Body and Russian Politics." In: University of California Television (Youtube), 11 February 2016 (https://www.youtube.com/watch?v=NBpm3CnGT30) [21 May 2023].

Grani.Ru (2017): "Viktor Shenderovich o dele Kirilla Serebrennikova." In: Youtube, 23 August 2017 (https://www.youtube.com/watch?v=1h35Ik6HfdU) [11 April 2023].

Jameson, Fredric (1991): Postmodernism, or, The Cultural Logic of Late Capitalism, Durham: Duke University Press.

Kun, Mishel' (2012): "Zastava Il'icha (1968)." In: Braginskii, Nikita/Vasil'eva, Ekaterina (eds.): Noev Kovcheg russkogo kino: Ot "Sten'ki Razina" do "Stiliag", Moscow: Globus, pp. 228–533.

Kushnir, Elena/Koėn, Tania (2018): "'Moia zhizn' – ne sovsem moia': Natal'ia Naumenko o fil'me 'Leto', svoem muzhe Maike, druzhbe s Viktorom Tsoem i nostal'gii." In: Meduza, 19 June 2018 (https://knife.media/naumenko-interview/) [08 April 2023].

Meerzon, Yana (2011): "Dancing on the X-rays: On the Theatre of Memory, Counter-Memory, and Postmemory in the Post-1989 East-European Context." In: Modern Drama 54/4, pp. 479–510.

Maiers, Masha (2023): "Personal'no Vash. Interview with Viktor Shenderovich." In: ĖkhoFM 07 April 2023 (https://echofm.online/programs/personalno-vash/personalno-vash-s-viktorom-shenderovichem-4) [01 May2023].

Roads L (2018): "Boris Grebenshchikov vozmushchen fil'mom Kirilla Serebrennikova o Viktore Tsoe." In: YouTube, 15 February, 2018 (https://www.youtube.com/watch?v=_inVuKLkIVc) [07 April 2023].

RTIVi Novosti (2019): "Aleksei Rybin: 'Tsoi nikogda ne igral russkii rok.'" In: YouTube, 28 May 2019 (https://www.youtube.com/watch?v=VE003zUOlCQ&t=911s) [11 April 2023].

Salys, Rimgaila (2016): "Hipsters." In: Salys, Rimgaila (ed.): The Contemporary Russian Cinema Reader 2005–2016. Boston: Academic Studies Press, pp. 114–135.

Shada 315 (2018): "Andrei Burlaka o fil'me 'Leto.'" In: YouTube, 07 August 2018 (https://www.youtube.com/watch?v=H9z06SpTFvA) [11 April 2023].

Solov'ëv, Vladimir (2008), "Ideologicheskii fil'm nastol'ko vazhnyi, chto ia by vsekh procil ego posmotret'" In: Beliy.ru (Otzyvy) (https://www.beliy.ru/work/stilyagifilm/-id=204-1.htm) [09 April 2023].

Telekanal Sankt-Peterburg (2018): "Kak kritiki i muzykanty vospriniali fil'm Serebrennikova 'Leto.'" In: YouTube, 25 June 2018 (https://www.youtube.com/watch?v=8gi_khfjMbo) [08 April 2023].

Troitskii, Artemii (2018): "O fil'me 'Leto' i Leningradskom rok-klube (ARU TV)." In: YouTube, 24 June 2018 (https://www.youtube.com/watch?v=nT5vxayAPN8) [08 April 2023].

Tsipursky, Gleb (2016): "Jazz, Power, and Soviet Youth in the Early Cold War, 1948–1953." In: The Journal of Musicology 33/3 (Summer), pp. 332–361.

Unamusic (2017): "Kirill Serebennikov. Fil'm 'Leto.' Viktor Tsoi. Mnenie Andreia Tropillo." In: YouTube, 16 September 2017 (https://www.youtube.com/watch?v=QzO8OMPbpqs&t=2s) [11 April 2023].

Vorob'eva, Irina (2009): "Osoboe mnenie. Interview with Artemii Troitskii." In: Ėcho Moskvy, 6 January 2009 (https://echo.msk.ru/programs/personalno/563726-echo/) [12 August 2020].

Zhang, Petr (2022): "Iurii Shevchuk o Viktore Tsoe. Kakoi konflikt byl mezhdu Shevchukom i Tsoem?" In: YouTube, 29 January 2022 (https://www.youtube.com/watch?v=az9ZHwJ3SRI) [09 April 2023].

## III. Sites of Trauma: Horror Fantasies, Weird Sceneries and Realms of Terror

Chapter 9:
# Dealing with Cultural Traumas
Popular Representations of the Past
in Contemporary Belarusian Prose

*Lidia Martinovich*

## 1. Belarus: 26 Years of the State Regulation of Everything

Work on this essay began in the period following the mass protests over the illegitimacy of the 2020 elections in Belarus, continued during the subsequent repressions and ended at the point when Russia's war in Ukraine had been going on for several months. All these events changed the context of the ideas and works discussed, further emphasising the importance of the trends noted in this essay: the significance of historical narratives for the present, the public role of the Belarusian language within this process as well as the tendency of repressing and censoring certain representations of the past from oppositional writers and intellectuals. In this, the Belarusian state policy seemed to be very similar to the Russian one, except that in the Russian Federation the state more actively engaged, also financially, in history politics. Before the war unleashed by Russia in February 2022, these trends might have looked like a nostalgic attempt to motivate the citizens of Belarus and Russia to be proud of their countries despite the lack of democracy, economic and technological development, a way of trying to cover up these deficits with an eye to the 'great past' and to revive the spirit of Soviet patriotism. After 24 February 2022, it became clear that these seemingly nostalgic representations and the pathetic celebrations of the 1945 Victory were also preparation on a psychological level for new wars.

What might have seemed like a selective approach to history during the 26 years of Lukashenko's [Lukashenka's] regime, privileging certain interpretations and laying emphasis on the state ideology, today becomes the only allowed reality, claiming to be absolutely true. And the ways in which historical events are memorialised and represented in feature films, documentaries, and city festivals can no longer claim to have the cute flair of kitsch, amusing in its fabulousness and addressed to a deliberately naïve viewer. Depicting historical events through entertainment has been a way for the dominant (i.e., state) discourse to disguise the coercion and lack of alternatives to the official version of history.

In contrast to the Russian case, in Belarusian society the commercial component of this entertainment format was virtually absent; turning history into a nostalgic product was mainly a matter for state cultural actors. Movies, TV-documentaries, military parades and mass shows, as well as museums and memorial complexes (the most striking example being the Stalin Line, a museumised complex of defensive structures not far from Minsk) have become the main media for broadcasting an ideologised version of history.

But the Belarusian literary community has not mirrored this development by producing a similar kind of popular historical fiction prose, portraying historical events in a way that expresses the writers' vision and interests a wide range of readers. This, at first glance, is even more astonishing as in the literatures of neighbouring countries, such as Russia, Ukraine and Poland, we can observe in recent decades a boom in alternative histories, historical fantasy, radical rewritings of traditional Soviet historical narratives, and reappropriations of national narratives with very different ideological orientations and media implementations. Such a widely varied and pluralistically diversified, playful approach to one's own history is clearly absent from Belarusian literature and culture.

This absence is partly due to the fact that Russian mass cultural products enjoyed much greater popularity and were better financed for many years, whereas many local, Belarusian products were poorly financed and hardly stood a chance of enjoying a broader reception. The overwhelming Russian-speaking majority of Belarusian readers preferred popular books, films and other media products from Russia, whose mass media market – at least until recently – was also more pluralistic and freer than in Belarus. But a more profound cause for this absence could be that the literature of independent Belarus (from 1991 to the present) developed in a sociopolitical context that was itself traumatic for both society and authors. The first years after the collapse of the USSR gave rise to hope for the possibility of cultural, political and creative self-expression for all social forces and actors, but this period was replaced by a revanche of state control over all spheres of life and the dying out of a wide public field.

The daily life of literary production consists of restrictions on freedom of speech, the marginalisation of the Belarusian language (the state only occasionally uses it in the public sphere for decorative purposes), and an extremely narrow range of what is considered acceptable. A vivid example of a critical reaction to this cultural policy is the existence of two unions of writers in Belarus: the pro-governmental one, which enjoys preferential treatment from the state, and the independent one, which, along with the Belarusian PEN Centre, is essentially engaged in defending the interests of writers under constant pressure. These circumstances restricted commercially profitable projects, while traumatic and problematic social issues gained increasing importance and critical writers were rather focused on the moral overcoming of their own 'invisibility', isolation and even marginalisation. Therefore, entertainment, as already noted, was for many years at the opposite pole from those critical and tragic ways of speaking, the pole chosen by most Belarusian authors.

Another factor that complicates the situation is the bilingualism of Belarusian society, in which only a small minority of the country's residents can actively use, understand

and read the Belarusian language. In the national survey "Culture of reading and literary preferences of Belarusians" from 2014, the respondents answered the question "In what language do you prefer to read books" as follows: 93.7 per cent prefer to read in Russian, 5 per cent – in Belarusian, and less than 0.5 per cent – in other languages (Mikheeva 2014a). These figures do not reflect the share of those who know Belarusian (it is much higher), but preferences and reading habits. This situation is also connected with the informal division of the literary community into Russian-speaking (with a potentially large audience) and Belarusian-speaking (oriented towards the Belarusian-speaking minority). Until recently, there was even a discussion within the literary community whether Russian-speaking authors living in Belarus should be included in Belarusian literature at all, as their works enter into a common literary market with Russia. The discussion ended with the introduction of a rule that does not give Russian-speaking works the right to be nominated for the country's main literary prize – the Jerzy Giedroyc Literary Award.[1] The Jerzy Giedroyc Literary Award is given every year for the best book of prose (including non-fiction and collections of essays) written in the Belarusian language. The award was co-founded by the Embassy of Poland in Belarus, the Polish Institute in Minsk, the Belarusian PEN Centre, and the Union of Belarusian Writers and is dedicated to the Polish essayist and politician Jerzy Giedroyc (1906–2000). In general, it can also be noted that Russian-speaking authors more often choose to work with popular literary genres. Natal'ia Batrakova's love novels or Olga Gromyko's humorous fantasy are good examples of this tendency.

Historical narratives became the prerogative of Belarusian-speaking authors, who are more focused on the values of national revival and therefore choose to depict periods when Belarus was part of the Grand Duchy of Lithuania (this period is considered the heyday of the Belarusian lands), the Polish Rzeczpospolita, or a short period of national-cultural renaissance in the early 20th century. The most popular author of fiction and documentary historical books in Belarusian for several decades has been Uladzimir Arloŭ, who received the Jerzy Giedroyc Prize in 2018 for the book *Dances Above The City.* (*Tantsy nad goradam*, 2018), and the most popular historical book of recent times is his illustrated children's encyclopaedia *Motherland: A pictural history from Rahnedy to Kastsiushki* (*Aichyna: Maliaŭnichaya historyia. Ad Rahnedy da Kastsiushki*, 2017). The book's release was a notable public event, with queues of people wanting to buy it, lining up to get an autograph from the author as well. In online bookshops it is still on the list of top non-fiction books. The media wrote about the book as an essential that every Belarusian should read and every Belarusian family should have at home. Although *Motherland: A pictural history* does not present any new facts, it presents a sequential overview of events from the first mention of the Belarusian lands in chronicles to the 1794 uprising of Tadeusz Kościuszko [Tadevush Kastsiushka], who tried to resist the encroachments of the Russian Empire on the Rzeczpospolita and stop its partitions. In all likelihood, adults will also use the book

---

1 The Jerzy Giedroyc Literary Award is the main prize for independent writers. This award was the most visible and important among the existing non-state ones. These prizes have only been actively monitored by the independent media, which have now been completely shut down in Belarus. In contrast, state awards followed the Soviet version of award distribution, honouring propagandist writers supported by ministerial offices.

as a handy source of knowledge about Belarusian history, and Pavel Tatarnikaŭ's vivid illustrations are in many cases stylised reconstructions of real historical images (landscapes, portraits, maps), making them especially valuable for readers.

Not only non-fiction books, however, but also fictional works in Belarusian have been published in the last decade more often, targeting a broader audience. This popular genre prose (detective, historical detective, travel novel, adventure novel) followed the tradition of the great Belarusian writer of the Soviet period Uladzimir Karatkevich. For example, Liudmila Rubleŭskaia's cycle of novels *The Adventures of Prancish Vyrvich* (*Avantury Prantsisha Vyrvicha*, 2012–2020) can be compared to both the novels by Karatkevich and to the quasi-historical detectives of the extremely popular Russian writer Boris Akunin. And Uladzislaŭ Akhromenka's novels *The Theory of Conspiracy* (*Těoryia zmovy*, 2011) and *Muses and Pigs* (*Muzy i svinni*, 2014) combine a historical detective component with postmodern play and irony.

Also worth mentioning are books by other well-known Belarusian authors of recent years like Alhierd Bakharevich, Artur Klinaŭ, Viktor Martinovich, and Ihar Babkoŭ. None of them works in the genre of historical fiction, but for all of them working with history is an important part of today's life or even of the imagined future. For example, Alhierd Bakharevich sneers at a lot of historical stereotypes about Belarus (for example, the common love contemporary Belarusians have for the medieval castles in Belarus, almost all of which are now ruins, as well as for the national revival in the early 20th century) and incorporates these ironic reflections also indirectly into his novels.

Another example is Ihar Babkoŭ, who created a whole pseudo-historical novel about a figure from Belarusian culture called *Adam Klakotski and His Shadows* (*Adam Klakotski i iahonyia tseni*, 2001) who never actually existed, thus committing a kind of historical hoax. But many readers took it seriously as a 'discovery' of a previously unknown historical character, even students and teachers of the Philosophy Faculty of the Belarusian State University (BSU) and the Belarusian Collegium, who were among its first readers. However, several intellectuals and writers admitted that Klakotski could be a real, but unknown figure. Thus Babkoŭ, who is known for researching little-known and forgotten thinkers from the Belarusian lands throughout history, demonstrated, intentionally or not, how little Belarusians, even those interested in cultural history, actually know about it and could have intrigued his readers to engage more with the past.

The novel itself is a collection of fragments representing the memories, reflections, dreams and diary entries of several characters living in Belarus during different historical epochs. These fragments are linked through the main character, Adam Klakotski, who at the beginning of the book is presented as a real-life enlightener and encyclopaedist, allegedly born on the territory of Belarus in 1793, the year of the second partition of the Rzeczpospolita. Klakotski's life seems to resonate with the lives and ideas of characters from other eras, as if setting major questions, dramas, discussions and themes of reflection for generations to come. The part devoted to Klakotski is stylised as a biography and is replete with many vivid details, as if putting his character in the context of the 1830s, which were rich in historical events in Europe. Importantly, Adam Klakotski is shown as a bearer of the European tradition, for whom Paris, Warsaw and Minsk are equally accessible and important centres of culture. The other characters seem to echo him in their reflections and experiences.

Furthermore, Artur Klinaŭ's novel *Empties* (*Shklatara*, 2013, the term in Belarusian denotes empty bottles and jars) literally includes as a 'novel within a novel' the text of a quasi-historical screenplay written by the protagonist. These historical inserts reference the 19th century, when the Belarusian territories became part of the Russian Empire, and among the Belarusians there were many of the so called 'narodniks', politically active people from the intelligentsia who organised the rural population in opposition to tsarist power, the most prominent of whom was the Belarusian Ihnat Gryniavitski [Ihnatii Grinevitskii; Ignacy Hryniewiecki], who threw a bomb at Tsar Aleksandr II in 1881. These events are intertwined in the 'novel within a novel' with folk legends and a free interpretation of the 19th century Belarusian author Ian Barshchėŭski's work *Nobleman Zaval'nia, or Belarus in Fantastic Stories* (*Shliachtsits Zavalnia, abo Belarus u fantastychnych apaviadanniach*, 1844). This plot clearly resonates with events of the present, when Belarus is still experiencing a political crisis and the intelligentsia is searching for its role in this situation.

In his other writing, Viktor Martinovich also works with historical references, for example, in his most acutely political novel *Paranoia* (2009). Here the fictional present is compared with the era of Belarusian Kastus Kalinoŭski's uprising against Russian tsarist power, which took place in 1863, and the fictional Belarusian president is named after General Muravyov, who then suppressed this uprising and conducted the execution of its leaders. The fantasy novel *Mova* (2014), on the contrary, in a way transports the activities of Belarusian national revivalists of the late 19th – early 20th century to the near future, when Belarus has become part of the global Russian-Chinese state. Here, learning and writing in the Belarusian language is a form of opposing the state-imposed Russian and Chinese languages. Despite all their differences, both novels *Sphagnum* (*Sfagnum*, 2013) and *Night* (*Noch*, 2018) present the Belarusian people as a society without historical memory. In *Sphagnum*, the worldview of the characters is based on fragments of Soviet ideologemes about the Great Patriotic War, folk legends and village prejudices. In the novel *Night*, historical memory seems to be completely destroyed, so that the characters lose all ability to think critically and unconditionally believe the false news broadcast to them on the radio by a mad crank.

What all these works have in common is a critical and often ironic attitude toward historical narratives. Instead of creating romantic historical works designed to enchant the reader with the atmosphere of a certain era, these authors highlight critical reflection on history and its complex, debatable aspects, many of which have been culturally traumatic for Belarusians.

## 2. Regressive Sociality as a Traumatic Core of Belarusian Literature

A critical and ironic approach to one's own history is not, however, the main feature of contemporary Belarusian literature. In 2017, in cooperation with the Belarusian Journal, I conducted an expert survey (Mikheeva 2017) on the 500th anniversary of book printing in Belarusian lands, starting with Francisk (Frantsishak) Skaryna's (1470–1551) work in the first half of the 16th century. I asked fifty experts to name the most important Belarusian books of those 500 years. The experts named a total of 175 books – from Skaryna's

Bible to prose published in the 2010s. This list of 175 books helped me formulate the hypothesis that the contemporary code of Belarusian literature consists of a kind of traumatic core connected not only with the problem of identity (who, what are we, Belarusians?), but also with the always conflicting and painful experience of the social reality in which Belarusians exist.

To elaborate on this hypothesis, in this essay I have chosen novels from the expert list that were written in the 2010s and received a wide public response, gained awards and became bestsellers. They all in many ways echo the most influential classics of 19th and 20th century Belarusian literature like Yanka Kupala's [Ianka Kupala] tragicomedy *The Locals* (*Tutėishyia*, 1922), Vasyl' Bykaŭ's short novel *The Ordeal* (*Sotnikaŭ*, 1970), Barshchėŭski's *Nobleman Zaval'nia* (1846), mentioned above, Maksim Harėtski's *Two Souls* (*Dzve dushy*, 1919) and several postwar novels by Uladzimir Karatkevich. In these works, the topic of an unsatisfactory, traumatic sociality, of a deficit of solidarity, a ruptured cultural landscape, discordant due to a lack of social conventions on all meaningful occasions, is added to the issue of problematic local identities. The only situations when solidarity among people becomes evident are in 'negative' deficit or traumatic circumstances, a sort of 'negative solidarity' when people rally around something that, though vitally necessary, is currently missing, stolen or destroyed.

When analysing these literary works, I would like to use a concept introduced in 2005 by the most influential Belarusian political philosopher Vladimir Fours – the concept of "regressive sociality" (Fours 2012). In Fours's analysis of the Belarusian social field, regression is "a specific reaction to one's own inconsistency in a changed situation of action or in a situation of serious uncertainty" (ibid.: 111), a decrease in the aims and expectations of citizens, apoliticality, the shifting of responsibility to a charismatic leader, the uncomplaining acceptance of social roles approved by the state, and finally the acceptance of the status quo as the only possible and natural one. It is the state that the majority of Belarusians were in before the 2020 protests and the state to which the Belarusian authorities hope to return.

This "regressive sociality" in my view can also be described as a feeling of being engulfed in the present (without a vision of the future and without a consensus about the past), in the private (without access to public spaces), without solidarity and collectivity. It is condition that is enforced by a sovereign state, which opens no possibility to participate politically in the government or ministries and allows no freedom of speech or a public sphere where open discussions and independent culture could be created. Of course, there is no space in such a state to cope with the historical traumas of Belarusian society listed above. However, it is worth remembering, as the Polish sociologist Piotr Sztompka states, that the concept of cultural trauma should not be understood as a single event, but as a process that includes many components: the initial situation, the event itself, the description of the event with the help of available cultural resources, the appearance of certain social symptoms, and a subsequent adaptation, and, in positive cases, processing and curing of cultural trauma (Sztompka 2001: 6). In other words, one cataclysm may not become a trauma, while another, on the contrary, may significantly shake the social foundations and the usual model of the self-understanding of society.

Another factor is time, as we know from studies about the temporal range of communicative memory, which does not extend further back than a few generations. For example, events prior to the 20th century are mostly perceived by contemporaries as unproblematic, causing no heavy and negative emotions nor being associated with a sense of irreparable historical damage. So, the naïve, heroic film *Anastasiya Slutskaya* (*Anastasia Slutskaia*, 2003), directed by Yuri Yelchov (Iurii Yelkhov) and produced by the film studio Belarusfilm, tells the story of a princess who lived in the late 15th – early 16th century, and who, after the death of her husband, ruled the principality of Slutsk on her own and repelled the attacks of Tatar invaders. The film is one of the most entertaining productions of Belarusfilm and includes elements of a love narrative. Also, Liudmila Rubleŭskaia's most popular novels take place in the 18th century, completely detached from any negative emotions. But the further we move toward the 20th century, the less ironic and more problematic the filmic and literary representations are, depicting past events rather as uncorrected misfortunes, having fatal consequences until today.

Based on the aforementioned analysis of the list of the 175 books named as the most significant literary works, we can specify the following *traumatic* events in a chronological order:

1. World War I, which has been displaced from official discourse by the memory of the *"heroic" Great Patriotic War*.
2. After the war, the incorporation of Western Belarus into Poland and its subsequent annexation to the BSSR (the western part of Belarusian lands went to Poland as part of the Peace of Riga in 1918, while the eastern part went to the USSR, then at the beginning of World War II Western Belarus was again annexed to the USSR). As a result of these events, society was divided and for decades existed in two different states with a radically dissimilar economic structure, political system, and state language.
3. Collectivisation in the Soviet Union in the late 1920s and beginning of the 1930s, which turned the owners of private farmsteads into a free labour force for collective farms and dekulakisation.
4. Stalinist repressions of the 1930s when the Belarusian national intelligentsia was purposely destroyed in the so-called Night of Executed Poets in October 1937, with more than one hundred cultural figures and politicians being killed during one night without trial), but also during the NKVD shootings of citizens in Kurapaty from 1937 to 1941.
5. World War II, accompanied by the extermination of the Jewish population and civilians, as well as the partisan movement.
6. Participation of Belarusians along with other Soviet citizens in the Afghan war from 1979 to 1989.
7. Explosion at the Chernobyl Nuclear Power Plant in April 1986.
8. The collapse of the USSR and the socio-economic crisis that affected the last years of the USSR and the first years after its collapse in the 1980s and 1990s.
9. Repression of national intelligentsia and politicians under Lukashenko, peaking with demonstrations of disagreement with the results of elections and referendums.
10. The Niamiha tragedy in May 1999, an accident in which 53 people died in a crush while fleeing a downpour in an underpass.

11. The April 2011 explosion in the Minsk metro, in which 15 people died and 400 were injured, as well as its investigation, the results of which were not accepted by public opinion.

During the past 26 years, in the absence of public debate and in the context of state pressure on independent media, it is precisely these catastrophic, traumatic events that have acted as triggers for an increase of informal communication between a variety of subjects and groups, that united society situationally, forcing it to search for internal resources for collective processing. What is important here is that state ideology essentially blocked any open conversation about these events, either by ignoring, glossing over, or directly disputing the existence of a certain occurrence (for example, the shootings at Kurapaty are not officially recognised). It is precisely because of this lack of a truly universal ethical reflection on the Soviet past that the cultural traumas of the 20th century are still so crucial for civil society and literature.

Interestingly, the traumatic events of the more recent past are thus often unofficially discussed as a kind of mirror image of older historical traumas: Thus, the pressure on Belarusian-speaking and opposition-minded citizens and authors was linked to the Stalinist repression of the national intelligentsia, the activities of contemporary Belarusian security forces evoked the actions of their Soviet predecessors and the Niamiha tragedy and 2011 terrorist attack in the Minsk metro were associated with the silencing and inadequate elimination of the consequences of the Chernobyl disaster.

In spite of this engagement with traumatic events in the past, mainly in non-state and unofficial media and formats, there is one state-approved trauma in the Belarusian public sphere, which is intensively used for the official ideological metanarrative, namely that of the Great Patriotic War from 1941 to 1945. In December 2021, the Belarusian parliament even passed a bill "On the Genocide of the Belarusian People" (during World War II), which essentially aims to legally enshrine something like the Holocaust as applied to citizens of the BSSR.

The state monopolises the discourse about this period, masking everything painful and unspoken about the war with the mythology of the feat of the Belarusian people, which has no dark chapters or controversial figures. Even the old Soviet Museum of the Great Patriotic War was closed, rebuilt, and reopened in a new location in 2014. The concept of the new museum smoothed over the suffering and horrors of the war and celebrated the heroic deeds of ordinary Belarusian people as part of the Soviet Union in an even more sublime way, emphasised by innovations in the museum's exhibition and architecture. The museum is filled with compositions in which human-sized figures of partisans or invaders play out various scenes of military life or battles. Museum visitors can entertain themselves by taking selfies with plastic partisans or models of Soviet military equipment. (Mikheeva 2014b).

*Figure 9.1: Glass dome in the Minsk Museum of the History of the Great Patriotic War.*
© *Lidia Martinovich*

*Figure 9.2: Representation from soldats in the battle. Scene in the Minsk Museum of the History of the Great Patriotic War.* © *Lidia Martinovich*

## 3. Traumatic Experience through the Eyes of Belarusian Writers

This tension between an official glorification of the Great Patriotic War while negating all other traumatic experiences and a multilayered unofficial engagement with the negative experiences of the 20th century can also be found in Belarusian literature. We can identify two sense-forming centres of attention, which in general characterise the thinking of significant Belarusian prose writers today. First, comprehending the traumas of the late Soviet and post-Soviet transformations is still relevant. Until 2020, this relevance was based on the policy of 'preserving the best of the USSR' conducted in Belarus. In 2021, this relevance is fuelled by the realisation in society that not only the 'best' was preserved. Such phenomena as the absolute power of the police, security and supervisory agencies, the planned economy, the bureaucratisation and ideologisation of all spheres of society, and militaristic rhetoric were all carried over from the USSR. All the more relevant are the books that have been published in recent years rethinking the Soviet past and the period of post-Soviet transformation by the Nobel Prize laureate Svetlana Alexievich (Sviatlana Aleksievich), for instance *Secondhand Time* (*Vremya sekond khėnd*, 2013), as well as the laureate of the Jerzy Giedroyc Literary Award Ihar Babkoŭ's *A Minute* (*Khvilinka. Try historyi*, 2013). Second, many Belarusian prose writers think not only about the experience of 'the Soviet' and overcoming 'the Soviet' as central to society, but also raise the question of the uniqueness of life in Belarus, which emerged from an incredible superposition of various factors. Barys Piatrovich's novel *The Square. One Lovestory* (*Ploshcha. Historyia adnaho kachan'nia*, 2011) for instance was inspired by the events of the 2006 protests and reflects on the specific pressure on dissenters. At the same time, this uniqueness is comprehended and experienced as a cultural trauma. For example, novels by Viktor Martinovich *Sphagnum* and *Night*, novels by Klinaŭ *A Helmet* (*Shalom*, 2011) and *Empties*, the short stories by Eva Vezhnavets from the collection *The Way of the Minor Bastard* (*Shliakh drobnai svolachy*, 2008) and many other texts problematise the totality of circumstances in which their characters, placed in contemporary Belarus, have to exist.[2] These novels describe various social dis-synchronisations, anomalies and lacunae, which can be found in various spheres of social life. All these failures and gaps are seen by the authors as directly connected with the local specificity and historical epoch, that is Belarus during Lukashenko's reign, which one could designate as a perspective that marks the whole state of 'Belarus as a trauma.'

The formula 'Belarus as a trauma' in my view (and, I believe, for many intellectuals in our country as well) is not only a reflection on the dissatisfaction with current developments or the breakdown of many social institutions, but signals also the transition of previously suppressed political and cultural conflicts into an articulated form. For me, the main meaning of this form is in the real, daily experience of fear of state violence behind each of the social problems listed above. By designating the current situation with

---

2 At the same time, works appeared that rediscovered the old trauma of the marginalisation of the Belarusian language, an old, unhealed trauma from the imperial 19th century like Martinovich's *Mova* or Alhierd Bakharevich's *Alindarka's Children* (*Dzetsi Alindarki*, 2014) while Sasha Filipenko offered his interpretation of cultural trauma associated with the mass crush near Niamiha metro station in the novel *Ex-Son* (*Byvshyi syn*, 2014).

'Belarus as a trauma' many authors I am talking about in this text relate the memory of the Soviet and post-Soviet years to episodes of state violence in contemporary Belarus, trying to comprehend their present situation through the prism of history and images of the future, and based on this drawing conclusions and offering explanations of the apparent traumatic situation. To illustrate more precisely what I mean by this, in the following I will examine some of the abovementioned novels in more detail.

## 4. The Double Trauma of the Transition from Soviet to Post-Soviet Society

My first example is the novel *A Minute* (*Khvilinka*, 2013) written by Ihar Babkoŭ, one of the most iconic authors of recent years. It deals in a way with a double trauma affecting Belarusian society. Undoubtedly the greatest trauma of the recent past was the collapse of the Soviet Union with all its well-known consequences: the crisis of social institutions, the economic breakdown, the sudden impoverishment of the population, the dissolution of the army, the new borders and military conflicts of former 'brotherly peoples', the vanishing of a monolithic ideological metanarrative, and so on. In parallel to this, behind this present traumatic situation it became more and more obvious, that the Soviet Union itself was a conglomerate of social traumas, which gradually were publicly acknowledged: Stalinist repression, the Soviet devaluation of human life (the lives of its own citizens in war and in everyday life), the undermining of trust in the state after the Chernobyl tragedy, and so on.

It is this double Soviet and post-Soviet trauma that is depicted in Babkoŭ's novel *A Minute*. Its plot begins just before perestroika and the Chernobyl tragedy in the 1980s and extends to the early stage of state independence of Belarus. In the novel, the trauma of the post-Soviet period takes on a metaphysical and generalised political meaning. It is composed of several intricately intertwined stories involving the narrator himself, the poet Franciszak, the political activist Bahdan, the singer Eva Daminika, and the bartender Leo at their favourite coffee shop, Khvilinka. Through the intertwining of the lives of these characters, Babkoŭ depicts the decline of the Soviet era and the social transformations of the 1990s. The Soviet is described in the categories of boredom and indifferent detachment. The novel offers us large-scale generalisations, filled with the experience of deadness, the frozenness of social life, lasting seemingly forever. Babkoŭ's protagonist experiences the feeling of isolation, disconnection, and non-inclusion in sociality as a satori. Thus, the negative social effects of alienation and atomisation of the individual are transformed into a productive and refreshing state of mind associated with the establishment of a salutary distance in relation to an alien and already deadened Soviet society. Observing the flow of city life from the window of a coffee shop one day, the narrator apprehends his own separateness as a liberation from any illusions about social life. He feels mild disgust, nausea towards Soviet Belorussia. The source of these feelings is described not as a sense of injustice at the social order, but as an intellectual and aesthetic protest against the inviolability of social automatisms. In this perspective, the main problem of the late Soviet is the inertness, the lack of alternative to the total ideological spectacle, in which citizens participate simultaneously as obedient actors and mesmerised spectators.

This perception of Soviet life is also present in a rather carnivalesque way in a fragment which depicts a scene when the three main characters, Franciszak, Bahdan and Eva Daminica, become acquainted and accidentally find themselves in the "Leninist room" of the student dormitory, partying, drinking wine, listening to records, thereby risking, perhaps, not only their well-being, but also their freedom. The characters throw the works of the classics of Marxism and Brezhnev's book *The Minor Land* out of the window, and later leave the room locked from the inside in an imaginary hot air balloon. Thus, the 'Soviet' in Babkoŭ's novel is described in the categories of a dead, mechanistic spectacle, the traumatic consequences of which are represented latently but discernibly. The reprisal of alien, unnecessary, dead books, embodying the code of the decrepit system, becomes a game, an act of freedom and carefreeness, the opposite in its modus operandi to any obsolete rituals produced by the system itself.

The author as narrator contrasts this 'pain' caused by Soviet society to him and the other characters with the microcosm of the coffee house Khvilinka, which gives its name to the entire novel, where the protagonist feels that it is "not so painful to live" (Babkoŭ 2013: 8). At this alternative, almost underground place the protagonist can finally be alone with himself or meet friends. In the case of Babkoŭ, this is a gesture of demonstrative artistic escape. The author is telling us: I know all about the traumas of my homeland, but I intend to confront this collective experience with my own individual world as a piece of art and a project of self-salvation.

However, it is no coincidence that this centre of the new microcosm is a small, modest coffee shop, overlooking the main avenue of the capital. This café represents the antithesis of Soviet kitchens, in which people criticised the government in the 1960–70s. Because in contrast to the private kitchen, a coffee house is a public place not hidden from the system, but it appears as if it slips out of the system's field of vision by being in full view. It is both part of the city and life and an island of privacy, solitude and mutual respect. At the same time, a cup of coffee is a symbol of pure, aesthetic pleasure of taste, unrelated to the profane nutritional content of food or the intoxicating effects of alcohol. Coffee is a drink with a flavour of Europeanness and ties in with the tradition of intellectual conversation in urban cafes of the fin de siècle. Its very existence symbolises a failure of the Soviet system, providing additional resources for a 'less painful' existence within it.

Hence the descriptions of the 1990s in the novel stress the urge to transform reality, the hope of establishing a path for Belarus of its own, although not without stating the other side of the coin, also referring to theft and the redistribution of everything 'that is bad', which ran parallel to the struggle for democratic freedoms. But this hope for a new less painful life of the early 1990s fails and Babkoŭ's heroes are confronted with a relatively smooth turn into the well-known 'stability' of Lukashenko's reign. According to the narrator, the responsibility for this turnaround lies not only with the corrupt, the men in power or the hapless 'revolutionaries', but also with the majority of those who have chosen the path of loyal consumption, rejecting the opportunities of a radical change. The novel describes this development as a vicious circle: The main characters start with critical contemplations and thereby detach from the 'society with a deficit of sociality' of the late Soviet Union, then actively participate in social change, before they return to the initial position of mere contemplators, but already with the experience of an unfulfilled, unrealised social project of a new Belarus. Both author and his heroes are puzzled by the present: the crisis-ridden 1990s led them to the still crisis-ridden 2000s. There seems to be no way out of the double trauma of late and post-Soviet experience.

## 5. *Empties* and *Sphagnum:* Belarus as a Trauma

Another perspective on the traumatic entanglements of Belarusian past and present is opened up in the novels *Empties* by Artur Klinaŭ and *Sphagnum* by Viktor Martinovich, which were both published in 2013 and became bestsellers.[3] Both novels share quite similar images of Belarus, depicting a social crisis which can be characterised in Vladimir Fours words as a 'regressive sociality'. Martinovich and Klinaŭ tell us about heroes from different social strata (Klinaŭ's heroes are Minsk intellectuals and artists, Martinovich's are provincial gangsters), which allows us to see this regressivity from different perspectives.

The action of the novel *Empties* develops around a contemporary art gallery that used to be housed in a building that once was a drop-off point for recyclable empty glassware. The prototypes of its characters are real people, artists, designers, philosophers, publishers, writers. The narrator is Artur Klinaŭ himself, an artist, writer, and screenwriter. The novel has two plot layers – the story of falling in love with a girl and parting with her, as well as the story of the script written for Partizanfilm-Studio (Belarusfilm), which is a pseudo-historical narrative on the *narodnik* Ihnat Gryniavitski, a Belarusian revolutionary, a member of the underground revolutionary-terrorist organisation Narodnaya Volya (People's Will). In 1881, he threw a bomb at the Russian Emperor Aleksandr II who died from his injuries.

Like Artur Klinaŭ's previous, more phantasmagoric novel *A Helmet* and *Empties* can be read, on a plot level, as a novel about a rejected artist. Empty glass bottles and jars here are a metaphor for the marginalisation and desolation of Minsk's intellectuals and artists. The gallery is not at all an optimistic public place. On the contrary, this public space is deeply broken, and its participants (as the novel's metaphorical title emphasises) are almost garbage, spent material that struggles for the right to be useful again and again. People of art in the novel are aware that they are on the margins, but retain enough courage and irony to continue to live their bohemian existence and work even under the conditions of neglect and humiliation by society and the state.

While the hero of Klinaŭ's previous novel *A Helmet* consciously chose a radical artistic position of self-exclusion, in *Empties* an outlet for the protagonist becomes a painful love affair. His struggle for the script, in other words, his attempt to defend his authorial self in public space, is paralleled by constant battles for his personal happiness, and in the end the hero's downfall awaits him both in his private and public life. The pathological environment, deaf and insensitive to the intellectual and artistic processes that exist in spite of everything somewhere on its margins, repeatedly nullifies all of the hero's efforts. The leitmotif of *Empties* is needlessness and loneliness.

---

3   The Belarusian independent literary scene is, for reasons mentioned above, very modest. When we talk about a "bestseller", we have to consider a print run of no more than 2000–5000 copies.

Traumatic collective experiences are present in Klinaŭ's novel on several levels. On the one hand, the terrorist attack of April 11, 2011, is central to the plot of the novel, a certain inexplicable excess of violence, the subjects of which are not fully defined due to the distrust of the official version of events. And so, it is not clear where this violence came from, what its meaning or message was, and what conclusions can be drawn from the event. But what it exposes is a terribly rigid, clumsy, bureaucratic system in the face of deadly and blind outbreaks of undirected, illogical violence. Tellingly, the tragic events at Niamiha are interpreted in Sasha Filipenko's novel *Ex-Son* (*Byvshii syn*, 2014) in a very similar vein – as a burst of random, uncontrolled, 'nobody's' violence. In both novels, the tragedy has become something of a transition point between Lukashenko's early rule and the subsequent tightening of his regime and the constant pressure on civil society, which is what Filipenko's novel especially is about.

Another common trait of both novels is that the perpetrators of the terror act are almost impossible to identify, whereas the huge number of victims affects society as a whole, with it being incapable of rationally comprehending what actually happened, whereby the tragedy gains an almost mystical nature. This links the Minsk terror attack to earlier traumatic tragedies like the accident at the Chernobyl nuclear power plant where also no culprits were identified. Thus, the novel offers a model of a 'sinister subjectlessness' of traumatic events, which leads to a total mistrust towards the state authorities, who do not take responsibility and conceal the scale of the consequences not only from the public, but also from the forced liquidators of the disaster.

In summary, the traumatic echo of *Empties* is triggered by a disaster, namely the terrorist attack on April 11, 2011, which recalls the terrorist attack on the Tsar of Ihnat Gryniavitski in the screenplay written by the main character. This resonance between past and present spills over into social reality of the protagonists, who are confronted with distrust, their own futility and, in particular, personal catastrophes.

Viktor Martinovich offers a different perspective on Belarusian society and its historical memory and traumas in his work *Sphagnum*, a novel initially praised by the publisher as an entertaining read comparable to the films of Guy Ritchie and Quentin Tarantino. The novel tells the story of three men from the Belarusian countryside, who stole a bag of money from the scene of a mysterious murder and are on the run. The detective story develops into an exploration of small towns and villages, their everyday lives and social imagination. It depicts a Belarus whose life does not intersect in any way with the universe we find in Klinaŭ's *Empties*. At the same time, the countryside is obviously as isolated from a kind of 'Belarusian society in a vacuum' as, for example, Minsk's intellectual community. Moreover, glocalisation in the description of the Belarusian province reaches a new level. The 'regressive sociality' here consists not only in Belarus' self-isolation from the world, but also in the self-isolation of separate regions (the autonomy of Palesse, small similar worlds of the Hrodna, Brest, Vitebsk, Homel' regions, each of which has its own agenda, its own political guidelines and ways of doing business, and so on) and small towns and nearby villages, where residents seek to secure themselves by accepting imposed social contracts and social roles. The narrative strategy of *Sphagnum* is the creation of a kind of thread, stringing together the world of the dying and eventless modern Belarusian villages and provinces. The dramatic events of the detective plot expose all the elements of this frozen world that acts according to rusty social automatisms. The depicted social reality of the Belarusian wilderness is a motley palimpsest of various discordant layers of experience: some villagers exist in secluded archaicism, subordinating their lives to the everyday magic and rhythms of forest and agricultural life; others live by the rules of local bureaucracy; some are classical philistines, who have made a social contract with the state apparatus – loyalty in exchange for the status of a 'normal citizen.' This 'social contract' had often already been made during Soviet times and was then mechanically prolonged in the era of independent Belarus. In the novel, the Soviet debris (in the form of remnants of a bygone civilisation, traces of urban planning and centralised management – in the form of signs on stores, transport stops, local history museums, etc.) looks like one of the layers of a complex palimpsest of types of experience which one needs to have in order to be 'the true local' in the Belarusian village. It is governed by fear of authority, by a social atomisation as modus of everyday interactions and by archaic beliefs and values.

The titular swamp moss – *sphagnum* – in this sense is a metaphor for everything that replaces the social coherence of the Belarusian village: the partisans put it in their wounds as a disinfectant, and the inhabitants also use it during the construction of houses to fill in the cracks between the logs. Swamp moss exists in nature in abundance, it is an inexhaustible resource for those who want to survive on the margins of 'big society', in the land of forests and swamps. Moss in this way also becomes a symbol of compensation for the lack of real social connections between people.

Another 'unnecessary' social group is depicted in the novel with the three young protagonists who simply have no place to put themselves within society, being neither part of the village people nor of the philistines. Their search for a bag of money resembles some magical or adventurous treasure hunt linked with the hope that its discovery could change their hopeless lives at once. Just as Klinaŭ's hero compensates his lack of publicness with an unhappy love story, so Martinovich's gangsters receive compensation for all the shortcomings of regressive sociality in the form of magical trips through the marshes of the Belarusian province, where, as they hope, an alternate mystical world could be found.

In his novel *Night* Viktor Martinovich continued to develop this logic of thought. Here, the fragmentation of the social imaginary in which the Belarusians live is illustrated on the plot level as the actual disintegration of the whole society. After an energy apocalypse, the world is split into multiple subjects where everyone is living according to his or her own values, ethical principles and concepts. In a world without electricity, nation-states and societies disappear, people return to living in communities, each spontaneously invented from scratch, regressing to pre-modern forms of sociality. The novel describes this fragmentation of societies around the world into local groups sharing sometimes maximally contrarian views in detail. It presents followers of conspiracy theories who stormed the Capitol, religious traditionalists, living in communities and denying the need for any vaccines, but also radical feminists, or adherents of veganism and zero-waste, and paramilitary communities. At the same time, it shows precisely the disintegration of post-Soviet society – choosing not only global trends, but also recognisable Belarusian examples. The novel presents this development as a direct outcome of the post-Soviet situation: due to the inability to build real solidarity and effective social institutions after the collapse of the USSR, Belarusian society is falling apart into warring communities not bound by law and order, each with its own rules and vision of the future. Thus, the disappearing electricity – the central symbol of Soviet modernity – is not only an embodiment of technical and economic regression, but also a symbol of social regression, a regression of humanity and the expiration of the guarantee of law. It is an apocalyptic picture which resembles many developments happening in Belarus right now.

## 6. Conclusion

Comparing Babkoŭ's, Martinovich's and Klinaŭ's work with history in their best-selling novels, it is striking that all of them in a way mark a shift from writing that is concentrated directly on the traumas of the past (in the manner of Svetlana Alexievich, who gives 'ordinary people' a voice, the right to speak, and laments the personal dimension of social catastrophes) to the paradigm of conceptualising contemporary Belarus as a pervasively traumatic social reality due to its misunderstood or forgotten history. The authors represent this shift in fictional form, using the techniques of genre prose (mysticism, fantasy plots, detective stories), as well as the endless resources of postmodernist play and irony.

As I have already mentioned, it is largely thanks to the authors' desire to create fiction books for a broad readership that Belarusian literature in the 2010s and 2020s has become the most noticeable public platform of critical thinking about the social and political agenda of Belarusian society, more influential than, for example, political science or sociology, which experience permanent pressure. The entertaining and accessible nature of these novels made it possible to involve readers, regardless of their profession, education or status, in the reflection about history and collective memory.

These popular novels developed new literary ways of perceiving the history of Belarus as a series of cultural traumas, shifting the focus from the literary recollection of immediate traumatic experiences and their consequences (as is the case with Alexievich's prose) to a vividly entertaining narrative of active heroes building creative, diverse relationships with their history and its echoes in the present. These literary works were able to look at the image of the 'suffering Belarusian' with a certain distance, simultaneously with empathy, but also ironically. They also offered images of characters who challenge the traumatic reality and create their own alternative worldviews and even imaginary worlds in which trauma becomes surmountable, less frightening, sometimes even ridiculous. Instead of a documentary examination of past suffering heroes as passive witnesses, these works offer a multiplicity of views and characters who are acting, resisting, fantasising, and creative. In this way, literature potentially empowers and might motivate the reader to act themselves, in associating their own situation with the one of the literary protagonists.

## Filmography

*Anastasiya Slutskaya* (Anastasia Slutskaia), dir. Yuri Yelchov, Belarus 2003.

## List of Illustrations

Figure 9.1: The final halls of the Museum of Great Patriotic War express the continuity of the Belarusian authorities with the victory in the war and glorify the common bright future of the fraternal peoples of the former Soviet Union. © Lidia Martinovich.

Figure 9.2: The final halls of the Museum of Great Patriotic War express the continuity of the Belarusian authorities with the victory in the war and glorify the common bright future of the fraternal peoples of the former Soviet Union. © Lidia Martinovich.

## References

Alexievich, Svetlana (2013): Vremia second-hand, Moskva: Vremia.
Fours, Vladimir (2021): K voprosu "belorusskoi identichnosti." In: Fours Vladimir. Sochineniya 1, Vilnius: EHU, p.111.
Babkoŭ, Ihar (2013): Hvilinka, Minsk: Lohvinaŭ.
Filipenko, Sasha (2017): Byvshii syn, Moskva: Vremia.
Klinaŭ, Artur (2013): Shklatara, Minsk: Lohvinaŭ.
Martinovich, Viktor (2013): Sphagnum, Minsk: Knihazbor.
Martinovich, Viktor (2017): Noch, Minsk: Knihazbor.
Mikheeva, Lidia (2014a): Culture of Reading and Literary Preferences of Belarusians, Report, Minsk: Laboratory of Social Research NOVAK.
Mikheeva, Lidia (2014b): "Voina: Niashno i ne strashno," 19 July 2014 (http://journalby.com/news/voyna-nyashno-i-ne-strashno-209) [30 September 2023].
Mikheeva, Lidia (2017): "Nashy lepshyia 50. Samyja vazhnyia knihi belarusskai litaratury pavodle ekspertau," 1 September 2017 (http://journalby.com/news/nashy-lepshyya-50-samyya-vazhnyya-knigi-belaruskay-litaratury-pavodle-ekspertau-1026) [30 September 2023].
Sztompka, Piotr (2001): "Socialnoie izmenenie kak travma." In: Sociologicheskie issledovanija 1, p. 6.

## Chapter 10:
# Nostalgia for Trauma
## Russian Prize Literature and the Soviet Past

*Valery Vyugin*

## 1. Introduction

Much, or perhaps even most, of contemporary Russian culture, including literature, can be interpreted in terms of recycling – the 'recycling' of one's own historical, and above all Soviet, experience.[1] This term is convenient as an alternative to the two concepts that are commonly used to describe attitudes to history – "nostalgia" and "trauma". From the point of view of recycling, history appears primarily as a resource that can be reutilised and resold. Understood in this way, "cultural recycling" is an extremely basic, primal category, not an ideological one like "nostalgia" and "trauma" (V'iugin 2021). The benefit of addressing it lies primarily in the removal of the familiar, albeit more complex, interpretative frameworks.

Recently, Russian writers have displayed a great interest in the Soviet ideological and aesthetic experience, which is especially evident in the phenomenon that can be roughly called 'prize literature.' Over the past two decades, the institution of Russian literary prizes have proved to be an effective tool for shaping the writers' 'elite.' Award nominations, of course, are not always and by no means the only important criteria for a writer's significance. However, prize literature – at least, within the domestic context – is extremely influential. Although its audience is not large compared, for example, with that of popular television shows and blockbusters, it actively participates in the circulation and production of topoi that are characteristic of popular mainstream culture. Some of them will be discussed in more detail in this essay.

---

[1] This work was prepared with support from the Russian Science Foundation, Project No. 19–18-00414 (Soviet Today: Forms of Cultural Recycling in Russian Art and Aesthetics of the Everyday. 1990s-2010s). I am also deeply grateful to Mark Lipovetsky for his invaluable moral support at a critical moment of my research. All translations of Russian quotes are mine, unless noted otherwise.

The institutional mechanisms of Soviet and contemporary Russian literary awards have not yet been studied in detail (Svin'in/Oseev 2007; Akhmanaev 2016; Zubkov 2021; Gorski 2023). While this aspect is undoubtedly important, this essay does not address questions of the sponsoring, nominating and selecting of finalists nor the question, to use a well-known aphorism, 'who judges whom?'. The focus is not on what James English calls the "cultural economics of prizes and awards" (English 2005: 4), but on literature as such, on the literary works themselves, which have been selected according to certain criteria, and as a result form a specific 'genre' that is shaped not by the authors, but by the prize jury. This essay examines several works of such prize literature that meet these criteria. In doing so, it is important to emphasise that the rather complex process of selecting and nominating certain literary works directly influences the career success of authors in the genre of prize literature. Prize literature is the specific result of those who, among other things, endorse and promote certain trends in contemporary literature.

To interpret such trends, this essay analyses selected literary works that were included in the 2019 longlists of arguably Russia's four most prestigious literary prizes: *Bol'shaia Kniga*, *Natsional'nyii Bestseller*, *NOS* and *Iasnaia Poliana*. This small selection of award-winning literature reflects not only one year's performance but a general trend in contemporary Russian literature over the past decade. Moreover, it is worth taking into account the specificity of 2019, which I could not imagine when I started, at the beginning of 2020, to read and write about the latest prize-winning novels. Indeed, this undertaking would ultimately turn out to be a dive into a preapocalyptic culture. Back then, I only vaguely felt what now becomes more and more obvious to me: the ideas and emotions of this kind of fiction from 2019 absorbed, if not foreshadowed, the upcoming catastrophic future, and today, at least, can contribute to a better understanding of why the social cataclysm which followed the pandemic became possible.

About a third of the overall corpus of prize literature of 2019, comprising almost a hundred texts, is represented by works which can be categorised as a "retrospective genre", i.e. a genre which includes historical novels and "novels of the recent past" (Fleishman 1971: 3). These are either explicitly historical narratives or narratives in which history occupies a central position. The vast majority of them refer to the Soviet period in one way or the other, and when one considers that other writings – novels and stories about modernity, future worlds or fantastic tales – also refer to the same time period in many cases, the picture becomes even more impressive: at the beginning of the 21st century Russian literature is obviously actively recycling the Soviet past.

The focus therefore will be on authors whose works deal with the Soviet past. The essence of the trend they reflect can be characterised as an ongoing attempt to 'harmonise' and 'normalise' Soviet history, to mask all contradictions, and to find something positive even in the seemingly worst stories. It is also important to note that this rhetorical strategy is not carried out through explicit declarations, but latently, through a kind of suggestive poetics that sometimes may not even be fully reflected by the author himself. The literary works examined here are also united by what can be broadly described as allegorical poetics: a very significant part of contemporary Russian literature, which aspires to the status of 'serious' literature, seems to be governed by it. This technique is reminiscent of the traditions of Soviet literature, drawing on both socialist realist and more recent aesthetics, though of course it is not a unique post-Soviet phenomenon, but a general characteristic of the global literary mainstream. Moreover, the selected works resemble what Boris Engel'gardt (1924) in analysing Dostoevskii's work, called the 'ideological novel', wherein one can easily identify certain ideas behind the main characters. In rhetorical terms, the characters serve as examples illustrating – metaphorically, metonymically, or otherwise – a general thesis. In other words, these novels feature in addition to the usual story a more or less developed 'allegorical plot' – a gradually unfolding argument in defence of a certain ideology and ethical values. The reader is invited to identify them as a specific intellectual and aesthetic exercise. This essay focuses on these ideological presuppositions inscribed into the narratives through the 'enigmatic' way of an 'allegorical plot'.

No less interesting, however, are the ethical premises on which these narratives are based, which are not necessarily included deliberately, but always at least unintentionally (Booth 1961). If, from the point of view of allegorical hermeneutics, literature about the past can be described as intellectual entertainment, from a rhetorical perspective it turns out to be a very serious matter, serving the formation of identity and social consolidation. But what are the ideological and ethical presuppositions with which the authors of the selected literary works seek to consolidate their readers' attitudes and which literary devices do they employ to achieve this? These are the questions that will be discussed in this essay.

## 2. Idyllic Stagnation

It is to a certain extent unsurprising that the so-called period of stagnation of the 1970s-1980s is mostly represented as a harmonious time. If we look at the 2019 prize literature, the most telling illustration of this observation is perhaps the novel by Vasilii Aksënov, *Ten Visits of My Beloved* (*Desiat' poseshchenii moei vozliublennoi*, 2018), which was included in the 2019 Iasnaia Poliana longlist.[2] It is an autobiographical novel, and, if we relate the situation to the Soviet tradition, a kind of new village prose.

'Ancient' Russian history is presented by Aksenov as a Golden Age: "Our ancestors, the Cossack pioneers, knew how to choose the place where to build" (Aksenov 2018: 17), but the story set in the Soviet time is also quite idyllic in the way it portrays the period. This depiction clearly contrasts with the personal melodramatic plotline, which is based on a story of unhappy adolescent love. Aksenov's village exists almost outside of Soviet ideology, almost beyond politics and even agricultural production. The author of the novel is more fascinated by the leisure culture of its inhabitants than in the 'battle for the harvest'. Social conflicts are depicted as coming from the outside into the community's life: "Only my Ialan is falling apart, it's a pity [...] after the announced enlargement. And who invented it? Some enemy. Someone, but no one from Ialan" (Aksenov 2018: 17–18). Group

---

2   According to the author's dating the novel was written in 2009–2010. It was first published in 2011 in *Moskva* magazine (No. 1/2), and the author won the magazine's award for best publication of the year. In 2014, a play based on the novel was staged at the Maiakovskii Moscow Academic Theatre with the title *V.O.L.K. (That's What Love Is)* (*V.O.L.K Vot Ona Liubov' Kakaia*)), directed by Svetlana Zemliakova. The first book edition was published in 2015, the second in 2018.

conflicts, for example, over the honour of a village girl, are also provoked not by their own people, but by outsiders. Even vehement arguments about the painful past, about Stalin, do not turn Aksenov's characters against one another, even if one is a convinced communist and the other is a believer and former kulak, a victim of the Bolsheviks' policy. After each quarrel the characters reconcile with each other. Apart from an unfortunate teenage crush, life in the Soviet countryside according to Aksenov appears quite prosperous.

But even when the author is clearly concerned with demonstrating the hidden conflicts of the Soviet system, the portrayal may end up being similar. In the novel *Verification Bureau* (*Biuro proverki*, 2018), for example, the officiousness and internal social contradictions are numerous.[3] This 'urban Moscow' novel by Aleksandr Arkhangelskii was shortlisted for the *Bol'shaia Kniga* Award in the 2017–2018 season, and a year later, in 2019, for the Iasnaia Poliana longlist. The main tension in the novel emerges as a confrontation between the party-state apparatus and the intelligentsia and all the other plotlines in Arkhangelskii's piece of art are based on this. And yet, Arkhangelskii, like Aksenov, manages to resolve the conflict. *The Verification Bureau* is essentially a novel about unity, – unity which is achieved on 27 July 1980, the day of Vladimir Vysotskii's funeral, functioning as a symbol that reconciles all the 'actors' of late Soviet history. In the final scene, the narrator – who is also the main character – witnesses the coffin of the deceased poet being carried through the city. Someone in a large crowd hands out Vysotskii's poems, and a policeman holds out his hand for them: "'But you are, excuse me, the police!' The policeman blushed. – 'And what,' he asked offended, 'do you think policemen aren't human?'" (Arkhangelskii 2018: 412) Arkhangelskii combines the utopian character of the phrase "the policeman blushed" with an apocalyptic expectation of a 'new world' to come – some fundamental social changes. Thus, contemporary Russian prose settles every conflict situation and attempts to harmonise history.

One motif that concerns both authors of these 'stagnation' novels is religion. In Arkhangelskii's work, the conflict of antagonistic social groups also means a religious opposition to the atheist state. Moreover, the topic of religion in *The Verification Bureau* is so crucial that one gets the impression that all private and public life in the Soviet Union revolved, if not exclusively then mainly, around this question. In *Ten Visits to My Beloved*, by contrast, religion is not brought to the forefront. Aksenov mentions it rarely, but each reference is symbolically weighty. His characters, who argue vehemently about Stalin, are wary of arguing about religion.

Aksenov and Arkhangelskii are by no means unique in their attention to this motif. Contemporary Russian literature in general draws extensively on this previously taboo subject. But what is new is that religion in these works turns out to be a part of the harmoniously constructed past. This aspect also characterises the novels discussed below, which focus on other periods of Soviet history.

The fact that in this 'stagnation' literature the late Soviet era is often portrayed as relatively prosperous is hardly surprising. But it is worth remembering that under the conditions of censorship during the Brezhnev era the Stalin regime was also not depicted as particularly disastrous. The situation did not change significantly until perestroika,

---

3   The novel, according to the author, was written between 2014 and 2018. It was first published in 2018 in the journal *Oktiabr'* (No. 3/4).

when it was mostly shown as a traumatic period, while today, after a different historical-political turn, there is a pluralism of different positions, to which award-winning writers have contributed.

Many of them are by no means inclined to present the pre-1953 Soviet Union as a conflict-free environment. The repressions and their consequences are often described in such detail that this literature may well be called 'traumatic'. This leads to the curious and, at first glance at least, paradoxical situation that this 'traumatic' literature, which highlights the dark sides of Soviet history, at the same time promotes the normalisation of that history, a constellation worthy further consideration.

## 3. Peacemaking Pantheism

Guzel Yakhina [Guzel' Iakhina] occupies a special place among contemporary writers who made it into the circle of prize-winners in 2019. She is truly a bestselling author, whose works are discussed not only by experts or in literary circles. Yakhina's novel *Zuleikha Opens Her Eyes* (*Zuleikha otkryvaet glaza*, 2015) was turned into a television series in 2020 and aired on the TV channel Russia-1. The series immediately became the subject of a heated public debate with some even calling for the series to be banned. As for the awards themselves, Yakhina is a regular on domestic shortlists. Her award-winning second novel *A Volga Tale* (*Deti moi*, 2018), discussed below, was written after *Zuleikha Opens Her Eyes*, but is no less, and perhaps even more, revealing in its theme of Soviet history under Stalin.

The novel, as already mentioned, is written in an allegorical manner typical of many contemporary authors, including Aksenov and Arkhangelskii. Only the degree of its symbolism clearly exceeds the norm. Yakhina's eventful plot – unlike, for example, Aksenov's account of everyday life – is almost entirely subordinate to the allegorical message. Since the mid-1970s, Soviet literary critics have referred to a special genre, the 'novel-parable,' which unites such diverse authors as Vasil' Bykaŭ, Chingiz Aitmatov, Bulat Okudzhava and many others. Yakhina's work, perhaps, embodies the qualities of this genre to an even greater extent.

*A Volga Tale* made the longlists for the 2019 *Natsional'nyii bestseller* and *Iasnaia Poliana* awards and was ranked third among the winners of the 2018–2019 *Bol'shaia Kniga* season. The novel spans two decades, from 1918 to 1938, but the story is also accompanied by references to both the more distant past and a brief excursion into the characters' future.

Throughout the entire novel, Yakhina's narrative is devoid of any complacency: a love story unfolds against the backdrop of a brutal revolutionary reality. Meanwhile, the immediate prehistory is again characterised as "calm, full of penny joys and little worries, quite satisfactory. Somehow happy" (Iakhina 2018: 24).

Yakhina's protagonist, a young German teacher named Bach, leaves his community together with his beloved Klara – because the community did not accept the young people's relationship – to settle some distance away, on a farm on the other side of the Volga. The characters thus drop out of society, and even time begins to flow differently for them, as their connection with the real calendar is gradually lost. This is one of the basic devices in the novel: the author replaces the historical, objective time in the spirit of 'neo-mythological' poetics or magical realism with 'legendary', symbolic time.

The fugitives are occupied only with themselves, so much so that even the continuation of their family seems not only unnecessary, but also undesirable. The hero only visits his former neighbours when necessary, each time witnessing the changes taking place in the abandoned settlement. Thus, the narrator, or, more precisely, the author[4] describes the Sovietisation of the Volga region from the perspective of a – in the sense of Viktor Shklovskii – 'defamiliarising' observer. This is the second characteristic device used by Yakhina that determines nearly everything in the novel.

A turning point in the novel is a bandit attack, which Bach is unable to prevent. His beloved was raped. That is, an outside force invades the lovers' asylum and destroys their idyll. After that, *A Volga Tale* turns mostly into an account of regular violence, which, although primarily inflicted by the new authorities, is also caused by the acts of ordinary people. *A Volga Tale* concludes with a phantasmagoric allegorical scene, in which the hero, plunging into the Volga, observes the riverbed filled with the victims not only of Soviet but also of Russian history: at the bottom of the Volga, he sees an endless row of dead people and animals as well as artifacts. Moreover, all these bodies and items have not decomposed despite the passing of time.

Thus, violence, brutality, and confrontation form the basis of Yakhina's novel, as if to dispose the reader to fear and reject Soviet history, assuming, of course, that violence is meant to deter. But around this chronicle of violence, Yakhina constructs her own 'historiosophy', in whose light terror looks somewhat different. Apart from her main character, the former teacher Bach, who has a marginal social status, Yakhina devotes quite a lot of attention in her novel to the person who held the highest position of power in the Soviet Union, namely Stalin. Yakhina's Stalin possesses traits that are quite often attributed to him. He is extremely suspicious, it is impossible to contradict him and it is better to anticipate his wishes even regarding trivial things. For example, although he firmly decides on a particular carp for dinner, the cook prepares him three different ones, since the leader can change his mind at any time. In addition to these generally known character traits, Stalin is also depicted through allegorical gestures, among which relations with animals, especially fish and dogs, occupy a special place. Stalin feeds the carp, personifies them and treats them as he treats people: he encourages the most zealous one, the one that grabs the feeder by the finger, and then demands that the fish be fried. The dictator repeats the same experience with a pack of feral dogs, whereby he is also attacked and, on this occasion, much more seriously.

Yakhina's Stalin fails to tame animals, but it is obvious from the novel that he is a much more successful tamer when it comes to people – primarily those close to him who set the mechanisms of terror in motion. In this sense, for example, Ezhov in Yakhina's novel becomes the first contender for the role of the zealous carp, which is about to be delivered for frying. This extended analogy is only one of the allegorical links in the chain

---

4   It is important for me to disavow here a well-known opposition between the terms 'author' and 'narrator', stressing the fact that, ultimately, it is the author (writer) who is responsible for the ideas and values which she or he imposes upon the reader. In this respect, my approach is close to the "optional-narrator theory" (Boyd 2017; Patron 2021).

of figurative identifications – identifications and oppositions – in which the specificity of the author's axiology in relation to the subject of the story, that is, national history, is expressed most clearly.

If we start again with Stalin, there are clearly two figures alongside him, literally, in the text: One extremely famous, Hitler, and the other less well known, a man named Chemodanov, who teaches Stalin billiards in between matters of national importance.[5] From the point of view of the author, which is expressed stylistically, Hitler clearly loses out to Stalin because the latter is endowed only with minor negative connotations. Hitler is discredited *ad hominem*. For example, in contrast to the Soviet dictator, the *Führer* is portrayed as hysterical: "Hitler is insane, hysterical and an undoubted demagogic genius […]" (ibid.: 458). Stalin, on the other hand, is in most instances characterised either neutrally or complimentarily, despite his inherent fear: Whatever he may be, he stands above everything, with Yakhina constantly repeating the word 'leader'.

At the same time in the novel, Hitler remains the only equal political rival to Stalin, against whom the Soviet dictator is literally and figuratively still learning to 'play'. Chemodanov, a billiards genius, helps him in this business. During one of the games with him, Stalin finally overcomes his master in a game of billiards and simultaneously, imagining that Chemodanov is Hitler, acquires a certain feeling – 'courage' – which, the author believes, will give him an undeniable advantage over his enemy in the coming great war. Yakhina's Stalin has no doubts that the war will take place, which makes him a shrewd (complimentary rhetoric) politician. Yakhina uses the war as an ethical motif by which to evaluate all of Stalin's activities, including repression, as they occupy much of the writer's attention.

Yakhina's form of evaluation of Stalin's character implies a suggestive strategy rather than an explicit ethical judgment. On the basis of the central text fragment in which the author's position is expressed, it is impossible to say clearly whether the idea of unity being used as a justification for oppression when faced with an imminent military threat should be attributed to the character, the narrator or the author. I am specifically referring to the following phrase: "Only by cleansing the organism of sores and ailments can one expect to win the inevitably approaching war" (ibid.: 461). In other words, we have a narrative which looks too much like a legitimising narrative typical of the oppressor's discourse about terror, which necessarily discredits the victim of this terror, presenting them as an enemy and depriving them of their human qualities.

The fact that in this dual situation the reader is left to make an ethical choice on his own is not so important for understanding the axiology of the narrative. The main thing, as far as the latter is concerned, is that the ambivalence of Yakhina's expression of the author's position takes Stalin and Stalin's repressive policies out of the category of unconditional, absolute, evil. The ethics manifested in the novel allows for the possibility of repression. The absolute evil is attributed to the external enemy, Hitler – a character who appears episodically and plays a service role. The future war also appears in the novel only when the author makes an ethical – not accusatory and therefore already apologetic – assessment of Stalin.

---

5   This fact is most probably fictitious.

The dictator's other opponent in the novel is, of course, the Volga German Bach, who fulfils this role, however, only on the allegorical level of the plot: the characters never meet, and Stalin certainly knows nothing about Bach. The characters, who are situated at opposite ends of the social ladder, are initially opposed to one another, although this conspicuous antagonism is again not so unambiguous.

In a sense, *A Volga Tale* is a hagiography of Bach: an account of the hermit's movement toward some truth of life, to sanctity. Bach begins his reclusive journey by serving his only woman, Klara. The climax of his feeling is when Klara, who died just after giving birth, is placed in the ice shed, and the hero realises that this is exactly what he has always strived for: to contemplate his undying beloved. He understands that this is the only thing he ever really wanted. At the same time, from this moment on he must look after the child she left to him.

Bach, who at first dislikes the child of an unwanted pregnancy caused by rape, gradually focuses all his attention on caring for it. Soon, another child appears in the house – an orphan, to whom Bach is also averse at first, but slowly Bach gets used to seeing him at the farm. Now the hero serves the two children. The orphan who appears in Bach's home is also a phenomenon of the new world (the world which once already destroyed Bach's idyll), so he begins to serve the children of revolution and modernisation, and gives himself to this cause wholeheartedly – first on the farm, then in the orphanage where the children are taken, and then in other, somewhat more distant places.

In this manner, Yakhina connects Bach, children and revolution in a demonstrative way. The protagonist makes his 'contract' with the Soviet regime immediately after the loss of his beloved: to obtain milk for his infant, he composes fairy tales, which the local activist uses to agitate for the new regime among the main character's former neighbours.[6] In the last episode of the novel, Bach also sets up an orphanage in his own house, no longer for his two wards, but also for other children.

Finally, having accomplished his mission – raising his wards and building a common home for others – he readily accepts his fate to end his life in the camp: "I am ready," he claims during his arrest (ibid.: 484). Thus, Bach, who rebels against his own ethnic community at the beginning, becomes a convinced builder of the new, Soviet world and a 'convict' at the same time by the end of the novel.

He builds an order in which he himself has no place. Even his two children, having found themselves in a Soviet orphanage, soon stop thinking about him. In Yakhina's novel, the children are happy, interacting with their peers, and they do not need anyone else. In a key scene of happiness, the adults beside them are simply absent: "By the gleam in their eyes he felt: here they are happy" (ibid.: 437); "Laughing, hurrying, bumping foreheads and laughing again. There were no adults" (ibid.: 430). That is, the author portrays a real utopia of childhood and the orphanage.

It is precisely in this role of selfless servant to the new regime that Bach is equal to Stalin: one readily sacrifices others for the sake of a certain unity, the other does not hesitate to sacrifice himself. (As the iconic Soviet comic character Iurii Detochkin would

---

6   "Tales" refers to the collection of Leonid Lerd (1935), a reference which the writer does not hide. In particular, the book mentions the 'storyteller' Hoffmann, the namesake of one of Yakhina's characters.

say: "And together we make a common cause: you in your own way and me in mine.") In other words, Yakhina, in her novel about Stalinist repressions, is implementing the same strategy of 'normalising' Soviet history as the prize-winning authors who write about the 'calm' Brezhnev era, albeit in a somewhat more elaborate way.

It is not difficult to see this if one again pays attention to the 'animalistic code' in the novel. In Yakhina's work, it is not only Stalin, but also Bach who interacts with wild animals. In one episode, when Bach is wandering in the steppe between the farm and the village, he runs into a pack of wolves. The wolves run across the steppe, approaching Bach, but instead of attacking him, they simply 'streamline' him from all sides. If we proceed from the gift of taming animals, Bach – a kind of Francis of Assisi or Egorii the Brave – wins in a tacit contest with the dictator. Ultimately, the symbolism of emotions separates the leader and the outsider: Bach, who is afraid of losing his beloved more than anything else in the world, loses his fear by the finale, while Stalin, on the contrary, experiences it constantly, albeit concealing it from others. In this way, the idea of total violence as an ethical value loses out somewhat to the idea of personal sacrifice. But in a didactic and instructive sense this means only one thing: Yakhina teaches humility. The author offers nothing else in her novel equal to these two ethics (for example, the ethics of rebellion). The only ethical reference point remains the harmony between the executioner and the victim.

In Yakhina's novel, the truth of this new world, for which some killed and others sacrificed themselves, is unambiguous. When Bach's two children of the revolution are grown up, having had so far a quite shabby and crippled life (Iakhina 2018: 485–486), they eventually meet to spend the rest of their days together, in a sense echoing the fate of Bach and Klara. At least, this is how the cycle of the family saga closes.

The final scene in *A Volga Tale* – the one in which the hero plunges into the Volga, can be easily read as a manifesto of pantheism – a hymn to nature, which equates and includes everyone and everything, friends and enemies. Drowning in the Volga, observing history and grasping its truth, the hero feels that he simultaneously merges with the whole earth: "His toes were carried to the quiet backwaters of Sheksna and Mologa [...] his hair – spread out on the Akhtuba, dipped end into the Caspian Sea. Bach dissolved into the Volga" (ibid.: 483). In other words, one kind of religious discourse, the Christian one, has just been replaced with another, 'pagan' one.

## 4. The Geopolitics of Eros

In the novel *Paradise on Earth* (*Rai zemnoi*, 2018) by Sukhbat Aflatuni, which was shortlisted for the *Bol'shaia Kniga* Award, the repressive past is a seemingly negative phenomenon: at least one of its main characters – though not the main one – is entirely immersed in the work of exposing the crimes of the repressive regime. Taken as a whole, the novel depicts Soviet history, starting with the 1930s and ending in the early 2000s – in the final scene, we hear the 2004 song *Black Boomer* (*Chernyi Bumer*) by Seëga which was very popular at that time. The main character Pliusha grows up in the Brezhnev period. At the same time the novel features important secondary characters. One of them belongs to the generation socialised during the Stalin period, another – to the generation socialised during the Khrushchev and Brezhnev periods. Thus, the main character is dragged into the ideological and ethical clash between these generations, and this generational confrontation serves as the main plot of the novel, which, just as the novels previously mentioned, also has an allegorical level.

At the beginning, the action unfolds within the framework of interpersonal relations, touching upon gender rather than historical and political issues. The main character has a close female friend. When it comes to their attitudes toward men, the two girls differ from their peers. They do not want to get married and in general, their relations with the 'strong' sex are not easy. At the same time, they are opposites in terms of character: if Pliusha is an introvert, her friend Natali is very active and sociable and not averse to the pleasures of life, except for sex.

In its most extreme form, gender conflict manifests itself in Natali's story. One day, when Natali comes home from a party, she is attacked and raped by a local guy called Grisha. However, Natali, who is strong by nature, is not distressed for long, but learns karate and beats Grisha unconscious, only just refraining from depriving him of the signs of manhood. Grisha, in turn, coming out of the hospital, begins to pursue Natali again, and one day he almost catches up with her. The conflict is finally resolved only after the death of the male character for reasons beyond the woman's control. The relationship between Grisha and Natali is, of course, a typical rape-revenge story, a plot about a woman's vengeance on her abuser. However, it also has an allegorical meaning, which only becomes apparent towards the end of the novel, an aspect to which I will return.

Pliusha, on the other hand, has a different paradigm for communicating with men. She gravitates toward artists and intellectuals, humanities scholars, and somewhat older men. Relationships with them do not lead to sexual intimacy, although the affectionate touches of one of them, a teacher and academic supervisor at the institute, at least at first, do not disgust her. At the climax of the novel, Pliusha unexpectedly finds herself caught between two men – mentors, people of different generations (the generation of Stalin and Khrushchev-Brezhnev) who, having been friends and even co-authors for a long time, suddenly break off all relations. Moreover, the case ends with a public slap in the face. Thus, a political and historical conflict related to the theme of repression breaks into the narrative: the reason for the end of the friendship is that the younger scholar discovered that his older colleague was involved in the execution of the Polish population living in the city until the 1930s. Not yet aware of the reasons for the quarrel between the two men, Pliusha gradually begins to distance herself from the compromised hero, switching over to the side of the indignant truth-seeker. This manifests itself in her losing interest in art history and choosing a new supervisor, a historian-archivist, to investigate the mass murder of the Poles together with him.

As in Yakhina's case, Aflatuni presents the events from the point of view of a naïve 'ordinary' hero, who clearly does not understand what is going on, in a way that avoids making ethical judgments about the actions of characters and events in real history. His text, like Yakhina's, lacks clear markers that clarify the point of view of the narrator, and thus of the implicit or biographical author. The reader is given the chance to make their own choices, which of course they will make in accordance with their ethical and ideological background. For instance, after a certain period of successful activity, the truth-seeking character, whom Pliusha assists, begins to have difficulties. A new chief appears who, unlike him, believes that: "There is no need to imagine that some were only executioners and others only victims. We need to show everything in a more complex, broader way" (Aflatuni 2019: 196). The reader is quite free to identify with either point of view, accepting or not accepting them.

The fundamental ambivalence of the narrator's position allows each interpretation. At first glance, Aflatuni perceives his truth-seeking hero positively – already by virtue of the fact that he rebels against detected injustice and 'meanness.' This gives reason to think that the narrator ethically stands and, in this sense, identifies with the inquisitive historian, attracting the reader to his side as well. To put this in other terms, in the eyes of the author, Pliusha's new supervisor, a historian, ethically surpasses his predecessor, the art historian and, as we already know, traitor. This ethical hierarchy, exactly as in Yakhina's case, is supported by using the rhetorical device *ad hominem*. If, in Yakhina's novel, Hitler looks worse than Stalin because he is explicitly hysterical, in Aflatuni's narrative, the art historian is worse not only because he is a traitor but also because he is older.

Aflatouni emphasises that his heroine, the unaware Pliusha, is uncomfortable with the signs of old age that she notices in her first mentor, the art historian: "When he first embraced Pliusha, she was frightened by the pungent smell of tobacco and old age" (ibid.: 26). In contrast to this negative physical attraction between Pliusha and her first mentor, her connection with her second mentor, the younger archivist and historian is purely intellectual or 'spiritual'.

But this obvious assessment is only one side of the coin, with the allegorical plot complicating the picture. As we know, Grisha rapes Natali. However, this is not self-sufficient violence, but violence with a special 'historiosophic' meaning. Aflatuni mentions that Natali is of Russian origin, from the Cossacks, while Grisha turns out to be a Pole: "We are Poles. – Anton slows down slightly. – Poles [...]" (ibid.: 44). Moreover, Grisha catches up with Natali not just in some wasteland, but in a field where the grave of his compatriots executed in the 1930s is located. It is a sexual act on a grave – a motif not common in Russian and Polish literature but one gaining popularity today.

This means, the rape can be read on an allegorical level also as Polish revenge against the Russians for the crimes committed by them in the 1930s against the Poles. This revenge can hardly be called successful, but it is not completely unsuccessful either. A child does not appear in this case, but there is a 'sadomasochistic' connection between the characters after this encounter, at the breaking off of which the heroine feels a distinct sense of loss. And after finding out about the death of her 'offender', Natali immediately proposes to marry his older brother. Thinking of this in terms of geopolitical abstractions – the Russian offers to create a family for the Pole. Such a Russian-Polish relationship does not cease to be a love-hate relationship, because in response the Pole offers the Russian a bowl of soup into which he pours a glass of salt, and in the end, plagued by nausea, they eat the soup together and the matter ends in marriage.

The unity between the Russian and the Polish nation is also realised in another form, not erotic, but thanatological. Before dying of illness, Natali demands that her friend scatters her ashes over the wasteland where the Poles are buried. In death and in nature, Aflatouni thus argues, all are equal. Putting it all together, the reader is faced at this moment with the same concept of pantheism which we witnessed in Yakhina's novel.

There is little to be added to this finale. Unlike Yakhina, in Aflatuni's novel, the final harmony, however, is achieved within also religious, but this time again, like in Aksenov's and Arkhangelskii's narratives, Christian, discourse. At the very end of the novel, near the field where the repressed Poles are buried, it is decided that two chapels should be built, one Russian and one Polish, with a garden between them as neutral territory. This is how Aflatuni constructs that 'earthly paradise', where everyone is reconciled or, more precisely, where the hope for universal harmony and forgiveness, which is declared in the title of the novel, is anchored. All this is presented through the eyes of Pliusha, who in her detachment from earthly matters appears increasingly like a nun or a saint.

What is noteworthy, however, is that despite the presence in the novel of a truth-seeker investigating a crime in the past, the idea of repentance or a confession of guilt is hardly articulated in the novel, or rather, it is suppressed by the thesis of reconciliation. In terms of trauma, the point is that the novel depicts not how the victims, the Poles, are trying to get rid of the physiologically painful consequences of trauma, but how their oppressors, the Russians, do so. It is 'traumatic literature', but upside down.

## 5. Conclusion

In summary, several very different novels of so-called prize literature about Soviet history have something in common in the way they reutilise the topoi of the Soviet past. Whatever different writing styles their authors adopt, whatever time period they concentrate on, in their portrayals history invariably comes to a certain kind of harmony. The idea of ethical acceptance of the past, even when it comes to mass terror, becomes central to them. The writers construct a system of evaluations such that, ultimately, any experience of the past, including mass terror, is presented as positive.

This is curious, but not entirely new. The ethical normalisation of the social crisis, if we bear in mind the domestic tradition of the present and past centuries, is by no means a recent innovation. A similar situation was observed in the 1920s. Many writers, as well as representatives of other arts, tried to talk about the revolution and civil war, not censoring, but rather explicating its horror. Significant writers of this trend were Isaak Babel', Boris Pil'niak, Artëm Vesëlyi, the aforementioned Andrei Platonov, Vassilii Grossman and Vladimir Zazubrin. An 'objective' narrator proved to be an appropriate device to deal with the recent past under the conditions of the new order. If at first, in the chaos of the 1920s, such a literary strategy for many writers proved to be a wise choice, it clearly did not appeal to Stalin: Stalin demanded a beautiful story, and instead of 'objectivism' socialist realist camouflage and pathos.

Something similar is happening nowadays: the normalisation of history, including the history of mass violence, its evaluation as ethically acceptable, is a proposal with which contemporary writers successfully enter the market of cultural products. This is the economic side of the cultural recycling they are undertaking, but at the same time, of course, it is also an ethical and socio-political choice.

The rhetoric that allows contemporary writers to effect "reconciliation with history" can be summarised as follows. First, it is based on an explicit or implicit appeal to religiosity. In other words, contemporary literature is actively included in the process of the desecularisation of culture, which once surprised one of the first researchers of recycling in the post-Soviet space, Sonja Luehrmann (2005). Secondly, it is important that despite the dissimilarity of the narratives, in Yakhina's, Arkhangelskii's and Aflatuni's novels the main character's death turns out to be the key argument for harmonising the past. This recurrent thanatological interest lends itself to various forms of rationalisation – for example, in terms of sociality as the priority of the origin over the individual or in the Christian paradigm, which interprets the earthly life of man as a preparation for the greater and supreme afterlife. But whatever the case, the topicality of death is important to the writers, both as a rhetorical device and as a self-promoted value. Of the authors mentioned above, only Aksenov does not focus on the idea of death in this form in his village prose.

Finally, in some cases (as in Yakhina's horror novel of terror) the idea of forgiveness and harmony is reinforced by the motif of love, and by the motif of sacrifice: the authors sacrifice a concrete person for the love of an abstraction. Thus, one can conclude that the keywords of this new ethical program of so-called prize literature are sacrifice, humility, death and religion.

If we look at these novels discussed above in a larger context, we find that they are by no means unique in their kind. A similar 'poetics of harmony' can also be found in Nikolai Kononov's resolutely anti-Stalinist novel *The Uprising. Documentary novel* (*Vosstanie. Dokumental'nyi roman*, 2016), which was shortlisted by the *NOS*. Somewhat earlier, in 2014, the first *Bol'shaia Kniga* prize was awarded to Zakhar Prilepin for his novel *The Abode* (*Obitel'*, 2014), where the apologetic rhetoric of concentration camp politics is seen with much greater clarity. Prilepin's *Abode* was, among other prizes, awarded the 2016 Russian Government Cultural Award (Government Order 2017). But even without this, it is clear that the 'harmonisation' of history, which boils down to the elimination of internal conflicts in favour of universal unity, is a state-encouraged line of recycling the past in contemporary Russia. It turns out that a notable number of Russian authors, whose names are prominently mentioned, voluntarily or involuntarily act in accordance with it. Only the need for a thorough and evidentiary parsing of texts stops us from giving other examples of the same kind.

In 2004, Anne Whitehead published her book *Trauma Fiction*. Against the backdrop of countless studies on the aesthetic narrativisation of negative experiences, this work by a representative of the first wave of trauma studies attracts attention given that its title contains the very term that captures the phenomenon. Whitehead drew attention to the paradox presented by works of fiction that address traumatic events: their authors spell out what, according to the essence of the notion of trauma, should seem to resist language and representation. According to Whitehead, the extraordinary authority of trauma studies has only strengthened the desire of contemporary writers to bring the traumatic to the surface. Their appropriation of the ways of conceptualising historical events suggested by trauma studies has resulted in a vast and significant body of fiction (Whitehead 2004: 3), to which Whitehead devotes her research.

If we consider that trauma studies are not only fed by theoretical interest, but are conceived as a kind of social therapy that helps to deal with negative collective experiences, the trauma fiction they provoke must serve the same purpose. The essence of the process to which it thus contributes is not only to make sense of and remedy the effects of trauma, but also to prevent its recurrence; or at least, the recurrence is accepted by default as highly undesirable.

This is not at all the case with the trend in Russian fiction discussed above, as with Russian cultural production as a whole. Drawing parallels with the USSR of the 1930s-1950s, it could be considered a kind of reincarnation of the then so-called literature of non-conflict. Although fiction of this type deliberately 'visualises' trauma, it does not care about overcoming it. On the contrary, if you continue in the logic of therapy, it promotes a permanent return and adaptation to the traumatic experience, transforming it from an anomaly to the norm. From a political and rhetorical perspective, the latter means a more or less veiled call to maintain the status quo, to freeze both history and modernity. Finally, since this kind of narrativisation does not deny the stressful experience of the past as something ethically unacceptable, but, on the contrary, legitimises its reproduction, the apologetic recycling of the past that it facilitates is more suitable for description in terms of nostalgia studies rather than trauma studies. Based on its predilection for the cultivation of social 'wounds' without any attempt to comprehend and address their causes, it could well be characterised as nostalgia for trauma.

Obviously, the 'harmonisation' of history is not a unique phenomenon and is characteristic not only of the Russian context. Popular mass culture in general tends to transform conflictual subjects, including the discourses of horror, terror, pain and death, into entertainment and pleasure. What should be highlighted however is that Russian cultural production with pretensions to intellectuality – and the prize literature in question often makes a claim to be 'realist', 'serious' and even 'elitist' – is in this respect voluntarily or involuntarily converging with popular culture. The only difference is that it is not aimed at the ordinary mass reader, but at a fairly well-prepared reader who expects obstacles and puzzles from art of various kinds and who is able to enjoy multi-layered allegorical, intertextual, and not just one-dimensional plots. Just as in the case of adventure novels or computer games on a historical theme or, for example, in the case of the reenactment movement, in this new 'literature of non-conflict' the entertainment function begins to supplant the critical function. In this sense, we are confronted with a typical case of the 'gamification' of history. On the other hand, no matter to what degree fiction is entertaining, by virtue of its ethical and rhetorical nature – let us recall Wayne Booth's *Rhetoric of Fiction* again – it always imposes on the audience a certain "fictional world", that is, specific moral values and norms of behaviour.

## Filmography

*Zuleikha Opens Her Eyes* (Zuleikha otkryvaet glaza), dir. Egor Anashkin, Russia 2020.

## References

Akhmanaev, Pavel (2016): Stalinskie premii: Istoriia uchreezhdeniia i praktika prisvoeniia i vruchniia Stalinskikh premii, Moskva: Russkie Vitiazi.
Booth, Wayne (1961): The Rhetoric of Fiction, Chicago: University of Chicago Press.

Boyd, Brian (2017): "Does Austen Need Narrators? Does Anyone?" In: New Literary History 48/2, pp. 285–308.

Ėngelgardt, Boris (1924): "Ideologicheskii roman Dostoevskogo." In: Arkadii Dolinin' (ed.): F.M. Dostoevskii: Stat'i i materialy 2, Leningrad/Moskva: Mysl', pp. 71–105.

English, James (2005): The Economy of Prestige: Prizes, Awards, and the Circulation of Cultural Value, Cambridge: Harvard University Press.

Fleishman, Avrom (1971): The English Historical Novel: Walter Scott to Virginia Woolf, Baltimore: Johns Hopkins Press.

Gorski, Bradley A. (2023): "Literaturnyi kapitalizm i ekonomika prestizha (Rossiiskie literaturnye premii 1990 – 2000-kh godov. Ot 'Triumfa' do 'Bol'shoi knigi')." In: Novoe literaturnoe obozrene 1/179, pp. 202–218.

Iakhina, Guzel' (2018): Deti moi, Moskva: AST.

Kononov, Nikolai (2019): Vosstanie: Dokumntal'nyi roman, Moskva: Novoe izdatel'stvo.

Lerd, Leonid (1935): Skazki [nemtsev Povolzh'ia], Saratov: Saratovskoe gos. izd-vo.

Luehrmann, Sonja (2005): "Recycling Cultural Construction: Desecularisation in Postsoviet Mari El." In: Religion, State & Society 33/1, pp. 35–56.

Prilepin, Zakhar (2014): Obitel', Moskva: AST.

Patron, Sylvie (ed.) (2021): Optional-Narrator Theory: Principles, Perspectives, Proposals, Lincoln: University of Nebraska Press.

Rasporiazhnie Pravitel'stva (2017): Rasporiazhenie Pravitel'stva Rossiiskoi Federatsii ot 07.02.2017 g. No. 209-r. O prisuzhdenii premii Pravitel'stva Rossiiskoi Federatsii 2016 goda v oblasti kul'tury: http://government.ru/docs/all/110388/ [30 September 2023].

Svin'in, Vladimir/Oseev, Konstantin, (eds.) (2007): Stalinskie premii: dve storony odnoi medali: Sbornik dokumentov i khudozhestvenno-publitsisticheskikh, Novosibirsk: Svin'in i synov'ia.

V'iugin, Valerii (2021): "'Kul'turnyi resaikling': k istorii poniatiia (1969–1990-e gody)." In: Novoe literaturnoe obozrene 3/169, pp. 13–32.

Whitehead, Anne (2004): Trauma Fiction, Edinburgh: Edinburgh University Press.

Zubkov, Kirill (2021): Stsenarii peremn: Uvarovskaia nagrada i ėvoliutsiia russkoi dramaturgii v ėpokhu Aleksandra II, Moskva: Nove literaturnoe obozrenie.

Chapter 11:
## The Affective Landscapes of S.T.A.L.K.E.R.
Domesticating Nuclear Disaster in a Video Game

*Oleksandr Zabirko*

## 1. Introduction

Computer games allow millions of people to play with and within the past.

Although, even in the realm of pop culture, games are often considered crass entertainment and are generally less respected than movies or literary texts, the rapidly increasing sophistication of history-based game titles leads to an assumption that the cultural impact of the gaming industry will keep growing.

Today, some bestselling games already compete with historiography itself in the way they render facts and events to elaborate a sense of reality for almost every historical epoch. For instance, the *Assassin's Creed* series, famous for using real historical events as a backdrop to the games, has covered multiple scenarios – from Viking expansions into the British Isles, via the Crusades and up to the American Revolution.

The modes of ludic interaction with history vary considerably depending on the game's genre. In strategy games, players may experiment with counterfactual history while commanding ancient armies, running a business enterprise, or ruling a medieval dynasty, whereas a first- or third-person shooter game can offer cinematic depictions of historical drama, for example, on the battlefields of World War II.

Experiencing history through virtual reenactment is probably the most obvious, yet not the only way of interacting with the past. Far less evident is the engagement with history in the games, which are set not in the historical past, but in the present time, and which rely on the player's deeper emotional resonance with the memories of a bygone era rather than on its detailed presentation or simulation. This emotional impact is particularly important for various horror games. Certainly, as digitally created works of art, all video games depend on player input to trigger the majority of in-game events, thus contributing to the player's engagement in the unfolding of the storyline or activating new game levels, however more than other settings for digital games, horror contexts go beyond this 'technical' kind of interaction as they are primarily designed to produce strong emotional responses.

The locale of horror games, i.e., the space in which the player moves, lives, and survives, is usually saturated with elements of gothic aesthetics such as decaying, ruined scenery, 'dark' music, and the ubiquity of monsters. Merging the gothic entourage with the elements of action-oriented games (e.g., shooters or adventures), the 'survival horror' games place the player character, who is usually vulnerable and under-armed, in the middle of this uncanny environment.

Ever since the release of its originator, *Resident Evil* in 1996, the genre of the survival horror has been gradually expanding its aesthetic features, for instance, by incorporating 'ecogothic' elements for modelling the in-game landscapes or for the representation of ecological crises. If gothic is understood as centring around some profoundly historical motifs like the "return of the repressed" (Clemens 1999) or revealing the "unburied past" (Etkind 2013), ecogothic mediates cultural anxieties about the human relationship to the non-human world through uncanny apparitions of a monstrous nature (Deckard 2019: 174).

However, a clear boundary that separates the non-human world of nature from the human realm of history is often impossible to draw. Their interconnectedness is particularly evident in the case of the Chernobyl nuclear accident, where the environmental disaster is often regarded as a pivotal point in history – a dark metonym for the fate of the Soviet Union (Milne 2017: 95).

Chernobyl has been the subject of historical documentaries, crime thrillers, and haunting photo installations – all focusing on both historical and ecological features of the nuclear catastrophe. Similarly, the gaming industry has been invoking the ghostly area of Chernobyl with striking regularity. This paper explores the representation of Soviet history and culture in the main instigator of this trend, the *S.T.A.L.K.E.R.* game series, which combines the elements of survival horror and ego-shooter against the backdrop of the Chernobyl nuclear disaster.

## 2. From Cossacks to Stalkers

Roughly at the time when the scholarly community was arguing whether Ukraine has a history (while discussing the eponymous article by Mark von Hagen), a small, Kyiv-based studio of game developers, GSC Game World, was working hard on making this very history playable. The outcome of their efforts was a real-time strategy computer game titled *Cossacks: European Wars*.

The game was released in 2001 and immediately became a massive success both in Ukraine and abroad. By December 2001 *Cossacks* had sold over 500.000 copies globally, thus becoming one of the most popular game titles at the time (Bye 2001). The game is set in the 17th and early 18th centuries in Europe and is divided into several campaign scenarios ranging from Stepan (Sten'ka) Razin's rebellion to the War of the Austrian Succession.[1] Drawing heavily on Microsoft's best-selling strategy game *Age of Empires*,

---

1 The game consists of four "campaigns", which are divided into "missions" or "scenarios". For example, at the beginning of the "Russian Campaign" the player takes on the role of a tsar general who must supress the Cossack uprising led by Stepan Razin.

the *Cossacks* offer four military campaigns: the English, the French, the Russian, and the Ukrainian campaign. Against the backdrop of the colonial powers' fight for supremacy, a ubiquitous motif in strategy games, the Ukrainian campaign seems out of place, but the product's original title coupled with a fragment of Ilya Repin's *Reply of the Zaporozhian Cossacks* (rus. *Zaparozhtsy pishut pis'mo turetskomu sultanu*; ukr. *Zaporozhtsi pyshut' lysta turets'komu sultanovi*, 1880–1891) on the CD cover leaves few doubts that the Cossacks are the real protagonists of this game.

Apart from its exotic, East European flavour, the game became renowned for its massive battles with a seemingly infinite number of units that players may control. However, the GSC's attempts to apply the same game design and mechanics to different historical epochs and countries were far less successful: for instance, *American Conquest* (2002), a game deliberately designed to appeal to the United States computer game market, failed to build on the success of *Cossacks*.

*Figure 11.1: The original cover of the computer game* S.T.A.L.K.E.R.: Shadow of Chernobyl *(2008)*

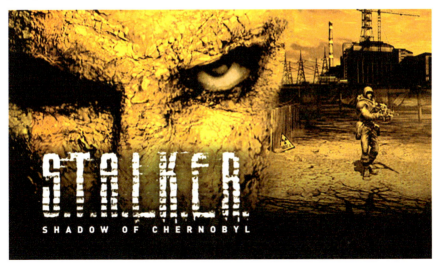

It was only in 2008 that GSC Game World managed to produce another global bestseller: an ego-shooter *S.T.A.L.K.E.R.: Shadow of Chernobyl*. This game has had three iterations since 2008 and supports an energetic fan community all around the globe. In August 2021, GSC and its partner Koch Media GmbH claimed over 15 million total sales for the *S.T.A.L.K.E.R.* franchise (GSC Game World 2021b).

Having changed the game's original title from *Stalker* to *S.T.A.L.K.E.R.* due to copyright issues[2], the game still borrows many of its key elements from Andrei Tarkovskii's famous film *Stalker* (1979) based on the science-fiction novel *Roadside Picnic* (*Piknik na obochine*, 1972) by Arkadii and Boris Strugastkii. However, *S.T.A.L.K.E.R.* is set in the Cher-

---

2   S.T.A.L.K.E.R. is a backronym for Scavengers, Trespassers, Adventurers, Loners, Killers, Explorers, and Robbers.

nobyl Exclusion Zone, in present-day Ukraine. The game's backstory assumes that in 2006 another nuclear disaster occurs in Chernobyl, turning the natural environment into a contaminated "Zone" full of physical anomalies, mysterious objects, and aggressive mutants. S.T.A.L.K.E.R. starts a few years later, after people have begun coming to the Zone in search of money, valuable artifacts, and scientific information. These people call themselves "stalkers" (*stalkery*), while their activities in the Zone and the corresponding ethos are referred to as *stalkerstvo*, a term which is by no means synonymous to the modern English word 'stalking', but rather designates exploration, trailblazing, and economic exploitation of the Zone.[3]

## 3. Welcome to Wasteland

Starting from the first game of the series, *Shadow of Chernobyl*, S.T.A.L.K.E.R. was designed as an open-world game: although it introduces its own plot and storyline, which the player has to uncover by accomplishing a certain number of missions (quests), the developers place the player in a self-sustaining ecosystem in which game situations arise from the random interaction of different components such as weather conditions, elements of the natural environment (mutants, zombies, and animals) as well as from occasional fights between rival gangs and fractions, who are 'stalking' in the Zone. The great deal of randomised activity taking place in the game, no matter whether or not the player chooses to interact with it, creates an illusion of a living, open universe. Unlike other shooters, which deliberately place the player in the centre of the world, S.T.A.L.K.E.R, on the contrary, constructs a self-sufficient environment, which seemingly does not require the player's presence and attention. In terms of the gameplay, this particular kind of 'worlding' also means that the terrain continually shifts its topologies so that strategies that worked before no longer apply.

Being primarily a first-person shooter, S.T.A.L.K.E.R. naturally centres weapons and ammunition as one of its key elements, but it also incorporates features more typical for adventure and role-playing games, including interactions with non-player characters (NPCs): the player may talk, trade or fight with the NPCs, but he also may listen to their conversations, which usually include jokes or stories of the everyday life in the Zone. Other features, like the scary ambience and ominous background music, are typical for the genre of survival horror as they are designed to instil a sense of fear and anxiety in the player. The horror aesthetics are amplified by certain gameplay properties, which make the hero vulnerable to several problems such as radiation, hunger, and bleeding. As is typical for post-apocalyptic tales, the player always has to pay attention to the hero's diminishing forces. Yet unlike most survival horrors of the early 2000s (e.g., *Doom 3*, *Silent Hill*, the *Resident Evil* series) which try to frighten the players by the sheer number, aggressiveness, or ugliness of different monsters, S.T.A.L.K.E.R. offers a setting of striking tranquillity – the Zone produces an atmosphere of suspense rather than that of an action-oriented shooter. To be sure, the flesh-eating, blood-sucking monsters are all there,

---

3   The Russian term "stalker" is probably borrowed from Rudyard Kipling's book *Stalky* (1899), a collection of stories with a pronounced imperial subtext.

but, irrespective of a player's preferences and strategies, the far larger part of the playing time in *S.T.A.L.K.E.R.* is always devoted to the exploration of the Zone's natural and urban spaces rather than to shooting down its aggressive inhabitants.

By privileging ludic experience over narrative content, the game shifts its emphasis from characters towards the landscape, thus offering its own ecogothic version of the genre of survival horror. If the players of real-time or turn-based strategy games spend most of their time contemplating and changing the geopolitical map of the respective game worlds (thus treating the map as an aestheticised object), the players of the *S.T.A.L.K.E.R.* series focus predominantly on the natural or urban environment, which they, however, can only observe and study, but hardly alter.

Unsurprisingly, the prominent role of the environment in the game design leads to an assumption that the real protagonist of *S.T.A.L.K.E.R.* is the Zone itself. Matthew Sakey concludes:

> If characters in narrative are primarily responsible for the evocation of emotional response, and assuming that a character can be anything, then certainly a place can take center stage as easily as a person. The Zone is the star of this show. (2010: 97)

Thus, according to Sakey, the agency of the Zone is rooted in its capacity to evoke emotional responses such as the feeling of peace, threat, wonder, or loneliness. This agency anchors the Zone firmly in the context of the so-called affective landscapes, which consider space and place beyond their material properties while recognising that this "beyond" of "imaginary places, ideals, and real but intangible objects underpin and produce material places and social spaces" (Berberich et al. 2013: 314). The interaction between the material and virtual, which comprise the semantic core of the term "affective landscape", is particularly relevant in the context of video games. While people connect themselves to and detach themselves from topographical areas in complex ways, video games, as a specific medium, highlight our ability to interact with virtual, in-game landscapes through contemplation, exploration, destruction, etc. Although this experience usually remains within the borders of virtual simulation, the empirical dimension of this interaction saturates the corresponding landscapes with powerful associations and symbolic meaning.

The Zone as an affective landscape has a glocal character. It links legacies of the industrial past (e.g., industrial ruins, depopulated settlements, etc.) with geographical and natural space, thus addressing the common experience of de-industrialisation, which the countries of the former USSR share with many other regions of the Global North. But while for Western, particularly American, players the Zone may function as an estranged version of the "old west" or Yukon (Sakey 2010: 101), it cannot be denied that the Zone is also an archetypical no-go-area on the eastern side of the former Iron Curtain and as such it is burdened with specific historical connotations, semantics, and aesthetics. Anton Bolshakov, creative director at GSC Game World, explained this particular meaning of the Chernobyl Exclusion Zone:

> Ruins of old Soviet industrial complexes, blocks of flats, military and civil facilities, vehicles and so on are still plentiful around ex-USSR. However, those traces of old empire can hardly be felt as keen and striking as in the Chernobyl zone. To me it's living history,

as life has been still there for over twenty years now, ending back in USSR times. It was only after visiting Chernobyl that we were able to render the atmosphere of true post-apocalyptic Soviet world which we intended to deliver. (Rossignol 2007)

Interestingly enough, the choice of the Chernobyl Exclusion Zone as the game setting was not a spontaneous decision, but a result of a long and arduous development process. The initial concept of the game with the working title *Oblivion Lost* had no references to Chernobyl whatsoever. Instead, the game relied heavily on the plot of Roland Emmerich's *Stargate* movie (Iatsenko 2008). The game was supposed to take place not in contemporary Ukraine, but in the distant future, an era of interstellar voyages, with thousands of inhabited planets and intelligent races. The player and his comrades were supposed to take the role of intergalactic pioneers – the first to encounter new, previously unknown, and possibly hostile worlds. However, the developers soon abandoned the initial concept as both labour-intensive and trivial (ibid.). Between 2002 and 2007 the project had undergone some significant changes both in terms of gameplay and storyline. In 2002–2003, GSC staff went to the real Chernobyl Exclusion Zone twice, to film footage of rusting machinery and collapsing buildings. As mentioned above, these excursions became an important source of inspiration for the game: what came with the material was not just the images of the decaying architecture, but also myths and narratives of the Chernobyl catastrophe.

An influential British computer games journalist and critic Jim Rossignol, who wrote extensively on *S.T.A.L.K.E.R.*, goes as far as to valorise the natural and cultural environment of the Zone as "a world that sits apart from the Americanised homogeneity that exists across the spectrum of gaming" (Rossignol 2011). This statement may sound somewhat exaggerated with regard to a game, which basically offers the same ludic activity as *Half-Life 2* (an ego-shooter by American game developer Valve Inc.) and draws heavily on the aesthetics of the post-apocalyptic America of the *Fallout* series (created by Interplay Entertainment). For instance, *S.T.A.L.K.E.R.* painstakingly follows power fantasies of atomic health in *Fallout*, where the toxic effects of radiation exposure become an element of gameplay that can be easily overcome by wearing "power armor" and consuming "Rad-Away", a chemical solution that bonds with radioactive particles and removes them from the user's body (unsurprisingly, in the East European setting of *S.T.A.L.K.E.R.*, these healing qualities are attributed not to some futuristic potions, but to vodka). *S.T.A.L.K.E.R.* provides its own ironic comment on the (dis)continuity of the post-apocalyptic theme in video games: in *Shadow of Chernobyl* (2008) and in *Call of Pripyat* (2009), the second iteration of *S.T.A.L.K.E.R.*, the player may find the dead bodies of Myron (one of the main characters in *Fallout*) and Gordon Freeman (the protagonist of *Half-Life 2*), who obviously did not manage to survive in the Ukrainian wasteland.

Critics however point to some more fundamental differences between Ukrainian and American post-apocalyptic shooters: according to Mukherjee (2008: 235–236) the dissimilarities lay in the affective experience and in the fictional setting of the games, while Rossignol (2010) highlights the authenticity of the Soviet landscape as one of the main factors for the worldwide success of *S.T.A.L.K.E.R.* With regard to the game's Soviet ambience, some statements made by the gamers in the comment section beneath Rossignol's texts are even more telling. For instance, an Estonian gamer with the nickname "irve" concludes:

> So the S.T.A.L.K.E.R was a thing I (literally) waited for years and as someone from the former Soviet bloc (Estonia): the whole architecture in Ukraine was utterly standardized so I got to be nostalgic about some concrete fences and small checkpoint houses, which got the "exact right" childhood window bar designs... I didn't enjoy the plot of the game: I just trespassed whenever I could: the buildings had lots and lots of places I could climb and they didn't reward me with any stuff or ammo: they were their own rewards. I could spend hours climbing half-built buildings, overlooking abandoned trainyards or just admiring rusty cars from my childhood. (Rossignol 2010)

Another gamer, who obviously does not have any personal ties to the Soviet era, summarises his (or her) playing experience as follows:

> The whole mythos of the Zone, Chernobyl and the Cold War has been churning around in my brain for far too long without reason, and then I realised just what an impact the actual history surrounding the zone had on me when I was playing. There's something engrossing about it, something unpeaceable, and feeling as if you're not only within the games [sic] mythology, but that of the real world only makes it more believable and immersive. (Ibid.)

## 4. Observing the Ruins

What are the main fascinations with this appropriation and playful transformation of the Soviet past in *S.T.A.L.K.E.R.*? Anton Bolshakov describes the 1986 accident in Chernobyl as "one of the black pages in the history of Ukraine", yet in the same interview he also highlights the unique combination of factors, which led to the success of the game's concept: "global public awareness of the setting, mysteriousness of the place, radioactivity dangers, talks about mutations – all combines into a solid concept of a horror-filled atmospheric shooter" (Rossignol 2007). The 'atmosphere' of Chernobyl remains utterly historic, since the affective landscape of the exclusion zone seems frozen in time, on the eternal 'black page' of 1986.

Paradoxically, in the game, the Soviet past is both omnipresent and inaccessible. It appears, for instance, as an overtone in the soundscape of the haunted town of Prypiat, where the game's sinister background music is intertwined with road noise and children's laughter, but also with a fragment of a radio broadcast that informed Soviet citizens about the death of Leonid Brezhnev. The epitome of this inaccessibility is the time machine from the popular Soviet children's miniseries *Guest from the Future* (*Gost'ia iz budushchego*, 1984), which, quite in line with the plot of the miniseries, can be found behind a secret door in the basement of one of the abandoned houses. However, the gameplay allows no interaction with the device – the time machine is, therefore, a typical 'easter egg', a secret feature or image which is hidden in a video game. The tension between the presence of Soviet history and the player's inability to interact with it can be traced back to the level of game characters. For example, *Call of Pripyat*, features two NPCs, Captain Tarasov and Corporal (*praporshchik*) Volentir from the Soviet cult action movies *In the Zone of Special Attention* (*V zone osobogo vnimaniia*, 1978) and *Hit Back* (*Otvetnyi khod*, 1981). In the game, the two characters appear as members of the Ukrainian airborne unit that supports the protagonist in one of the decisive battles against his adversaries. Yet again, in the heat of battle, the interaction with both Soviet heroes is reduced to a couple of banal phrases.

A player's limited freedom to act is an inherent feature of computer games, hence the inaccessibility of Soviet history is not a deliberate ideological or philosophical message but results predominantly from the gameplay properties. However, combined with an affective landscape of the Zone, full of the remnants of the Soviet past, this technical limitation offers a particular perspective on history: the Soviet characters, cultural artifacts, and, ultimately, the collapsing Soviet architecture may evoke the feeling of sorrow and majesty, but the world it belongs to remains ultimately out of reach. Instead of ludic interaction with history (like in *Cossacks: European Wars*), S.T.A.L.K.E.R. offers the contemplation and exploration of its visible remnant – a landscape full of ruins.

*Figure 11.2: The town of Prypiat'. Screenshot from S.T.A.L.K.E.R.: Call of Pripyat (2009)*

As uncanny reminders of the passing of time, ruins inevitably trigger meditations on mortality and life's transience, thus providing an ideal scenery for a survival horror. Yet at the same time, the omnipresence of the decaying architecture in S.T.A.L.K.E.R. makes this scenery programmatically and affectively past-oriented: a place, where an unexpected catastrophe left behind a post-human space of disaster naturally produces a haunting affect, which makes it impossible to see "what now is" without constantly reflecting on "what once was" (Lee 2017: 2).

*Figure 11.3: The town of Prypiat'. Screenshot from* S.T.A.L.K.E.R.: Call of Pripyat (2009)

Indeed, juxtaposing the lively past with the decaying present is a commonplace in literary and cinematographic romanticisations of all kinds of ruins – from ancient amphitheatres to the sites of industrialisation. A popular subject of ruins photography ('ruin porn') and dark tourism, the real-life Chernobyl Exclusion Zone certainly fits into this paradigm of aesthetic romanticisation. Although with regard to Chernobyl the thinking of "what once was" inevitably conflates the nuclear catastrophe with the 'geopolitical disaster' of the collapse of the Soviet Union, in *S.T.A.L.K.E.R.*, the Zone as a haunted place privileges emotional turbulence over the rational reflections on history: rather than providing ideological or political conclusions, it triggers the melancholic mood of childhood memories or, as shown above, an unspecified feeling of 'something engrossing and unpeaceable'.

Unlike photos and historical documentaries, the game turns the melancholic experience of loss into a ludic experience and thus into a form of entertainment and satisfaction. For instance, *S.T.A.L.K.E.R.* breathes new life into the dilapidated Soviet buildings by making them a haven for dangerous monsters and mutants. These ruins, however, may also harbour valuable artifacts and other treasures, thus, in the game, the player is constantly drawn to what he fears most. This hypertrophied, affective response to decay and material degradation is what drives the 'ruin gaze' in *S.T.A.L.K.E.R.*, but it also frames the perception and the historical contextualisation of the Chernobyl' nuclear catastrophe.

For instance, Svetlana Bodrunova argues that the non-memories of gamers familiar only with a "virtual Chernobyl" of *S.T.A.L.K.E.R.* obfuscate the tragic events of the nuclear disaster and effectively substitute them with "a warmed-up interest in mutations, abandoned and dead cities, stalkerism, and romantics of the place where time stopped" (2012: 23). However, this place is not just a virtual replica of Chernobyl infested by mutants: apart from the real places of the disaster (e.g., the town of Prypiat') the game's topography features some utterly fantastical locations such as the swampy area of Zaton with its grounded ships and dock cranes or the secret research town of Limansk, thus offering an estranged, de-familiarised version of the real Chernobyl Exclusion Zone.

Moreover, the 'ruin gaze' also makes the game's aesthetics programmatically ambiguous in political and ideological terms. The mythology of S.T.A.L.K.E.R. cannot be reduced either to the mere nostalgia for Soviet imperial grandeur or to the blank rejection of Soviet heritage. On the level of the landscape, this ambiguity may be illustrated by one of the most spectacular Soviet artifacts that can be encountered in the game – a gigantic wall of antennae, the *Duga* radar system, which is located within the Chernobyl Exclusion Zone.

*Figure 11.4: Photograph of the DUGA Radar Array near Chernobyl from 2014*

In the game, however, *Duga* features twice: in its historical role as an early-warning radar system developed for Cold War defence, but also as a sinister "brain scorcher", a psychotropic weapon capable of destroying people's psyche by provoking hallucinations, nightmares, and panic attacks. The two devices are not identical, the "brain scorcher" is smaller in size and does not take the form of the real array, but the resemblance of their metallic structures is by no means accidental – it points at popular conspiracy theories that *Duga* was used for mind control experiments. Thus, within the game universe, the old Soviet radar system manifests the legacy of the perished high-tech civilisation as well as the history of the ruthless, totalitarian regime. Additionally, the aggressive side of the Soviet Union comes to light in the form of military bases and secret bunkers, weapons, and classified documents, yet in the post-apocalyptic, and, by extension, post-

Soviet world of *S.T.A.L.K.E.R.*, the Soviet history also symbolises the state of the world prior to the Chernobyl disaster, i.e., the 'normal world' without mutants and physical anomalies.

## 5. Mutants from the Past

In the game, elusive Soviet history becomes visible and tangible not on the level of objects and topography, but rather on the level of characters. Conflating Tarkovksii's *Stalker* and the novel *Roadside Picnic* by the Strugatskii brothers with the real events in Ukraine in April 1986, the game revives the "stalkers" as a profoundly Soviet subculture.

The starting point of the stalker trope, the Strugatskiis' *Roadside Picnic*, is set in a post-visitation world in which aliens have left six zones full of mysterious artifacts that defy the laws of physics. The stalkers are tough survivalists and explorers who venture out into the dangerous zones in search of these extra-terrestrial objects. Tarkovskii reinvented his Stalker as a mystical wanderer on a search for spiritual knowledge rather than for wealth or power, but he also modified the Strugatskiis' zones by reducing them into a singular, forbidden, and enigmatic Zone, which features in the film as an area cordoned off behind an army-patrolled border. For Tarkovskii's Soviet audience, the Russian word *zona* (as *singulare tantum*) gave rise to various associations, ranging from the network of prisons and labour camps (GULag) to the walled-off West. Famously shot in the ruins of chemical factories in Tallinn, the film created a powerful image of a contaminated ecology and decaying architecture, but the Zone as a territory of technological disaster and human debris was only one possible interpretation among many others. However, when the Chernobyl accident occurred, Tarkovskii's *Stalker* was the first ready-to-hand model for interpreting it. Due to the film's eerie foreshadowing, the evacuated 30-km exclusion zone around Chernobyl's nuclear plant came to be called *zona*, while illegal scavengers and tour guides to the evacuated area began to call themselves *stalkery*.

Obviously, despite all the differences in terms of genre specifics, the concept of the Zone unites the science-fiction novel by the Strugatskii duo, Tarkovskii's art drama, and the ego-shooter by the GSC Game World. The Zone as a place to which some men are irrevocably drawn, despite the dangers and in search of all-powerful artifacts, resonates through all three instalments.

Less evident, however, are the roots of stalkers as a cultural milieu. The continuity of the stalker theme in literature and cinema suggests that the post-Soviet stalkers follow the role-models of their predecessors from Soviet science fiction or, speaking more broadly, from what Mark Lipovetsky calls "the poetics of the ITR discourse" (Lipovetsky 2013). As a common denominator for various strata of the scientific intelligentsia, the term ITR (*inzhenerno-tekhnicheskii rabotnik*, engineer-technical employee) is both a misnomer and a widely used label for a cultural milieu that constituted the leading group in the liberal movement of the late Soviet period. The ITRs were the main audience of the bard song festivals, their humour dominated the competitions of amateur student comedians (known as KVN: *klub veselykh i nakhodchivykh*), but they were also the backbone of the tourist and alpinist movements, and, last but not least, of the energetic Soviet sci-fi community.

The most prominent Soviet science-fiction authors, the Strugatskii brothers, effectively summarised the self-identification of the ITRs in the perennial figure of the progressor, an agent of a highly developed civilisation secretly planted into a repressive and backward society. The idea of progressorism is to facilitate the development of primitive civilisations and to diminish casualties inflicted by historical processes or inevitable crises. According to Lipovetsky (2016: 32–33), the progressor trope primarily offers the intelligentsia reader an identification not with a "colonized subject", but with a "colonizer", a bearer of progress to the passive and backward community of "natives". Thus, the central characteristics of the "ITR discourse" epitomised by the figure of the progressor are essentialism, double confrontation of the authorities and the "masses", and the subsequent exceptionalist position of the intelligentsia (Lipovetsky 2013: 130). This catalogue may also include the inherent urge for escapism, manifested in the zeal for long expeditions or open-air song festivals in the woods, which promised temporary freedom from the pressures of Soviet ideology as well as from the routines of everyday life. The late Soviet intelligentsia's wanderlust combined with the urge for "inner freedom" also predetermined the popularity of a stalker as a subcultural role-model. The strange neighbourhood of ragged bounty-hunters (stalkers) and extra-terrestrial know-alls (progressors) as identification symbols has little to do with the "biographies" of their literary prototypes. However, while in the literary universe of the Strugatskii duo, stalkers and progressors are detached from each other both ethically and aesthetically, the Zone serves as a link between both these figures as it places the stalkers on the opposite end of the progressorism theme: in *Roadside Picnic* the Zone, a remainder of progressorship by some higher-level civilisation, attracts and terrifies the stalkers, while in Tarkovskii's film the stalker treats the Zone with almost religious awe. Although the stalker does not exhibit the elitist superiority typical for the progressors, in the film he still shows an exceptionalist stance of a prophet or a holy fool, as he leads his companions in the path of knowledge and righteousness.

The post-Soviet stalkers from the video game appear, at first glance, as pop versions of their highbrow predecessors mutated beyond recognition. Indeed, the heavily armed men on steroids seem light-years away from the Romantic truth-seekers of late Soviet literature and cinema, yet behind the protective suits and gas masks, one easily recognises the same archetypes of rugged survivalist and mystic seer, which fuse in the figure of the stalker in the works of Tarkovskii and the Strugatskiis. Eavesdropping on conversations between the NPCs in *Shadow of Chernobyl* or in *Call of Pripyat* reveals the stalkers' self-fashioning as aristocrats of the spirit, who would fill their leisure time with music and books: "Oh, I wish I was home now, lying in a hammock with a good book in my hands."

A seven-string acoustic guitar, a frequent companion of the conversations around a campfire or in an improvised bar, anchors stalkers within the Soviet bard subculture as represented by Vladimir Vysotskii or Aleksandr Galich. In the game, the description text for a guitar in the dialog box for equipment features a quote from the song famously performed by Vysotskii "talk to me, my seven-string friend." To be sure, the long echo of the "ITR poetics" comes to light only in the form of hints, brief references, or allusions – often with an ironic undertone. No bard song is actually performed here in full length and the 'conversations' mentioned above are, in fact, nothing more than short exchanges of phrases, but *sapienti sat* – for those, who are at least vaguely acquainted with late Soviet tourism subculture or with sci-fi fandom, there is no need for lengthy explanations.

*Figure 11.5: Screenshot from S.T.A.L.K.E.R.: Call of Pripyat (2009) Stalkers at the campfire*

Unlike the stereotypical landscape of industrial and military ruins from the Cold War era, which remains accessible for the Western audience, the nostalgic subcultural allusions to 'stalkerism', were designed primarily for post-Soviet gamers. Being kept on a low level, these allusions, however, establish no visible links to the heroes of Strugatskiis' novels or to the enigmatic protagonist of Tarkovskii's film, but rather to a generalised, stereotypical figure of stalker, which served as a role model for the late Soviet intelligentsia. As a subcultural role model, the stalker mirrors neither the identities of its fictional prototypes nor the collective identity of the Soviet ITRs, instead, it exhibits a certain set of values and qualities, which the educated urban dwellers (i.e., the audience of Tarkovksii and the Strugatskii duo) eagerly ascribed to a fictionalised figure of a hardened adventurer, thus constructing an easily identifiable ideal of a 'real man'. By adapting this ideal to the genre conventions of an ego shooter, the game resemantisises the fictional archetype of a stalker by conflating it with the universally recognisable figure of a modern action hero, thus placing the aesthetics and the values of 'stalkerism' in a global context.

Modelling its playground as a new frontier to be explored by heroic male adventurers, who value courage, risk, and technical innovations, *S.T.A.L.K.E.R.* presents these values as explicitly gendered. The Zone is undoubtedly a man's world and a realm of literally toxic masculinity. However, a glaring absence of female characters in all three iterations of the game is rather a sign of escapism than of an explicitly sexist attitude. In the game, this escapism is presented with a sense of self-irony, which can be illustrated by the joke about a stalker, who always carries a picture of his mother-in-law – a reminder that for him the contaminated Zone, full of dangerous anomalies and aggressive mutants, is, in fact, a less hostile environment than the one he calls home.

Furthermore, in the Ukrainian context, the Zone as a terrain of wild nature and the hub of a heroic homosocial society inevitably evokes references to Cossacks and their military stronghold, the Zaporozhian Sich. However, in *S.T.A.L.K.E.R* these references remain marginal – *Cossacks* appear here as a vodka brand, widely renowned among the stalker community as an effective "medicine" against radiation sickness (in the game, the label of the "Cossacks Vodka" is identical to that of *Cossacks: European Wars* by GSC Game World).

Even though the game ironically downplays the connection between Cossacks and stalkers, it would not be an overinterpretation to emphasise the transgressive, liminal qualities of both groups. Similar to the fictional Cossacks, who, in the literary texts of the Romantic era[4], inhabit the frontier between the 'civilised world' and the 'wild field' of the Ukrainian steppe, the stalker, as a liminal figure, connects the 'normal' world of post-Soviet Ukraine with the fantastical realm of the Zone. This liminal status is potentially burdened with political meaning since in liminality people often comply with power in unusual, often irrational ways and tend to create communal structures, which 'interrupt' the routines of the known world. At this point an otherwise redundant plot of the series becomes important.

## 6. The Stories behind the Story

In *Shadow of Chernobyl*, the first game of the series, the protagonist named Strelok (Shooter) who has lost his memory at the beginning of the story, has to explore both the Zone and his own identity. Typically for all three iterations of *S.T.A.L.K.E.R.*, the game features more than one ending, but only one of them is happy: if the player manages to kill all his enemies, he gets a chance to destroy all things in the Zone that contain the Zone's mystic "consciousness" and the Zone will vanish. The alternate endings imply a self-mutilation of the player: he may, for instance, wish the disappearance of the Zone, which will cause his own blinding, or he may choose immortality, which will turn him into a statue (Schmid 2013: 4). According to Ulrich Schmid (ibid.), these endings show the two fundamental modes of the relationship between the individual and the surrounding world: either the protagonist shapes reality according to his wishes or he changes himself in order to comply with external challenges. More importantly, this scenario resonates with the self-perception of post-Soviet societies dominated by values of survival that imply passive or reactive behaviour to social change (ibid.). Thus, *Shadow of Chernobyl* echoes the gothic aesthetics of Russian popular movies and bestselling book series from the early 2000s, such as *Night Watch* (*Nochnoi dozor*) by Sergei Luk'ianenko, in which the groups that adhere to the archaic principles of clan loyalty and the rule of force appear far superior to the societies organised by moral and legal judgement (Khapaeva 2009: 373–374; Zabirko 2020: 273–280). In the hostile environment of the Zone, neither state nor society can provide the feeling of security, the protagonist's survival results here (quite in line with the conventions of the ego-shooter genre) exclusively from his

---

4    E.g., Nikolai Gogol's *Taras Bulba* (1835) or Henryk Sienkiewicz's *With Fire and Sword* (*Ogniem i mieczem*, 1884).

readiness to kill. In fact, the game's backstory assumes an erosion of the state, which is incapable of guarding the exclusion zone: as soon as anomalies start 'throwing' artifacts with fantastic physical properties, a black-market trade springs up, as scientists and collectors offer massive bounties for the bizarre items. As the precious objects grow in value, the military cordon becomes permeable – this leads to an assumption that, in the game, the whole stalker movement ultimately results from the corruption of the Ukrainian state institutions.

However, the second game of the series, *Call of Pripyat*, shifts the emphasis, as it centres Major Aleksandr Degtiarev, an officer of the Ukrainian Secret Service (SBU), who travels to the Zone to investigate the crash of five military helicopters. Thus, unlike in the first iteration of the series, the protagonist of the game is not a homeless adventurer in search of his own identity, but a government agent on a mission. Yet, in the Zone, Degtiarev is cut off from the resources of his powerful organisation and has to earn his living as a simple stalker, thus making contacts with other inhabitants of the Zone such as criminals, environmentalists, traders, scientists, and simple wanderers. Degtiarev's cover allows him to work for various faction members within the Zone and become involved in factions' politics and conflicts. He may support or attack certain factions or may try to remain neutral. In the course of events, the protagonist has to rescue the pilots, defeat the evil forces of the militant renegades responsible for the crash of the helicopters, but he may also save the life of Strelok, the hero of the first game of the series. If the player and his companions manage to escape the Zone after the final battle, the ending slideshow appears, telling the player what has happened after the escape. Major Degtiarev is given the opportunity to be promoted to the rank of Colonel which he declines – however, he later becomes the head of the Security Service in the Zone. Strelok – if he survives the finale – gives all the materials he had found in the Zone to the Ukrainian government, prompting the creation of a Scientific Institute for Research of the Chernobyl Anomalous Area, with Strelok taking up the position of chief scientific consultant.

Against the backdrop of the game's post-apocalyptic aesthetics and the general focus on mutations and anomalies, this somewhat simplistic happy ending appears strikingly normal, if not trivial. However, in post-Soviet countries, an image of a state, in which the agents of the secret service rescue those in need, the government funds scientific research, and the idea of the common good prevails over greed and social climbing, is anything but trivial. Furthermore, the overall 'progressive' tone of the plot can be interpreted as the long echo of the ITR discourse and the corresponding social ideals (epitomised by the progressor trope). If, following Lipovestky, we read the progressors' history as an allegory of the modernising efforts of ITRs from the 1960s' generation onward, then the post-Soviet transformation of the fantastic freedom Zone "into an elite settlement, where modernization works for the modernizers only" (2013: 125), certainly manifests the defeat of this modernising zeal. The rag-tag teams of stalkers are the losers of the post-Soviet transformation, but instead of simply feeding on each other, they swarm to the Zone in search of answers, mysterious artifacts, and, above all, the mythical Wish Granter – a nod to the secret Room from Tarkovskii's *Stalker*, which is said to grant the wishes of anyone who steps inside. Yet, what they usually find in the Zone are rather models of social interaction, and ethical ideals, which the player, however, may share or not, since the plot and the storyline of *S.T.A.L.K.E.R.* does not diminish or regulate the scope of possible interpretations of what the Zone might be and what kind of stories may happen in this fantastic realm.

In terms of its gameplay, *S.T.A.L.K.E.R.* offers a 'sandbox,' which, in video games, usually means a large, relatively free-roaming world, sometimes combined with a non-linear narrative structure. In a typical sandbox, narrative does not limit a particularly free way to play the game and to interact and move around in the world.[5] This is true for all three iterations of *S.T.A.L.K.E.R.*, where the respective plot functions only as a possible story (out of many others supposedly occurring in the Zone) and does not restrict the player's freedom of movement and interaction.

Over the years, *S.T.A.L.K.E.R.* has developed a strong 'modding' scene. The game modifications, commonly referred to as "mods", allow ambitious players to create their own modifications, which alter various aspects of the original game. These changes may range from minor details to complete gameplay overhauls. While most of the mods tackle certain aspects of the game mechanics (e.g., introducing a new weapon upgrade system or enhanced graphics), others aim at providing new content with a more or less clear political subtext. For example, the yet unfinished mod *S.T.A.L.K.E.R. – The Cursed Zone* addresses the ongoing Russian-Ukrainian war, as it features the Zone as a battleground, where Ukrainian guerrillas fight against the Russian occupation.[6]

Ego-shooters are not famous for their ability to deliver extensive political or philosophical messages; instead, *S.T.A.L.K.E.R.* offers a wide range of open conflicts, stories, and characters, which can be further developed both in video games and in other media. For instance, the fierce rivalry between two clans of stalkers, the anarchistic Freedom and the paramilitary Duty, runs like a thread throughout all three games of the series without being solved or extensively commented upon, thus leaving a lot of space for interpretation of the reasons and possible outcomes of this conflict. The same applies to Scar, the protagonist of *Clear Sky*, the third game of the series, who earns his living by escorting groups of ecologists to the Zone. Scar never vocally speaks in the game; therefore, his personality and biography are open for interpretation. Thus, the fundamental restrictions of ego-shooter as a genre allow for the basic models and the aesthetic of *S.T.A.L.K.E.R.* to be transplanted into literature, cinema, and television.

## 7. Intermediality of *S.T.A.L.K.E.R.*

Soon after the release of *Shadow of Chernobyl*, the post-apocalyptic mode of the game spread to the book market. The Moscow publishing house EKSMO launched a series with the programmatic title *Russian Apocalypse* and with the covers clearly modelled on the aesthetics of *S.T.A.L.K.E.R.* In 2009, the *S.T.A.L.K.E.R.* book series was launched by the same publisher. Today, the Russian-language novelisations of *S.T.A.L.K.E.R.* are hard to estimate, as they include several dozens of novels and even a larger number of short stories,

---

5 A prototypical example is the widely known *Minecraft*, where the player controls a character in a world composed of blocks, where the blocks can be combined into objects and buildings (e.g., swords, doors, rails, beds) depending on their components.
6 The mod is available online, see [Anon.] (2019/2022).

blogs, and other forms of fan fiction.[7] The plots of the books are usually set in a devastated world after an atomic war or, similar to the game's plot, after a second nuclear accident in Chernobyl. In both cases, the hero has to fight for his own survival in the contaminated and hostile environment.

*Figure 11.6: Typical book titles of the S.T.A.L.K.E.R series (2008–2019)*

Most of these books are rather plain and simplistic stories – their protagonists are stereotypical action heroes, while their plot and story are usually of minor importance as they only provide a framework for a seemingly endless chain of shooting and fighting scenes. Although the print-runs of these books remain comparatively small, the sheer scope of such a kind of literary production shows that the bleak and haunted world of S.T.A.L.K.E.R. generates particular excitement among the post-Soviet reading public, even if the authors of these texts seem to abandon the very idea of literature as a more sophisticated kind of entertainment compared to video games.

Standing alone against the background of stalker-fiction, Dmitrii Glukhovksii's bestselling novel *Metro 2033* (2002) borrows extensively from S.T.A.L.K.E.R. but transplants the Zone into the heart of modern Moscow. In 2007, Glukhovskii was awarded the prestigious Encouragement Award of the European Science Fiction Society at the Eurocon (the biggest European science fiction convention) for *Metro 2033*. Finally, a video game adaption of *Metro 2033* was released in 2010 by Ukrainian developers 4A Games – a studio, which was founded by some former members of GSC Game World, who formed the core team of *Shadow of Chernobyl* (Wordsworth 2014). Providing a vivid example of the wanderings of a fictional topic through different media in contemporary pop culture, *Metro 2033*, however, presents its particular version of survivalist horror and its own metaphys-

---

7   Russian-language Wikipedia lists more than 50 titles: "Spisok literaturnykh proizvedenii po miru S.T.A.L.K.E.R." Wikipedia, last modified 16 September 2022, https://ru.wikipedia.org/wiki/Список_литературных_произведений_по_миру_S.T.A.L.K.E.R. The online book store *Labirint* lists 178 books set in the S.T.A.L.K.E.R. universe: "Serii/S.T.A.L.K.E.R.". The fandom-page S.T.A.L.K.E.R. – *Books* counts more than 1800 book titles, including more than 1300 fan fiction texts (written by amateur writers and published online) as well as 524 novels published by the Moscow-based publishing houses AST and EKSMO, see [Anon.] (2010-), [Anon.] (2016-).

ical vision of toxic modernity, which differs both from the original S.T.A.L.K.E.R. series as well as from their low-quality novelisations.

The latter show a clear tendency towards imperial imaginary (e.g., in the works of Fëdor Berezin or Aleksandr Zorich), providing a particular form of Soviet nostalgia, which sometimes goes along with the possibility of traveling in time. On the level of narrative structure, this implies merging two time layers: the present-day post-Soviet world and the Soviet Union in 1986, on the eve of the Chernobyl accident. The notion of time travels places the literary stalkers from the S.T.A.L.K.E.R. book series, published by EKSMO and AST (two major Russian publishing houses), firmly in the context of the books about *popadantsy*, the revanchist time travellers, who are usually preoccupied with saving various forms of Russian statehood (e.g., the Tsarist empire or the Soviet Union) from their historical collapses (Weller 2019: 167–178; Zabirko 2020: 287–294). However, the most prominent variation of stalkers travelling in time can be found not in a work of literature, but in the TV series *Chernobyl: Zone of Exclusion*, which was launched in 2014 by the Russian federal TV channel TNT. The series centres on a group of young men, who travel to the town of Prypiat' where they accidentally find a time machine capable of bringing them back to 1986, on the day before the Chernobyl disaster. In the course of events, the protagonist of the series manages to change the future – in the end, he finds himself in the alternate year 2013, where the USSR did not collapse and the nuclear accident took place not in Chernobyl, but at the Calvert Cliffs nuclear power plant in the United States, ultimately leading to the dissolution of the USA and a new American civil war.

Obviously, this particular kind of revanchist alternate history is only loosely connected to S.T.A.L.K.E.R. Although the game provides its own alternate historical scenario of a second nuclear accident in Chernobyl, neither the storyline nor the gameplay offers any deliberate attempts at changing the past, in order to either prevent the collapse of the Soviet Union or to avoid the original Chernobyl disaster of 1986. Instead of altering history, the S.T.A.L.K.E.R. series provides its own model of coming to terms with the disaster that has already happened.

## 8. The Zone Lives!

The affective landscape of the Zone, in which catastrophe is "reincorporated into the ordinary" (Palmer 2014: 16), comes close to the alternate history scenario of the *Fallout* series set in a fictionalised United States after atomic war. But while *Fallout* satirises the 1950s' and 1960s' fantasies of the American "post-nuclear-war-survival" by making them available for comic play, S.T.A.L.K.E.R. rejects a satirical attitude and treats the nuclear apocalypse with what Jim Rossignol (2011) calls "Eastern pessimism" – a strange mixture of fear, brutality, and despair. Countering Rossignol's assumption of the game's specifically East European attitude, Bartłomiej Musajew (2016) argues that despite its local flavour, S.T.A.L.K.E.R. is "embedded in globalized popular culture, usually associated with the USA". Indeed, the conventional post-apocalyptic setting integrates S.T.A.L.K.E.R., and by extension both Soviet and Ukrainian history, into the global aesthetic framework of survival horror, but the game's roots in the progressorism of Soviet science fiction allows it to treat the apocalypse in a way that differs from Western "doomwriting literature" (from Isaac Asimov to Roberto Vacca) and its contemporary pop versions, which are usually pervaded by a sense of anxiety over planetary problems such as the nuclear apocalypse, overpopulation, and ecological disasters.

Some widely acclaimed Western TV productions from recent years deliberately target the Atomic Age optimism of a nuclear-powered future. Thus, in the American science-fiction horror drama *Stranger Things*, a laboratory, connected to the U.S. Department of Energy, appears as an ominous site of dangerous experiments and paranormal activities. Similarly, in the German series *Dark*, the cave system beneath the nuclear power plant hides a "wormhole", which enables time travel. In both series, the anomalies created by atomic energy bring the world to the verge of the apocalypse. The narrative, which unfolds as a recovery story, highlights the endeavours of the protagonists, who desperately try to bring the world to the *status quo ante*.

On the contrary, the "Eastern pessimism" (Rossignol 2011), if not downright fatalism, of the *S.T.A.L.K.E.R.* series offers no way back to "normality". Instead, it gives the player a chance to settle in a new, uncanny, and terrifying world. This world is undoubtedly a toxic wasteland, its countryside is dominated by horrifying mutants, while in the abandoned buildings bandits lay in wait for travellers, but after hours of playing, the Zone can be perceived, above all, as a living space, where the world is continuing in its own way. The holistic image of the 'domesticated' apocalypse survived all three iterations of the game and is likely to remain its key element in the future.[8]

In 2021, after years of dormancy followed by scandals, lawsuits, and break-ups, GSC Game World finally announced the revival of the legendary series, with the release of the new *S.T.A.L.K.E.R. 2: Heart of Chernobyl* scheduled for April 2022. A short gameplay trailer published on YouTube in June 2021, presents a group of rugged stalkers, who are sitting by a campfire playing guitar. Rendered from the viewpoint of the player's character, the scene is interrupted, as soon as the player approaches. A laconic "How was it?", asked by one of the men, sets off a sequence of combat scenes overlaid with fast, dynamic music.

The Zone seemed ready to produce new stories of stalkers, monsters, and physical anomalies.

It was, however, not to be.

In the afternoon of 24 February, 2022, the first day of the 2022 Russian invasion of Ukraine, the Russian armed forces launched an attack to capture the Chernobyl Exclusion Zone. By the end of the day, they had seized control of the defunct nuclear power plant and the surrounding area. The pictures of armoured vehicles and camouflaged soldiers in front of the plant went around the world triggering speculations about further damage to the radioactive site due to fierce fighting, the potential of leaking nu-

---

8   The question about the origins of the supposed fatalism of *S.T.A.L.K.E.R.* is, of course, debatable. This fatalism might be traced back to the game's national origin or to its overall retrospective stance, but it can also be described more broadly as a genre convention of the survival horror, which lacks national or cultural specificity. However, it cannot be denied that most post-apocalyptic video games present the nuclear apocalypse as an event that has changed the entire world. *S.T.A.L.K.E.R.*, instead, implies the normal world outside the Zone and therefore presents a radioactive wasteland as an integral part of this world.

clear waste or even a possible terrorist attack on the plant: what seemed like the plot of a bizarre video game, suddenly appeared on newsfeeds and came dangerously close to reality.

In the meantime, the official Twitter account of *S.T.A.L.K.E.R. 2: Heart of Chernobyl*[9] stopped posting updates of the game's development process and launched a fundraising campaign to support the Armed Forces of Ukraine.

With Russian missiles raining down on Ukrainian cities, turning them into areas full of ruins, the question, which remains to be answered, is not whether Ukraine will endure and domesticate yet another apocalypse on its territory, but rather, how soon the gaming industry will catch up with the new reality and what new versions of survival horror it will produce.

## Filmography

*In the Zone of Special Attention* (*V zone osobogo vnimaniia*), dir. Andrei Maliukov, USSR 1977.
*Guest from the Future* (*Gost'ia iz budushchego*), dir. Pavel Arseno, USSR 1984.
*Hit Back* (*Otvetnyi khod*), dir. Mikhail Tumanishvili, USSR 1981.
*Stalker*, dir. Andrei Tarkovskii, USSR 1979.
*Stargate*, dir. of Roland Emmerich, USA/France 1994.

## List of Games

*Age of Empires*, produced by Xbox Game Studios, PC/MAC, 1997.
*American Conquest*, produced by GSC Game World, PC/MAC, 2002.
*Assassin's Creed*, produced by Ubisoft, PC/MAC, 2007.
*Cossacks: European Wars*, produced by GSC Game World, PC/MAC, 2001.
*Fallout series*, produced by Cain, Tom, Interplay Entertainment, PC/Mac, 1997–2004.
*Half-Life 2*, produced by Valve, PC/MAC, 2004.
*Resident Evil*, produced by Capcom, PC/MAC, 1996.
*S. T. A. L. K. E. R. Shadow of Chernobyl'* (*S.T.A.L.K.E.R. Ten' Chernobylia*), produced by GSC Game World, PC/MAC, 2007.
*S.T.A.L.K.E.R. Clear Sky* (*S.T.A.L.K.E.R. Chyste Nebo*), produced by GSC Game World, PC/MAC, 2008.
*S.T.A.L.K.E.R. Call of Pripyat*, (*S.T.A.L.K.E.R. Poklyk Pryp'iati*) produced by GSC Game World, PC/MAC, 2009.
*S.T.A.L.K.E.R. The Cursed Zone* (*S.T.A.L.K.E.R. Prokliata Zona*) produced by GSC Game World, PC/MAC, 2013.
*S.T.A.L.K.E.R. 2: Oblivion Lost*, produced by GSC Game World, PC/MAC, 2015.
*S.T.A.L.K.E.R. 2: Heart of Chernobyl* (*S.T.A.L.K.E.R. Sertse Chernobylia*), produced by GSC Game World, PC/MAC, 2024.

---

9   See the official *S.T.A.L.K.E.R.* account on Twitter: S.T.A.L.K.E.R Official (@stalker_the game): https://twitter.com/stalker_thegame?lang=de [30 September 2023].

## List of Illustrations

Figure 11.1: The original cover of the computer game *S.T.A.L.K.E.R.: Shadow of Chernobyl*, developer GSC Game World, Ukraine 2008.
Figure 11.2: The town of Prypiat'. Screenshot from *S.T.A.L.K.E.R.: Call of Pripyat*, developer GSC Game World, Ukraine 2009.
Figure 11.3: The town of Prypiat'. Screenshot from *S.T.A.L.K.E.R.: Call of Pripyat*, developer GSC Game World, Ukraine 2009.
Figure 11.4: Photograph of the DUGA Radar Array near Chernobyl from 7 August 2014, copyright: Wikimedia Commons, https://commons.wikimedia.org/wiki/File:DUGA_Radar_Array_near_Chernobyl,_Ukraine_2014.jpg [01 February 2023].
Figure 11.5: Stalkers at the campfire. Screenshot from *S.T.A.L.K.E.R.: Call of Pripyat*, developer GSC Game World, Ukraine 2009.
Figure 11.6: Typical book titles of the *S.T.A.L.K.E.R* series, various authors, publisher AST/Eksmo: Moscow 2008–2019.

## References

[Anon.] (2010-): "Izdatel'stvo AST/Seriia S.T.A.L.K.E.R." In: labirint.ru (https://www.labirint.ru/series/14450/) [19 October 2021].

[Anon.] (2016-): "Literaturnaia ėntsiklopedia S.T.A.L.K.E.R." In: S.T.A.L.K.E.R.-knigi.fandom (https://stalker-knigi.fandom.com/ru/wiki/Заглавная_страница) [19 October 2021].

[Anon.] (2019/2022): "S.T.A.L.K.E.R. The Cursed Zone: Dimkas Story." In: moddb.com: https://www.moddb.com/mods/stalker-the-cursed-zone-dimkas-story-day-zero [30 September].

Berberich, Christine/Campbell, Neil/Hudson, Robert (2013): "Affective Landscapes: An Introduction." In: Cultural Politics 9/3, pp. 313–322.

Bodrunova, Svetlana (2012): "Chernobyl in the Eyes: Mythology as a Basis of Individual Memories and Social Imaginaries of a Chernobyl Child." In: The Anthropology of East Europe Review 30/1, pp. 13–24.

Bye, John (2001): "The Art of Cossacks." In: Eurogamer, 14 December (https://web.archive.org/web/20030228091306/http://www.eurogamer.net/content/i_cossacks) [30 September 2023].

Clemens, Valdine (1999): The Return of the Repressed: Gothic Horror from the "Castle of Otranto" to "Alien," New York: State University of New York Press.

Deckard, Sharae (2019): "Ecogothic." In: Maisha Wester/Xavier A. Reyes (eds.): Twenty-First-Century-Gothic: An Edinburg Companion, Edinburg: Edinburg University Press, pp. 174–188.

Etkind, Alexander (2013): Warped Mourning. Stories of the Undead in the Land of the Unburied, Stanford: Stanford University Press.

GSC Game World (2021a): "S.T.A.L.K.E.R. 2: Serdtse Chernnobylia – Ofitsialnyi geimpleinyi treiler" ["S.T.A.L.K.E.R. 2: Heart of Chernobyl – Official Gameplay Trailer."]

In: YouTube, 13 June 2021, (https://www.youtube.com/watch?v=ZNLaKOlXVvw) [30 September 2023].

GSC Game World (2021b): "Koch Media and GSC Game World partner up for the physical release of S.T.A.L.K.E.R. 2: Heart of Chernobyl." In: Plaion, 11 August 2021 (https://press.kochmedia.com/de/STALKER-2-Heart-of-Chernobyl-Koch-Media-und-GSC-Game-World-kooperieren) [30 September 2023].

Iatsenko, Maksim (2008): Istoriia razrabotki S.T.A.L.K.E.R. In: WINLINE. Mir Operatsionnykh Sistem, 26 February, 2008 (http://winlined.ru/articles/istoriya_razrabotki_s_t_a_l_k_e_r.php) [30 September 2023].

Khapaeva, Dina (2009): "Historical Memory in Post-Soviet Gothic Society." In: Social Research: An International Quarterly 76/1, pp. 359–394.

Lee, Christina (2017): "Introduction: Locating Spectres." In: Christina Lee (ed.): Spectral Spaces and Hauntings: The Affects of Absence, New York: Routledge, pp. 1–18.

Lipovetsky, Mark (2013): "The Poetics of ITR Discourse." In: Ab Imperio 1, pp. 109–131.

Lipovetsky, Mark (2016): "The Progressor between the Imperial and the Colonial." In: Klavdia Smola/Dirk Uffelmann (eds.): Postcolonial Slavic Literatures After Communism, Frankfurt am Main: Peter Lang, pp. 29–59.

Milne, Drew (2017): "Poetry after Hiroshima? Notes on Nuclear Implicature." In: Angelaki: Journal of the Theoretical Humanities 22/3, pp. 87–102.

Mukherjee, Souvik (2008): "Gameplay in the Zone of Becoming. Locating Action in the Computer Game." In: Stephan Günzel/Michael Liebe/Dieter Mersch (eds.): Conference Proceedings of the Philosophy of Computer Games, Potsdam: University Press, pp. 228–241.

Musajew, Bartłomiej (2016): "Stop Calling Eastern European Videogames Pessimistic." In: Kill Screen, 24 June 2016 (https://killscreen.com/previously/articles/stop-calling-eastern-european-videogames-pessimistic) [30 September 2023].

Palmer, Christopher (2014): "Ordinary Catastrophes: Paradoxes and Problems in Some Recent Post-Apocalypse Fictions." In: Gerry Canavan/Kim Stanley Robinson (eds.): Green Planets: Ecology and Science Fiction, Middletown: Wesleyan University Press, pp. 158–178.

Rossignol, Jim (2011): "On the Importance of S.T.A.L.K.E.R." In: Rock Paper Shotgun, 10 December 2011 (https://www.rockpapershotgun.com/on-the-importance-of-s-t-a-l-k-e-r) [30 September 2023].

Rossignol, Jim (2010): "Ghosts of The Future: Borrowing Architecture from the Zone of Alienation." In: BLDGBLOG, 17 May 2010 (https://www.bldgblog.com/2010/05/ghosts-of-the-future-borrowing-architecture-from-the-zone-of-alienation/) [30 September 2023].

Rossignol, Jim (2007): "S.T.A.L.K.E.R. I.N.T.E.R.V.I.E.W." In: Rock Paper Shotgun 10 December 2007 (https://www.rockpapershotgun.com/stalker-interview) [30 September 2023].

Sakey, Matthew (2010): "Alone for All Seasons: Environmental Estrangement in S.T.A.L.K.E.R." In: Drew Davidson (ed.): Well Played 2.0. Video Games, Value and Meaning, Carnegie Mellon University: ETC Press, pp. 92–114.

Schmid, Ulrich (2013): "Post-Apocalypse, Intermediality and Social Distrust in Russian Pop Culture." In: Russian Analytical Digest 126, pp. 2–5.

Weller, Nina (2019): "Gestern wird Krieg sein. Zeitreisen als neoimperiale Wunschmaschinen der russischen Erinnerungskultur." In: Riccardo Nicolosi/Brigitte Obermayr/Nina Weller (eds.): Interventionen in die Zeit. Kontrafaktische historische Narrative und ihre erinnerungskulturelle Dimension, Paderborn: Schöningh, pp. 167–198.

Wordsworth, Rich (2014): "Games from the Real-World Post-Apocalypse. It Came from Ukraine – How One Team and Two Studios Changed Gaming's Wasteland Forever." In: IGN, 28 January 2014 (https://www.ign.com/articles/2014/01/28/games-from-the-real-world-post-apocalypse) [30 September 2023].

Zabirko, Oleksandr (2020): "The Magic Spell of Revanchism. Geopolitical Visions in Post-Soviet Speculative Fiction." In: Alexander Etkind/Mikhail Minakov (eds.): Ideology after Union. Political Doctrines, Discourses, and Debates in Post-Soviet Societies, Stuttgart: ibidem, pp. 251–304.

Chapter 12:
# Come and See, Once Again
A Russian Television Series on the Seventh Symphony in Defeated Leningrad

*Matthias Schwartz*

## 1. Introduction

*Come and See* (*Idi i smotri*) by Ėlem Klimov was a sensation in 1985 when the film was finally released after years of being blocked by Soviet censors. It won the main prize at the Moscow International Film Festival and became one of the most successful films of the year in 1986 in the early days of glasnost and perestroika.[1] No one had ever portrayed the horrors of the German war of extermination from 1941 to 1945 so radically, the situation of the Soviet partisans so hopelessly and bitterly, the German scorched earth policy so relentlessly and clearly. Without ideological filter, without scrupulous symbolism, it showed how deadly and merciless the German occupation of the Belarusian territories of the Soviet Union was: 'Come and see', the terse request referring to the four horsemen of John's Apocalypse, was a sensation even in West Germany, where the myth of the 'clean Wehrmacht' was still officially upheld, a country where Chancellor Helmut Kohl had laid wreaths at SS soldiers' graves together with US President Ronald Reagan as late as May 1985 (Stieglegger 2020: 169–178; cf. Bulgakowa/Hochmuth 1992: 127–132). But the film remains in the memory above all through the main actor, 14-year-old Aleksei Kravchenko in the role of the boy Flëra, through whose eyes, or more precisely: in whose face we as viewers perceive all the horrors depicted, mirrored, seen. Children's faces have always been the most credible witnesses to the horrors of the adult world for cinema directors – but rarely has the expression of a youthful face been so cruelly destroyed as in Klimov's work.

Four decades later, Aleksei Kravchenko, now 52, is once again starring in a film about World War II, in Aleksandr Kott's eight-part television series *The Seventh Symphony*

---

[1] I thank Nina Weller and in particular Franziska Thun-Hohenstein for their extremely helpful comments on an earlier version of this essay. All translations from Russian quotes are mine if not noted otherwise.

(*Sed'maia simfoniia*, 2021), which, on the occasion of its 80th anniversary, tells the story of the performance of Dmitri Shostakovich's *Symphony No. 7 in C major* in Leningrad while besieged by the Germans in August 1942. The broadcast of the television series had been associated with high expectations not only because of its subject matter. After all, Aleksandr Kott, who on 24 February 2022 immediately positioned himself against the war (Popogrebskii et al. 2022),[2] is a successful cinema and television director who had previously made demanding literary adaptations such as Mikhail Lermontov's *A Hero of Our Time* (*Geroi nashego vremeni*, 2006,), eight-part television series, exciting biopics such as *Trotsky* (*Trotskii*, 2007), eight-part television series, but also patriotic World War II films such as *The Brest Fortress* (*Brestskaia krepost'*, also known as *Fortress of War*, 2010). The cast also included many star actors (Mel'nikova 2021; Morozova 2021; [Anon.] 2021). Accordingly, when the series was first broadcast in the second week of November 2021 on Russian state television's second channel Rossiia, it achieved the highest viewing figures (Al'perina 2021). The critical response was largely positive, both at home and in Russian-speaking communities abroad ([Anon.] 2022c), with the only criticism being the sometimes considerable deviations from historically verified facts, but also the underlying "anti-Soviet" attitude (Kudriashov 2021; Karev 2021; Litov 2021; Timuka 2021). Other critics praised the fact that this was not the typical "militarism" of other series about World War II (Maliukova 2021; Dubshan 2021). And so, in January 2022, on the eve of the full-scale Russian war against Ukraine, the series was awarded the most important jury prize, *Zolotoi orël*, as the best television series of the year ([Anon.] 2022a).

## 2. Aleksei Kravchenko Now and Then: The Poetics of Popular Culture

Aleksandr Kott knows exactly who he has in front of the camera with Aleksei Kravchenko, from the very first scene. *Come and See* ends with Flëra, who, enraged, shoots repeatedly from his rifle at a picture of 'Hitler the Liberator' (*Hitler Asvabadzitsel'*) lying in the mud, while black and white documentary film images run backwards before the audience's eyes to atonal musical sounds, tracing the entire history of the horrors of the National Socialists from the end, beginning with pictures of the extermination camps and the destruction of the war, through repeatedly shown images of Hitler caressing children. It is only when the reverse documentary history pauses on a photograph with Hitler as a baby on his mother's arm that Flëra stops shooting, and his child's face freezes in close-up with his eyes wide open. In the moment of freezing, the choral voices of the *Lacrimosa* from Mozart's *Requiem in D-minor* are heard, under whose dramatic singing Flëra rejoins the partisans in the Belarusian forests. The inconceivable horror brought upon humanity by the politician from Austria cannot be undone by the music of the great composer from the same country, but it can give expression, at least for the moment, to the child's speechless anguish of the soul.

The first scene of the first episode in *The Seventh Symphony* begins on 20 September 1941 at a jetty in Leningrad on the river Neva, where Kravchenko, playing the role of the

---

[2] Aleksandr Kott signed the appeal "No to war!" initiated by the president of the Cinema Association of Russia, Aleksei Popogrebskii, directly on 24 February 2022. Cf. Popogrebskii et al. 2022.

NKVD lieutenant Anatolii Serëgin, is taking his wife and two children to be evacuated by steamboat. Mozart sounds again, now from the public radio speakers, but this time it is the *Piano Concerto No. 23 in A major*, to the sounds of which Kravchenko runs around dancing a little with his son on his shoulders. But the cheerful major sounds instead of the minor of the *Requiem* are deceptive. As he waves on the shore, looking after the departing ship, there is a bombing raid by the German Luftwaffe and he has to watch his wife and children being sunk in the Neva: again, with the same eyes wide open in horror, an expression that we know so well from *Come and See*. As if the horror never stops, but rather catches up with him, again and again. Even four decades later. Even almost eight decades after the end of World War II.

And yet there are huge differences between the 1985 cinema film and the 2021 television series, not only because almost twice as much time has passed since the end of the war on the eve of a new war and because Aleksandr Kotts' television series was made in a completely different socio-political environment. In the mid-1980s, in the face of the debacle of the Soviet mission in Afghanistan, which was discussed more and more openly in the Soviet press and in which a generation of conscripts had gained traumatic experiences of war, the anti-war film *Come and See* undoubtedly struck a chord with the times, in which heroic war narratives could hardly be conveyed. During Vladimir Putin's fourth term as President of Russia, on the other hand, the state-funded production of films, television series, novels, exhibitions and educational initiatives presenting the Great Patriotic War in all its heroic and patriotic facets reached new heights. The defamation of the Red Army and the defence of the fatherland was made a punishable offence and the mass cultural preoccupation with the war became a central propagandistic *lieu de mémoire* staged and celebrated in all media and on all possible occasions as an obligation of subsequent generations for the future.

But the decisive difference between the advanced cinema film of 1985 and the successful television series of 2021 lies in the different genre, since the popular format of mass-culture television productions follows a completely different logic than the auteur cinema of the time, which worked under the conditions of state censorship and regulation. While here the director has to assert his work of art above all against the ideological and aesthetic control authorities, popular culture in today's Russia, although dependent on state support as well, is mostly tied to audience success and therefore reacts much more strongly to current moods in the population or among certain target groups. Popular culture signals and reinforces what is considered fashionable and relevant, and in its products makes offers to give a social unease, widespread longings and fears, social questions and political concerns an affective and imaginary space to be articulated and adapted to certain realities (cf. Hermann 2008; Borenstein 2011; Boele et al. 2020). All kinds of music cultures with their scene locations, dress codes and habits of behaviour, but also mass commodity products such as popular literature or TV series function in this way.

In capitalism, such popular mass cultures are generally analysed as consumer offers that help people come to terms with the relations of exploitation, insecurities and fears of decline in neoliberal market economies. Since popular culture gains its attractiveness through the participation and involvement of consumers, it can certainly become the catalyst and motor of protest movements and revolutions, but it can also contribute to defusing and neutralising radical resistance in the field of culture, just as conversely, it may also strengthen populist and reactionary movements (cf. Storey 1996; Hall 2009: 508–518). In authoritarian or dictatorial societies like the Russian Federation, this relationship between adaptation and protest is much more ambivalent. On the one hand, popular formats are an instrument of state actors to attune the population to existing social conditions and ideological narratives, but since popular culture – unlike mere propaganda – always remains dependent on the interest and participation of consumers, it constantly produces contradictory and conflicting signals and semantics (György 1999: 53–72; Bassin/Poso 2017; Stephen 2022). A concert or blockbuster movie that no one attends is just as worthless as audience flops or news programmes solely watched by foreign correspondents.

This mode of operation of popular television series will be analysed in the following using the example of Aleksandr Kott's *The Seventh Symphony* against the general background of the enormous production of film and television series about World War II in the contemporary Russian Federation. The aim is not so much to work out a general characteristics of this mass cultural genre, but rather to show the specific pragmatic and poetic function of this series between narratives prescribed by the state, affectively and imaginatively appealing offers of identification and the compensation of collective fears and target group interests.

## 3. World War II in Contemporary Russian Television Series

In the Russian Federation of the first two decades of the 21st century, the Stalinist era and World War II were probably the most controversial period of history to which the increasingly professional commercial and state film and television industry devoted itself (cf. Beumers 2006; Norris 2012; Brouwer 2016). The sides of the war that had been taboo or little discussed in Soviet times could now be dealt with in an audiovisually sophisticated form using digital techniques and exciting scripts. Punishment battalions with criminals and political prisoners from the Gulag who were burnt out at the front (the series *Penal Battalion*, *Shtrafbat*, 2004, directed by Nikolai Dostal'), (former) NKVD officers and spies spreading fear and terror (like in the series, *Execution Impossible to Pardon*, *Kaznit' nel'zia pomilovat'*, 2017, directed by Kim Druzhinin), incompetent and scheming party politicians, collaboration with the occupiers or anti-Semitism even in their own ranks became the subject of melodramatic war adventures just as much as rousing action thrillers (cf. Norris 2021: 48–75).[3] Often, novels that were banned, well-known or popular in Soviet times served as scripts, such as Vasilii Grossman's *Life and Fate* (*Zhizn' i sud'ba*, series 2011–2012, directed by Sergei Urusliak) or Anatolii Rybakov's *Children of the Arbat* (*Deti Arbata*, series 2004, directed by Andrei Ėshpai), but just as often there were series whose scenarios were developed specifically for the production. At the same time,

---

[3] The expression "Kaznit' nel'zia pomilovat'" is a catchphrase in Russian, which carries opposite meanings depending on the emphasis or comma placement: "Execution impossible, to pardon" or also "Execution, impossible to pardon". Its written or oral origin is unclear; it is attributed to various tsars such as Peter the Great.

in addition to curiosity about that which was forbidden and hidden behind the official scenes, these series often confirmed, but sometimes also questioned and subverted certain clichés and prejudices of their viewers. For example, Sergei Ursuliak's series *Liquidation* (*Likvidatsia*, 2007) showed the criminal milieu in Odessa in the immediate post-war period, reproducing many familiar topoi about Jewish shrewdness, Ukrainian collaborators and the sunny life in the port city, but also openly problematising anti-Semitic prejudices (cf. Noordenbos 2021: 150–169). Series thus also function on an affective and intellectual level as imaginary offers to the viewer to become immersed in a fictional reality full of adventure, exoticism and unexpected challenges.

In cultural-political terms, these series productions primarily followed the function of familiarising the viewers with the harsh everyday reality of war, whereby the focus of the plot was often not on the battles and combat life at the front, but on what was happening behind the front. Either the action took place in the enemy's territory, where one had to cope as a saboteur or agent, or behind one's own lines, where one was confronted with treason, sabotage and espionage. This function of normalising and portraying the everyday realities of war can be observed in exemplary fashion in the Russian-Ukrainian co-production *Under Military Law* (*Po zakonam voennogo vremeni*, 2016–2023), six seasons so far. The series, directed by Maksim Mekheda, Evgenii Serov and Sergei Vinogradov, deals with all the fears of machinations and intrigues within the security services, addresses corruption and arbitrary violence in the army as well as the illusion of a supposed infallibility of the party and its commissioners. In many episodes, however, simple naivety, egoism, jealousy and plain opportunism within their own ranks often provide drama and suspense. Civilian life can only be adapted to the titular 'military law' with great difficulty. At the same time, the four main heroes, the conscientious investigator of the military prosecutor's office Ivan Rokotov (played by Evgenii Volovenko) and his chauffeur Grigorii Fedorenko (Aleksandr Pankratov-Chërnyi), always up for a joke, both from Kyiv, as well as the attractive investigator of the Supreme Military Prosecutor's Office of the Red Army, Svetlana Elagina (played by Ekaterina Klimova), and her superior Nikolai Mirskii (Maksim Drozd), both from Moscow, survive all the dangers and difficulties they are confronted with on their countless missions from Kyiv in the summer of 1941 to Königsberg in the autumn of 1945. The fact that this series primarily serves to convince viewers at home of the 'just cause' of the war is shown by the fact that the German enemy and his war crimes appear at most in passing and as background events, while the criminal cases mostly revolve around uncovering grievances and misconduct in one's own ranks. The aim is not to play down the scepticism towards the secret services and the military by concealing and 'varnishing reality', as was still common in Soviet times. Rather, the credibility of the fictional reality is suggested by the fact that personal failures and criminal violence are depicted, but then always in the end the state authorities find a resolution as a necessary and essential instrument of power. The series (the last two seasons of which were only produced by the Russian side) also deals extensively with the mistrust and disagreements between Kyiv and Moscow, which are, however, always resolved by the protagonists in a productive Russian-Ukrainian cooperation, symbolically embodied in the love affair between Elagina and Rokotov. The series, which was launched after the Euromaidan in 2013/2014, the incorporation of Crimea into the Russian Federation and the proclamation of the separatist 'People's Republics' in Luhansk and Donetsk, is in this respect also a popular cultural response to how the military-political conflict with Ukraine should be overcome from the Russian point of view.[4]

Yet, at the same, this series, like many others, follows the global model of Hollywood cinema in its aesthetics and even in its "military-patriotic" textbook, as a critic noted:

> It is as if there is a textbook, no more elaborate than the primer on which most local war serials are diligently filmed. The plotting is admirably clear. If our guys are in the picture, they are mostly good, although villains and traitors and not always fair NKVDs are allowed. If the Germans are in the frame, they are mostly bad, but clever and formidable opponents are tolerated, and in a sense, sometimes even almost positive characters. And if love occurs, it is usually with a distinct flavour of doom. (Legostaev 2020)

This pattern "with a distinct flavour of doom" is also followed by the series *The Seventh Symphony*, but it undertakes significant shifts, attempting to unite war and art, entertainment and high culture in its subject, which almost inevitably means a lot of kitsch.

## 4. History and Fiction: The Leningrad Symphony Myth and NKVD Terror

The story of the performance of Dmitri Shostakovich's *Symphony No. 7* is one of the best-known episodes from the 900-day German siege of Leningrad during World War II and has been the subject of many artistic representations. After the invasion of the Soviet Union on 22 June 1941, the German Wehrmacht had advanced rapidly across the Baltic, while from the north Finland recaptured the territories lost in the Winter War of 1939/1940. After the Wehrmacht had captured Shlisselburg on Lake Ladoga, Leningrad was surrounded from 9 September 1941 to 27 January 1944. After the German leadership decided not to conquer the city with Lenin's symbolic name but to systematically starve its population, more than a million inhabitants died during the blockade, which lasted almost 900 days, mainly from hunger, but also from air raids and artillery fire, as well as from cold and deprivation, since the people could only be supplied through makeshift routes via Lake Ladoga and by air.[5] Shostakovich was in besieged Leningrad in September 1941 when he was already writing a new symphony, but he did not complete it until he had been evacuated to Kuibyshev (Samara) at the end of the year. After its premiere by the evacuated orchestra of the Moscow Bolshoi Theatre in Kuibyshev in March 1942, premieres took place in Moscow, London and New York, among other places, before *Symphony No. 7* could also be performed in Leningrad on August 9, 1942 by the radio

---

4   It is certainly no coincidence that some of the Ukrainian actors who appeared in the series also played prominent roles for Volodymyr Zelensky's production company "Kvartal 95" and its television series *Servant of the People* (*Sluga naroda*, 2015–2019), three seasons, such as Stanislav Boklan or Viktor Saraikin.

5   There is an ongoing debate about whether and if so to what extent the Soviet side also willingly contributed to the famine, but the film does not take any explicit position on this. For more recent research on the siege of Leningrad, cf. Kirschenbaum 2006; Ganzenmüller 2007; Reid 2011; Bidlack/Lomagin 2012.

orchestra that had remained in the city and the conductor Karl Eliasberg in the hall of the Philharmonic. The performance was broadcast live nationwide on the radio so that the besieged city and the entire Soviet Union could follow it (cf. Reid 2011: 356–369; Redepenning 2011: 169–193).

Thus, the symphony entered the canon of anti-fascist art worldwide already during World War II, dramatically giving musical expression to the inconceivable suffering and resistance of the Leningrad population. Nothing was better suited as a symbol of the triumph of art and civilisation over the barbarism of German National Socialism than classical music. The performance is also portrayed as such a collective human effort in the face of the horror of the siege in the black-and-white film *Leningrad Symphony* (*Leningradskaia simfoniia*, 1957, Mosfilm) by the dramatist and director Zakhar Agranenko, which was released in Soviet cinemas on the 15th anniversary of the performance. However, this film was soon forgotten, still heavily influenced by the narrative schemes of the late Stalin era, where Eliasberg is given a Russian name and oddball elderly gentlemen, motherly women and strong young men overcome the most difficult dangers. The heroic pathos inherent in this performance under the conditions of the blockade resonates even in William T. Vollmann's great epic novel *Europe Central* (2005) about the fate of the continent in the short 20th century, whose narrator devotes central passages to Shostakovich and the radio broadcast of the Symphony on 9 August 1942:

> How should I tell this tale? [...] The Great Hall Philharmonic, that dull yellow, not particularly ornate building, with it white-on-yellow rococo decorations sparse and faded, this was now the brain of our national telephone; and Shostakovich had braided the sub-waves of his immense signal so as to most beautifully and loudly carry the commands of the automatic central office in a rhythm as reassuringly steady as Red Army men with up-pointed files filing past our trapezoidal shelter for the Bronze Horseman. [...] Many wept. Leningrad was transformed into gold. (Vollmann 2005: 218–219)

Aleksandr Kott avoids such pathos. Instead, he follows the narrative patterns of popular television series that demand dramatic conflicts, emotional shock, unexpected twists and multiple opportunities for identification that captivate the viewer by combining the strange and the familiar, the unfamiliar and the mundane, the exciting and the comforting into an exciting story. For this, Kott changes the historical reality considerably in some points. It is the heartbreaking story of about a dozen largely fictional orchestra members and helpers, whom we get to know better while they practise the performance of the symphony under the terrible and deprived conditions of the Leningrad blockade. At the centre of the plot, he puts the enmity between the NKVD lieutenant Anatolii Serëgin, played by Kravchenko, and the conductor of the radio orchestra Karl Eliasberg, played by Aleksei Gus'kov. Whereas there is no historical precedent for Serëgin, the conductor, who then was actually 35 years old, now becomes an older man, whose wife is even arrested. While Serëgin is a typical 'achiever' (*vydvizhenets*) of the 1930s, coming from humble proletarian beginnings, believing in iron self-discipline, masculine toughness and uncompromising rigour, Eliasberg in the film is from the Baltic German and Jewish bourgeois upper classes, living entirely for art and music. He is the conductor of the Leningrad Radio Orchestra and refuses to be evacuated in order to stay with his orchestra, which had to remain in the besieged city alongside the choir and the comedy theatre on the orders of Andrei Zhdanov, secretary of the Communist Party and at the time a member of the Leningrad Front war council, in order to raise the spirit of resistance among the population. A little later, Eliasberg receives direct orders from Zhdanov himself to perform *Symphony No. 7*. At the same time, Serëgin, who has absolutely no interest in classical music, is ordered to ensure the proper performance of Shostakovich's work and at the same time to spy on the orchestra for agents and traitors. But in practice this order means, above all, that he must find capable musicians in Leningrad and at the front and forcibly recruit them for the orchestra.

But this mission turns out to be difficult for Serëgin, not only because often the people he is looking for have already died of hunger, cold or at the front and are severely physically injured. As an NKVD officer, his person inspires fear and terror above all. The memory of the Great Terror of 1936 to 1938, when the chekists took innocent people from their homes at night, when anyone could be denounced as an enemy of the people and a traitor, when people were arbitrarily shot or banished to the Gulag, is still too dense, and the cultural intelligentsia in particular suffered from the purges. And this fear seems to be more than justified, as becomes clear in the very first episode of the series, when Eliasberg's wife is personally arrested by Serëgin before the conductor's eyes. A few scenes later, people in the air-raid shelter talk about how it is better to die under bombs than to be taken away at night by the NKVD (episode 1, min. 42:25-43:00). Accordingly, when the lieutenant first appears, people panic and anticipate their immediate arrest and shooting. When Serëgin is looking for an urgently needed violinist, his mother at first refuses to give him any information for fear that he might be captured, and when he finally finds the son in the front line, he flees in panic: the violinist would rather die at the front than in the torture cellars of the NKVD. An oboist whom he fetches from her bombed-out flat insults the chekists as inquisitors from the Middle Ages. And when, just before the premiere, the orchestra's agitated viola player Leonid Kleiman (played by Timofei Tribuntsev), exasperated to hysterical with despair, wants to volunteer for the front, he curses the whole orchestra as cowards, blurting out the following while standing right next to the NKVD lieutenant Serëgin:

> "I didn't think I would say this, but he was telling the truth from the beginning, you're all cowards, eighty people gathered to play a little concert, and you all happily hid behind him.... Do you know what will happen after the concert? Maybe not right away, maybe not even this year, but people like Lieutenant will devour you, one by one, the masses will crush you and kill you like new enemies, because they are many and you are eighty..." (Episode 7, min. 33:05-34:00)

The fear of the cultural intelligentsia of the terror of the NKVD, which culminates in this tirade, is historically accurate and to a certain extent prophetic here, since it could be understood as a reference to the repressions of the post-war period.[6] Within the logic of the

---

6   On the repression during the blockade, cf. Ganzenmüller 2011. On the postwar period, cf. Bljum 2011.

plot, however, it represents a complete misjudgement of the situation, since the television series has previously made it more than clear, in particular through the character of Serëgin, that the fear is not only unfounded but also unjust. The lieutenant is anything but a merciless inquisitor and ruthless murderer.

Rather, the chekist in the series is himself a deeply traumatised person, as the viewers know from the opening scene with the death of his wife, son and daughter, a person who is initially completely incapable of expressing his feelings other than through anger and aggression. Accordingly, after the scene at the jetty we see him for the first time on a professional assignment, where he almost beats a prisoner to death in an NKVD cell and can only be stopped at the last moment. But it is not murderousness that speaks from his eyes, but pure desperation and helplessness. Just as the boy Flëra in the film *Come and See* desperately shoots at the portrait of the *Führer*, the adult Serëgin strikes here without sense and reason. He does not torture due to political or other motivations, but out of despair, which is psychologically immediately understandable for the audience. And with each subsequent scene and series episode, the empathetic, compassionate camera eye makes the NKVD lieutenant more sympathetic and familiar, for behind the tough façade lies a soft character who has difficulty putting his feelings into words and initially tries doggedly to suppress his own pain and grief. He helps people out of difficult situations, supports the weak, saves lives or signals understanding and compassion through his silence alone. The more often he manages to shed his body armour of an iron chekist in the course of the series, the more human he becomes. This 'humanisation' of Serëgin takes place primarily through three characters: a little red-haired boy, a woman who loves him and the conductor Eliasberg as his actual opponent.

## 5. The Boy, the Beloved and the Conductor: The Humanisation of a Chekist

Popular television series explain the world through the experiential horizons of their main protagonists, often bringing the enigmatic and mysterious ways of big politics into conflict with private issues and personal interests, which adds drama and suspense. This is also the case with NKVD Lieutenant Anatolii Serëgin, who is supposed to be monitoring the orchestra for traitors and informers, but at the same time has to reconcile his deeply traumatised, yet still intact world view of an uncompromising chekist with the partly eccentric and completely alien world of the orchestra musicians. This contrast between the world of state violence and suspicion and that of culture becomes most obvious in the encounters with Karl Eliasberg.

In this confrontation, the sympathies of the script and camera are clearly on the side of the arts. For while the repressive policy of the NKVD is discussed as an anti-human and false understanding of order that only causes fear, chaos and suffering, the order of music is no less strict and rigorous, but it provides harmony, stability and security. And this other, better order is embodied from the very beginning by the conductor of the radio orchestra, who states in one of his very first appearances: "There is no excuse for hackwork, especially now… the more chaos around, the more order should be here" (episode 1, min. 18:55-19:10).

Eliasberg's role is to uncover the narrowness and falseness of Serëgin's world view. Already at their second encounter (after the arrest of Eliasberg's wife), when the NKVD lieutenant is still grumbling about why he has to look for musicians for this needless orchestra, the following dialogue develops between him and the conductor:

– "If you had gone to the front, there would have been no problem."
– "I went to the enlistment office and they turned me down. They said I'm needed here."
– "You mean waving the baton? With your name, comrade Eliasberg, there's nothing to do at the front. They'll shoot you."
– "Were you at the front?"
– "No, I've been catching your countrymen here."
– "By the way, I'm half German. My father is German. My mother is Jewish."
– "And even worse."
– "You don't like the latter?"
– "Well, let's put it this way: I don't trust them."
– "Karl Marx was a German Jew. You don't trust Marx?"
– "Marx? I had no idea."
– "I was named after him."
– "But you don't look much like him."
– "Thank God for that."
– "Why so?"
– "Because. Marx has to be the one and only." (Episode 2, min. 18:34-20:07)

Serëgin embodies the typical careerist from a simple background, characterised by his semi-education and anti-Semitic prejudices, while Eliasberg even emphasises that he comes from an educated communist family by referring to his first name, Karl. Accordingly, the two despise each other, as becomes clear in their next conversation:

– "I'm not such a moron."
– "Who told you that you're a moron?"
– "Well, this is why I said it? You have it written on your face that you despise me, just like the working class."
– "I love the working class. It's just that putting people in jail, torturing women, whipping children, that's not a job."
– "I don't torture women, at least I don't put them in a cell with murderers according to the eighty-first article. Well, I could. But I don't torture." (3, 15:20-19:09)

Eliasberg expresses this abysmal dislike for the NKVD lieutenant repeatedly, with anger over his arrested wife certainly playing a role.

Only gradually does Eliasberg realise that Serëgin also has human sides when, for example, he does not impose a punishment on a young man who has reported to the front with false papers. Conversely, thanks to the conductor, the chekist begins to understand why music is so important to the state and what an important role culture apparently plays for people, so that he even steals a popular booklet on the *Myths of Ancient Greece* (*Mify Drevnei Gretsii*, 1941) from a destroyed library, which he also reads.[7]

But the decisive impulse for his 'humanisation' in the series comes from someone else, namely the flutist Vera Preobrazhenskaia (played by Elizaveta Boiarskaia), whose name already symbolically indicates this, since her first name in Russian means "faith" and her last name means something like "The Transforming One": she has to convey both qualities to him in the course of the series.[8] Her first appearance in the series is when she gives birth to a boy in a hallway under German bombardment, but in the very next scene with her we see a broken woman with ruined hands at the front, from whom Serëgin learns in an 'interrogation' that she lost her son shortly after birth and that the illegitimate father was killed in the war: he orders her to come back to the orchestra anyway. However, already in the third episode we learn in a flashback that Preobrazhenskaia's relationship with the child's fallen father was not a happy one: Vera was actually in love with the Jewish viola player Leonid Kleiman, but despite all her familiarity with him, he preferred the blonde estrada singer Lidia at the time, which is why she consoled herself with the soldier.[9] When Vera Preobrazhenskaia is ordered back to the orchestra, the guilt-ridden Kleiman's affection for her flares up again, but she now seeks support and closeness with Anatoly Serëgin, who keeps his distance from her for a long time.[10]

Serëgin only begins to visibly show emotion when, while searching for orchestra musicians in a bombed-out flat, he comes across the striking red-haired boy Kolia Vasiliev (played by Makar Mozzhevilov) hiding in a wardrobe, staying with his slain grandfather.[11]

---

[7] In the series, the booklet is attributed to the historian Nikolai Kun (1877–1940), whose popular science book on the ancient stories, previously revised and expanded several times, first appeared in 1940 under the title *Myths and Legends of Ancient Greece* (*Mify i legendy Drevnei Gretsii*). In fact, the cover of the booklet *Myths of Ancient Greece* (1940) by Vsevolod and Lev Uspenskii, published in the same year, is shown in the film.

[8] Her surname has an ambivalent connotation in Russian, since the main hero of Mikhail Bulgakov's well-known satirical story *The Heart of a Dog* (*Sobach'e serdtse*, 1925), the surgeon Professor Filipp Filippovich Preobrazhenskii, bears the same eloquent surname, who implants the dog's heart in a human being, thus transforming him into a fanatical animalistic Bolshevik. Aleksandr Kott to a certain extent symbolically reverses this "transformation" from a human being into a bestial creature, albeit not through surgery but through music.

[9] Leonid Kleiman also married Lidia, but she leaves him during the siege, preferring the adventurous life of a front-line orchestra. When Lidia's lover is killed before her eyes in a bombing raid, she returns to Leonid in despair, emaciated by hunger and losing her mind, she buys fake chocolate on the black market in exchange for her last piece of jewellery, which she then fatally poisons herself with.

[10] Thus, the pre-war constellation between Vera and Leonid is repeated under the opposite sign: Kleiman is now alone and despises the NKVD man just as he hates military men, but Preobrazhenskaia courts Serëgin this time not for comfort but out of actual affection.

[11] Red-haired boys have been considered headstrong and rebellious at least since O. Henry's legendary short story *The Ramson of Red Chief* (1907), so also in the Soviet O. Henry movie adaptation *Strictly Business* (*Delovye liudi*, 1962) by Leonid Gaidai. Tom Sawyer, modelled on his red-haired creator Mark Twain, is often portrayed as a redhead in films too, as in the 1981 Soviet television series *The Adventures of Tom Sawyer and Huckleberry Finn* (*Prikliucheniia Toma Soiera i Gekl'berri Finn*, dir. Stanislav Govorukhin). The headstrong Kolia shares some of the characteristics of these role models.

Ten-year-old Kolia refuses to stay at the children's home, so he takes him to the orchestra and Vera agrees to take him into her flat while Anatolii Serëgin gets treats for him on the black market and builds him a makeshift bed. For the first time, the chekist shows a hint of *joie de vivre*: he smiles with the boy and makes jokes. But Kolia demands more from "Uncle Tolia" (the short form of Serëgin's first name Anatolii), he should not only put him to bed and be near him, but take him seriously, give him his attention. One evening Kolia asks him if he will go to the front, repeating word for word the last words of Serëgin's dead son. This childlike, naïve importunity bursts Serëgin's emotional shell: with eyes wide open, a face expression we know so well since *Come and See*, the horrible memory overwhelms him, and we see fragmented flashbacks of the last moments until his son's death, whereby Serëgin almost collapses, drenched in sweat. A little later he is sitting on the edge of Vera's bed alone with her, who tells him face to face:

> "You are terribly afraid. Then no, you are a brave man, you are not afraid of the enemy, of the battlefield of death, but you are terribly afraid to live. [...] you can't live in the past all the time... yes, I don't know what will happen tomorrow, what will happen the day after tomorrow... I only understand about now, there's you, there's me, we're alive, what else?" (Episode 7, min. 22:55-24.00)

With these words his resistance is broken and they spend the same night together in her bed.

The series thus performs a double therapeutic function: on the one hand, Vera Preobrazhenskaia succeeds in curing the NKVD man of his private traumas and turning him into a living human being. On the other hand, the series also cures the traumas of *Come and See* on an emblematic level: Now Kravchenko plays the symbolic father to the ten-year-old boy Kolia, a father who the 14-year-old Flëra he played then never had. The war in *The Seventh Symphony* is also cruel and senseless, but love in solidarity and human empathy can at least temporarily bring fleeting happiness and relief. However, this overcoming of traumata doesn't last for long. For the very next day, before Serëgin can even leave for the front, he is surprised by a bombing raid while saving the life of Karl Eliasberg, but he is so badly wounded that he ultimately dies as a result of his injuries. After this next dramatic event, the conductor at last recognises the humane side of Serëgin, and so Eliasberg, standing next to the chekist's corpse, has to confess: "I was wrong to think Anatoly Ivanovich Serëgin was a stranger. I was wrong. I failed to tell him that while he was alive. This is how wars begin when we think other people are strangers" (Episode 8, min. 22:52-23:10).

Thus, in the end, the series exposes a double misjudgement: the secret services have wrongly persecuted the cultural intelligentsia in the Great Terror and murdered many of its representatives, but the artists have also been mistaken in their disdain for the ordinary 'new men,' whom they perceived as 'strange' transformed beasts, and therefore in a sense share at least a certain responsibility for their own persecution. So, the series suggests that war does not begin with an external threat or the German attack on the Soviet Union, but at the moment when people perceive the other in their own country as a 'stranger', an enemy of the people and a traitor.

## 6. Imperfect People: The Leningrad Blockade as an Existential Challenge

In the end, the 'transformed' chekist remains a tragic hero who only realises what life is all about just before he dies. For life, as the series shows in many small scenes, means the acceptance of strangeness and otherness, of even deviant feelings and acting according to one's own needs, which also sometimes includes transgressing rules and regulations. This is shown most clearly with the Jewish viola player Kleiman, who in his eccentricity and desperation repeatedly transgresses all boundaries of decency and tolerability without ever being malicious or unsympathetic.[12] But this also applies to the behaviour of the nurse Anna, who deserts from the front for fear of being raped by her battalion commander, while her beloved trumpeter illegally gets her food and forged food stamps. Rather almost grotesquely carnivalesque, this irregularity of transgressive behaviour is demonstrated by the double life of the orchestra's oboist and party organiser (*partorg*), Ekaterina Prudnikova (played by Elena Velezheva), who, even before the war, has charged the fun-loving timpanist and womaniser Valerii Korneichuk (played by Jurii Anpilogov) with a council tribunal for publicly imitating a sex act at a festive event. The accused, however, ridicules the charge by making sexual remarks to the party woman, which the audience approves with general laughter, while she is at a loss for words due to indignation. After his heroic death at the front, however, it turns out that this very prudish and strict party organiser was the last secret lover of the heartbreaker.

Even behaviour that is clearly harmful to society goes unpunished in the film. The fat oboist Semënov, for example, prefers to be fed by his no less obese mother, who works in a canteen, through stolen food rather than take on the stress of orchestra rehearsals. But when his mother dies and he is caught stealing cabbages, he is forgiven because he now conscientiously attends rehearsals. And even the denunciator of Eliasberg's wife, the young violinist Tusia from Belarus, is forgiven in the end, since she acted out of unhappy love and jealousy.

Thus, in its depiction of interpersonal relationships, the series is also a plea for generosity and solidarity, according to which different population groups, regardless of class and nationality, must come to terms with their private wars and social conflicts. Yet, one would misunderstand the series if one were to see it as unreserved advocacy of tolerance and diversity, since it is clearly demonstrated that the transgressions, going to the point of grotesque frenzy, are motivated above all by private or war traumas. In other words, the German siege of Leningrad is only the backdrop, which has a cathartic effect on the protagonists as an existential challenge. The micro-world of the orchestra is staged as humanism actually lived, which represents a clear counter-world to the official propaganda image of the 1930s with its conservative values and heroic narratives. Reports from the front and the war only appear indirectly in conversations and news fragments, official socialist slogans as well as Christian Russian Orthodox or Soviet patriotic tones are completely absent. However, the series is not concerned with conveying a 'more truthful' or

---

12   Especially in the character of Kleiman – but also in that of Eliasberg – the series addresses many anti-Semitic stereotypes common in Russia by indirectly invoking them, but then unmasking them clearly as inaccurate projections and prejudices through the behaviour of the respective protagonists.

even 'realistic' picture of everyday blockade life or with deconstructing common myths around heroic suffering and the 'Leningrad Symphony'. Rather, it incorporates everything into its immersive and narrative logics, even fine arts, especially classical music and the titular *Symphony No. 7*, but also literature through the poetry of Ol'ga Berggolts.

## 7. The Third Zone: Classical Music and the Poetry of Ol'ga Berggolts

Aleksandr Kott not only takes the performance of Shostakovich's *Symphony No. 7* during the Leningrad Blockade as grateful material for a partly tragic, partly melodramatic plot, but also skilfully incorporates the motif of music into the symbolic-affective level of the story, as he shows from the first scene, when the radio broadcast of Mozart's *Piano Concerto No. 23* segues directly into the death of Serëgin's children and wife in the hail of bombs. But music is not only used as a soundtrack to intensify emotions, tension and drama, as is otherwise common in popular films, it is also a direct object of reflection. Karl Eliasberg for instance, in the first scene that shows him as a conductor at an orchestra rehearsal, a broken man after the arrest of his wife by Serëgin, in his despair quotes from the so-called 'Testament' of the 31-year-old Ludwig van Beethoven, who wrote that it was art alone that prevented him from committing suicide. Whereupon the rehearsal of Beethoven's *Symphony No. 9* begins.

This opening with Beethoven's famous letter to his brothers from 1802 is already symbolic, as he writes it because of his incurably progressing deafness, and by the time he completed *Symphony No. 9* in 1823 he already could not hear anything. Thus, the motif of performing or not-performing, hearing or not hearing music is put forward as a varied motif in the series from the beginning. So, many musicians initially refuse to continue working in the orchestra because of personal grief, since music seems to be pointless in times of war, but then they realise that making music is more important than killing.[13] Conversely, Serëgin's inability to grasp the beauty and expressiveness of music is a consistent theme in his relationship with Preobrazhenskaia. She repeatedly tries to cure him of his 'deafness', but initially without success. It is only when she plays Beethoven's *Symphony No. 5*, the 'Fate Symphony', on the gramophone at her bedside in the evening that he slowly begins to sense what music means, even if he cannot yet put it into words. And it is not only Serëgin's 'fate' that is softened by Beethoven's music: the 'officers of the Third Reich' blockading Leningrad, who have been listening via radio on the other side of the front, are so thrilled by a live broadcast of Beethoven's *Symphony No. 5* by the radio orchestra that they give Eliasberg a German *Volksempfänger* by parachute as a thank-you.

And for Eliasberg himself, Beethoven's fate is also decisive, since he not only owes his stamina to Beethoven's 'Testament', but he himself almost completely goes deaf due to the fatal bomb attack that costs Serëgin his life. Thus, the performance of Shostakovich's *Symphony No. 7* in Leningrad is also a symbolic quotation of Beethoven's premiere of his

---

13   The orchestra's blind percussionist, for example, immediately reports to the front when he hears that blind people are also wanted there. Thanks to his absolute hearing, he identifies all enemy aircrafts, but returns to the orchestra in the end because he considers music more important than the war effort.

*Symphony No. 9* in 1824, which the already completely deaf composer himself conducted. It is the same with Eliasberg; he hears very little, but still knows his cues as a conductor at every moment. At a dress rehearsal, he even exaggerates this contrast between making music and making war, addressing the orchestra:

> "I don't know anything about the war, yet I don't want to know either. When I hear what Beethoven sounds like, when it sounds exactly as he intended, I cannot believe that a human is capable of such harmony. But war, that's disharmony. And Beethoven is German, and I'm not ashamed of him. But war, that's a shame. A shame!" (Episode 7, min. 34:20-35:25)

It is these words that, in a sense, sum up the quintessence of the television series, making it a pathetic anti-war work. War between nations, but also between people fighting each other as strangers and enemies, is a moral disgrace, "a shame", whereas music can transform this disharmony into a higher harmonic order that does without false morals and mendacious words. And it is precisely this transformation of disharmony into harmony that Kott also stages in the more than ten-minute-long central final scene of the series: the performance of Shostakovich's *Symphony No. 7* in the Leningrad Philharmonic. In the first movements, we experience this acoustically and visually as an extreme disharmony: we hear the music excerpts with the damaged ears of Eliasberg, who can only distinguish some distorted sounds from the noise in a very selective and fragmented manner, or with the ears of the radio listeners, as they hear the fuzzy and shrill excerpts played through loudspeakers across the Soviet Union. The camera work, which is otherwise usually quite conventional in the series, also visually underlines this disharmony by daring to use bird's-eye views and extremely subjective shots before Shostakovich's musical sounds are gradually 'harmonised' audio-visually and the images take on a more phantasmatic, dreamlike dimension, when the orchestra members also see the figures of fallen relatives and acquaintances sitting in the rows of Philharmonic visitors, before the last sounds of the *Allegro con troppo* are shown through close-ups of the exhausted, tense-looking faces of the musicians and the conductor as a final collective physical and psychological act of strength on the podium.

But Kott does not leave it at this crowning conclusion, which tends towards heroic kitsch in its audio-visual harmonisation of the orchestra collective to Shostakovich's dramatic, droning final chords, but allows the performance to be followed by a short, no less pathos-filled speech by Eliasberg in the small circle of musicians.[14] This, however, is then abruptly broken by the conductor with his last, slightly mumbled words ironically distancing: "Somehow, that was a lot of pathos, let's go home, robbers!" (Episode 8, min. 41:23-41:28) Though in saying this, he indirectly underlines that musicians are not soldiers and conductors are not political orators, but with their arts they rather undermine the state order and the war pathos, resembling more "robbers" (*razboiniki*), gentleman

---

[14] "And we may be forgotten, forgotten by name. But the performance of Shostakovich's music from the besieged, tormented city will not be forgotten... They won't forget... our children, our grandchildren, their grandchildren's grandchildren will remember and know: music is stronger than death!" (Episode 8, min. 40:36-41:12)

thieves, criminals of lost honour. Such an anti-pathetic stance is further emphasised by the fact that Shostakovich's symphony is not the last piece of music in the series, but after a few more exchanges in which Eliasberg once again refuses to be evacuated, the 'robber chief' goes to the stone steps of the Neva shore, to which the hauntingly moving piano sounds from the *Adagio* from Johann Sebastian Bach's *Concerto in D minor (BMV 974)* resound to the noise of the waves. Sad minor sounds at the end as in *Come and See*, but this time not by Mozart, but by Bach. Not to return to partisan war, but to draw stamina for further 'robber' actions. Classical music is thus not only the art that overcomes man's disharmony and wars, but also purifies human hearts and leads them back to the harmonious state of nature, for which the stone Neva shore with its long Petersburg mythology has long served as a cultural-historical trope since the founding of the city.[15]

A similar, but different function to music is fulfilled by the poetry of the Leningrad poet Ol'ga Berggolts (1910–1975) in the series, who remained in the city throughout the blockade period and makes a total of five appearances in the film (played by Viktoriia Tolstoganova), reading sometimes lengthy excerpts from her poems written between 1940 and 1942. Her recitals are connected to the plot only by the fact that her verses are broadcast live on the radio, just like the concerts by Eliasberg's radio orchestra. Only in the first scene is there a brief cool encounter with Serëgin in the broadcast studio and at the end she also sits in the audience at the performance of *Symphony No. 7*. But her appearance has strong symbolic significance for viewers educated in literary history, since Berggolts as the most prominent poet of the Leningrad blockade embodies the tragic fate of the cultural intelligentsia under Stalinism like no other: she had written poetry from childhood, was a convinced communist, worked as a journalist, war correspondent and newspaper editor since the end of the 1920s, wrote reportages and poems for adults as well as children's books, before she was caught up in the mills of the Great Terror in Leningrad at the beginning of 1937, when she was drawn into the fabricated accusations against former RAPP leader and critic Leopold Averbakh (1903–1937), initially only as a witness. After her first husband was shot as a 'Trotskyist' in February 1938, the charges against her were initially dropped, but in the same year she was again imprisoned as an 'enemy of the people' for 171 days, before she was released and rehabilitated in July 1939. In February 1940, despite everything, she joined the Bolshevik Party, and during the nearly 900-day blockade, she made almost daily live radio broadcasts to encourage Leningraders to hold on and to testify to the world outside of the inhabitants' heroic struggle for survival. Her

---

15   However, the series does not follow the so-called 'Petersburg text', according to which the founding of Petersburg represents a civilisational taming of the wild element of water, which, in the form of the river, repeatedly challenges man's fate through fog and floods. In Kott's work, in contrast, the deadly threat comes from the sky in the form of German bombs, as the very first scene makes clear when Serëgin's family drowns after a bombing raid. In *The Seventh Symphony*, the river has rather a religious connotation of the purification of souls. Again and again, the protagonists go alone or in pairs to the banks of the Neva, let their feet be washed by water on the stone steps, seek comfort and relaxation by the river, which is also visually underlined by shots of the calming, unshakable rippling water that are filmed in ever-changing ways. Instead of mortal danger, in Kott's work the river is a consoling confidant and silent witness to human fate.

second husband, the literary critic and journalist Nikolai Molchanov, died of starvation during the siege of Leningrad in 1942.[16]

Added to this was another tragic private fate: she had lost two daughters at a young age because of serious illness already in the 1930s, and during the interrogations and arrests 1937 to 1939 she was pregnant twice, but lost both children due to torture by the NKVD, the first while still pregnant, the second as a stillborn child. After that she could no longer bear children. By no means could Berggolts speak publicly about all this at the time, but her destiny is well known to today's educated Russian citizen, at least since the publication of her secret diaries in the late Glasnost period. And Aleksandr Kott deliberately alludes to this, when Serëgin, in response to Eliasberg's accusation, feels compelled to categorically emphasise twice that he does not torture women – the viewer may relate this dialogue directly to the nowadays well-known poet's own experience with chekists. Accordingly, when Serëgin loses his own two children on the quay, when Preobrozhenskaia's child dies shortly after birth under bombing, and they both symbolically adopt Kolia, and Kravchenko intertextually recalls his role as Flëra from *Come and See*, then all this points unequivocally to the subtext of Berggolts' biography. In a sense the fictious protagonists thus act out her experience of suffering, whereby the German bombs from the sky also become detectable as an allegory for the torture cellars of the NKVD.

At the same time, Berggolts is depicted in the series as an alternative role model to Eliasberg for the cultural intelligentsia during times of terror and war: while the conductor does not want to know about the chaos and 'disharmony' of the world, the poet knows all the abysses of suffering and dying, but she is not allowed to tell this truth publicly. Outraged, she yells at the radio recording supervisor in her very first appearance in the series: "There, in Moscow, no one knows anything about us, do you understand, no one! […] We are all going to die here, they just don't know about us. So I'm going to go and say all this live on air!" (Episode 2, min. 25:55-26:06) The latter desperately tries to stop her from doing so, which is overheard by Serëgin who happens to come in, whereupon she indignantly shouts at him:

> "Standing here and spying! For how long? […] I was in Moscow. Nobody knows anything there. Everyone keeps talking about the Leningrad heroism, but no one knows about the real situation. And it is forbidden to speak! How do you think that is?" (Episode 2, min. 26:25-27:05)

To which the chekist only tersely replies, "Some truths you don't need to know." (ibid.) But that is precisely the role of Berggolts and her poetry in *The Seventh Symphony*: she knows the whole truth, she knows what immeasurable suffering and death mean, but she is forbidden to speak about it publicly. And the viewer won't see her anymore in a private conversation. Instead, she recites poems live on the radio. Radio is thus also a medium of censorship, a censored venue of public speech that is only allowed to broadcast artistic truths, saying in verses, but also in music, what is not allowed to be said in plain language. Lidiia Ginzburg (1902–1990) has already indicated the "very hysterical note" with

---

16  For biographical details, cf. Gromova 2017. I thank Franziska Thun-Hohenstein for all her valuable advice on Berggolts.

which Berggolts tried to encode the private and the collective in her poetry after the personal "catastrophe", and Polina Barskova has recently pointed out how polysemous, fluid, ambiguous her "lyrical invocations" actually were, expressing the inner turmoil of her poetic voice and speaking to different addressees inside and outside the city, to the suffering and the powerful, alive and dead (cf. Ginzburg 2011: 111–113; Barskova 2017: 104–108; ibid. 2020: 65–67).[17]

And it is precisely this ambivalence of truth and prohibition due to censorship, this tension between saying and concealing, hope and despair, concrete biographical allusions and general human 'hysterical notes' that the radio readings also convey in Kott's television series. In a way, her poems are woven into the series plot like musical counterpoints, often but not always at the end of an episode. And they invite not just the older viewers – as they were used to do in Soviet times under the conditions of censorship – to interpret her words and accordingly the series' plot allegorically. For example, in the second episode, after we learn of the death of Preobrozhenskaia's baby and Serëgin has found Kolia, she reads the third stanza from her poem *Europe. The War in 1940. For Il'ia Erenburg* (*Evropa. Voina 1940 goda. Il'e Erenburgu*, 1940), in which the lyrical I dreams of a recreation of the world as a kingdom of children who will live there like birds in accordance with an undestroyed nature (episode 2, min. 28:08-29:30):

> Perhaps, these times are close:
> No howl of sirens, screech of bombs,
> But silence the children will hear,
> In their bomb-shelter sealed up tight.
> [...]
> All slaughtered... Only the children
> Saved, under the scorched earth.
> They do not remember those times,
> They do not know who they are and where.
> Like birds, they wait now for sunrise
> And warm themselves, splashing in the water.
> [...]
> Thus, will the childhood on the world arrive,
> And the wise dominion of children.
> (Berggolts 1988: 195)
> (Translation by Daniel Weissbort)[18]

---

17  The only one in the series, who still sometimes says in plain language and with a 'hysterical note' the truth about the real situation in besieged Leningrad, is Leonid Kleiman, who in a certain way performs as the poet's revenant, endowed with a fool's licence in his desperation close to madness.

18  Berggolts 1996. Quoted from: https://arlindo-correia.com/040704.html [30 September 2023]. Berggolts 1988: 195: "Быть может, близко сроки эти:/ не рев сирен, не посвист бомб,/ а тишину услышат дети/ в бомбоубежище глухом. [...] ...Все перебиты. Только дети/ спаслись под выжженной землей./ Они совсем не помнят года,/ не знают – кто они и где./ Они, как птицы, ждут восхода/ и, греясь, плещутся в воде. [...] Вот так настанет детство мира/ и царство мудрое детей."

Obviously, the unspoken truth of these verses is that this 'dominion of children' is also the realm of her own dead children, "slaughtered" by the NKVD, which here poetry, like music, raises to a certain stage of lyrical harmony. Meanwhile, we see Serëgin – alongside recordings of the poetry recital – walking through barricades and tank traps in Leningrad, lost in thought; whether he has heard the verses, and what he may think, remains open.

Even more suggestive is the associative linking of Stalinist terror with German besiegement in the scene when the dead Serëgin, lying on an open truck next to the sitting Preobrazhenskaia and Kolia, is driven away to the gravesite to the first three stanzas of her poem *29 January 1942* (*29 ianvaria 1942*, 1942), which Berggolts dedicated to her husband Nikolai Molchanov, who died of malnutrition that day (episode 8, min. 25:20-26:05):

> Despair and sorrow aren't enough
> to get this cursed sentence over with!
> [...]
> Why?
> I can't even rock your child
> to sleep or swaddle him.
> (Berggolts 1989a: 33)
> (Translation by Venya Gushchin)[19]

Serëgin here symbolically takes the place not only of her dead husband, but also of Berggolts' and Molchanov's common child, whom they lost during the 'cursed sentence' (*prokliatyi srok*) in NKVD prisons: the cruel constellation of her private catastrophe is revised in the series' fiction: here the chekist made human has to die instead of the child Kolia.

But the series cites not only a certain 'Soviet aesthetic' of coded truths, but also one of artistic defamiliarisation. When Serëgin seeks out the denunciator Tusia at her work in a tank factory in order to forcibly recruit her for the orchestra, she only stares at him wordlessly when they meet, whereupon Berggolts reads lines of poetry from the *February Diary* (*Fevral'skii dnevnik*, 1942) about how only hatred and the need for revenge can still unite and warm us. In Berggolts' poem, these verses are clearly directed against the Germans, but here they can also be related to the relationship between the two protagonists (episode 4, min. 48:56-49:40).[20]

Just as Berggolts' verses are thus taken out of context, the poems in this way alienate the plot in the television series, in a sense replacing the protagonists' possible thoughts

---

19   Berggolts 1989a: 33: „Отчаяния мало. Скорби мало./ О, поскорей отбыть проклятый срок! [...] Зачем, зачем?/ Мне даже не баюкать,/ не пеленать ребенка твоего." Berggolts 2022: 64–65.
20   "No, we do not cry. There is not enough tears for the heart. Hate keeps us from crying. Hate is our guarantee of life: it unites, warms and guides. That I will not forgive, that I will not spare, that I will avenge, that I will avenge as best I can, cries out to me the mass grave on the Okhtensky, on the right bank." Berggolts 1989b: 35: "Нет, мы не плачем. Слез для сердца мало./ Нам ненависть заплакать не дает./ Нам ненависть залогом жизни стала:/ объединяет, греет и ведет.// О том, чтоб не прощала, не щадила,/ чтоб мстила, мстила, как могу,/ ко мне взывает братская могила/ на охтенском, на правом берегу."

and feelings, giving them an intertextual meaning of self-reflection through Berggolts' biographical experience, but also a more general allegorical dimension. So, the lines of poetry interrupt or disrupt the otherwise stringently narrated plot, imaginatively opening up a "third zone", as the famous Blockade poem *The Third Zone* (*Tret'ia zona*, 1942) by Berggolts is called, which is quoted in full length: A zone where words are disoriented and feelings confused:

> How do you cry, rejoice, beckon,
> who told you what is wrong with me?
> I am joyful today to the point of pain,
> I myself do not know why. (Episode 6, min. 50:25-50:42)[21]

But in 'defamiliarising' depicted events and experiences in this way, the lines of poetry at the same time also elevate the plot of the series in besieged Leningrad during the one year from September 1941 to August 1942 to a more general, human level, thus 'familiarising' it for contemporary viewers, who may recognise as educated people in Berggolts' poetry the general fate of the cultural intelligentsia under Stalinism and war, but a less historically savvy audience may also project their own topical feelings and thoughts onto the hardships and pains, conflicts and catastrophes suffered by the protagonists.

## 8. Conclusion

Whereas Elem Klimov's film *Come and See* attempted to capture the horrors of war with cinematic devices on a formal and aesthetic level, Aleksandr Kott's *The Seventh Symphony* works with the conventional patterns of representation and narration of contemporary television series, which are, however, constantly enriched with allusions and signs of distinction from high culture. Moritz Baßler characterises this form of storytelling as the "international style" of "popular realism," which presents itself as sophisticated high culture, as demanding on a formal aesthetic level and offering complexly constructed plots. But as a popular form of realism, it is in fact decidedly directed against any artistic modernism and renounces any "poetic function" in the sense of Roman Jakobson, any effective "defamilarisation" in the sense of the formalists that could lead to a "new seeing" of reality. Instead "popular realism" constantly confirms the existing symbolic order and an "educated bourgeois basic trust" ("bildungsbürgerliches Urvertrauen") (Baßler 22: 86). Precisely this narrative dynamic can also be observed in *The Seventh Symphony*, which does indeed integrate defamiliarising elements and avant-garde devices on an audio-visual level, among other things with Berggolts' poems and Shostakovich's music, but these defamiliarisations only temporarily disrupt the fictional diegesis, temporarily delay it, but in no way lastingly impede its narrative logic and a straightforward reception of the series' episodes.

---

21  Berggolts 1989c: 58: "Как ты плачешь, радуешься, манишь,/ кто тебе поведал, что со мной?/ Мне сегодня радостно до боли,/ я сама не знаю – отчего."

With the melodramatic reenactment of Shostakovich's *Symphony No. 7* in the popular television series format, the film *The Seventh Symphony* thus provides a double integration offer in the context of Russian culture on the eve of Russia's 'special military operation' against Ukraine: vis-à-vis the state authorities, it stages the 'humanisation' of the chekist in the figure of Anatolii Serëgin by presenting the terror of the 1930s as a historical aberration that had already been fundamentally revised during World War II; and towards the Soviet socialised and post-Soviet educated and art-loving classes, this cinematic reinterpretation of the past signals that it shares the discomfort with a glorification and sacralisation of Great Patriotic War that increasingly is performed in the state media since the 2010s, presenting with Eliasberg and Berggolts alternative role models of how to behave in times of repression and censorship.

When Karl Eliasberg exclaims in an indignant voice: "I don't know anything about the war, yet I don't want to know either. [...] But war, that's a shame. A shame!" then this exclamation can be understood in various ways. It can be understood as a clear anti-war statement. But it can be taken also as the exact opposite of what Elem Klimov's *Come and See* did: one does not want to come and see the horrors and cruelties of war, but prefers to stay behind the front in his 'harmonious' world of art and music. Instead of a rejection of war out of experience and observation, this is rather a refusal of war out of demonstrative disinterest and ignorance. Even more, the quotation marks this 'ignorant' attitude as morally superior by describing war as something inferior, indecent, as 'a shame' (*stydno*). In this way, however, the television series also makes an offer to the anti-war sentiment of the cultural intelligentsia within Russia: you are welcome to consider the war a dirty affair and devote yourself to culturally superior matters; the 'shameful' dirty work will be done for you by others. But then the cultural intelligentsia (like the fictional Eliasberg) also doesn't have to interfere with official state decisions on warfare and peace. And if you absolutely do not want to remain silent about the truth, then you have to censor yourself, as (the fictional as well as the real) Berggolts has done in her poems and radio addresses (and this series does too!), choosing an artistically coded form. At the same time, the series pleads for 'humanised' interactions within society in all its diversity, including ordinary military men and chekists like Anatolii Serëgin, who must not be treated as 'morons' or 'strangers' but as equal human beings with feelings and compassion.

It is precisely such characteristics, contradictory at first sight, that make popular culture products attractive: they deal with political sensitive issues and social aversions (against the NKVD, the terror of the chekists, the war), dangerous resentments (anti-Semitism, nationalism, class prejudices), uncontrolled aggressions and fears, and bring them together in an exciting plot. As a work of 'popular realism' the series at the same time addresses the specific target group of the cultural intelligentsia or people who see themselves as such, to whom it presents slightly encoded sophisticated high art, starting with the intertextual allusion to the film *Come and See*, classical music and Berggolts' poetry, and offers – in the shape of its protagonists – various options for integrating into the respective society despite all obstacles and reservations. And it is this specific offer of socialisation that makes the television series *The Seventh Symphony* still relevant and topical after 24 February 2022, even if the space for divergent cultural agency is increasingly limited within the contemporary Russian Federation.[22]

If one considers *The Seventh Symphony* in the broader context of Russian popular culture before 24 February 2022 it is – as some critics have claimed – not so much or, at least, not alone an exception to the rule, but in a way also fits into the general development towards a gradual militarisation of public discourse. However, it does not call the cultural intelligentsia to the front; on the contrary, it uses the fictionalised story from besieged Leningrad to formulate an option to participate in the social and cultural life of one's own society with moral integrity and even critical consciousness, staying in the civilian, though permanently threatened and endangered hinterland.[23] In doing so, it represents the performance of Shostakovich's *Symphony No. 7* as well as Berggolts' poetry readings on radio as a civilisational act of high culture in contrast to the inhuman cruelties and horrors of an ongoing war, which the film *Come and See* once depicted so vividly. The series prefers rather not to speak of these horrors, not to come and see, once again.

## Filmography

*A Hero of Our Time* (*Geroi nashego vremeni*), dir. Aleksandr Kott, Russia 2006.
*Children of the Arbat* (*Deti Arbata*), dir. Andrei Ėshpai), Russia 2004.
*Come and See* (*Idi i smotri*), dir. Ėlem Klimov, USSR 1985.
*Execution Impossible to Pardon* (*Kaznit' nel'zia pomilovat'*), dir. Kim Druzhinin, Russia 2017.
*Leningrad Symphony* (*Leningradskaia simfoniia*), dir. Zakhar Agranenko, USSR 1957.
*Life and Fate* (*Zhizn' i sud'ba*), dir. Sergei Urusliak, Russia 2011–2012.
*Liquidation* (*Likvidatsia*), dir. Sergei Ursuliak, Russia 2007.
*Penal Battalion* (*Shtrafbat*), dir. Nikolai Dostal', 2004.
*The Adventures of Tom Sawyer and Huckleberry Finn* (*Prikliucheniia Toma Soiera i Gekl'berri Finn*), dir. Stanislav Govorukhin, USSR 1982.
*Servant of the People* (*Sluga naroda*), dir. Oleksii Kyriushchenko, Ukraine 2015–2019.
*Strictly Business* (*Delovye liudi*), dir. Leonid Gaidai, USSR 1962.
*The Adventures of Tom Sawyer and Huckleberry Finn* (*Prikliucheniia Toma Soiera i Gekl'berri Finn*), dir. Stanislav Govorukhin, USSR 1981.
*The Brest Fortress* [also known as *Fortress of War*] (*Brestskaia krepost'*) dir. Aleksandr Kott, Russia/Belarus 2010.
*The Seventh Symphony* (*Sed'maia simfoniia*), dir. Aleksandr Kott, Russia 2021.
*Trotsky* (*Trotskii*), dir. Aleksandr Kott, Russia 2007.

---

22   It is certainly no coincidence that in May 2022, when the military disaster and the brutality of the Russian invasion of Ukraine (like in Bucha) were already obvious, the series was awarded the prize for best patriotic series of the year at the St Petersburg film festival "Viva Russian cinema!" ("Vivat kino Rossii!"), cf. [Anon.] 2022b.

23   Just as official Russian rhetoric has appropriated and recoded many other Soviet topoi and narratives in imperial and national garb, here Socialist humanism, the civilising mission of Soviet internationalism and the cultural front against anti-fascism reappear in the guise of and in the name of classical music.

## References

Al'perina (Susanna): "'Sed'maia simfoniia' stala samym prosmatrivaemym serialom na TV." In: Rossiiskaia Gazeta, 18 November 2021 (https://rg.ru/2021/11/18/sedmaia-simfoniia-stal-samym-prosmatrivaemym-serialom-na-tv.html) [30 September 2023].

[Anon.] (2021): "'Budem smotret' vsei sem'ei': pochemu zriteli zhdut 'Sed'muiu simfoniiu'", In: VestriRu, 8 November 2021 (https://www.vesti.ru/television/article/2636672) [30 September 2023].

[Anon.] (2022a): "'Zolotoi orel': luchim serialom stala 'Sed'maia simfoniia'." In: VestiRu, January 28, 2022 (https://www.vesti.ru/television/article/2668726) [30 September 2023].

[Anon.] (2022b): "'Sed'maia sinfonia' nazvana luchim serialom na festivale 'Vivat kino Rossii!'" In: VestiRu, 16 May 2022 (https://www.vesti.ru/television/article/2744988) [30 September 2023].

[Anon.] (2022c): "Sed'maia simfoniia: mneniia i somneniia. Pressa a serial." In: Muzykal'noe obozrenie 3:492/493 (https://muzobozrenie.ru/sedmaya-simfoniya-mneniya-i-somneniya/) [30 September 2023].

Anderson, Matthew T. (2015): Symphony for the City of the Dead. Dmitri Shostakovich and the Siege of Leningrad, Somerville: Candlewick Press.

Barskova, Polina (2017): Besieged Leningrad. Aesthetic Responses to Urban Disaster, Ithaca: Northern Illinois University Press.

Barskova, Polina (2020): Sed'maia shchëloch'. Teksty i sud'by blokadnykh poėtov, Sankt Petersburg: Izdatel'stvo Ivana Limbakha.

Bassin, Mark/Poso, Gonzalo (eds.) (2017): The Politics of Eurasianism. Identity, Popular Culture and Russia's Foreign Policy, London: Rowman & Littlefield.

Baßler, Moritz (2022): Populärer Realismus. Vom International Style gegenwärtigen Erzählens, Munich: C.H. Beck.

Berggolts, Ol'ga (1988): "Evropa. Voina 1940 goda. (Il'e Erenburgu.) Tretii. 'Byt' mozhet, blizko sroki ėti'." In: ibid.: Sobrannie sochineii v trekh tomakh. Vol. 1. Stikhotvoreniia. 1924–1941, Leningrad: Khudozhestvennaia literatura, 195.

Berggolts, Ol'ga (1989a): "29 ianvaria 1942 goda. 'Pamiati druga i muzha Nikolaia Stepanovicha Molchanova'" In: ibid.: Sobrannie sochineii v trekh tomakh. Vol. 2. Stikhotvoreniia i poėmy. 1941–1953, Leningrad: Khudozhestvennaia literatura, 33.

Berggolts, Ol'ga (1989b): "Fevral'skii dvenik 'Poėma'." In: ibid.: Sobrannie sochineii v trekh tomakh. Vol 2. Stikhotvoreniia i poėmy. 1941–1953, Leningrad: Khudozhestvennaia literatura, 34–39.

Berggolts, Ol'ga (1989c): "…Tret'ia zona, dachyi polustanok." In: ibid.: Sobrannie sochineii v trekh tomakh. Vol 2. Stikhotvoreniia i poėmy. 1941–1953, Leningrad: Khudozhestvennaia literatura, 58.

Berggolts, Ol'ga (1996): "Europe – 1940 – War (to Ilya Ehrenbourg)." In: Daniel Weissbort (ed.): Modern Poetry in Translation (New Series 10), London: King's College London (https://arlindo-correia.com/040704.html) [30 September 2023].

Berggolts, Ol'ga (2022): "29 ianvaria 1942 / 29 January 1942." In: ibid.: The Blockade Swallow. Selected Poems, Grewelthorpe: Smokestack Books 2022, 64–65.

Beumers, Birgit (2006): "The Serialization of the War." in: KinoKultura 12, 04/2006, (http ://www.kinokultura.com/2006/12-beumers.shtml) [30 September 2023].

Bidlack, Richard/Lomagin, Nikita (2012): The Leningrad Blockade, 1941–1944. A New Documentary History from the Soviet Archives, New Haven/London: Yale University Press.

Bljum, Arlen (2011): "Blockierte Wahrheit. Blockadeliteratur und Zensur." In: Osteuropa 8/9, 297–299.

Boele, Otto/Noordenbos, Boris/Robbe, Ksenia (eds.) (2020): Post-Soviet Nostalgia: Confronting the Empire's Legacies, New York: Routledge.

Borenstein, Eliot (2011): Overkill: Sex and Violence in Contemporary Russian Popular Culture, Ithaca/NY: Cornell University Press.

Brouwer, Sander (ed.) (2016): Contested Interpretations of the Past in Polish, Russian, and Ukrainian Film: Screen as Battlefield, Leiden: Brill.

Bulgakowa, Oksana et al. (1992): "Geh und sieh/Idi i smotri (UdSSR 1985)." In: Bulgakowa, Oksana/Hochmuth, Dieter (eds.): Der Krieg gegen die Sowjetunion im Spiegel von 36 Filmen. Eine Dokumentation, Berlin: Freunde der Dt. Kinemathek, 127–132.

Dubshan, Fedor (2021): "'Sed'maia simfoniia': vnezapnaia peredyshka ot militarizma v zomboiashchike." In: Rosbalt, 8 November 2021 (https://www.rosbalt.ru/blogs/2021/11/08/1929900.html) [30 September2023].

Ganzenmüller, Jörg (2007): Das belagerte Leningrad 1941 bis 1944. Die Stadt in den Strategien von Angreifern und Verteidigern, Paderborn: Schöningh.

Ganzenmüller, Jörg (2011): "Mobilisierungsdiktatur im Krieg. Stalinistische Herrschaft im belagerten Leningrad." In: Osteuropa 8/9, 117–134.

Ginzburg, Lidiia (2011): Prokhodiashchie kharaktery. Proza voennykh let. Zapiski blokadnogo cheloveka, Moskva: Novoe Izdatel'stvo.

Gromova, Natal'ia (2017): Ol'ga Berggol'ts. Smerti ne bylo i net: opyt prochteniia sud'by, Moskva: Izdatel'stvo AST.

György, Péter (1999): "Popular Culture and Nationalism: Challenges and Possibilities of the Postmodern Politics of Identity." In: East Central Europe – L'Europe du Centre-Est. Eine wissenschaftliche Zeitschrift, 26/2, 53–72.

Hall, Stuart (2009): "Notes on Deconstructing 'The Popular'." In: John Storey (ed): Cultural Theory and Popular Culture: A Reader, Harlow: Pearson Education, 508–518.

Hermann, Sebastian M. (ed.) (2008): Ambivalent Americanizations: Popular and Consumer Culture in Central and Eastern Europe, Heidelberg: Winter.

Hutchings, Stephen (2022): Projecting Russia in a Mediatized World: Recursive Nationhood, London: Routledge.

Karev, Igor' (2021): "Bez antisovetchiny ne oboshlos'". Zriteli o seriale "Sed'maia simfoniia." In: Argumenty I fakty, 9 November 2021 (https://aif.ru/culture/movie/bez_antisovetchiny_ne_oboshlos_zriteli_o_seriale_sedmaya_simfoniya) [30 September 2023].

Kirschenbaum, Lisa (2006): The Legacy of the Siege of Leningrad, 1941–1995. Myth, Memories, and Monuments, New York: Cambridge University Press.

Kudriashov, Konstantin (2021): "Dissonans 'Sed'moi simfonii'. Chto ne tak s 'glavnoi prem'eroi sezona'?" In: Argumenty i fakty, 09 November 2021 (https://aif.ru/culture/

movie/dissonans_sedmoy_simfonii_chto_ne_tak_s_glavnoy_premeroy_sezona) [30 September 2023].

Legostaev, Il'ia (2020): "Chto ne tak s rossijskimi serialami o vojne. Zriteli v gneve: 'Snimaiut kak amerikosy v svoem Gollivude'." In: Moskovskii komsomolets, 9 Mai 2020 (https://www.mk.ru/social/2020/05/09/chto-ne-tak-s-rossiyskimi-serialami-o-voyne.html) [30 September 2023].

Litov, Il'ia (2021): "Serial 'Sed'maia simfoniia' ostavil voprosy. V proekte uvideli antisovetchinu." In: Moskovskii komzomolets, 11 November 2021 (https://www.mk.ru/culture/2021/11/11/serial-sedmaya-simfoniya-ostavil-voprosy.html) [30 September 2023].

Maliukova, Larisa (2021): "'Chinovnitsa' na fone 'Sed'moi simfonii'." In: Novaia Gazeta, 3 November 2021 (https://novayagazeta.ru/articles/2021/11/03/chinovnitsa-na-fone-sedmoi-simfonii) [30 September 2023].

Mel'nikova, Mariia (2021): "Personifitsirova' pobedu: serial 'Sed'maia simfoniia' vyidet na ekrany v nojabre." In: Peterburgskii dnevnik, 10 October 2021 (https://spbdnevnik.ru/news/2021-10-27/personifitsirovat-pobedu-serial-sedmaya-simfoniya-vyydet-na-ekrany-v-noyabre) [30 September 2023].

Morozova, Oksana (2021): "Chto izvestno o fil'me 'Sed'maia simfoniia' na telekanale 'Rossiia'?" In: Argumenty i fakty, 3 November 2021 (https://aif.ru/culture/movie/chto_izvestno_o_filme_sedmaya_simfoniya_na_telekanale_rossiya?from_inject=1) [30 September 2023].

Moynahan, Brian (2013): Leningrad: Siege and Symphony. The Story of the Great City Terrorized by Stalin, Starved by Hitler, Immortalized by Shostakovich, Eastbourne, London: Quercus Publishing.

Norris, Stephen M. (2012): Blockbuster History in the New Russia: Movies, Memory, and Patriotism, Bloomington: Indiana University Press.

Norris, Stephen M. (2021): "The Great Patriotic War Serial. Penal Battalion (Shtrafbat), Historical Taboos, and the Beginnings of the New National Idea." In: Prokhorov, Alexander/Prokhorova, Elena/Salys, Rimgaila (eds.): Russian TV Series in the Era of Transition: Genres, Technologies, Identities, Amsterdam: Academic Studies Press 2021, 48–75.

Noordenbos, Boris (2021): "Fighters of the Invisible Front: Re-imagining the Aftermath of the Great Patriotic War in Recent Russian Television Series." In: Anton Weiss-Wendt/Nanci Adler (eds.), The Future of the Soviet Past: The Politics of History in Putin's Russia, Bloomington: Indiana University Press, 150–169.

Popogrebskii, Aleksei et al. (2022): "Net voiny!" In: Kinosojuz, 24 February, 2022 (http://kinosoyuz.com/news/?pub=2614) [30 September 2023].

Redepenning, Dorothea (2011): "Das Werden eines Mythos. Dmitrij Šostakovičs 7. Symphonie, 'Die Leningrader'." In: Osteuropa 8/9, 169–193.

Reid, Anna (2011): Leningrad. Tragedy of a City under Siege, 1941–44, London: Bloomsbury.

Stiglegger, Marcus (2020): "Komm und sieh /Idi i smotri (1985). R: Ėlem Klimov." In: Matthias Schwartz, Barbara Wurm (eds.): Klassiker des russischen und sowjetischen Films 2, Marburg: Schüren, 169–178.

Storey, John (1996): Cultural Studies and the Study of Popular Culture: Theories and Methods, Edinburgh: Edinburgh University Press.

Timuka, Tat'iana (2021): "Elena Frumina-Sitnikova: dissonans 'Sed'moi Simfonii." In: Argumenty nedeli, Novembber 27, 2021 (https://argumenti.ru/society/2021/11/748776) [30 September 2023].

Vollmann, William T. (2005): Europe Central, London: Penguin Books.

# Epilogue

# Public History, Popular Culture, and the Belarusian Experience in a Comparative Perspective
## A Conversation

*Aliaksei Bratachkin in conversation with the editors*

*In recent decades there has been a worldwide boom in the didactic and educational promotion of national history, which since the 1970s became known in English as 'public history'. State or privately sponsored institutions, museums, schools, universities started to engage in memory culture, sites of memory, monuments, and also TV stations and internet platforms began to broadcast specific programmes, documentaries, series or movies dedicated to historical topics. What is the role of public history in Belarus today? Can we observe a similar boom?*

Public history in my understanding is not only what different institutions and political actors do with historical material, but also how history is perceived by ordinary people, who are also participants in public life. In the last thirty years, Belarus has undergone a number of important changes, first of all, related to the way post-Soviet public life has evolved and the way history is perceived and consumed.

Firstly, in the early 1990s, the state lost its exclusive right to interpret historical events. Back in the mid-1980s, the communist regime's monopoly on the interpretation of history was ensured through control over traditional media, control over the school education system, museums, political censorship of historical research, etc. After the collapse of the USSR, new modes of publicity began to form in Belarus, and the beginning of this new post-Soviet publicity coincided with the revision of interpretations of Soviet history – the problem of Stalinist repressions was raised, the national narrative began to be constructed. History became a subject of debate for ordinary people, not just historians.

In the late 1980s and mid-1990s, we see a real boom in the dissemination of historical materials of both a professional and popular nature. The 'public history' of the late 1980s-early 1990s in Belarus became a search for a new collective identity, for example, the first disputes about 'colonialism' applied to Belarus took place, attempts were made to deal with the traumas of the Soviet past, a wave of renaming Soviet street names changed the symbolic landscape, a democratisation of the very idea of history was set in motion. In this atmosphere, people wanted to discover the history that 'really was', it was a search for 'truth'.

The second important change is the emergence of new media channels for the dissemination of historical materials. During the collapse of the USSR, everything was quite traditional – historical fiction and academic literature were published in mass circulation, there were many publications in newspapers, debates were held on state television, etc. In a number of cities (not only in Minsk) something like debate clubs appeared during the perestroika period. These channels of distribution were quite easy to control centrally even in the early 1990s, until independent media (newspapers, radio and TV channels) began to gain more influence.

More radical changes in the 2000s were associated with digitalisation, the spread of the Internet, the emergence of new media and social networks. Large online news portals appeared (such as Tut.by, which appeared in 2000 and was closed for political reasons in 2021), which also began to publish historical materials. From the mid-2000s the Live Journal platform, then social networks like Facebook or VKontakte (until it was censored), the development of Wikipedia, YouTube, and later Telegram channels created a new public and social infrastructure that also affected the representation of historical knowledge and the visibility of personal views on history significantly. Since the 1990s, the commercial distribution of historical knowledge and, for example, the book market also developed its own logic.

After the establishment of the authoritarian regime in 1994 in Belarus, some of the new freedoms, as well as historical debates, were restricted again. However, there has been no complete return to Soviet practices, although the authoritarian regime has tried and is trying to regain 'total' control over the interpretation of history. Describing the situation in Belarus today, we can speak about the so-called 'authoritarian public sphere', which is characterised by a peculiar hybridity. On the one hand, the authoritarian regime controls most of the media, controls the education system, research institutes and universities, at the same time there are phenomena that can be referred to as counter public spheres. Independent publishing projects, magazines, conferences, educational projects, independent researchers still exist.

This situation is dynamic and depends largely on political factors. For example, after the Euromaidan events in Ukraine and the annexation of Crimea by Russia, the authoritarian regime of Aleksandr Lukashenko [Lukashenka] pursued a more 'liberal' policy. Thus, in 2015–2019 we see a large number of historical projects and initiatives of an activist, grassroots type, which have a significantly expanding audience, also because it coincides with the development of digital technologies and new media in Belarus. These initiatives undermined, to some extent, the official narrative focused on the history of World War II, the Soviet past, the selective acceptance of pre-Soviet history, and the legitimisation of authoritarian institutions after 1994.

But after the mass protests of 2020 and the attempts to suppress them, the authoritarian regime turned its memory policy into an important instrument of political control, and a series of laws were passed, by means of which – through labelling them as 'extremist' or 'rehabilitating Nazism' – certain interpretations of history are persecuted. All independent media outlets have been shut down, and independent publishing houses have been banned. Digital platforms are also controlled – for example, YouTube channels, websites, or Telegram channels are declared extremist.

The regime is trying more actively than before to impose specific interpretations of history on society, for example, by promoting the idea of a "genocide of the Belarusian people".[1] This idea is promoted in school education, museum and exhibition activities, and the media. The regime's ideologists are also trying to master such platforms as YouTube, posting propaganda materials there and encouraging the population to comment on them. My colleague Gundula Pohl, hinting at the fact that the regime actually avoids all kinds of participation, has aptly and ironically called this phenomenon "participatory propaganda" (Pohl 2023). This approach, well known from the USSR, is achieved, for instance, by filming and releasing propaganda fiction films about life in interwar Belarus like *On the Other Side* (*Na drugom beregu*, 2023) with funds from the state budget, ensuring box office income with the help of administrative resources. Newly erected places of memory connected with the contradictory sides of history of World War II are destroyed in the public space for example, memorial signs or the graves of the members of the Armia Krajowa ("Home Army") are destroyed. This anti-Nazi Polish resistance movement, which during German occupation operated within the borders of Poland, which in 1939 included Western Belarus, was already disparaged during Soviet times, because given its anti-Bolshevik orientation it did not collaborate with the Soviets. Nowadays, this negative attitude to the Armia Krajowa is renewed by the ruling regime for its anti-Western and anti-Polish propaganda.

Thus, within the last three years of the aggressive official memory policy everything that characterised 'public history' so far has been destroyed – all the narratives which allowed it within the public space to see the variability of Belarus' history from the perspective of different actors and communities. Because, in the last 10–15 years the appropriations of history including the Holocaust, women's history, local history, history of different ethnic groups (Tatars, Roma, etc.), queer history or urban landscape studies from the perspective of forgotten "places of memory" have become much more differentiated than before. If in the early 1990s, when the construction of a national narrative began, we spoke mostly about the dominant cultural group, the Belarusians, now, for example, we speak about the Jewish culture within Belarus of the 20th century. A Belarusian-Jewish festival has started to be held, translations of Jewish writers of the interwar period are published, including repressed ones, such as Moishe Kulbak (1896–1937). All this has been made possible not only by civil society activists and historical initiatives, but also by the fact that state officials occasionally cooperated. Now all this pluralism is clearly under threat.

---

1    In 2022 the law "On the Genocide of the Belarusian People" was adopted, which defines genocide as "systematic physical destruction" of "Soviet citizens" living in 1941–1951 in Belarus committed by "Nazi criminals and their accomplices". This definition ignores the Stalinist repressions and the history of 1939–1941, and blurs the memory of the Holocaust.

*How does this conflict over 'public history' in Belarus relate to popular culture? In particular among the post-Soviet Eastern European states the Soviet past has become a widespread topic also in popular culture formats, beginning from tabloids and social media to popular songs, music or comics. Would you confirm such a boom also for the Belarusian case and do you see differences to the cultures of remembrance in neighbouring countries like the Baltic states, Poland, Ukraine or Russia?*

The authoritarian regime established in Belarus in the mid-1990s relied exclusively on the Soviet experience in the first years of its existence. This created a different dynamic, for example, for the memory of the Soviet or the use of references to 'the Soviet' in popular culture. The lack of critical reflection on the recent past led to the fact that throughout the whole of society tropes of Soviet culture, elements of the former everyday life were incorporated into the new, westernised reality and culture, forming bizarre collages. We see such collages in the visual language of urban space, where fast food advertising signs overlap with Soviet mosaics and metaphorical sculpture monuments to the proletariat, in the combination of modern digital technologies with the language of 1930s-1970s propaganda in state media, or the attempts to combine the Bologna educational system with old, barely reformed Soviet university education.

In Belarus, there was no symbolic break with the Soviet past also on a political level, because the initial democratic reforms were replaced already in the second half of the 1990s by authoritarian rule and a re-Sovietisation of politics and, subsequently, by the reestablishment and instrumentalisation of a Soviet memory and history policy on the part of the ruling regime since the early-mid 2000s. However, I do not share the thesis that Belarus remains 'Soviet', we see a more complex configuration. The state violence of the years 2020 to 2023 in Belarus is often compared to the repressions of the Stalinist period, but even here I believe we should see the uniqueness of what is happening.

We did not pass decommunization laws like in Ukraine in 2014–2015. There was no such radical distancing from the Soviet experience as in the Baltic states immediately after the collapse of the USSR and directly before it, when the concept of two 'occupations' – Soviet and Nazi – appeared. Also, in neighbouring Poland the Soviet period was shorter and different and accordingly is remembered in a different way. In neighbouring Russia, Soviet history was also transformed in a very specific way. Here a peculiar hybridisation of Soviet history with the history of the Russian Empire took place, although everything that happened after 1917 was once denoted by Soviet propagandists as the complete opposite of the imperial history of Russia before the October Revolution.

Belarus is still connected with post-communist Russia through a common space of information – Russian-language Russian media (newspapers, radio, television) broadcast the Russian agenda and there is also a transfer of Russian (post-Soviet) culture. For some time, the 'Soviet past' in Belarus played a similar role as in Russia – in the mid-1990s, both in Russia and Belarus there was the first strong wave of nostalgia, symbolised by the TV musical shows *Old Songs about the Main Things* (*Starye pesni o glavnom*, 1995–1998), offering a kind of remake of Soviet 'popular' culture in new conditions. Perhaps, we can say that this wave of nostalgia, on the one hand, stressed a certain crisis of cultural production (the new westernised culture could not displace the former Soviet cultural codes in any way), on the other hand, it functioned as a kind of reconciliation with the past after the political mobilisation of the perestroika era and the collapse of the USSR, one could even say, it enabled a certain 'depoliticisation' of this past and of the attitude to it.

Later on, nostalgia about the Soviet, as well as critical reflection about Soviet history followed different dynamics in Russia and Belarus. This was due to the diverging political context, market transformation of the economy, etc. In Belarus, the process of defragmentation of the Soviet experience was much slower, and, I think, this slow and, to some extent, more 'natural' gradual death of Soviet cultural forms due to generational change and globalisation processes created certain opportunities for society and researchers.

I rather tend to believe that in Belarus the Soviet 'outlived' and outlives itself in a rather peculiar way, not by means of radical negation, but rather, as one scholar once noted, by gradually establishing the hegemony of the subject over the discourse itself, which no longer evokes feelings of oppression but became a subject for reconfiguration. This confident approach to the past is supported by such details as the rather low prevalence of representations of nostalgia that reproduce 'the Soviet' as an everyday living condition.

The first signs of such a new approach to nostalgia, already quite far from the desire to restore the USSR, can be observed in Belarus around the turn of the 2000s-2010s. This manifested itself in the opening of cafes or bars with a 'Soviet atmosphere'. One of the first cafes in this style was the "Tovarishch café" ("Comrade café") in Minsk, placed in the basement of the 1950s building of the Palace of Culture of Veterans, which retained the 'classical' pretensions of Stalinist architecture, which was followed by attempts to create such cafes also in some other cities. However, these were mostly designed more for tourists and did not turn into particularly successful or iconic projects.

By the end of the 2010s, the 'Soviet' was being appropriated and digested by hipster culture. Media, for instance, reported about the opening of a brow-bar (beauty salon for eyebrows) called Brezhnev or a barbershop with the name Chekist. The opening of the latter caused a political scandal and raised ethical questions about the 'consumption' of history. Similar reactions were provoked by the partial restoration and inauguration in 2005 of the so-called Stalin Line, a barrier of defensive military installations built in the 1930s on the western border of the USSR near Minsk. Despite the protests of a part of society, the Stalin Line memorial near Minsk, exploiting narratives about the Great Patriotic War, turned eventually into a commercial attraction for tourists.

Similar to the Soviet narrative but much earlier, the new 'national' narrative began to be promoted already in the late 1980s and the first half of the 1990s and quickly became part of popular culture. Specific representations of national history even became forms of kitsch. This was also due to the fact that the 'national' was already present in the culture of the late Soviet era. Rock scene, art, literature, academic environment – everywhere there were people, activists promoting 'Belarusianness'. For example, in 1990, the Pahonia association was founded within the state Union of Artists, which was closed in 2023 for political reasons. The project of 'national revival' became part of the public discourse in the late 1980s – mid-1990s, in the course of the political struggle of that time. Of course, this was also visible in the field of popular culture. References to the national history of the pre-Soviet period were also used by state structures in attempts to create commercial cinema. For example, the 2003 film *Anastasia Slutskaya* tells the story of events that took place in the early 16th century, when the lands of the Grand Duchy of

Lithuania were attacked by Tatars, and the defence of one of the towns, Slutsk, was led by the wife of the dead prince, Anastasia.

However, different versions of collective national identity competed in the public space, including references to different historical narratives and the use of the Russian or Belarusian language. The state actually discriminated against speakers of the Belarusian language despite the adopted laws to preserve it, and this all the time influenced additionally the dynamics and political meanings of cultural phenomena. For example, after another dispersal of protests in December 2010, many activists came to the conclusion that public politics was impossible, but it was possible to shift some of the activity into the sphere of cultural projects.

This activity coincided with digitalisation and the acceleration of Belarus' inclusion in a more global context. The processes of marketisation of the economy also played a certain role. In the period of 2013–2019, commercially successful projects in the Belarusian language appeared, which were no longer situated solely in the field of independent culture and activism and promoted the 'national idea' in new ways, for example, through the production of clothing brands referring to Belarusian history and identity. In part, one can speak of a specific 'commodification' of Belarusianness. But in times of a relative 'liberalisation' of the regime the very same projects and activists also tried to influence the political agenda, and were the organisers of events like the 2018 celebration of the centenary of the formation of the non-Soviet Belarusian People's Republic (BNR). During World War I, when the German imperial troops occupied the territory of Belarus, then part of the Russian Empire, in March 1918, representatives of the Belarusian national movement proclaimed the BNR, which existed until December 1918. In the USSR, the history of the BNR was not recognised, and in the historical narrative under Lukashenko's regime, the BNR was also not considered a state for a long time, until this changed around the year 2018.

*What does this 'commodification' of history, in which there are various commercial and state appropriations of the past, mean for the conflict between the authoritarian regime and the opposition movements? What role does the Great Patriotic War, but also the short-lived Belarusian People's Republic of 1918 or the Grand Duchy of Lithuania play in these controversies? To what extent is this conflict over competing images of history also played out in popular culture and mass culture?*

The conflict you are talking about was rather characteristic for the culture of remembrance in Belarus in the mid-1990s and early 2000s. This split was formed and intensified after Lukashenko came to power and a certain re-Sovietisation of the historical narrative in official memory policy took place. Over the last ten to fifteen years at least, we can see a gradual convergence of two narratives – the official narrative oriented towards the Soviet past and the memory of the Great Patriotic War with the competing narrative referring to the history of the Grand Duchy of Lithuania (13th-16th centuries), the Polish-Lithuanian Commonwealth (16th-18th centuries), and the short-lived Belarusian People's Republic in 1918.

The sociologist Aliaksei Lastoŭski, who describes this merging of the two narratives, when official historians and regime ideologists even appropriated the oppositional narrative, as a process of convergence and proposes the thesis that in Belarus, finally, an understanding of a "long genealogy of statehood" was established. According to this new genealogy history is no longer limited only to the Soviet period, a phenomenon which is typical for nation-building and the construction of the national narrative in Eastern Europe (Lastouski 2019). This merging of narratives accelerated after Russia's annexation of Crimea, when Lukashenko tried to balance between Russia and the European Union, which also affected the official politics of remembrance.

Even now, when Lukashenko practically gave up the country's independence in exchange for Russia's support during the events of 2020, this tendency of building a "long genealogy" of the history of Belarus persists. But it can also be said that this narrative minimises critical reflection on the relationship between Russia and Belarus during the Soviet period; it is more a history of state power and institutions than a history of society, its social groups, resistance and divergent behaviour. One of the goals of this narrative is to legitimise the authoritarian institutions of power in Belarus. Perhaps, we can say that the split of the memory culture of the mid-1990s was transformed into a new phase in which the conflict has become more complex.

To what extent this merging of the two national narratives will have an impact on popular culture in the future is difficult to say. But in the 30 years since the early 1990s, references to the history of the Grand Dutchy of Lithuania, the Polish-Lithuanian Commonwealth, and the BNR have become more extensive and stable, also because these references to 'Europeanness' underline the non-Russian context. However, now the regime is trying to reverse this process.

*But if popular culture is defined as a specific way of appropriating some cultural products, formats, topics or symbols, which gains a certain popularity among people, as we do in our book, can we then speak at all about 'popular culture' within Belarus today, where the state aims to control all channels of public communication and representation?*

We can still talk about 'popular culture' in Belarus today, if only because there is no longer an iron curtain, there is YouTube, Instagram, TikTok, and other social media. Until 2022 when the sanctions started to take effect, film distribution worked without interruptions, Hollywood blockbusters were shown, and so on. All cultural industries were functioning. However, all this coexisted alongside two phenomena – the renewed old authoritarian aesthetics and also attempts to censor and ban this or that cultural product for political reasons. Also important in the cultural field were the lines of division around the political struggle which took place in the late 1980s and early 1990s and were mainly concentrated on the problem of language use and the support for a 'Belarusianisation' of national culture. Today we can talk about another problem – the problem of forced emigration after 2020, and the emergence of new lines of division within society – those who left and those who stayed.

But authoritarianism in Belarus has also produced its own aesthetics, which claims to become part of popular culture – it is not only about mass spectacles inherited from the USSR associated with state holidays and parades, or official festivals, such as the Slavianski Bazaar, a music festival that has been held since 1992, in which musicians from

Belarus, Russia, and Ukraine have participated. Often attended by Lukashenko and officials from Russia, the festival is seen as a political event, not just a cultural one. In 2022, representatives of Ukraine refused to participate in the festival. But also in literature or propaganda cinema we can of course find this authoritarian aesthetic, which on the verge of thrash or kitsch presents history in a pseudo-democratic manner for 'ordinary people'. We can observe here a kind of cultural populism that mirrors authoritarian political populism. Yet, authoritarian aesthetics has so far not matured to a specific style in Belarus.

Authoritarianism in the period of its liberalisation also tried to appropriate popular culture in order to demonstrate its own 'achievements' – like in sport – outside and inside Belarus. Thus, partly due to personal interference by Aleksandr Lukashenko, the ideologists of the regime participated for some time in the local selection of contestants for the Eurovision Song Contest. And winning places at the children's Eurovision or adult Eurovision were regarded as almost a political success; they were even mentioned in the sections of school history textbooks dedicated to culture. A similar phenomenon can also be observed in the film industry. On the one hand, the state retains control over film production (Belarusfilm studio) and finances some obviously ideological projects, on the other hand, there are sporadic statements about the need to create commercially successful products.

In the late USSR there was an official culture committed to Socialist realism with its institutions of censorship and control, and there was an underground culture, which developed according to its own logic, often staying outside the public space. Nowadays authoritarian control over culture, which has been reestablished in Belarus since the mid-1990s, in a way resumes this late Soviet situation: there are so-called 'black lists' of representatives of other cultural spheres (musicians, artists, writers, etc.) who for political reasons are not allowed to perform in public in state media or at various event venues and clubs. This situation worsened drastically after the mass protests of 2020, when all blacklists were updated. Some representatives of the art scene, theatre, literature, etc. were forced to emigrate. Those who participated in the protests but stayed in the country were mostly dismissed from cultural institutions, the absolute majority of which are state-owned. Some independent cultural institutions were closed and destroyed, such as the Ў Gallery in Minsk which had a long history or a number of creative spaces and independent galleries in other cities of Belarus like in Brest or Hrodna.

Another important aspect is the language in which this or that cultural product is made. Until the mid-1990s a policy of 'Belarusianisation' dominated the cultural sphere. In 1995 this was stopped, and although it was prohibited by law, those who spoke Belarusian were discriminated against, for example, when educational programmes in it were significantly reduced. Only in the independent culture scene did Belarusian continue to prevail, and people started to describe this increasingly isolated use of the Belarusian language metaphorically as existence in a 'ghetto' because authoritarian aesthetics mainly represented itself in Russian, also in popular culture.

However, in the 2010s this whole configuration started to change slowly. We see the professionalisation of independent culture that I already mentioned, which uses new ways of marketing and makes Belarusian more popular. Belarusian was increasingly used for advertising to mark distinctive styles or acquire symbolic value. Some authors tried to work for the Russian-speaking market as well, but at the same time insisted on their belonging to an independent Belarusian culture. Even Russian-language media started to use Belarusian expressions. The Russian-language sector was still larger in terms of consumption, but the more exciting things seemed to happen in the sector of Belarusian language culture, a tendency that nowadays has practically been stopped inside Belarus.

Some people left Belarus after 2020 and are trying to make cultural products and build up new institutions outside the country within a completely different cultural environment. These works of new emigrants are made in the Belarusian language and there, of course, the question arises of how to work in a commercially successful way and of how to attract the target audience.

*If we take this tension into consideration: on the one hand, the digitalisation and professionalisation of cultural production in the last decade, on the other, the massive emigration since 2020: Are there any particular historical events, figures or motifs from the Soviet past that play a special role for appropriating, rewriting or deconstructing history by certain state actors or independent institutions? How would you assess, for instance, the role of the Soviet-Belarusian partisan in the field of popular culture? Are there other figures that could compete with him?*

Late Soviet and post-Soviet official projects of collective identity in Belarus were built largely on the memory of the Great Patriotic War. Representations of this subject in popular culture, media, education system, etc. fulfilled an important political role. The metaphor of the "partisan republic", images of 'partisans' in particular, as described by Michael E. Urban (2008) and Simon Lewis (2017), were not only a successful project to combine 'national content' with an overall Soviet identity, but also represented a colonial construct, imposing a new identity and also acting as a defence against the trauma of the actual war. In the 1990s – 2010s in Belarus, one can observe a specific dynamic of remembering World War II and its functioning in the public sphere: the 'nationalisation' of the Soviet discourse of remembrance by the authoritarian regime led to a certain gamification of war images in popular culture and at the same time to the emergence of various counter-narratives and images in social media and publishing projects.

The mass protests against Lukashenko's regime in 2020 and the beginning of Russia's war in Ukraine in 2022 reinforced the reframing of World War II by different actors. Inside Belarus, on the part of the repressive regime, the idea of a genocide of the Belarusian people perpetrated by the Germans is instrumentalised, references to Nazism and fascism are manipulated, memorials of the Armia Krajowa are physically destroyed, and critical analyses of World War II are criminalised. Instead, a certain militarisation of history and a synchronisation of propaganda in Belarus and Russia can be observed.

Because of this dynamic, I think the widespread image of the Soviet partisan has also changed in popular culture. For example, one of Artur Klinaŭ's most famous projects, an art magazine and publishing project in Belarus was named *PARTizan*, but at the same time there existed also an edition in this series called "Partizanka" which was an attempt to review the art field from a feminist perspective. And also during the 2020 protests, a hacker group called Cyber Partisans emerged that paralysed government websites. All these new appropriations of the partisan figure vary widely from the Soviet discourse on the topic.

Is there a competing figure to the partisan in popular culture today? I would say that for quite a long time the image of Kastus Kalinoŭski, one of the leaders of the anti-Russian uprising of 1863–1864 in the former Polish-Lithuanian Commonwealth, has been quite popular. A programme for students and teachers repressed in Belarus was named after him, the reburial of the remains of Kalinowski and other rebels in Vilnius in 2019 became an important event. After the protests of 2020 and the beginning of the war in Ukraine a Kalinowski regiment was formed by Belarusians, fighting on the side of Ukraine. By the way, official Russian historians-propagandists like Aleksandr Diukov tried to deconstruct this popular Belarusian image of him for quite a long time, focussing on his biography and personal views (Diukov 2021).

Other images of the Soviet (or anti-Soviet) couldn't compete so far. Pre-war history for many is the history of Stalinist repressions. The history of such absolute evil is for instance depicted in the comic strip *The Last Vampire* (*Poslednii vampir*, 2019) by Andrei Skurko and Filipp Kokosha, which deals with the late Stalinist era in Belarus and was printed in the popular history magazine *Nasha istoriia* (*Our History*). Military history is also actively exploited by the authoritarian regime, whereas post-war history is still only beginning to be actively discussed. One could even say that there is almost an empty space between 1945 and the 1986 disaster in Chernobyl with regard to the representation of post-war Soviet Belarusian history in mass culture.

Recently the TV series *For Half an Hour to Spring* (*Za polchasa do vesny*, 2022), which tells the history of the most successful musical group in Soviet Belarus, *Pesniary*, was released. Its leader, Uladzimir Muliavin, started his career in Soviet Belarus in 1963, having moved from the Russian part of the USSR. The *Pesniary* ensemble performed Belarusian folk songs in modern arrangements and rock compositions which had huge success in the 1970s-1980s. The series caused controversial reactions and was suddenly subjected to unexpected political censorship because one actor took part in the 2020 protests against Lukashenko's regime who was therefore removed from a number of scenes.

In my opinion, the place Lukashenko's image occupies in mass culture is also interesting. He was the subject of anecdotes, caricatures, satire. Within the authoritarian culture, a specific cult of Lukashenko's personality even began to form. The 2020 protests strongly deconstructed this authoritarian image of the 'leader'.

*This aspect of a certain 'personality cult' around Lukashenko, even in satirical and critical popular culture, is interesting. Because it points to the fact that popular culture always works very strongly with emotions, channelling hatred and anger, but also longings and empathy, providing symbolic form and stories for feelings. How is this 'emotionalised' relationship with history being dealt with officially these days? Does this also affect the role and function of history museums and (school) textbooks in Belarus today? Or is there a specific aesthetics or mode of representation that differs from global developments? Are there frictions and diversions within this discourse and imaginary?*

More than twelve years ago, Tatsiana Ostrovskaya's first study on school history textbooks in Belarus was published, which analysed how they had been rewritten three times since independence due to political changes (Ostrovskaya 2010). By today we can already speak about a long "tradition" of textbook rewriting and instrumentalisation of history in independent Belarus under the authoritarian regime. After the mass protests of 2020, a new stage of this rewriting has come. Among the authors of textbooks we find not only historians and methodologists from the National Institute of Education, but also representatives from state authorities and the General Prosecutor's Office. This concerns, first of all, textbooks for pupils of all ages about the "genocide of the Belarusian people", in which the contemporary protesters are accused of links with the legacy of the Nazi collaborators during World War II. We can observe here a process of 'securitisation' of history politics – control over interpretations of the past becomes the main task of "security" for the regime.

The school system of historical education and museums in Belarus are financed and controlled by the state. School teachers, including history teachers, are appointed as members of election commissions, and many of them, either under duress or consciously, become participants of political manipulations and falsifications. Using school buildings for polling stations and teachers for election commissions, is still a Soviet tradition. But we have to bear in mind that history textbooks used by teachers and children are the same throughout the whole country and are compulsory. The curriculum as well as lists of additional, extracurricular literature on history have to be approved by the Ministry of Education. Of course, there are always exceptions and people who have the courage to teach critical thinking, but this is not the rule and the goal of this system is oriented towards political loyalty.

This systematic monitoring and controlling of all aspects of the past is not a unique Belarusian phenomenon, also in Russia we can observe such an "affective management of history" (Oushakine 2013) to emotionally connect new generations to a national collective, but in Belarus this practice has its own peculiarities. Back in 2010, the Russian-Belarusian film *The Brest Fortress* (*Brestskaia krepost'*, also known as *Fortress of War*) was released in mass distribution, in which naturalistic, even hyperrealistic scenes of Nazi crimes ensured an instant emotional connection to the lived experience of the past events in June 1941 shortly after the German invasion. The film's distribution was quite successful, but at the same time, the way of representing the historical events of the Brest Fortress defence against the Nazi aggressors followed the typical Soviet narrative that has been established since the late 1950s. In fact, the film updated this construct of distorted memory, which omitted many historical circumstances, for new generations.

As it seems to me, in today's Belarus, the emotional modes of connecting to the past, if we are talking about the official politics of memory, are as distanced as possible from any critical reflection. In the case of the film *The Brest Fortress* this can be somehow explained by the logic of mass cinema and its particular artistic demands, such an excuse however does not work if we speak about school history textbooks or museum exhibitions. In the latest editions of school textbooks, we find for instance photos of excavations of the remains of Nazi genocide victims, but the corresponding descriptions of the crimes are not aimed at working 'with sensitive topics', but propaganda. It's 'affective mechanism' aims not at explaining the past but at legitimising the present.

There is no Holocaust Museum in Belarus, but a special type of various museums, which are dedicated to different groups of victims, to the mechanisms of genocidal practices, to trauma, to the problem of political responsibility for history. Large museum projects, such as the Museum of Modern Belarusian Statehood, which was inaugurated in 2011, or the new Museum of the Great Patriotic War, which opened in 2014 with the relocation of part of the exhibition, rather work as obvious political and ideological projects that use modern equipment, but they themselves are archaic in a certain sense, as their task is not to act as independent institutions that stimulate debates about memory and history, but to represent quite specific official interpretations of historical events.

Museums in Belarus are not autonomous and independent in their activity. But in the 1990s, part of the state museums' exhibitions changed, they became more modern, topical, and until recently, museums employed people who tried to promote some new ideas which were even partly implemented during the period of political liberalisation in 2015–2019.

The last 10 years were a time when some museums began to work orientated on the principles of participatory museums, but after mass dismissals of museum workers who participated in the 2020 protests or allowed this freedom, the situation has worsened, political control and censorship of exhibitions leave almost no opportunity to act creatively. Outside Belarus today we see attempts to create independent museum institutions. Such as, for example, the Museum of Free Belarus in Warsaw, which emerged after 2020 and is focused on collecting documents and artefacts of the protest movement. However, there is a problem of identity of such institutions – for whom are they intended: for Belarusians inside Belarus, for Poles, for those Belarusians who emigrated?

*Let us come back to the more general questions that concern us in our volume. One thesis is that the global trends in popular culture with regard to the appropriation of history find a very specific form within the post-Soviet condition of Belarus, Ukraine and Russia. This is shaped in particular by a widespread distance or scepticism to official state-supported representations of history and its ideology, inherited from the distance to the uniform Marxist-Socialist hegemonic history narrative. Would you confirm this thesis for the Belarusian case?*

I would rather agree with this thesis than oppose it. Perhaps, I will supplement it a little, looking from the Belarusian context. The collapse of Soviet Marxism (if we speak about Belarusian historiography) does not coincide with 1991, it is a slower process, the language of many researchers and their optics are often still influenced by the old methodological habits. But in general, yes, distrust in the public sphere towards the way historical knowledge was and is produced in Belarus exists, and it is connected with the long-lasting manipulations of the Soviet period. Even though historians once started their struggle for a national narrative. This distrust is also reinforced by the participation of some historians in the creation, promotion and legitimisation of propaganda narratives of Lukashenko's authoritarian regime.

It is important, perhaps, to think about the implications of this scepticism. On the one hand, we see the coexistence in the public sphere of both the professional work of historians and its reception by a broader audience, along with the entire different spectrum of popular representations of history, which include conspiracy narratives, more or less marginal alternative versions of history and all kinds of mythologies and propaganda stories, but also the widespread publication of various forms of 'folk-history', fulfilling the mass demand for books dealing with national identity. In this context we see also how non-fiction, such as Svetlana Alexievich's books on the Soviet past, which are not documentary studies, play the role of 'sources' on Soviet history for mass readers.

On the other hand, I have a hypothesis, which I am now trying to confirm or refute in my own research, that in the case of Belarus, but also in a broader context of authoritarian regimes in general we can still speak about peculiar manifestations of 'citizen science' and the phenomenon of 'shared historical authority'. I mean with this the phenomenon that when public, civil pressure is exerted on the authorities and academic institutions, many nevertheless feel obliged to work honestly, to conform to standards, to refuse the manipulation and instrumentalisation of scholarship.

In this sense, the struggle for the memory of the victims of Stalinist repressions in Belarus, which started in the late 1980s, or the political and environmentalist struggle after the Chernobyl accident in 1986, the consequences of which were silenced – all this shows how the mechanisms of power and knowledge function in the Belarusian context, how people try to re-establish 'science' in terms of ethics, responsibility, etc. This is, of course, a very contested, very slow process, and often does not say anything good about science itself, but it is still worthy of attention. In the context of our conversation, it also means that popular culture in Belarus, public history outside the academy, can also be analysed from this perspective. Scepticism towards manipulation does not mean rejecting the notion of history as a science.

*But is there not another aspect to this conflict? Can we see here – as in many other post-Socialist states – also a sort of longing for constructing one's own 'national history' which is promoted by state institutions but also finds wide resonance in the population and especially among nationalist groups. How would you describe this constellation with regard to the extremely polarised political situation in Belarus?*

Belarus has its own trajectory here, if we talk about the construction of the national narrative and collective identity after the collapse of the USSR. Researchers tried to define it in various ways, mostly pointing to a kind of 'lack' of national identity both within the society and among the politicians who came to power in the mid-1990s. Or by labelling the existence of several collective identity projects at the same time. The picture of history and identity from below is quite diverse.

Such a 'search for identity' (and for legitimacy) is also characteristic of the authoritarian regime: at some point in time, references and reliance on Russian support were less, the regime even used references to Europeanness, and in 2015–2019, some media experts announced a 'soft Belarusification' and that in this way the historical narratives of the political opposition were about to become mainstream. This was because, as I have already mentioned, in 2018 the authorities gave permission to celebrate the centenary of the non-Soviet version of Belarus's statehood – the Belarusian People's Republic. And in the same year, an official monument to the victims of Stalinist repressions was finally erected near Minsk, in Kurapaty.

Since 2020, this trend towards a soft Belarusification seems to be over. The authoritarian regime and other groups, including those with a nationalist agenda, have different political resources. At the moment, the Lukashenko regime controls the public space, supports Russia's war in Ukraine, and these are all signs that the historical narrative will be minimally 'national', at least within official history policy.

*Could you elaborate on this highly intriguing aspect of how the 'search for identity' penetrates the mainstream within an authoritarian regime with a concrete example?*

As an example, I would like to talk about a case study from 2015. In Minsk, on 7 November the most important Soviet holiday, October Revolution Day, which is still celebrated in Belarus, the opening of the Leningrad shopping centre took place on Lenin Street. This street adjoins Kastrychnitskaia vulitsa/Street, the gentrification of which quickly became an example of new processes in Belarus, where offices, creative spaces, cafes opened inside old Soviet factory buildings, etc. In 2014, the same street started hosting a street art festival with the participation of foreign artists called Brasil Street, thus making the street a hangout for the city's flaneurs.

When the Leningrad shopping centre was opened, they invited an actor portraying the leader of the world proletariat Vladimir Lenin, hung a Soviet flag, portraits of Stalin, and arranged a 'solemn meeting'. On 9 November the BBC website published an article "Soviet-themed shopping centre opens in Minsk", which ironically commented on the opening (BBC monitoring 2015).

Indeed, the opening of such a private enterprise was impossible in Soviet Belarus, just as it is ironic that "Soviet marketing" is used to promote capitalist values. The reaction to this Soviet opening in the media and social networks was quite negative, and then expert interviews were published, which criticise this 'Sovietisation' of brands and nostalgia in Belarus. However, a number of brands have remained from the Soviet era, but generally references to the Soviet era do not play a big role in the market, on the contrary, there is a process of 'Belarusification' of names, replacing them with local or Belarusian-language names that also refer to history. From all this history we can only draw the conclusion about how interestingly and asynchronously different historical narratives are combined in contemporary Belarus, but also notice that we are moving away from the Soviet past.

*To conclude, let us move on from this peculiar conflation of a 'Belarusification' of history and a simultaneous 'Sovietisation' of contemporary consumer goods to a more general question. How would you describe this partly antagonistic condition in a broader global context? Where are the common trends, where do you see disruptions and exceptions? How important is history nowadays for political developments, be it democratic upheavals or state repression? How do you envisage the development of public history and its appropriations in popular culture for the near future?*

Such representations of the Soviet past in the Belarusian context are to some extent in line with global trends. Together with other countries in the eastern part of Europe, in the late 1980s-early 1990s we went through a period of active political mobilisation and active criticism of the Soviet and state socialist experience. We then faced different types of nostalgia about the Soviet, which can be "reflexive" or "restorative", as Svetlana Boym put it (2001). Then we saw a process of defragmentation of the Soviet and its "commodification", turning it into a material for "consuming history", as Jerome De Groot writes (Groot 2015). Eventually, attempts at the museification of the Soviet began, although this process was very slow in Belarus, and a number of exhibition projects took place, showing and displaying Soviet things, posters, and everyday life.

Of course, the specificity of Belarus is the preservation of authoritarianism and, due to this, the absence of open and large reflection about the Soviet period with clear political decisions, also on the societal level. But, perhaps, this gave a chance for greater preservation of the Soviet material heritage, which, from a distance, can now be treated differently than in the early 1990s. Also, the term "Soviet" still evokes associations with state violence, the responsibility for which has not been fully formalised and discussed.

If we talk about the future, much depends on whether and how our society will be able to get out of authoritarianism. For example, will the Soviet in mass perception be associated with its continuation in the form of Lukashenko's regime and intensively destroyed (for example, at the level of monuments, is it possible that we will repeat the Ukrainian decommunisation, etc.) or will there be some other configuration? In any case, if we talk about public history in Belarus in the future, we should, first of all, talk about a new democratisation of the public sphere and an open dialogue about history.

*The conversation by Aliaksei Bratachkin with Nina Weller and Matthias Schwartz took place in December 2023.*

## Filmography

*Anastasiia Slutskaia* (*Anastasiya Slutskaya*), dir. Yuri Yelkhov, Belarus 2003.
*The Brest Fortress* [also known as *Fortress of War*] (*Brestskaia krepost'*), dir. Aleksandr Kott, Russia/Belarus 2010.
*For Half an Hour to Spring* (*Za polchasa do vesny*), dir. Stepan Korshunov et al., Belarus 2022.
*Old Songs about the Main Things* (*Starye pesni o glavnom*), dir. Leonid Parfënov/Konstantin Ėrnst, Russia 1995–1998.
*On the Other Side* (*Na drugom beregu / Na drugim beragu*), dir. Andrey Khrulyov, Belarus 2023.

## References

BBC monitoring (2015): Belarus: Soviet-Themed Shopping Centre Opens in Minsk, 9 November 2015 (https://www.bbc.com/news/blogs-news-from-elsewhere-34768381) [20 December 2023].
Boym, Svetlana (2001): The Future of Nostalgia, New York: Basic.

Diukov, Aleksandr R. (2021): Neizvestnyi Kalinovskii. Propaganda nenavisti i povstancheskii terror na belorusskikh zemliakh, 1862–1864 gg., Moskva: Fond "Istoricheskaia pamiat'".

Groot, Jerome de (2015): Remaking History: The Past in Contemporary Historical Fictions, London/New York: Taylor & Francis Ltd.

Lastouski, Aliaksei (2019): "Return of the 'Long Genealogy' to School Textbooks on the History of Belarus." In: Ideology and Politics Journal 2/13, pp. 185–197.

Lewis, Simon (2017): "The Partisan Republic: Colonial Myths and Memory Wars in Belarus." In: Fedor, Julie/Kangaspuro, Markku/Lassila, Jussi/Zhurzhenko, Tatiana (eds.): War and Memory in Russia, Ukraine and Belarus, New York: Palgrave Macmillan.

Ostrovskaia, Tat'iana (2010): "Genealogiia istoriccheskoi pamiati belorusov v kontekste obrasovatelnykh praktik." In: Belarusian Institute for Strategic Studies [biss], 20 October 2010 (https://belinstitute.com/be/article/genealogiya-istoricheskoy-pamyati-belorusov-v-kontekste-obrazovatelnykh-praktik) [20 December 2023].

Oushakine, Serguei (2013): "Remembering In Public: On The Affective Management Of History:" In: Ab Imperio 1, pp. 269–302.

Pohl, Gundula (2023): "Participatory Propaganda? The YouTube Project 'Dialogue with the Prosecutor' as a History-Political Practice in Belarus." Report [not published] on Workshop "A Short History of Digital Publics at War" 1–3 May 2023 in Berlin, organised by FernUni Hagen.

Urban, Michael E. (2008): An Algebra of Soviet Power. Urban An Algebra of Soviet Power. Elite Circulation in the Belorussian Republic 1966- 86, Cambridge: Cambridge University Press.

# Appendix

## Acknowledgments

The idea of this book goes back to the workshop *'History goes Pop?' On the Popularization of the Past in Eastern European Cultures*, which was organised by the editors at the European University Viadrina in Frankfurt (Oder) from 10–12 December 2019 in cooperation with the Leibniz Center for Literary and Cultural Research (ZfL) as part of the BMBF research project "Designing the Past. Imagined History, Fiction and Memory in the Belarusian, Russian and Ukrainian Cultures", headed by Nina Weller.

Since then, the world and Europe have changed drastically: The corona pandemic, the protests and repressions in Belarus against critics of the regime, the Russian invasion of Ukraine and the ongoing war, and the authoritarian legislation in Russia against opponents of the war affected also the lives and works of the authors of this volume substantially. Ukrainian colleagues had to flee Russian bombings and war crimes, colleagues from Belarus and Russia emigrated because of repressions, while some stayed in their home countries sometimes under extremely challenging conditions. We are thus all the happier that most of the invited authors were able to contribute to the volume. However, due to the difficult personal situation of repression, war, flight and exile some had to resign, so the volume shows some imbalances in the representation of the various formats and forms of popular culture within the three countries. In this way, the book is also a document of the period of upheaval before and after the outbreak of full-scale war in February 2022.

Many thanks go to the workshop participants in 2019 for the inspiring discussions and to all authors who contributed to this book. We would like to thank the European University Viadrina and the ZfL for the organisational support and in particular the German Federal Ministry of Education and Research (BMBF), as part of the programme "Kleine Fächer – Große Potentiale", as well as the Leibniz Collaborative Excellence funding programme and the Leibniz Open Access Monograph Publishing Fund for the financial support. We are grateful to Miriam Galley from transcript publishers for their support, patience and companionship throughout the lengthy publication process. We would like to thank Roman Boichuk and Yaroslava Hryhorchuk for their support in organising the workshop, Charlotte Bull and Margarita Schäfer for the language editing and Katharina Kelbler for the formal editing of the whole volume.

The transliteration of names and geographical designations follows the ALA-LC style standard (Library of Congress for Belarusian, Russian and Ukrainian Cyrillic). For better-known names already introduced in English, however, we have used the internationally most common spelling. In case of Belarusian names, we sometimes also give the alternative variant Belarussian or Russian spelling in brackets.

# Authors

**Eva Binder** is a senior researcher at the Department of Slavic Studies and head of the Centre for Eastern European Studies at the University of Innsbruck, Austria. Her research interests include contemporary Russian and 20th-century Soviet auteur cinema, documentary aesthetics in film and literature, and transcultural and postcolonial approaches to Eastern European cultures. Recent publications include "Of Lipovans, Meria and Mari: Denis Osokin's Poetization of Ethnocultural Diversity" (in *Zeitschrift für Slawistik* 1:2023, in German), *Victim Narratives in Transnational Contexts* (co-edited, 2020, in German), "Odessa 2014: Alternative News and Atrocity Narratives on Russian TV" (in the volume *»Truth« and Fiction. Conspiracy Theories in Eastern European Culture and Literature*, 2020, co-authored with Magdalena Kaltseis) as well as articles on the cinema of Aleksei Fedorchenko (2021) and the documentary films of Nikolaus Geyrhalter (2023).

**Aliaksei Bratachkin** is a Belarusian historian and researcher at the Chair of Public History at the Institute of History at the FernUniversität Hagen, Germany. Until its closure in 2021, he headed the Public History Department at the independent European College of Liberal Arts in Belarus (ECLAB). His sphere of research includes politics of memory, post-Soviet transformations, and civic education. He is the co-author of the collective monographs *After Soviet Marxism: History, Philosophy, Sociology and Psychoanalysis in National Contexts (Belarus, Ukraine)* (2013, in Russian) and *Pathways of Belarus Europeanisation: Between Politics and Identity Constructions (1991–2010)* (2011, in Russian). He was co-editor and author of the online journal *Novaia Europa* (2009–2013) and is the author of numerous articles on the politics of memory, post-Soviet transformations, civic education and public history.

**Maria Galina** is an independent researcher, prose writer, poet, literary translator, literary critic and cultural sociologist who has lived in Odesa, Ukraine since 2021. Until 2022 she was a columnist and critic at the literary magazine *Novyi Mir* in Moscow, for which she wrote a regular column on speculative fiction. As a critic and cultural sociologist she has worked on contemporary mass literature and written several monographs dedicated to Soviet and post-Soviet science fiction as a social and cultural phenomenon. Recent articles include "Post-Imperial Resentments: Alternative Histories of World War II in Popular Post-Soviet Speculative Fiction" (in the volume *After Memory*, 2021, co-authored with Ilya Kukulin) and "Ressentiment and Post-traumatic Syndrome in Russian Post-Soviet Speculative Fiction: Two Trends" (in the volume *The Post-Soviet Politics of Utopia*, 2021).

**Ilya Kukulin** is a literary critic, cultural historian, and cultural sociologist. Currently, he is a visiting research fellow at the Amherst Center for Russian Culture, Amherst, USA. His research interests include the history of Soviet unofficial poetry, the sociology of today's Russian culture, the cultural history of the Soviet Union and post-Soviet Russia, the gender history of post-Soviet literature, Soviet science fiction literature, the politics of childhood and children's literature of the Soviet Union and post-Soviet Russia, Russophone social networks, as well as trauma and memory in today's Russia. Recent books include *Machines of the Noisy Time: How Soviet Montage Became an Aesthetic Method of the Unofficial Culture* (2015, in Russian), *Breakthrough to an Impossible Connection: Essays and Articles on Russian Poetry* (2019, in Russian) and the co-authored monograph *A Guerilla Logos: The Project of Dmitry Aleksandrovich Prigov* (2022, together with Mark Lipovetsky, in Russian).

**Daniil M. Leiderman** is an art historian at the School of Performance, Visualization, and Fine Art at Texas A&M University, USA. He wrote his PhD dissertation entitled *Moscow Conceptualism and "Shimmering": Authority, Anarchism, and Space* (2016, Princeton University) on Moscow's unofficial art scene of the early 1970s and its relationship to contemporary post-Soviet and post-Crimean artistic resistance. His current research focusses on the representation of Eastern Europe and Russia in contemporary video games and related media. Recent articles include "Seeing Lenin's Double: the Visuality of Soviet Childhood" (in the volume *Pedagogy of Images: Depicting Communism for Children*, forthcoming, together with Marina Sokolovskaia), "Moscow Conceptualism and Shimmering: Not Conforming with Nonconformism" (in *Russian Literature* 2018: 96–98), "Zombies, Russians, Plague: Eastern Europe as a Sandbox for Utopia" (in *Digital Icons* 15: 2016).

**Mark Lipovetsky** is a professor at the Department of Slavic Languages at Columbia University, New York, USA. His research interests include Russian postmodernism, New Drama, Soviet literary and cinematic tricksters, Soviet underground culture as well as various aspects of post-Soviet culture. He is the author of twelve monographs and more than a hundred articles. He has also co-edited twenty collections of articles on Russian literature and culture of the 20th-21st centuries. Recent monographs include *Charms of Cynical Reason: The Transformations of the Trickster Trope in Soviet and Post-Soviet Culture* (2011), *Postmodern Crises: From Lolita to Pussy Riot* (2017), and *A Guerilla Logos: The Project of Dmitry Aleksandrovich Prigov* (2022, in Russian, co-authored with Ilya Kukulin). Lipovetsky is a co-editor of *The Oxford Handbook of Underground Soviet Culture*.

**Lidia Martinovich** holds a master's degree in sociology from the European Humanities University (Vilnius, Lithuania) and is an independent researcher in visual arts and literature. Her research interests include contemporary Belarusian literature, memory culture and vernacular photography in post-Soviet countries, the cultural history of landscapes in Belarus, and contemporary Belarusian cinema. Recent publications include "The Belarusian Forest as a Cultural Landscape" (in volume *Liudzi lesu* 2022: 13–30, in Belarusian and English); "Why Watch Weddings and Funerals? Studying Family Archives of Wedding and Funeral Photographs of Belarusians" (in *Dziavochy vechar* 2021: 3–7, in Belarusian); "Family Archive Photography as a New Iconography: Self-Representation of Belarusian Villagers in Mid- and Post-War Portraits" (in *Nailepshy bok* 2018: 16–26, in Belarusian); "Contemporary Belarusian Literature: Three Ways to Talk About Trauma" (in Sygma.ma 2019, in Russian). (The latter was published under her birth name Mikheeva).

**Svitlana Pidoprygora** is a professor of literary studies at the Petro Mohyla Black Sea National University in Mykolaiv, Ukraine. She was a URIS-Fellow (Ukrainian Research in Switzerland) at the University of Basel (01.08.2023-31.07.2024). Her research interests include the Ukrainian historical novel, Ukrainian experimental literature, and 20th century and contemporary popular culture with a special focus on comic culture and visual culture in a digitally globalised society. Recent publications are "Ukrainian Comics and War in Ukraine" (in *TRAFO. Blog for Transregional Research*, 2022), "Ukrainian Fiction: the Possibilities of the Digital Age" (in the volume *Role of Science and Education for Sustainable Development*, 2021), *Ukrainian Experimental Prose of the 20th and Early 21st Centuries. An 'Impossible' Literature* (2018, in Ukrainian).

**Olga Romanova** is an independent researcher, literary theorist and specialist in cultural studies. Until 2021 she was the head of the Department of Popular Culture and Media at the European College of Liberal Arts in Minsk, Belarus. Her research interests include the theory and history of Soviet and post-Soviet cinema and culture, and Belarusian cinema. Recent publications include "Between the Town and the Countryside. Utopian images and expanses within Belarusian Soviet Films" (in the volume *Urban Space on Screen. Cinematographies of Belarus, Poland, and Ukraine*, 2024: in print), "Victory Day in Belarus. State policy of memory and its alternatives" (in the internet magazine *Urokii istorii*, 2019, in Russian) and the forthcoming monograph *Another History of Soviet Belarusian Cinema. Research Stories* (2024, in Russian).

**Matthias Schwartz** is co-head of the program area World Literature and head of the project "Adjustment and Radicalisation. Dynamics in Popular Culture(s) in Pre-War Eastern Europe" at the Leibniz Center for Literary and Cultural Research (ZfL), Berlin, Germany. His research interests involve Eastern European contemporary literatures, memory cultures and popular cultures in a globalised world; documentary aesthetics and Socialist travel literature, the cultural history of Soviet and post-Soviet adventure literature, science fiction, science popularisation and space travel. Recent publications include *Documentary Aesthetics in the Long 1960s in Eastern Europe and Beyond* (co-edited, 2024); *After Memory. World War II in Contemporary Eastern European Literatures* (co-edited, 2021); *Sirens of War. Discursive and Affective Dimensions of the Ukraine Conflict* (co-edited, 2020, in German); *Eastern European Youth Cultures in a Global Context* (co-edited, 2016).

**Valery Vyugin** is a leading researcher at the Centre for Literary Theory and Interdisciplinary Studies of the Institute of Russian Literature of the Russian Academy of Sciences

(Pushkin House) St. Petersburg and a professor at St. Petersburg State University. His research interests include Russian Soviet and post-Soviet culture, especially literature and film, literary awards in contemporary Russia, history of the Soviet and post-Soviet spy fiction and cinema, memory studies, and rhetorical criticism. Recent publications are "Cultural Recycling' in the 21st Century. What Does It Mean Now?" (in *Antropologicheskii forum* 58:2023, in Russian), "Make Love, Not War. Russian Spy Comedies, 1990s–2010s" (in *Osteuropa* 11:2022, in German), "Cultural Recycling': A Contribution to the History of the Concept (1960s — 1990s)" (in *NLO* 196:2021, in Russian), "Soviet Conspiracy Drama of the 1920s and 1930s" (in the volume *"Truth" and Fiction. Conspiracy Theories in Eastern European Culture and Literature*, 2020) as well as the collective monograph *The Second All-Union Congress of Soviet Writers, 1954. The Ideology of the Historical Transition and the Transformations of the Soviet Literature* (co-author, 2018, in Russian).

**Nina Weller** holds a Ph.D. in comparative literature and is a postdoctoral researcher in the research project "Adjustment and Radicalisation. Dynamics in Popular Culture(s) in Pre-War Eastern Europe" at the Leibniz Center for Literary and Cultural Research (ZfL) in Berlin, Germany. Her research interests involve contemporary Eastern European literature, especially Belarusian, Ukrainian, Russian literature, popular culture, memory cultures, alternative history and documentary aesthetics. Recent publications include *"Everything is more Expensive than Ukrainian Life". Texts about Westsplaining and the War* (co-edited, 2023, in German), "'Let's be Belarusians!' On the Reappropriation of Belarusian History in Popular Culture" (in the volume *Memory as a Dialogue? History for Young People*, 2022) and *After Memory. World War II in Contemporary Eastern European Literatures* (co-edited, 2021).

**Oleksandr Zabirko** holds a PhD in Slavic literatures and cultures and is a researcher at the Slavic Department of the University of Regensburg, Germany. His major fields of research are literary models of spatial and political order, contemporary literature(s) from Russia and Ukraine, and fantasy literature in general. Recent publications include *"Literary Forms of Geopolitcs. The Modelling of Spatial and Political Order in Contemporary Russian and Ukrainian Literature* (2021, in German), *Figurations of the East. Between Literature, Philosophy and Politics* (co-edited, 2022, in German), *Protest Movements in the Long Shadow of the Kremlin. Awakening and Resignation in Russia and Ukraine* (co-edited, 2020, in German) and "The War in Neverland: The History of Novorossiia as Literary Project" (in the volume *Official History in Eastern Europe*, 2020).